STUDIES IN EVANGELICAL HI

Nonconformity's Romantic Generation

Evangelical and Liberal Theologies in Victorian England

STUDIES IN EVANGELICAL HISTORY AND THOUGHT

A full listing of titles in this series appears at the end of this book

STUDIES IN EVANGELICAL HISTORY AND THOUGHT

Nonconformity's Romantic Generation

Evangelical and Liberal Theologies in Victorian England

Mark Hopkins

Foreword by
Geoffrey Rowell

PATERNOSTER

First published 2004 by Paternoster

Paternoster is an imprint of Authentic Media,
9 Holdom Avenue, Bletchley, Milton Keynes, MK1 1QR, U.K.
and
P.O.Box 1047, Waynesboro, GA 30830-2047, U.S.A.

09 08 07 06 05 04 10 7 6 5 4 3 2 1

British Library Cataloguing in Publication Data
A catalogue record for this book is available from the British Library

ISBN 1–84227–150–4

Typeset by Sunday Asoso and Ed Greening
and printed and bound in Great Britain by
Nottingham Alpha Graphics

Studies in Evangelical History and Thought

Series Preface

The Evangelical movement has been marked by its union of four emphases: on the Bible, on the cross of Christ, on conversion as the entry to the Christian life and on the responsibility of the believer to be active. The present series is designed to publish scholarly studies of any aspect of this movement in Britain or overseas. Its volumes include social analysis as well as exploration of Evangelical ideas. The books in the series consider aspects of the movement shaped by the Evangelical Revival of the eighteenth century, when the impetus to mission began to turn the popular Protestantism of the British Isles and North America into a global phenomenon. The series aims to reap some of the rich harvest of academic research about those who, over the centuries, have believed that they had a gospel to tell to the nations.

Series Editors

To two of our daughters:

Patience Chule, who died in Christ's transforming joy through his power and special grace while I was preparing this book for publication, with gratefulness for an education in love as we shared Christ's death and life: in memory, anticipation and partnership still;

and Victoria Wang, who lives with us in Christ by another grace as special, and whose heart is truer than any I know: in our life sharing.

Contents

II THE BAPTISTS

Foreword

In this significant historical study Mark Hopkins analyses and explores some of the tensions in late nineteenth-century non-conformity between liberals and evangelical conservatives. Nineteenth-century controversies arising from the new critical study of the Bible originating largely from Germany (though with significant earlier English antecedents), and from the tension between Genesis and geology and later from Darwinian evolutionary theory have mostly been studied in relation to Anglican controversies. In focussing on Congregationalists and Baptists the different ecclesiological structure of these denominations and their less sacramentally focussed concept of communion provides an important counterpoise to such accounts. Credal issues were inevitably raised, yet could often not easily be answered in churches which had historically eschewed credal statements.

The influence of Romanticism (and Romantic idealism) is paramount, an influence in which 'Life' was given precedence over dogma. So too was the associated issue of a pervasive optimistic humanism which challenged traditional Christian ethics. One of the key points of dogmatic controversy was the doctrine of hell and future punishment which raised simultaneously issues of biblical interpretation and inspiration and the nature of revelation, together with the ethical challenge to a God who could arbitrarily condemn large numbers of men and women to an unrelieved eternity of torment in hell. Such punishment, albeit defended on grounds of just retribution, was offensive to a society increasingly wedded to reformatory ideas of punishment. Penal substitutionary ideas of atonement were likewise strongly ethically criticised.

Four names are prominent in this study – John Clifford, James Baldwin Brown, R. W. Dale and C. H. Spurgeon – and Mark Hopkins gives a well-researched re-assessment of their theology and contributions to the nineteenth-century debates. In particular his use of original papers bearing on the Downgrade controversy enables him to give the fullest account to date of one of the most significant theological controversies in Baptist history.

All churches in the nineteenth century had to confront the profound questions raised for traditional doctrine by science and biblical criticism, as well as by the subjectivism of Romantic theology and ethics. Questions of church authority were inevitably raised and different answers given. Catholic Ultramontanes, Tractarian appeals to the importance of tradition, and evangelical tensions between the plenary inspiration of the Bible and personal faith were all concerned with the same issues. Although the word 'liberal', as Hopkins reminds us, did not come into widespread use until the 1880s, the tensions were already evident at an earlier date. In many churches today, not least my own Anglican Communion, these tensions are still playing out between claims to revealed truth, its nature, character and biblical foundation, and appeals to new understandings of human nature which seem to enshrine culture relativism and subjectivism. The liberal/conservative tension again has an ethical dimension, this time focusing on sexuality. This careful analysis of an earlier nonconformist debate is not only historically illuminating, it may also throw important light from the past on contemporary tensions and debates. For both these reasons I am happy to commend this book, which has emerged from an exemplary doctrinal thesis and has been shaped by subsequent years of work in the very different circumstances of West Africa.

Geoffrey Rowell
Bishop of Gibraltar in Europe
September, 2003

Acknowledgements

My greatest debt is to the one person who has been with me throughout the twenty-one years that separate the start of my doctoral study from the publication of this book, my wife Isabelle. Her patient support has been essential at every stage, including encouraging me to go away for short spells in order to get the uninterrupted time I needed. In connection with that, I am grateful to the staff of Miango Rest Home for providing the conducive environment in which the thesis was revised.

In the Right Revd Geoffrey Rowell I had a courteous, helpful, understanding, stimulating and very accessible supervisor to whom I owe a great deal. I appreciate too his willingness to write the foreword. I would also like to acknowledge my external examiner, Dr David Bebbington, who was the first to encourage me to have my work published and who has continued to encourage me ever since.

I will not attempt to list the numerous other scholars and librarians who assisted me at various points, punctuating what was inevitably for much of the time a rather lonely pursuit – the memory that seems to have imprinted itself most strongly is of freezing in my overcoat during winter weeks spent poring over the Spurgeon Scrapbooks in the Heritage Room at Spurgeon's College. I must, however, mention Dr John Briggs, who was (if I remember rightly) the first person I consulted on my interest in research in church history, and who has been of help much more recently too.

The process of revision has been greatly eased by the efficient help of my assistant, Sunday Asoso – he has been everything from typist to compiler of the index. My friend Ed Greening has also helped immensely in preparing the book for publication.

Lastly, I would like to acknowledge Pieter Kwant for putting me in touch with Paternoster; also Dr Anthony Cross and especially Jeremy Mudditt, whose editorial advice I have appreciated at several points.

Abbreviations

BQ	*The Baptist Quarterly*
BQR	*The British Quarterly Review*
BW	*The British Weekly*
CQ	*The Congregational Quarterly*
CW	*The Christian World*
CY	*The Congregational Yearbook*
EI	*The English Independent*
JURCHS	*The Journal of the United Reformed Church Historical Society*
MB	Baptist Union Minute Book, 1887-89
Pulpit	*The New Park Street and Metropolitan Tabernacle Pulpits*
SS	Spurgeon Scrapbooks
ST	*The Sword and the Trowel*

CHAPTER 1

Introduction

The second half of the nineteenth century was not the time of stability and prosperity for the churches that beleaguered twenty-first century Christians may imagine it to have been. It was in this period that the numerical growth ushered in by the Evangelical Revival fell behind population growth, the prelude to the absolute decline of the twentieth century. It was also a time of extraordinary theological flux: abandonment rapidly overtook modification as the preferred remedy for the problems increasingly perceived in the old systems, and attempts at rebuilding were radically different, nevertheless varied, often confused, and generally desultory. The overall aim of this study is to deepen understanding of the complex causes, nature and effects of the theological turmoil in England, particularly as it affected Baptists and Congregationalists. It will be seen that they had to face a major crisis, that they were thrown into disunity and disarray, and that they did not succeed in recovering their poise. It is impossible not to entertain the theory that the theological crisis and numerical decline were linked, but establishing such a link is a major undertaking that goes beyond the scope of this work – indeed, it would be unwise to attempt it without preliminary study of the kind undertaken here.[1] Further interest is attached to the study of the period in which theological liberalism and conservative reactions to it began their careers by the fact that many of the issues discussed here have continued to be relevant ever since, often in not dissimilar guise.

In view of their close kinship and similar histories it is not surprising that Baptists and Congregationalists had well developed links in the late nineteenth century. Their theology and polity were

---

[1] Robert Currie, Alan Gilbert and Lee Horsley, *Churches and Churchgoers: Patterns of Church Growth in the British Isles since 1700* (Oxford: Clarendon, 1977), brings together some useful statistics, though none that bear directly on differing tendencies within denominations. Their theory of church growth and decline is however inadequate: its basic error is in almost completely neglecting internal factors after using a flawed argument to establish the supremacy of external factors (p. 97).

very similar: historically, baptism was the only substantial point that divided Congregationalists from the Particular Baptists. Both denominations were ultimately rooted in the Reformation and grew up in seventeenth century England; together they experienced both the eighteenth century's long drought and the refreshing showers of the Evangelical Revival. Their pattern of development of ministerial training, local associations and foreign missions showed many similarities. The resemblance becomes especially marked with the development of national denominational unions in the nineteenth century. After hesitant starts earlier in the century (the Baptist Union of 1813 did however keep going after a fashion, unlike the Congregational Union of 1808), both denominations established stronger organizations with new constitutions and similar aims in 1831-32. New life was injected into both in the early 1860s, which marked the beginning of a phase of centralization that reached its peak early in the twentieth century, causing anguished debates about the congregational polity. Patterns of numerical growth were also similar, with a five-fold growth in the first half of the century that was greater even in absolute terms than progress in the second half of the century; the latter was 71% for the Baptists and 56% for the Congregationalists.[2]

The Evangelical Revival was a major feature in the theological background to the late nineteenth century. It stimulated the development, by Andrew Fuller among others, of a Calvinist theology that gave priority to evangelism and spirituality; part of the inspiration for this derived from the Puritans, to whom the new mood was closer than to the rationalist high Calvinism that had developed in opposition to the equally rationalist trend toward Arianism and Socinianism. But in another sense the Revival broke with the Puritan tradition, in which theology had had a central place. The first generation of English evangelical dissenting theologians was also the last: they used the theological language of their tradition to give doctrinal sanction to a popular spiritual movement that looked upon theology as at best a simple ready-made arrangement of biblical doctrines providing adequate reference for preaching first a gospel of repentance and faith, and then a life of godliness. In the nineteenth century English Nonconformists who like R.W. Dale set out to do creative theological work

---

[2] Membership figures for 1800, 1851, and 1900 were 27,500, 140,000 and 234,114 for the Baptists (a combined figure for Particular and New Connexion General Baptists), and 35,000, 165,000 and 257,435 for the Congregationalists. Currie, Gilbert, and Horsley, *Churches and Churchgoers*, 147-52.

were rare; and C.H. Spurgeon, who did some such work in spite of sharing in the evangelical consensus that thought it unnecessary, was perhaps unique.

Evangelical Dissent was thus ill-equipped to stand up to the difficulties with which it was confronted in the nineteenth century. These can be arranged into five categories, the first of which was internal: the spiritual revival began to lose momentum, making Nonconformity increasingly vulnerable to external threats.

Very important but too often overlooked was the long-term change in ethical values which worked outward from high culture into society at large. Starting well before the nineteenth century, and continuing ever since, this movement has challenged evangelical Protestantism in fundamental ways: by its tendency to assert the authority of conscience over any ethical system emanating from an outside source; by stimulating the development of theories of punishment that juggled with deterrence, prevention and rehabilitation but excluded retribution; and by subjecting to increasing pressure a number of received doctrines, including election, atonement, justification, and future punishment.

The additional factor in the early nineteenth century which rendered that pressure more acute and formidable was Romanticism, together with its associated philosophies that differed radically from the dominant English empirical tradition. Rising as it did at a time when the great years of the Revival were over, it meant that evangelicals could no longer comfort themselves by comparing their own warmth and dynamism with a cold ethical rationalism. Romanticism was full of feeling, and spawned many varieties of immanental theology to give it expression.

Among the Romantic movement's many legacies was the stimulus it gave to modern historical studies and developmental approaches to science. The latter half of the century had more to cope with from this direction, but earlier on in the century evangelical Dissent had to begin to grapple with biblical criticism and scientific accounts of origins challenging the traditional theories based on Genesis.

The final category of difficulty was the variety of theological responses to these changes being produced in other Christian traditions. Part of the problem lay in deciding whether these constituted disguised capitulation to anti-evangelical ideologies or were authentically Christian theologies all the stronger for discerning and incorporating whatever was good and true in current movements of thought, or even – more difficult still – a mixture of both. The process of facing up to them was still in its infancy in 1850, and theologies that endeavoured to tackle critical and scientific problems were particularly scarce. The theological weakness of English evangelicalism meant that the major contenders were all of external provenance. Those that made most of the running in the middle of the century were the group of Scottish theologians associated with Thomas Erskine, and a linked Anglican group inspired by Coleridge and led by F.D. Maurice. German theology suffered from an aggressive campaign to highlight its most unorthodox elements and dismiss it *en bloc*, but with the help of the translations published by T. & T. Clark more conservative German theologians began to gain a hearing. Hegelian and Ritschlian theologies did not have much impact among Nonconformists before the closing years of the century: lesser foreign thinkers with a higher profile in the period of this study include the American Congregationalist Horace Bushnell.

Calvinism acted as a kind of crumple zone: the most exposed element in the theology of evangelical Dissent, its sacrifice deadened the shock of the collision with the juggernaut of change. Lack of interest in theological debate meant that the usual tendency was to relegate it imperceptibly from the practical domain of preaching to mere theory, in which state it quietly wasted away, rather than engage it in argument. Few drew attention to this process before it was well advanced. There was little effort invested in filling the theological vacuum, and certainly no proclamation of Arminianism; instead, the mid-century mood was an anti-theological exaltation of 'life' over 'dogma'. The rare would-be defenders of Calvinist orthodoxy felt the life oozing out of it but found it difficult to identify targets at which to lash out in its defence. John Campbell, the Congregationalist whose journalistic empire and combative disposition made him the most formidable champion of conservative ways in his generation, miscalculated in 1856 when selecting T.T. Lynch's inoffensive volume of poetry, *The Rivulet*, for an all-out assault. He exposed himself to the counter-attack of a dynamic new generation of young ministers, and never recovered from the loss of prestige he suffered. He might have been better advised to have waited another year and reserved his great effort for Samuel Davidson, a tutor dismissed from Lancashire Independent College because of an altogether more concrete publication based on a rare familiarity with contemporary German biblical criticism.

The older generation realized that these controversies of the 1850s were not to be the last word on the subject. John Angell James wrote after the Davidson affair that he was 'convinced that in ten or twenty years' time there will be another lapse in our body, on the side of heterodoxy, and the Baptists are as bad as we are – or perhaps worse'.[3] But the changes were to be far more radical than they imagined: just ten years later, with most of the last generation of the Revival years dead, James among them, the mediocrity of the intermediate generation allowed a group of ministers in their thirties and forties to take over the Congregational Union and transform the denomination. In spite of what James thought, Baptists followed more raggedly and less rapidly, yet mainly in the same direction: and it is the pilgrimage of that generation that supplies the unifying theme of this study.

* * *

Nonconformist theology of the Victorian period has been studied less intensively than contemporary Anglican theology. Relatively few works, often on particular themes, have sought to integrate the two, with Geoffrey Rowell's *Hell and the Victorians* (1974) and John Rogerson's *Old Testament Criticism in the Nineteenth Century: England and Germany* (1984) notable in this respect. Two published works had the field of late nineteenth century Nonconformist theological change largely to themselves for quite some time: Willis Glover's *Evangelical Nonconformists and Higher Criticism in the Nineteenth Century* (1954), and John Grant's *Free Churchmanship in England 1870-1940* (1955). These have many similarities: writing during the ascendancy of neo-orthodoxy, each sought to interpret what he considered a liberal parenthesis in Free Church history by identifying a particular area – higher criticism for Glover, ecclesiology for Grant – in which he thought the old evangelicalism had failed, with a resulting liberal interlude before the triumph of neo-orthodoxy, which they believed brought satisfactory answers in these as well as other issues. Neither entirely escapes the danger inherent in such studies of exaggerating the importance of his theme in the general scheme of things, but both remain useful within their limits. Glover's work is the more satisfactory: he is particularly successful in outlining a timetable describing how higher criticism established itself in Nonconformity; but his explanations of change are less convincing, the lack of a broad context making itself felt. Grant's book does not overcome the handicap of addressing a theme which received little attention during the period, and even that mainly weak and inconsequential: this made it hard for him to analyse the period in any depth.

---

[3] Quoted in Albert Peel, *These Hundred Years 1831-1931: A History of the Congregational Union of England and Wales* (London: Congregational Union of England and Wales, 1931), 231.

These two studies have more recently been joined by Mark Johnson's *The Dissolution of Dissent, 1850-1918,*[4] and Dale Johnson's *The Changing Shape of English Nonconformity, 1825-1925.*[5] They share more than a surname: both emphasize theological education and make Congregationalism their main base, though Dale Johnson ranges more widely. But they differ too, as their titles show: where Mark Johnson sees, and tries to explain, dissolution, Dale Johnson merely sees change and does his best to disassociate late nineteenth century theological change from twentieth century numerical decline.[6] Mark Johnson tries to establish an additional distinction, presenting his approach as a consideration of theological change in its social context, contrasting this with the usual intellectual historical method.[7] There is indeed little in it by way of intellectual history: Romanticism, idealism, Carlyle, and ethical change are among subjects that receive little, if any, attention. But he does not employ the methods of social history either. The only prominent social element is his central thesis, which he imposes on rather than draws out of his study: 'that a desire for political equality and social acceptability among a new and more prosperous generation of Nonconformists fostered a dramatic liberalization of religious doctrine';[8] and that the resulting new evangelicalism in the long run contributed to the assimilation of Nonconformity into mainstream national life. Before the closing years of the nineteenth century the link between political involvement and theological liberalism is highly suspect; for example, in the 1840s an influential theological conservative, John Campbell, was in trouble within Congregationalism as a political fire-brand, while a young theological liberal, James Baldwin Brown, was already distancing himself from political Dissent.[9] There is evidence for a link between theological liberalism and the higher levels of society, but Johnson does not delve into its nature, wrongly depicts it simply as the governing of theology by social goals, and subjects Congregational leaders to ill-grounded charges of hypocrisy, implying that they operated a theological

---

[4] New York: Garland, 1987.

[5] New York: Oxford University Press, 1999.

[6] Changing Shape, 7.

[7] Johnson, The Dissolution of Dissent, xiii.

[8] Mark Johnson, 'The Dissolution of Dissent: A Social and Institutional History of Congregational Theological Accommodation, 1850-1918' (PhD, University of Toronto, 1982), abstract (no page numbers).

[9] Peel, *These Hundred Years,* 147, 170-72; Baldwin Brown, *The Young Ministry: Its Relation to the Age* (London: John Snow, 1847), 39-40; Baldwin Brown, *Thomas Raffles, D.D., LL.D.: a Sketch* (London: Jackson, Walford & Hodder, 1864), 32-4.

strategy which exalted expediency over principle.[10] The inadequacy of Mark Johnson's theory is compounded by the weakness of his theological analysis: he uses R.W. Dale's term 'new evangelicalism' as a label for the theology of Dale's generation in a way that disguises the diversity and fluidity of the theological scene. But at least he shows a willingness to critique Dale's tendentious historical analysis of 'old evangelicalism', in contrast to Dale Johnson's flaccid acceptance of it at face value.[11] In reality both Johnsons have, like Glover and Grant, concentrated their study mainly in one corner of the field of nineteenth century Nonconformist theology, for about half of each book is centred on theological education. Like the earlier writers they have recovered useful detailed evidence, but like them also the limitations of a comparatively narrow focus are sometimes apparent.[12]

The method adopted in this study can be compared to a graph: the leaders, with the detailed information available as to the development of their thought in time, form one axis, and the controversies, with the broad view they permit of the state of denominational thought at one point in time, supply the other; together they allow the process of change to be plotted. There are reasons for the choice of denominations: the similarities between the Baptists and Congregationalists make their differences all the more illuminating. The development of liberal theology is a complex matter; it is therefore particularly helpful that in one respect it is simpler in Nonconformity than in the Church of England, for at that time the Free Churches lacked one of the dimensions of the Established Church: they had their equivalents of low and broad church parties, but nothing resembling the high church party.

Chronologically the study is not so much delimited by a period of years as by the life-span of a particular generation. The four selected

---

[10] Johnson, 'The Dissolution of Dissent' (thesis), 128, 155. The following is a sample: 'The irreverent way in which Dale's generation of Congregational leaders threw over a Calvinist tradition...reveals that religious doctrine was ultimately subject to the matter of survival' (p. 379). In reality they moved away from the theology they were taught because there were things in it they could not accept, not merely because these things were no longer acceptable in the religious market they were targeting.

[11] Johnson, *Changing Shape*, 91.

[12] An example of Mark Johnson's parochialism is the ignorance of the phenomenal impact of Spurgeon shown in his extraordinary statement that Dale was 'far and away the most publicly known and nationally visible Nonconformist minister in England' in the second half of the nineteenth century (*ibid.*, 19).

leaders of thought were born between 1820 and 1836, and represent the generation whose formative years, from the late 1830s to the 1850s, coincided with the period at which the influence of Romanticism was at its most pervasive, if not its most creative and dynamic, in England. They were all influenced by its ethos in a way that marked them out as radically different from their seniors; they ushered in a period rich in energy and power, but accompanied by change, instability and uncertainty. It was in this generation that Nonconformist liberal theology began its development. By the 1890s their work was largely done, and younger men were replacing them at the head of Nonconformity, with different ideas acquired through a different kind of upbringing and facing changing problems. The generation under scrutiny was pre-eminently *the* Victorian generation, for the most part their entire active lives being played out during Victoria's reign.

The four men selected, the Congregationalists James Baldwin Brown (1820-84) and Robert William Dale (1829-95), and the Baptists Charles Haddon Spurgeon (1834-92) and John Clifford (1836-1923), were leaders on opposite sides in the major denominational controversies of their time, the Congregational Leicester Conference Controversy of 1877-78, and the largely Baptist Downgrade Controversy of 1887-88; this fact helps bind together the largely self-contained individual chapters. The Downgrade Controversy selects itself, for it dwarfs all other Baptist quarrels, and has been served very poorly by its numerous historians. The Congregationalists engaged in disputes of similar magnitude to that occasioned by the Leicester Conference, on religious communion over *The Rivulet* in 1856-57 and the 'New Theology' in 1907, but these were largely shaped by the concerns of the preceding and succeeding generations. The selection of the leaders to be studied was guided by concern to choose prominent and influential men with intellectual and spiritual histories reflecting the diversity of their time: these criteria left few alternatives. Alexander McLaren was the other leading Baptist of that generation; but, though immensely gifted, powerful and influential as a preacher and expositor (not least through his publications), he deliberately gave his ministry a narrower focus than the two men selected. There was a larger peer group of Congregational leaders, but few – the popular preacher Joseph Parker not excepted – had much theological prominence, influence or weight. A.M. Fairbairn was a notable exception, but Baldwin Brown has been preferred because his thought, though less substantial, represented and mediated an important movement whose influence on English Congregationalism was earlier and arguably greater. Fairbairn was nearly forty when he left Scotland to begin his English career in 1877, and although he made an immediate impact through conveying a sense of being able to cope with the new intellectual challenges to faith, his thought and period of influence straddled the period between the Victorian generation and its successor. It might also be said of him that the most popular aspects of his thought tended to be the least distinctive. Others who meet the criteria, including P.T. Forsyth, R.F. Horton and the Baptist F.B. Meyer, belong to the following generation, whose influence did not reach its peak until the twentieth century.

The very prominence of the subjects of the various chapters means that they have attracted more attention from historians than many other aspects of the Nonconformist life of the period. Apart from Baldwin Brown, the factual structure of each life and controversy has already been set out in some detail (though not very satisfactorily in the case of the Downgrade Controversy). The function of the narrative sections of the present work is therefore rarely to break new ground, but to serve as a framework for the main purposes of tracing and explaining theological development and influence, and analysing the impact of theological change on the life of the churches.[13] The emphasis is thus more on the history of theology[14] than on ecclesiastical history. In this area existing work is much less adequate and extensive, a reflection of the gulf that too frequently subsists between historians of limited theological literacy and historically naïve theologians.

Two doctoral dissertations that discuss R.W. Dale provide good examples of these two types. William Blair Gould's 'The Theological Contribution of Robert William Dale' (University of Edinburgh, 1955) is lacking in historical perspective: he sets out Dale's theology systematically but is weak on its context, motivation and development. The chapter in Mark Johnson's published thesis utterly fails to make contact with the governing concerns of Dale's theology, presenting him as the inaugurator of a new evangelicalism whose underlying purpose was to give religious sanction to the attractions of secular living in increasingly prosperous times.[15] His work on the

---

[13] The historical section on the Downgrade Controversy is an exception, but in spite of the lengthier treatment it has been accorded, it should be supplemented by the extra detail on aspects of my reinterpretation that can be found in my two articles, 'Spurgeon's Opponents in the Downgrade Controversy', *BQ*, 32 (1988), 274-94, and 'The Downgrade Controversy: New Evidence', *BQ*, 35 (1994), 262-78.

[14] This phrase has been substituted for the usual 'historical theology' to underline my belief that it should not be any less historical than the allied discipline of church history.

[15] Johnson, 'The Dissolution of Dissent' (thesis), 24.

Leicester Conference Controversy has similar failings: the elucidation of its history supersedes all previous work, but his interpretation is compromised by his insistence that though the language was theological the central issue was political in nature.[16]

The best contribution to the ground covered in the Baptist part of the present study is M.R. Watts' doctoral dissertation, 'John Clifford and Radical Nonconformity (1836-1923)'. The only important recent study of John Clifford, it incorporates the development of the major themes of his theology in its full biographical coverage. Watts' theological analysis is generally sound, but is dominated by a simple distinction between Clifford's this-worldliness and the other-worldliness of the older evangelicalism; while this is a useful tool, he does not delve far into its background and applies it with a certain lack of finesse.[17] He also occasionally displays a tendency to imagine a line of development by selecting contrasting quotations, while neglecting the fact that these represent positions Clifford maintained in tandem over long periods.[18]

As in his lifetime, so more than a century after his death, C.H. Spurgeon is the recipient of more attention than other Nonconformist ministers of his generation. A definitive biography is still needed, but three post-war studies stand out from the rest. H.F. Colquitt's doctoral dissertation, 'The Soteriology of Charles Haddon Spurgeon Revealed in his Sermons and Controversial Writings' (University of Edinburgh, 1951), is very useful as a thematically arranged collection of excerpts based on a wide reading of the sermons, but his theological analysis lacks depth and is marred by two basic faults: a belief that Spurgeon entered on his ministry with a ready-made system that never changed, and a tendency to smooth away the more rugged features of his Calvinism.[19] Iain Murray's *The Forgotten Spurgeon* (second edition, 1973) is an interesting discussion of Spurgeon's theological controversies from a viewpoint very close to Spurgeon's own. Its usefulness in furthering understanding of the pattern of his career as a controversialist is however reduced by the fact that Murray is too eager to find ammunition to use in late twentieth century inter-evangelical polemics. In contrast, Patricia

---

[16] *Ibid.*,95.

[17] Michael R. Watts, 'John Clifford and Radical Nonconformity (1836-1923)' (unpublished D.Phil. dissertation, University of Oxford, 1966), 4, 62, 77.

[18] Watts, 'John Clifford', 446-7, 490-91.

[19] Henry Franklin Colquitt, 'The Soteriology of Charles Haddon Spurgeon Revealed in his Sermons and Controversial Writings' (unpublished Ph.D. dissertation, University of Edinburgh, 1951), i, 136.

Stallings Kruppa's *Charles Haddon Spurgeon: A Preacher's Progress* (New York 1982), the most scholarly recent work, is written from a theological perspective far from Spurgeon's. Whereas her account of the man Spurgeon is merely unimpressive, that of Spurgeon the theologian is thoroughly inadequate. A major flaw is the fact that her thesis is self-contradictory: Spurgeon was 'a representative Victorian who succeeded precisely because his values were those of the dominant middle class, who was unique only in his ability to present those values'; yet 'he remained an intellectual captive of the past, and in the end, he devoted his tremendous energies and talents to sustaining the religious convictions of another age'.[20] She cannot have it both ways.

Kruppa's weaknesses as a historian are nowhere more evident than in her chapter on the Downgrade Controversy. Indeed, nothing sorts out historians of the period more than the minefield that is the Downgrade Controversy, a subject discussed in varying depth in all the major works dealing with Baptists in this period. Not surprisingly, the broader-based studies of Grant and especially of Glover give the best accounts of the issues. The most detailed account of all, Ernest Payne's 'The Down Grade Controversy',[21] which aimed to defend the Union leadership against Glover's rather bold criticism, is let down by its narrow perspective. Watts' discussion was a great improvement, but does not altogether escape the dangers inherent in its similar bias. Although that of Murray is an exception, most conservative accounts are of very poor quality, following different versions of a mythical explanation for Spurgeon's defeat.

Murray and Kruppa are among the few historians of the Downgrade Controversy to have made even limited use of the important archival material relating to the controversy in Spurgeon's College. The correspondence, newspaper cuttings and other materials which constitute this are a major source for the account given in the present study. The other major source is the central denominational archival material which is now deposited at Regent's Park College, Oxford. Not even Payne, General Secretary of the Baptist Union at the time he wrote, made much use of this, and much of it only came to light when the Baptist Union moved from London to Didcot in 1989. But manuscript sources relating to the

---

20 Patricia Stallings Kruppa, *Charles Haddon Spurgeon: A Preacher's Progress* (New York: Garland, 1982), 6.

21 Baptist Church House, typescript (1955). His article ('The Down Grade Controversy: A Postscript', *BQ*, 28 [1979], 145-58) adds important documentary evidence but does not modify his interpretation.

people studied are few and far between, and it has therefore been necessary to rely on secondary works for most biographical material. Dale's son was responsible for much the best of these,[22] but later ensured that it would have no successor by destroying all of his father's correspondence and most of his manuscript sermons.[23] That story is typical. The main sources used for the theology of the leaders studied are their own published writings. The proportion used varies according to their output, with attention concentrated particularly on their most theologically significant, popular, and influential works. Newspapers are a major source for the controversies: a wide variety have been consulted, both national and local, daily and weekly, along with magazines. These are supplemented by all the other publications relating to the controversies, and also by available unpublished material.

* * *

The central area addressed by this study being the nature and development of theological and religious liberalism, it is necessary at the outset to address the problem of the definition of that term. Like any broad concept, liberalism is not easy to pin down in a sentence or two. The Oxford English Dictionary offers two invaluable guidelines: firstly, it gives openness to new ideas as the essence of this sense of the word 'liberal' – the other side of the coin of course being at least a degree of disenchantment with received ideas; and secondly, it indicates that this usage is largely a product of the nineteenth century. The analysis of liberalism contained in the present study suggests that it is also possible to attach some positive content to the word. Applied to nineteenth century Nonconformity, liberalism can be taken to denote the variety of new currents that used ethical criteria to question and replace elements that had hitherto been common to all types of orthodox evangelical theology. It follows that conservatism is a term applied to those who endeavoured to maintain the old limits of evangelical communion.

'Evangelical' is another problematic word – its meaning and ownership were in dispute in the nineteenth century, notably in the Downgrade Controversy. Overall, the word underwent a process of rehabilitation among liberals as the century drew to a close, a

[22] A.W.W. Dale, *The Life of R. W. Dale of Birmingham* (London: Hodder & Stoughton, 1898).

[23] Congregational Library, MS letter from A.W.W. Dale, 27 April 1910. This library, now housed at Dr Williams's Library, was still being catalogued at the time I consulted it.

development linked to a growing preference for a spiritual rather than a theological definition.[24] In the process, David Bebbington's widely accepted four characteristics of evangelicalism – biblicism, crucicentrism, conversionism and activism[25] – withered or disappeared. The tendency in this work has been to uphold the claims on the word of the conservatives, they being as it were the sitting tenants, but without attempting to attach to it any precise doctrinal content.

The difficulties involved in definition were felt acutely by people living amidst accelerating changes of all kinds. Baptists and Congregationalists alike were too confused to be able to agree on a set of theological labels: 'modern thought' and 'new theology' were but the most common of a great variety of appellations attached to anything new. Not until the 1880s did 'liberal' begin to come into widespread use, and then those who kept to the old ways began to hear that they were 'conservatives'. Though almost all were liberals in their politics, there are indications that they nevertheless accepted their new identity in good part.[26]

The most profitable way to begin an exploration of the nature and development of liberalism, the largest single concern in this study, is to look at the reasons that prompted people to seek theological change. As these are rarely explicitly declared, and are often to a considerable extent not consciously articulated, they must be elucidated by close examination of the process of change. This is a leading concern of the chapters on Brown, Dale and Clifford, the three leaders whose theology underwent considerable development. The factors can be sorted into categories, though not too neatly, for there is much overlap – psychological, ethical, social, political, philosophical, historical, scientific, cultural – and their interaction

---

24 Referring to half a century earlier, W.F. Adeney said in 1901 that though at that time 'people who considered themselves advanced thinkers repudiated the word "evangelical," as a title of narrowness, obscurantism and bigotry, this is now much less the case, and men who cheerfully accept the ripest results of criticism and are willing to adjust their minds to all ascertained truth, at the same time rejoice in the name "Evangelical"...' *A Century's Progress in Religious Life and Thought* (London: James Clarke, 1901), 14-15, quoted in Johnson, *Changing Shape,* 160.

25 David Bebbington, *Evangelicalism in Modern Britain: A History from the 1730s to the 1980s* (London: Unwin Hyman, 1989), 3.

26 See J. Collings, 'Conservatism in Religious Worship and Belief', a paper read at 1883 Midland Baptist Association meetings, and the adjoined report of the discussion which followed its delivery. There is a copy in Spurgeon's College.

and relative importance assessed. Too many studies have been spoilt by more or less exclusive attention to one or two of these: Mark Johnson gives disproportionate prominence to the social and political, while numerous conservative post-mortems are dominated by historical and scientific factors. The more important considerations are often overlooked as they tend to operate on a long time-span with little superficial visibility. An example is the very powerful optimistic humanism produced when mid-Victorian prosperity and achievement on a wide variety of fronts were put in harness with developmental thought. This was applied prolifically to society and politics, history and science. Even less visible was the great revolution in ethics that has transformed western culture, a movement that proved far more resilient than developmental optimism in the face of twentieth century testing.

The second focus of interest is the nature of the conservatism that resisted change: this is to the fore in the chapter on Spurgeon. A basic observation, but one that needs to be made, is that even the most uncompromising conservatism could not but be altered in the process of resisting liberalism. On the one hand, no-one is completely impervious to the leading forces of their milieu, and in the nineteenth century these were the ones that shaped liberalism; on the other hand, the very fact of having to redefine and regroup to face a fresh threat introduces some change, at least in apologetics, however unwelcome that idea may be. Something of each of these can be observed in Spurgeon.

The last two areas are mainly dealt with in the chapters on the controversies. One is the glimpse they allow of the relative strength, stage of development, and range of variants at one point in time among both liberals and conservatives. The other prominent theme of these chapters is the effect of theological change on the denominational basis of communion. The Leicester Conference Controversy took place when the liberal vanguard too far outpaced the main body, while in the Downgrade Controversy the conservative rearguard felt that the main body was not exerting sufficient control on the liberal van. In both cases the strain on the denominational basis of communion had become too great to be absorbed, and there was much heart-searching on the nature of the basis of communion under the congregational polity.

I

THE CONGREGATIONALISTS

CHAPTER 2

James Baldwin Brown (1820-84)

Introduction

James Baldwin Brown was born on 19 August 1820, the elder son of Dr James Baldwin Brown, an eminent London barrister who belonged to the intellectual and social élite of Nonconformity. He was sufficiently privileged and gifted to take full advantage of the new openings in higher education: in 1839 he was among the first to receive a degree at London University, graduating at the minimum age of eighteen. He then went to the Inner Temple, his father having from the first intended him to follow in his footsteps.[1]

It was while there that Brown became convinced that he was called to the Christian ministry. The idea had been in his mind since boyhood through the influence of his mother's brother, Dr Thomas Raffles of Liverpool, one of the most famous Congregational ministers of his generation.[2] But its rekindling was due to Dr John Leifchild, another prominent Congregational minister whose church he was then attending. 'Listening to his words, I first felt the inspiration of a preacher's spirit thrill through my being. He lit the flame of zeal and love, I might say passion, for the ministry, which, thanks be to God, has never burnt low on the altar of my heart.'[3] 'I so loved and honoured this man – to me the prince of preachers and the saintliest of saints – that while he lived I felt myself a disciple, in spirit, at any rate.'[4] Their relationship became closer through

---

[1] *In Memoriam: James Baldwin Brown, B.A., Minister of Brixton Independent Church*, edited by Elizabeth Baldwin Brown (London: J Clarke & Co., 1884), 1-3.

[2] Brown, *John Leifchild, D.D.: a Sketch of his Character and Ministry. With Brief Notes of His Last Days* (London: Ward & Co., 1862), 31.

[3] Brown, *Leifchild*, 3.

[4] Brown, *Leifchild*, 2. John Hunter ('Baldwin Brown', *Expositor*, eighth series vol. 21, (1921), 304) quotes these words as referring to A.J. Scott, apparently as a result of misunderstanding Joshua Harrison's quotation

Brown's marriage to Leifchild's brother's daughter, Elizabeth, whose father also impressed him deeply: 'The two brothers were just the two most remarkable men that I have ever known – fullest of character, of charm, I suppose because fullest of life.'[5]

Brown studied for the ministry at Highbury College; he referred to his time there in positive terms, although what he learnt in class does not bear comparison with his debt to A.J. Scott, the associate of Thomas Erskine, McLeod Campbell and Edward Irving, who became his mentor at this time. His first pastorate at London Road, Derby, was a mixture of success and controversy: after only three years he accepted an invitation from Claylands Chapel, Clapham Road, welcoming the opportunity to minister in London. For many years his congregation was restricted by the limited size of the chapel, until in 1870 most of them accompanied him in a move out to a large new building in middle class Brixton, which he managed to fill regularly until his death on 23 June 1884.[6]

Baldwin Brown's family connections and education gave him unrivalled advantages at the outset of his ministry, but the Congregational ministry was not an arena in which nepotism could flourish: his success in the ministry was principally due to his own qualities. The most obvious of these was the charisma of his personality: P.T. Forsyth believed that no Congregationalist of his time matched him in this, while another admirer thought the very poise of his body captured the admiration of the young. Next to this Forsyth listed his kindness and courage,[7] but Brown's ministry was one of exceptional power because these personal qualities were joined to lofty ideals and mental abilities of a high order.

Theology

Thomas Raffles and John Leifchild both came from a Methodist background, and never lost the fervour, simplicity and openness of their inheritance in the Evangelical Revival. The doctrine they preached was the moderate Calvinism of the Evangelical Revival, to which they had turned from their Arminian roots. Leifchild, whom he heard much more, Brown called 'perhaps the most soul-stirring, quickening, and successful preacher of his day';[8] he vowed that his

---

of them in his funeral address (Brown, *In Memoriam,* 89).

[5] Brown, *Leifchild,* 5, and *In Memoriam,* 3.

[6] Brown, *In Memoriam,* 6-9, 19-21; Hunter, 'Baldwin Brown', 310, 314.

[7] Brown, *In Memoriam,* 133, 138; F.J. Powicke, 'Frederick Denison Maurice (1805-72): A Personal Reminiscence', *CQ,* 8 (1930), 172.

[8] Brown, *Leifchild,* 32, also 8, 21-22, 30, 44, and *Thomas Raffles, D. D.,*

eloquent, practical, evangelistic ministry cast spells on him during his youth.

At the same time Brown's spiritual experience was also drawing nourishment from a very different source of life. He was reading the Romantic poets and thinkers – Goethe, Shelley, Keats, Coleridge, Emerson – and one book in particular stirred him very deeply, Thomas Carlyle's *Sartor Resartus*. He acknowledged this to the author a few years later:

> It gave shape to very much that I was dimly feeling, and a voice to very much that I was somewhat wildly thinking, and more than that it very much widened and deepened my understanding of the command, 'Walk by faith and not by sight.' To the course of study and thought to which the meditations of that period have led me, I owe it that I am not a member of a purely worldly profession for which I was then educating, but a preacher of the living Word, into the proclamation of which I can at any rate throw as much of earnestness and life as I have in myself.[9]

It was Carlyle's proclamation of honesty and truth that most impressed Brown; this convinced him that a style developed in the previous century was inappropriate for the needs of the mid-nineteenth century, even though it was the style of the man who had made him passionate about the Christian ministry.[10]

Soon after commencing his ministerial training Brown became the disciple of Alexander J. Scott (1805-66); dedicating his first major work to Scott, he called him 'the wisest teacher of the truth, as it is in Jesus, whom I have ever known'.[11] Scott was not a prominent figure: he published very little and his importance in the religious affairs of his time has consistently been underestimated. In calling him a disciple of F.D. Maurice and in judging Maurice to have been the greatest influence on Brown, Mark Johnson was merely repeating errors made by many previously.[12] Scott was a man of enormous

---

LL.D.: a Sketch (London: Jackson, Walford & Hodder, 1864), 19-21; Ian Sellers, 'Liverpool Nonconformity (1786-1914)' (unpublished PhD dissertation, University of Keele, 1969), 89.

[9] Quoted in Brown, *In Memoriam*, 4.

[10] Brown, *Studies of First Principles* (London: The Author, 1848-49), v, 18; see also an 1841 letter to his mother in *In Memoriam*, 5.

[11] Brown, *The Divine Life in Man* (London: Ward, 1859), preface.

[12] Johnson, *Dissolution of Dissent*, 69-70. His sources for the higher valuation of Maurice's influence are from the generation that undertook

intellectual powers – his friends Thomas Erskine, McLeod Campbell and Maurice all acknowledged his superiority – who placed great intellectual demands on his hearers and in consequence scarcely succeeded in communicating outside a small but select circle.[13] He entered the Church of Scotland ministry, and in 1828 cemented a triple bond with Erskine and Campbell during some weeks they spent together at Row; this productive life-long friendship was based on their common rejection of the theology of the Westminster Confession in favour of emphases on Christian experience, the authority of the spiritual conscience, and the universal fatherly love of God. That year he met Edward Irving and accepted an invitation to become his assistant in London. It was Scott who convinced Irving and the others of the continuing relevance of the charismatic gifts and again it was Scott who led Erskine and Campbell out of this phase when he became disillusioned with developments in Irving's church in 1832-33.[14]

When Brown first came across him in 1841, Scott was ministering to an independent congregation in Woolwich. He was won over by two lecture series, 'The Social Systems of the Present Day Compared with Christianity' (1842) and 'On Schism' (1842).[15] A comparison of these with Brown's early publications, *The Young Ministry: its Relation to the Age* (1847), and *Studies of First Principles* (1848-49), shows that the most fundamental lessons that Brown learnt from Scott were the authority of conscience and a belief that God's purposes were to be accomplished in the course of history, and not only beyond it. These two convictions were destined to mould all Brown's subsequent thinking.

Human capacity to discern spiritual things was a theme that threaded its way through all Scott's lectures. He did not expound his understanding of this systematically, but he accorded direct spiritual perception, as he termed it, a pivotal role, for he argued that it is through this spiritual faculty that God, the Bible and the Church

---

its theological studies in the 1870s – after Scott's death, and so not well placed to judge on the matter.

[13] William Hanna (ed.), *Letters of Thomas Erskine of Linlathen from 1800 till 1840* (Edinburgh: David Douglas, 1877), 311; Donald Campbell (ed.), *Memorials of John McLeod Campbell, D.D.* (London: Macmillan, 1877), 141, 160, 281; J. Philip Newell, 'A J. Scott and his Circle' (unpublished PhD dissertation, University of Edinburgh, 1981), 186, 343. This – the only major study of Scott – is followed in most of this account.

[14] Newell, 'A J. Scott', 37, 67, 69ff, 165.

[15] Both were published in Alexander J. Scott, *Discourses* (London: Macmillan, 1866).

have meaning.[16] Brown echoed Scott's conviction concerning the ability of the conscience to discern truth: 'Men have the faculty, and if they used it as wisely and simply as they use the organs of their sensual vision, it would never fail them – of discerning in others, and receiving in themselves *the truth of God*'.[17] Creativity and originality could be achieved by applying this faculty directly to study of the Bible.[18]

The major preoccupation of Scott's lectures was with unity. In 'The Social Systems' he analyzed different systems that aimed to bring about social unity, comparing them with Christianity which he believed shared this aim through its own system, the kingdom of Christ. He argued that recognition of the kingdom would begin with individual societies, with humanity in its nations following later. He restricted himself to discreet hints as to his optimistic belief that God's plans for mankind were to be realized in history, as he wished to maintain a spiritual unity with evangelicals who took a different view of the question.[19] For spiritual unity, his main concern in 'On Schism', was crucial to him: he held that it was the only satisfactory basis for social unity, and that conscience rather than an external authority ascertained the truth in which spiritual unity was to be attained.[20] The correspondence between Brown's ideas and Scott's on the programme of the church was as close as on authority in the church. Brown's clearest early claim that the purposes of God for man were to be achieved within history was couched in characteristic incarnational language even at this early stage:

> Not that He might so lead on humanity, that a crash must at last be inevitable, which should repeat, on a more direful scale, the scenes of the deluge and the destruction of Jerusalem, did the Word become flesh, making himself the elder brother of humanity, and taking all flesh into closer and living relation to himself.[21]

---

16 Scott, *Discourses*, 240, 254.

17 Brown, *Studies of First Principles*, ii, 20. Compare Brown, *The Young Ministry: Its Relation to the Age* (London: John Snow, 1847), 23.

18 Brown, *The Young Ministry*, 5-7, 13-16.

19 He argued that a belief in the impossibility of social unity should not prevent them from working towards it, in the same way that they strove for an unattainable perfection of love (Scott, *Discourses*, 224-8; also 60-61, 89).

20 Scott, *Discourses*, 231-3; 257-67; 72-6.

21 Brown, *Studies of First Principles*, vi, 13, see also iii, 10-11, and *The*

The accompanying package was the one Scott had opened up in his lectures: a belief in progress, a concern for social and political involvement, and a desire to integrate all the different fields of human thought and endeavour and bring them into submission to Christ.

Notwithstanding the influence of Scott, Brown spent the early years of his ministry trying to satisfy his conscience within Calvinism. The decisive break could not have occurred later than 1856-57, when Brown spent some time convalescing at Scott's home. It was at this time that he read McLeod Campbell's new book, *The Nature of the Atonement*, and wrote his first major work, *The Divine Life in Man*, though it was not published until 1859.[22] The heart of the shift was in his understanding of the nature of God, expressed in a sharp change of emphasis from the sovereignty to the fatherhood of God, a phrase that became the rallying cry for opposition to Calvinism.

But the prominent word in the title of Brown's book was 'life', a word characteristic of the ethical – frequently anti-theological – emphasis of the second half of the nineteenth century, and his preface to the second edition appeared to make the untheological aim of the book quite plain:

> I trust that I am fully sensible of the importance of maintaining sound doctrines in the Christian Church. But I doubt whether books on doctrine are the books which are chiefly wanted now. The great question now is, not what to believe, but how to live up to the true standards of life.[23]

In fact the book was much more doctrinal than he claimed. Brown's answer to his question on how to live centred on power, a second word characteristic of his theology. He interpreted the fall as a loss of power, and the gospel as God's power remedying the situation: salvation was essentially power to live regained in Christ.[24] That power was mediated by the Holy Spirit, but its source was in

---

Young Ministry, 5.

[22] Brown, *First Principles of Ecclesiastical Truth: Essays on the Church and Society* (London: Hodder & Stoughton, 1871), 352, and *In Memoriam*, 14; P.T. Forsyth, *Baldwin Brown: a Tribute, a Reminiscence, and a Study* (London: James Clarke & Co., 1884), 4.

[23] Second edition (London: Ward, 1860), 7-8. All subsequent references are to this edition.

[24] Brown, *The Divine Life*, chapters 3-5.

Christ's incarnation, death and resurrection. In consequence any tendency to marginalize these doctrines might result in disastrous interference with the flow of saving power. Brown therefore had grounds for his later opposition to the increasingly fashionable denigration of dogma that accompanied much contemporary reaffirmation of life:

> There are those who attach no meaning which appears to us to be substantial, having its ground in God, to such words as Inspiration, Incarnation, Resurrection, and Immortality; who yet express some amazement if we ask them, What is there left, then, of even the shell of a Gospel? They answer, and no doubt with entire honesty, There are left very beautiful, elevating, stimulating, sanctifying ideas; ideas which will work out in time what may be regarded as the salvation of the human race. But they have to learn that man never has been, never will be, never can be, saved by ideas, as Athens has taught us; it is the solid substance of Divine fact which is behind ideas, it is the vital *power* of God of which that fact is the conductor, which sanctifies and saves.[25]

John Howard Hinton, a leading Baptist of the older generation, fully appreciated the theological content of *The Divine Life in Man*, calling it 'the first open inroad into English evangelical Nonconformist churches of a theology fatally deficient in the truth and power of the gospel'.[26] The fatherhood of God was the subject of the first of the four strictures Hinton published in response; it was the only one to which Brown replied directly, for he was convinced that this was the decisive issue. Hinton held that a distinction should be drawn between God's two relations with men, as ruler and as father. Certain actions, such as condemnation to hell, would be reprehensible in a father but were appropriate to a sovereign judge – and God was judge and not father of the damned. In reply Brown argued that this introduced unacceptable duality into God; that all God's actions sprang from his love; and that his rectoral activity was subordinate to and derivative from his fatherhood.[27]

---

[25] 'Our Theology in Relation to the Intellectual Movements of our Time', *CY* (1879), 70. The emphasis is mine.

[26] Hinton, *Strictures on Some Passages in the Revd. J. B. Brown's "Divine Life in Man"* (London: Houlston & Wright, 1860), 47.

[27] Brown, *The Doctrine of the Divine Fatherhood in Relation to the Atonement* (London: Ward & Co., 1860), 1, 32-3, 35-6; Hinton, 8-11; *The Divine Life*, 26-8.

The main body of Brown's theological writing, from *The Divine Life in Man* to *The Doctrine of Annihilation in the Light of the Gospel of Love* (1875), charts his efforts to build a consistent theology on three basic principles: the universal fatherhood of God, freedom as the fundamental spiritual fact of man's nature, and righteousness. His motivation was overwhelmingly ethical: it is fair to summarize his theology as an attempt to answer two questions, 'How can God be righteous?' and 'How can humanity be righteous?' In the first case the difficulty was the existence of sin, in the second it was its removal.

Brown's answer to the first question rested firmly on human freedom:

> For freedom, and the responsibility which it brings, as the fundamental spiritual fact of our nature, we contend earnestly, yea vehemently, as for the only justification of God's constitution of the human world, the only key to the woes which He lets loose to afflict it and the discords with which he allows it to be torn.[28]

In 1859 he expounded this in a conventional way: 'And God, knowing all the possibilities of freedom, made us free; and saw for the time the wreck and ruin of His hope.'[29] But in 1864 he offered a more positive interpretation of the fall, involving a reinterpretation of the nature of freedom, along lines laid down by A.J. Scott much earlier. He argued that freedom, man's deepest power, had been developed (not merely exercised) in rebellion, leaving man higher in development although more alien in spirit from God. Man's free return to God would bring about a richer fellowship than that which preceded the fall. Sin was not therefore a disastrous accident that forced God to improvise, but the necessary precursor of redemption, with a view to which everything in the world was constituted. Only through sin could our humanity be fully realized.[30] He did not thereby wish to imply that God was the author of the human predicament, a role that he gave to Satan, nor did he equate freedom with independence: he believed that man was made to be dependent

---

[28] Brown, *Misread Passages of Scripture,* first series (London: Hodder & Stoughton, 1869), 72.

[29] Brown, *The Divine Life,* 347.

[30] Brown, *The Divine Treatment of Sin* (London: Jackson, Walford & Hodder, 1864), 2-6, 12; compare Scott, *Discourses,* 230-31. See also Brown, *In Memoriam,* 17-18 for Brown's awareness that this thinking was completely contrary to 'generally received notions'.

on God, and that there was a paradoxical freedom in that subjection.[31]

His argument that the present state of the world is a necessary stage on the way to a transcendently glorious goal was only part of Brown's vindication of God's righteousness; this was completed by his insistence that God be a participant in the pain and not just a spectator:

> I confess that this is the very core of my theology; that is, of such notions of the nature, methods and purposes of God, as I have been able to work out from my experience of life, and my study of his word. It would be all dark to me, utterly, hopelessly dark, if I did not believe that the travail of life and of the Creation is not watched and pitied only, but shared to its utmost depths of pain, by the Lord.[32]

This solidarity of God with humankind reached its climax in the incarnation and atonement; here the first question, as to the righteousness of God, merged with the second, concerning the righteousness of humanity. For the final vindication of God depended on the success of his plan to restore the human race to a deeper and righteous fellowship with himself.

Forsyth said of Brown's theology, 'Everything centred in the Incarnation, in the historic God.'[33] He continued to use it to affirm God's involvement in the entire spectrum of human activity, in the way that he had learnt from Scott.[34] But he saw incarnation as a composite fact, inclusive of Christ's life, death, resurrection and reign;[35] and within that progression the key element was his death, which Brown considered an atonement through which man could become righteous.

Brown's attitude to atonement was governed by a belief that God must deal with man justly in accordance with the reality of man's moral standing. This led him to oppose both of the current straightforward understandings of Christ's death. The subjective

---

31 Brown, *The Battle and Burden of Life* (London: Hodder & Stoughton, 1875), 5, 149-50.

32 Brown, *The Higher Life: Its Reality, Experience, and Destiny* (London: H.S. King, 1874), 151.

33 Forsyth, *Baldwin Brown*, 4.

34 E.g. 'The "Religious Life" and Christian Society', in H.R. Reynolds (ed.), *Ecclesia* (London: Hodder & Stoughton, 1870), 136-7.

35 Brown, *Battle and Burden*, 111.

view, that Jesus' death was the supreme manifestation of God's love, drawing forth man's love and moral reformation in response, incurred his criticism on the ground that it was incapable of making people righteous and therefore involved God in accepting sinners and condoning sin. He agreed with the forensic substitutionary view as to the necessity for both the condemnation of sin and the justification of the sinner, but dismissed the theory's account of these processes as an unrighteous tissue of legal fictions whereby God pretended that the guilty were innocent and vice versa.[36] Brown felt he needed to look for an understanding of the atonement that involved neither overlooking sin nor conjuring it away. For the obverse of his deep concern for true righteousness was a strong doctrine of sin: 'Sin, the sin of the first parent, which every child of Adam repeats, is the fundamental fact of man's being; no religion, no philosophy which makes light of it can lay firm hold of man's conscience and heart.'[37] There could be no alternative to dealing with sin, for sin and death were inseparable: '"The soul that sinneth it shall die." That "shall" is the utterance of a "must." It must be in the nature of things, as God has constituted them. He is the life of a spirit. Sin is schism from Him, and schism from Him is death.'[38] Brown was looking for an objective understanding of atonement that could explain both the expiation of sin in a righteous manner and the development of a true righteousness in forgiven men.

These were precisely the goals that McLeod Campbell had set himself in *The Nature of the Atonement*. Brown was at first impressed but not completely convinced by Campbell's work: it was the best yet, but he looked forward to more light being shed on the subject in the next few years. Later on, however, he became of the opinion that Campbell's book was the greatest theological work since the Reformation.[39] Brown's own published work on the atonement tends to confirm the natural inference that the expected increase in light failed to materialize, making Campbell's contribution more significant than he had anticipated.

He adopted Campbell's central idea that Christ made a perfect confession to the Father of man's sinfulness and guilt; this made it possible to claim that objective satisfaction for sin had been made

---

[36] Brown, *The Divine Life*, 116-18, *The Divine Mystery of Peace* (London: Jackson, Walford & Hodder, 1863), 54-5, and *Misread Passages of Scripture*, second series (London: Hodder & Stoughton, 1871), 11ff.

[37] Brown, *Misread Passages of Scripture*, first series, 89.

[38] Brown, *The Divine Fatherhood*, 37.

[39] Brown, *The Divine Life*, 115-16; Forsyth, *Baldwin Brown*, 4.

without having recourse to the penal theory.[40] Yet there were also differences between the two men. Whereas Campbell took extreme care to avoid any language that could be construed as legal fiction Brown did not shy away from the strongest biblical language on atonement; he favoured most that of representation, though he was even prepared to countenance that of substitution in a modified form.[41] And while Campbell held that Christ's death was merely the point at which his two-fold activity, witnessing to the love and righteousness of the Father, and confessing sin on our behalf, came into sharpest focus, Brown confined Christ's atoning activity to the cross in the belief that death was essential to atonement.[42]

Baldwin Brown's thinking on justification and sanctification maintained a close resemblance to McLeod Campbell's. Neither could brook a legal righteousness that was not at the same time an ethical righteousness, which meant that they could not subscribe to the conventional Protestant distinction between justification and sanctification: the former term contained the usual meaning of both, leaving the latter word redundant – Brown rarely used it. The point that they both emphasized was that the link between atonement and eternal life must be natural and not arbitrary. Campbell often described this in terms of human participation, variously in Christ's life, death and righteousness, as well as in the atonement; for both men faith was the act of entering into this participation.[43] However there was some divergence in the way they described this process. Whereas Campbell wrote of a previously hidden human capacity for good becoming apparent only in relation to Christ's atonement, and virtually omitted the Holy Spirit from his book, the Holy Spirit was very much to the fore in Brown's theology of the restoration of power to live: 'The doctrine of the Spirit is the essential complement of the Cross, and it is the glory of Christianity and its power'.[44] If

---

[40] Brown, *Divine Mystery of Peace*, 55; compare Campbell, *The Nature of the Atonement in its Relation to Sin and Eternal Life*, (London: Macmillan, 1867[2]), 134ff.

[41] Campbell, *Nature of the Atonement*, 161; Brown, *Divine Mystery of Peace*, 53-4, *Divine Fatherhood*, 138-40, and *Misread Passages of Scripture*, second series, 91ff.

[42] Campbell, *Nature of the Atonement*, 257ff; Brown, *Divine Fatherhood*, 36-9.

[43] Campbell, *Nature of the Atonement*, xv, 154, 308, 330; compare Brown, *The Divine Life*, 137-40, and *Light on the Way*, Elizabeth Baldwin Brown (ed.) (London: J. Clarke & Co., 1886), 211.

[44] Brown, *Light on the Way*, 290, compare 164; Campbell, *Nature of the Atonement*, 159-60, 334-6. It is interesting to note the affinities here

pushed, Campbell would have agreed with Brown that the righteousness involved in this process of justification was imputed as well as inherent.[45] However, imputation was restricted as much as possible, being seen as God's regarding someone's own righteousness, quickened by faith in Christ, as complete from the earliest stages of its development, an attitude that was possible because the power at work guaranteed the eventual completion of the process.[46]

That completion was evidently still unattained at death, and so the moral education of humankind was of necessity prolonged into eternity. This did not square with the traditional doctrine of a final judgement after death in which humanity was divided into the saved and the lost. This was a sensitive subject, and Brown rather avoided it until 1869, by which time others were beginning to take it up on all sides; at face value at any rate his earlier allusions did not clash with the old ideas.[47] But his first detailed exposition of his mature thought on the subject did not appear until *The Doctrine of Annihilation in the Light of the Gospel of Love* (1875), the work in which he completed the development of his theology by working out a coherent eschatology on the basis of his three principles of fatherhood, freedom and righteousness.

Earlier on he had begun to look for a broader entrance to heaven, adopting from Maurice the idea that the Holy Spirit witnessed to everyone, so that no-one is condemned without an opportunity to turn to God.[48] There remained a difficulty, for there was too marked an inequality of opportunity to receive the Gospel to be cancelled out by the strongest emphasis on the hidden workings of the Holy Spirit. There was also a parallel obstacle littering the Scripture in the form of the doctrine of election; this was by no means insignificant to one who believed, as Brown did, in the unity and authority of the Bible. He gave the subject detailed attention in two series of *Misread Passages of Scripture* published in 1869 and 1871, arguing that God's visible election of Israel and the Church was for service and witness,

---

between Campbell and Erskine on the one hand, and Brown and Scott on the other.

[45] Brown, *The Divine Treatment of Sin*, 85ff. Though Campbell was very reticent about imputation the idea nevertheless comes through in *Nature of the Atonement*, 177, 226-7.

[46] Brown, *Light on the Way*, 212, and *Battle and Burden*, 44-5.

[47] Brown, *Misread Passages*, first series, 38, *Divine Life*, 63-4, *The Divine Mystery of Peace*, 97, and *The Divine Treatment of Sin*, 69-70.

[48] Brown, *The World-Religion* (London: Ward & Co., 1851), 14, *The Divine Life*, 89-95, and *The Divine Mystery of Peace*, 97.

not for separation and privilege; that Romans 9 spoke of a providential election of peoples, not a spiritual election of individuals; and that the Bible taught the universality of God's love.[49]

This allowed Brown to believe that God did not determine people's fate, but for a while he remained mystified by the fact that some were more advantageously placed than others.[50] He resolved the difficulty by transforming the significance of death, which in evangelical theology ushered in the great eschatological judgement. He argued that as Christ's victory made death his subject it was no longer the realm of sin, but introduced a new phase in the endless operation of God's grace. 'Therefore the Father will never cease from yearning over the prodigals, and Christ will never cease from seeking the lost, while one knee remains stubborn before the name of Jesus, and one heart is unmastered by His love.'[51] He saw no reason to go back on his initial rejection of dogmatic universalism, for once death ceased to delimit the operation of God's fatherly grace it also ceased to be a barrier for the other two principles. He reasoned that if God could call sinning to an end and proclaim universal peace it would render the whole of life's struggle a mockery. Freedom must be preserved, which meant that universal restitution could not be assumed, however ardently hoped for, and righteousness had therefore to be attained through the continuation of the educational disciplines of life on earth:

> I see before me a great vision of pain; the suffering of the free spirits is not ended here. Nay, it is manifest that the righteous here have not finished their education; multitudes of good men pass to the gate of death laden with infirmity, with graces smirched and virtues crippled; halting disciples, whose culture has to be carried on and perfected on high. There will be struggle and discipline for many of us, but we shall bear it joyfully in the radiant light of hope, and in the cherishing, quickening atmosphere of love.[52]

---

[49] Brown, *Misread Passages*, second series, 27-8, 70ff, 77, 85, and *The Divine Treatment of Sin*, 179ff.

[50] Brown, *Misread Passages*, first series, 72-3, and second series, 84.

[51] Brown, *The Doctrine of Annihilation in the Light of the Gospel of Love* (London: Henry S. King, 1875), 118-19. For earlier statements that stopped slightly short of this see *The Higher Life*, 163, 327-8, and *First Principles of Ecclesiastical Truth*, 357.

[52] Brown, *The Doctrine of Annihilation*, 127, also pp. 128-9, *Misread Passages*, first series, 38-9, and *Light on the Way*, 32.

In spite of its rigours this purgatorial vision was more attractive to Brown than the traditional evangelical vision of eternal praise, which he dismissed as 'this restful and self-centred vision of immortality'.[53]

This discussion has shown the prominence of ethical considerations in the development of Baldwin Brown's theology. The extent of their dominance in his mature theology can be assessed by discussing his approach to the question of authority, and also his attitude to the Bible and science. There was much activity and change in the British religious world in both these fields, especially towards the end of Brown's life, and biblical criticism and Darwinian evolution have usually been accorded the lion's share of the responsibility for theological change in the period.

In *First Principles of Ecclesiastical Truth* (1871) Brown dealt with the human need for an infallible guide, defined as 'a knowledge of truth and duty which he can accept as final'.[54] Having first rejected Catholic claims on behalf of an infallible Church or Pope, Brown examined the similar claim made by Protestants about the Bible. He rejected its infallibility in detail but believed that it contained God's revelation, and affirmed that as God's own revelation of his mind it must be infallible. However difficulties in interpreting it meant that in practice it did not serve as an infallible guide; he was severely critical of what he considered the Protestant idolatry of treating the Bible as an infallible recipe book. In his view the Bible was not intended to spell truth out unmistakably, but to train the reader guided by the Holy Spirit. It was to the infallibility of the Holy Spirit that Brown turned last of all. He affirmed it, with none of the equivocation he had shown with regard to the Bible, but with the same sort of proviso as to its practical import: 'The guide is infallible, but we have no infallible apprehension of His guidance'.[55] Yet after reaching not dissimilar conclusions on the two authorities Brown allowed his personal proclivities to dictate a conclusion that took him beyond the bounds of his discussion: 'Our ultimate trust, then, is not in an infallible Church, nor in an infallible book, but in an infallible Teacher, who is leading us by ways of doubt and question and error, which we know not, to the knowledge of the mind of God.'[56] This was simply a reiteration of his belief in the authority of the conscience enlightened by the Holy Spirit, a belief held from the

[53] Brown, 'The Soul and Future Life', *Nineteenth Century*, 2 (1877), 513.
[54] Brown, *First Principles of Ecclesiastical Truth*, 9; this paragraph is based on 3-125.
[55] *Ibid.*, 121.
[56] *Ibid.*, 124.

outset of his ministry under the influence of A.J. Scott.

Brown's views on the authority of Scripture were not associated with any particular theory of inspiration: he had yet to find one that satisfied him. However he thought the books of the Bible differed in their degree of inspiration, with some of them entirely lacking divine inspiration. This idea had two main uses: it allowed scope for errors, and it helped him emphasize the role of the Holy Spirit in interpreting and applying the Bible. The example of errors to which he made allusion – the sun standing still and God's commanding the extermination of peoples – show where his concern lay: miracles that were particularly difficult to accommodate within a scientific understanding of the workings of the universe, and things that were simply unacceptable to Brown on moral grounds.[57]

In neither case was he concerned with biblical criticism. On the few occasions in his later writings when he alluded to matters undergoing critical debate it was always in a conservative vein – he joined in the widespread practice of noting with satisfaction that later critics were rebuilding what earlier ones had destroyed.[58] P.T. Forsyth had good grounds for saying that Brown was not quite at home on critical questions.[59] He was content in the belief that his broad spiritual approach to the Bible was impervious to criticism, in contrast with the vulnerability of verbal inspiration. It did however depend heavily on the unity of the Bible, something for which he argued conservatively to the end of his life.[60] There is no evidence that biblical criticism exerted the slightest influence on the development of Brown's theology.

A study of Brown's attitude to evolution draws a similar blank. His acceptance of the theory was a gradual process. In 1871 it was a possibility to be taken seriously, but not a matter of immediate concern; by 1874 he had thought it through theologically and saw no objections, prepared to accept that Genesis 3, as Genesis 1 before it, might convey spiritual rather than historical truth, while still thinking special creation more likely; in the late 1870s he gradually swung toward complete acceptance, with the proviso that man's

---

57 *Ibid.*, 92-3, 95.

58 *Nonconformist*, 5 December 1877, 1216; Brown, *First Principles of Ecclesiastical Truth*, 172, *The Higher Life*, 207-11, and *The Risen Christ the King of Men*, Elizabeth Baldwin Brown (ed.) (London: R. Fischer Unwin, 1887), 270-74.

59 Forsyth, *Baldwin Brown*, 3-4.

60 Brown, *First Principles of Ecclesiastical Truth*, 100, *The Higher Life*, 305-6, and *Light on the Way*, 177.

spirit was not a product of evolution.[61] While science and theology did not conflict in Brown's mind they did in the minds of many scientists and theologians in the 1870s. He blamed the theologians on two counts: for treating the Bible as an authority on the natural order, and for teaching 'a narrow, selfish, exclusive, and wholly incredible theology' – by which he meant Calvinism – the scientific reaction against which was 'simply at heart the inevitable protest of the honest human intellect'.[62] He concluded that there would be no revival of religion without a gospel 'in fair harmony with the immutable convictions of man's conscience, and the ineradicable instincts of his heart'.[63] In other word, scientific opposition to religion was basically on ethical grounds, and the solution was the promulgation of an ethical theology. This subsuming of the scientific problem into the ethical one reveals yet more clearly the moral dynamic that permeated all his thought.

In the twenty years it took Baldwin Brown to develop this theology the Congregational theological scene changed dramatically. His theological writing was usually practical and often polemical, and it is interesting to observe the way his emphasis changed over that period.

Brown was always on the theological left of the leading group of Congregational ministers, a fact that was demonstrated very clearly as late as 1878, when he refused to endorse the policy of the vast majority in pursuing a course of action condemnatory of the Leicester Conference on religious communion. But the climate in which he operated contrasted starkly with that pertaining in the 1850s. The tone and doctrine of *The Divine Life in Man* were considerably milder than those of *The Doctrine of Annihilation,* something reflected in Brown's evident nervousness on publishing the latter in 1875,[64] yet it was the earlier book that stirred up much more opposition. The explanation of this phenomenon centres on an extraordinarily rapid change of atmosphere that had occurred in the Congregational Union in the early 1860s. Brown's own book must be counted a contributory factor, for its challenge to the prevailing status quo showed up the weakness of its hold, but the main cause was the emergence of a new generation of leaders as the previous

---

[61] Brown, *First Principles of Ecclesiastical Truth,* 250, *Higher Life,* 4-9, *The Gospel of the Son of Man* (London: J Clarke, 1875), 3ff, *Nonconformist* 5 December 1877, 1216, 'Our Theology', 60-61, and *The Risen Christ,* 184-6.

[62] Brown, *Doctrine of Annihilation,* 10, and *First Principles of Ecclesiastical Truth,* 244.

[63] Brown, *Doctrine of Annihilation,* 11.

[64] *Ibid.,* 130.

one faded. Brown commented on the change as early as 1864: 'Happily, too, it is more easy to speak freely and to be judged Christianly, when treating, however imperfectly, yet with honest and reverent heart, of these high matters, than it was when I published the "Divine Life in Man," four years ago.'[65]

In the 1870s a new generation began to surface with approaches more radical than his own, and Brown shifted his stance to meet a very different threat than that he had perceived in his youth. After stating in 1859 that the need of the day was for life rather than theology, he balanced the two emphases in 1871, and in 1878 weighted the scales in favour of theology.[66] In his last years he even engaged in prophetic protests against 'some of our modern theologians, who simply leave out God from His Gospel',[67] in a manner similar to that for which his disciple P.T. Forsyth became well known.

His unease at the direction the Church was taking was paralleled in his outlook on political and social affairs, where a strident optimism progressively gave way to unrelenting gloom. There is no mistaking the change in the man who, having once described victory in the Crimea as 'this last noon-day triumph of progress over barbarism',[68] later anticipated that a terrible catastrophe would result from the crushing of the poor between armed national camps and the principles of industrial civilisation.[69]

This was particularly depressing in view of his belief that God's purposes were to be worked out in history. He sought compensation for this foreboding by adopting a long historical perspective in which to reaffirm his optimistic creed:

> I look forward to an anxious quarter of a century for you, young people, who will have to fight in the front of the battle when we have hung up sword and shield in the Temple of Peace on high. I contemplate, I confess, with grave anxiety, the immediate future, but without a shadow of fear as to its ultimate and not very distant

---

[65] Brown, *The Divine Treatment of Sin*, viii.

[66] Brown, *First Principles of Ecclesiastical Truth*, 362-3, and 'Our Theology', 70, compare 'The Soul and Future Life', 511.

[67] Brown, *The Risen Christ*, 208.

[68] Brown, *The Fullness of Time; or, the Advent of the Lord the Divine Key to History* (London, 1856), 8.

[69] Brown, *The Risen Christ*, 230-31.

result.[70]

A second response to the gloomy outlook was to stress the hidden progress taking place in individual lives, which he saw as the key to social progress.[71]

Baldwin Brown's theology has been summed up as 'Hegelian'.[72] On balance this is unhelpful, for it obscures the fact that, like the vast majority of Nonconformists of his generation, the sources of Brown's theology were predominately British. Brown was familiar with Hegel; he employed his dialectic in the pursuit of their common interest in philosophical history on the grand scale. Doctrinally, Brown had a Hegelian interpretation of the fall as a development, though his immediate source was probably Scott, but on the key doctrines of God, man and incarnation Brown's views lay within the mainstream Christian tradition, at some considerable distance from Hegel's.[73] P.T. Forsyth, who knew Brown very well, came up with a better epithet when he spoke of him as above all a moral theologian. He acknowledged that Brown was not quite at home in either metaphysics or criticism, but nevertheless called him 'a very genuine theologian'.[74] Baldwin Brown himself once declined the title of theologian, though admitting that he was intensely interested in the subject.[75] This modesty was directly linked to an awareness he shared with R.W. Dale and John Clifford among others that the rebuilding they were doing did not have the solidity of the structure they had felt obliged to do away with. It is of very general application to those of that generation involved in theological revision who, unlike many of their successors, tended to know what it was they were trying to revise. Brown confessed that he was still looking for the creation of a new instrument of thought to give mastery of a new world, a gospel 'in fair harmony with the immutable convictions of man's conscience, and the ineradicable instincts of his heart'.[76]

---

[70] Brown, 'Our Theology', 69.

[71] Brown, *Light on the Way*, 247-9, and *First Principles of Ecclesiastical Truth*, 263-4.

[72] E.g. Alan P.F. Sell, *Theology in Turmoil: The Roots, Course and Significance of the Conservative-Liberal Debate in Modern Theology* (Grand Rapids: Baker Book House, 1986), 110.

[73] Brown, 'The "Religious Life" and Christian Society', 139ff; Scott, *Discourses*, 230-31.

[74] Forsyth, *Baldwin Brown*, 3-4.

[75] Brown, 'The Soul and Future Life', 517.

[76] Brown, *The Doctrine of Annihilation*, 11; also 'The Soul and Future Life',

Influence

The way in which someone's name first attracts widespread attention can be of considerable importance in establishing the associations it will evoke thereafter: such was the case with Baldwin Brown. His earliest publications did not have any great impact,[77] and it took two controversies to make him widely known in Nonconformist circles. The first of these was the 'Rivulet' affair of 1856-57, occasioned by virulent conservative attacks on the theology of a book of poetry of that name by an obscure Congregational minister named T.T. Lynch. Brown was among the members of the fraternal of London Congregational ministers to which Lynch belonged who, joined by a few others, published a letter in his defence.[78] The signatories themselves became the targets of Lynch's opponents. Brown then published a pamphlet in which he hit back at the most formidable of these, John Campbell.[79] His most significant remarks were on the 'young school', about whose supposedly revolutionary intentions there was apparently much unease. In spite of claiming to be only speaking for himself he nevertheless assumed a representative role in saying that 'all that we want is, more simplicity, more reality, more life'.[80]

The second controversy, that surrounding the publication of *The Divine Life in Man* in 1859, was a smaller affair than 'Rivulet', but it brought Brown far more attention as this time he was the central figure. A strong condemnation has often been the making of a book; this service was done for *The Divine Life in Man* by John Howard Hinton, a prominent Baptist minister. Baptist participation, including that of C.H. Spurgeon,[81] was a feature of the controversy: Brown was becoming as well known in the sister denomination as in his own.

517.

[77] See F.J. Powicke, *David Worthington Simon* (London: Hodder & Stoughton, 1912), 17 for an isolated reference to their influence.

[78] Originally published in the *Eclectic Review*, the letter can be found in Brown, *In Memoriam*, 11-13. See also F.A. Freer, *Edward White, his Life and Work* (London: Elliot Stock, 1902), 315.

[79] Brown, *The Way of Peace for the Congregational Union; with Remarks on the Morale of its Religious Literature, the So Called Young School, and Negative Theology* (London: Ward, 1857), 3-17.

[80] Brown, *Way of Peace*, 23.

[81] Susannah Spurgeon and Joseph Harrald (eds.), *C.H. Spurgeon Autobiography*, revised ed., 2 vols. (London: Banner of Truth, 1962, 1973), I, 482-94.

This controversy marked an important turning point in Brown's life. The vague suspicions of him that had existed in many quarters now coalesced into a pronounced disapproval which Brown, a very sensitive man, felt deeply. Financial difficulties and overwork also contributed to a depression in which he seriously considered withdrawing from the Congregational ministry. A.J. Scott helped him decide against this course of action, warning him from his own experience of the isolation and loss of influence an independent ministry would entail.[82] This was a crucial decision, for the Congregational denomination was to be his pre-eminent sphere of influence.

The gloom of the aftermath of the Divine Life controversy soon lifted. The very theology and publicity that made him *persona non grata* in some quarters made him very popular among those who shared the disillusionment Brown had expressed with current Calvinist theology and the church life it engendered: *The Divine Life in Man* marked him out as the leading Congregational exponent of a theology that was to prove attractive to the young. His friends did not desert him,[83] and his sense of isolation did not last long. Brown's most implacable opponents were in the older generation that was rapidly passing from the scene.

The still more rapid decline in the control these men had exercised over the implicit definition of the denomination's basis of communion can only be appreciated when the nature of leadership in the two Congregational denominations is understood. This was well expressed during the Leicester Conference Controversy: 'We have no *episkopoi* amongst us in name, but we do expect that those in high places will "oversee" the churches, and take care that the all-paramount interests of Christian truth shall suffer no damage.'[84] These informal bishops were recognized in the churches, and were generally friendly with each other. The qualifications required for this status were varied. Culture, education and intellect were important; so too was the ability to give expression to these in preaching and other forms of public speaking. Their churches would provide solid evidence of these qualities: they would always be urban and contain a cultured element, and they would often be large and situated in London. The main platform for the demonstration of ability was provided by the twice-yearly meetings of the Baptist and Congregational Unions, which also gave opportunities for important personal contacts. Committee membership became increasingly

[82] Brown, *In Memoriam*, 16-17.

[83] *Ibid.*, 16.

[84] W.D. Ground, in *EI*, 10 January 1878, 36.

important, with the ultimate accolade being the chairmanship of the Union. Most important of all was acceptance by those already belonging to the leading group. Using a variety of ways to measure ministerial success several men would have figured more prominently than Joshua Harrison, but the respect of other leaders meant that he was as near as was possible in Independency an archbishop, counselling the other leaders and usually taking the most prominent place on representative occasions – it was he who preached Baldwin Brown's funeral sermon.[85] When a new generation of leaders took over in the 1860s Brown was accepted as one of their number. At the very moment his position in the denomination had seemed at its shakiest it was fast becoming more assured than it had ever been before. He was to be an embarrassment to his fellow leaders at times, especially in the Leicester Conference Controversy, but his theology never disqualified him from the group. His widow wrote that 'the tide seemed to turn' in the early 1860s. She attributed this to the impact of *The Divine Life of Man*;[86] that was important, but not so much for its creative theological impact as because it exposed the obsolescence of the old sanctions.

Brown's chairmanship of the Congregational Union in 1878 was the final recognition of his status. This came rather late, at least in part because he had for some time refused to be nominated. It is possible that he feared that theological opponents would defeat his nomination, or at least make it too disputed for comfort. If this is so, then he was too cautious, for only two people voted against him.[87]

Like most ministers, Brown devoted most of his time and effort to his own church. His congregation was drawn from all parts of London, 'embracing many men of intelligence and culture who occupied important positions in various walks of life'.[88] These were people with backgrounds similar to his own, who like him had been immersed in educated middle class metropolitan society, and who in consequence welcomed Brown's way of dealing with the tensions that had arisen between this milieu and the Calvinism of the Evangelical Revival. They were deeply involved in the contemporary ethical emphasis and were attracted to a theology that sought so explicitly to build on a moral foundation. They were also people

---

85 A.W.W. Dale, *R.W. Dale of Birmingham*, (London: Hodder & Stoughton, 1899[2]), 677-8 gives some clues as to how Harrison came to exercise this role.

86 Brown, *In Memoriam*, 17.

87 *CW*, 19 April 1878, 305; *Nonconformist*, 9 May 1877, 463-4.

88 Brown, *In Memoriam*, 9.

with a large vested interest in society, who wished to affirm it rather than adhere to a theology that reproved it and sometimes turned its back on it.

His second main occupation was writing. As the minister of a relatively small church Brown felt the need to supplement his income by writing for the press. Of most significance were his articles on religious subjects for *The Christian World,* which had by the 1870s much the largest circulation of any Nonconformist newspaper, enabling him to reach far more people than through any of his books.[89] The editorial support and publicity the newspaper gave him were very considerable. Brown confessed that he was surprised by the interest aroused by his 1875 lectures, *The Doctrine of Annihilation,* ascribing it largely to the publicity accorded them by the editor of *The Christian World* 'with that courage and love of free enquiry which have always been conspicuous in the conduct of that journal'.[90]

The vast majority of Brown's books and pamphlets resembled *The Doctrine of Annihilation* in that they started life as sermons or lectures. Even *The Divine Life in Man* was hardly an exception, for it is a series of unpreached sermons written during a period of convalescence.[91] As in other things, it marked the turning point in his publishing career: the steady flow of pamphlets now became a steady flow of books. Half of these went into a second edition, but just four went into multiple editions during his lifetime, all of them among his less theological and philosophical writings.[92] One of these more popular books, *The Soul's Exodus and Pilgrimage (1862),* opened up a new world for John Hunter when he read it while a student at Nottingham Congregational Institute, although it was only later, while at Spring Hill College, that he was introduced to Maurice's

---

[89] Circulation in the 1870s was 125,000 to 130,000 weekly – *CW,* 19 April 1878, 308; Arthur Porritt, *More and More of Memories* (London: G. Allen & Unwin, 1947), 76. *Light on the Way* is made up of articles republished from *The Christian World.* See also Brown, *In Memoriam,* 16, *Nonconformist and Independent,* 26 June 1884, 625, and 17 July 1884, 692.

[90] Brown, *The Doctrine of Annihilation,* vi. James Clarke's theological sympathies lay very much with Brown; his own contribution to the spread of the salient features of 'fatherhood theology' was immense.

[91] Brown, *In Memoriam,* 14; this contains a list of his published writings, complete except for his contributions to periodicals (pp. 185-8).

[92] Brown, *The Soul's Exercise and Pilgrimage,* 3 editions, 1862-70, *The Home Life in the Light of its Divine Idea,* 5 editions, 1866-70, *The Higher Life,* 5 editions, 1874-78, *Home; its Relations to Man and to Society,* 3 editions 1883-84 (*In Memoriam,* 186-8).

writings and moved decisively away from the Calvinism of his upbringing.[93] Another testimony to the influence of a book of Brown's on a leading Congregational minister was that of Alexander Mackennal, who told the Congregational Union in his presidential address of 1888 that *The Divine Mysteries* had alone made his life worthwhile.[94]

Hunter later found that Brown's personal influence was much more potent even than his writings:

> Elevating, quickening, helpful, as were his writings, they ever felt that the man himself in his whole spirit, bearing, and influence, far exceeded these... He had not only the qualities which placed him unquestionably among the great teachers of his age, which made his ministry an important factor in the history of religious thought in England – advancing that revolution in theology which had made the last thirty years a new and splendid epoch of reform in the progress of Christianity – but he had also the qualities in a rare degree which drew to him a personal respect, love, and reverence such as were accorded to few.[95]

Charisma, kindness, and commitment were the main qualities that combined to act so powerfully on the young. J.T. Stannard, John Hunter's closest friend, testified to the nature of Brown's influence in a memorial sermon:

> When I first went to him with grave difficulties and a heavy heart, it seemed to me, as I well remember now, comparative stranger as I was to him then, that I had not been five minutes in his presence before I felt as if I had known him intimately all my life, or before he had grasped the situation of my cares and burdens and made these his own. Nor did he simply place himself at my disposal with a brotherliness and a grace that took clear possession of my heart; he did what was more helpful and needful than that: in a few wise, weighty words he showed one, as with a divine clearness and impressiveness, the simple path of duty, what one ought to strive to do and to be, and though he seemed to make the

---

[93] Leslie Stannard Hunter, *John Hunter, D.D.: A Life* (London: Hodder & Stoughton, 1921), 20.

[94] Mackennal, 'The Life of the Spirit', in *CY*, 1888, 57. *The Divine Mysteries* was an 1869 republication of the 1863 *Divine Mysteries of Peace* and 1864 *Divine Treatment of Sin*.

[95] Brown, *In Memoriam*, 114-15.

> cross to be carried more sacred, more commanding, he sent one away feeling what an honour, what a means of education, what a spiritual blessing it was to have to bear it; and with every impulse and purpose of one's being stirred and enlisted to its fullest extent.[96]

The help Brown offered his proteges was not limited to advice. Thus he secured a first pastorate for Forsyth at Shipley, stood up for him when he got into trouble over the Leicester Conference Controversy, and then found him a new church in Hackney when his situation in Yorkshire became too difficult.[97] He greatly enjoyed the adulation he received in return for his considerable investment in young ministers and students.[98]

The obvious point at which to begin to assess the extent of Baldwin Brown's influence is the Leicester Conference Controversy of 1877-78, which provided the only figures that can be considered relevant. At the Congregational Union Assembly of May 1878 all the denominational leaders except two, Brown and Joseph Parker, supported resolutions that reaffirmed the Union's evangelical faith in response to the challenge posed to this by the conference on religious communion held during the Union's assembly in Leicester the previous autumn. Parker moved an amendment that attracted about sixty votes; Brown, not letting his position as chairman handicap him, opposed the resolution outright and lost by roughly a thousand votes to twenty-five. Parker then suggested that Brown should resign from the chairmanship, and thereby strengthen the loyalty of so many of the young to his leadership. Brown seriously considered this course of action, but decided against it, saying that he did not want to found a party and risk causing a schism.[99]

The voting figures would appear to suggest that Brown's influence, when measured against the collective influence of the other leaders of his generation, did not amount to very much. But appearances were deceptive. One consideration is the group of those who came under Brown's influence: tributes and obituaries agreed that his impact was mainly on the young, especially on the cultured

---

[96] *Ibid.*, 143.

[97] *EI*, 22 November 1877, 1283; W. L. Bradley, *P.T. Forsyth: The Man and his Work* (London: Independent Press, 1952), 34.

[98] Brown, *In Memoriam*, 68-9, *Doctrine of Annihilation*, 11-13; L.S. Hunter, *John Hunter*, 74.

[99] *CW*, 31 May 1878, 449; Brown, 'The Perfect Law of Liberty', *CY*, 1879, 82.

and educated.[100] That would include some who could no longer be considered young in Brown's last years – William Dorling considered himself Brown's disciple from the time he met him in the 1850s, just before beginning his theological training[101] – but Brown's two most distinguished followers, John Hunter and P.T. Forsyth, both born in 1848, believed that theirs was the generation he had influenced most. Having taken as his text 2 Kings 2:12 – 'My father, my father, the chariot of Israel and the horsemen thereof' – Forsyth began his tribute by saying, 'I am sure I truly speak the heart-feeling of at least the young generation of Independents, of the men who will give us our colour twenty years hence, when I put it in these words of Elisha to his departing master.'[102] Another disciple stated categorically that 'whatever might be the influence of other leaders over the older men of our churches during the great decade from 1875 to1885, Baldwin Brown was the one who, more than anyone else, captured the younger men'.[103]

Brown did this largely through figuring prominently in the college discussions of the 1870s – Forsyth said that Brown 'was himself one of our colleges'.[104] The crucial point in the life of a Congregational minister was usually the time he spent at theological college. Here contacts with peers were at their closest during a young man's most impressionable years: it was at college that students pooled their knowledge of the theologies and theologians of the moment, reading and discussing them together, providing each other with an alternative education that could be considerably more influential than that administered by their tutors.[105] Some students, especially in the London colleges, were able to get to know Brown in person: Forsyth was a member of his church, and F.B. Meyer, a leading Baptist minister of the same generation, was also in

---

100 E.g. Brown, *In Memoriam*, 92, 177.

101 *Ibid.*, 172-3; see also *CW*, 15 May 1878, special May meeting number, 3.

102 Forsyth, *Baldwin Brown*, 3; see also Hunter in Brown, *In Memoriam*, 114.

103 Powicke, 'Maurice', 172.

104 Forsyth, *Baldwin Brown*, 3; also Brown, *In Memoriam*, 130, 151.

105 Kenneth D. Brown, *A Social History of the Nonconformist Ministry in England and Wales, 1800-1930* (Oxford: Clarendon, 1988) makes much of the many negative features of Nonconformist ministerial education of the period, including the predominance of sheltered provincial backgrounds of teachers and taught, but neglects major counter-balancing factors such as the one discussed here.

contact with Brown while a student at Regent's Park College.[106]

In his tribute to Brown, a writer in *The Watchman* doubted whether even Thomas Binney, the man the young of the previous generation had followed, had been as influential as Brown had been in more recent times.[107] The Leicester conference figures can be accounted for in many ways: the radicals mishandled the debate, which was dominated by the skills of those two experienced politicians, R.W. Dale and Guinness Rogers; Brown was at some disadvantage through being in the chair; Parker's amendment introduced a confusion of issues that proved unhelpful to opponents of the Union line; more significantly, many of the generation Brown influenced were not yet ministers, and those who were were young and often in small and poor churches, and would therefore have been underrepresented in the Assembly – a state of affairs that would have been even more pronounced among lay delegates.

The fact that Brown was the Congregational leader with the most extensive following among the young and educated of the denomination in the 1870s marks him out as a man of some consequence, but a further question concerning the nature of the influence he exercised must be answered: after all, charismatic qualities and dedicated personal service had not resulted in a major theological contribution in the case of Thomas Binney.

Brown's theology of divine fatherhood was certainly very different from the varying forms of Calvinism that were the norm in Congregational churches at the time at which it was developed. It is also true that this kind of theology was rapidly gaining ground at the expense of the older forms; Brown was by no means alone in finding it more in keeping with his ethical outlook. Nor can it be disputed that Brown was unrivalled as an exponent of this new theology within his denomination, and thus presided over its growth.[108] But Brown's disciples were unanimous in casting him in the role of mediator rather than source of this theology, awarding that distinction to F.D. Maurice. F.J. Powicke's version of the pantheon is representative:

> I may be wrong, but I incline to say that a majority of our younger ministers in 1877 bore the Maurician stamp, if under that description may be included what they drew from Thomas Erskine, McLeod Campbell, A.J. Scott, and George MacDonald.

---

[106] *EI*, 22 November 1877, 1283; W.Y. Fullerton, *F.B. Meyer, A Biography* (London: Marshall & Co., 1929), 24-5.
[107] 9 July 1884, quoted in Brown, *In Memoriam*, 177.
[108] Forsyth, *Baldwin Brown* 7.

> These, I am sure, were the favourite authors of my own friends in the ministry; and the man to whom we looked up with enthusiastic trust as leader was James Baldwin Brown, who knew Maurice personally, corresponded with him, and sympathized fully with the spirit and scope of his teachings and very strongly with his efforts in favour of the working classes... He was the Charles Kingsley of the Free Churches, the mediator of Maurice to them.[109]

Maurice and the theologians these young men associated with him had their differences but also had much in common: a very well developed conscience; the desire to take both sin and atonement seriously; a belief in God's fatherly love that served as a basis for optimistic views as to the future of the human race; a spiritual emphasis that offered an attractive alternative to the immobile dependence on Scripture of increasingly beleaguered evangelicals. People were looking for an ethically satisfying theology that would also be invulnerable to the assaults of philosophy, criticism and science, and the efforts of Maurice, Brown and their like were the most attractive on offer. The primacy accorded to Maurice by no means meant that his version of the theology was considered the definitive one. For a start it was not very generally understood: Powicke was as deeply involved in the 'Maurician culture' as any student at Spring Hill College, yet in his early preaching demonstrated the salvation of Satan in the belief that Maurice was a dogmatic universalist.[110] Understanding of Maurice's theology was particularly complicated owing to the multiplicity of its sources – a strong Anglicanism grafted onto Unitarian and Platonic roots, with additional contributions from Roman Catholicism, Calvinism and Quakerism. Brown's more straightforward response to his Calvinist heritage was more accessible to his fellow Congregationalists. Forsyth astutely observed an allied factor that favoured Brown's influence: theologically he was near enough to the Congregational public 'to give him a greater leverage in the liberal direction, than men who go much further only to leave more behind'.[111]

In the nature of things it is not possible to make a precise assessment of Brown's share in the responsibility for theological change in his denomination. His kind of theology was carrying all before it in his later years, and he was clearly its pioneer and leader

---

[109] Powicke, 'Maurice', 172; see also Forsyth, *Baldwin Brown* 4; *BW*, 7 March 1907, 581; L.S. Hunter, *John Hunter*, 20.

[110] Powicke, 'Maurice', 171, 182.

[111] Brown, *In Memoriam*, 128.

in his own denomination, but his influence was certainly less than that of Maurice – whose vogue among Congregationalists may well have been greater than he enjoyed in his own Church – and also less than simplistic conclusions drawn from the facts recorded here might lead one to suppose.

One way to put it into perspective is to look at what happened to his reputation after his death. Baldwin Brown was sixty-three years old when he died in 1884, not too old to have outlived his reputation. On all sides it was said that the loss was irreparable.[112] There was certainly no one among his followers in a position to take up from where Brown left off. The one person who was widely regarded as his natural successor, John Hunter, never really assumed that status. He was proposed as the new pastor of Brown's Brixton Independent Church, but the church was divided, with the majority of the deacons vetoing an invitation to him; this was at least in part on theological grounds, for Hunter was more radical than his mentor. The prospect of Hunter nevertheless exercising leadership over a Brownian faction ended with his move to a church in Scotland in 1886.[113]

Lacking an acknowledged successor, Brown also went without a biography. His widow preserved and collected material with the intention of writing one, but it was never published; all that remains of her work is the memorial volume published soon after his death.[114] None of his own writings gained any long-term popularity, and his memory was destined to accompany to their graves those who had once been his followers. Although Brown's published output was so much greater than A. J. Scott's, his fate was similar, the transient fame of a man whose deepest impact on others had been personal.

This was not however the only reason for the eclipse that rapidly followed Brown's death. Something similar happened even to Maurice, if his pioneering Christian socialism is excepted. In the 1880s the main subjects of theological debate were new: biblical criticism and associated rationalistic theologies, along with new

---

[112] *Ibid.*, 115; Forsyth, *Baldwin Brown*, 18; *Spectator*, 28 June 1884, quoted in *In Memoriam*, 162.

[113] L.S. Hunter, *John Hunter*, 74-5; Charles Kirkby, *The Late Baldwin Brown's Pulpit: a Protest and a Defence Addressed to the Congregational Ministers of England and Wales* (London: Christian Union Office, 1886), 5-7.

[114] *In Memoriam*, vi. She edited three posthumous works, the last in 1893. There are no surviving descendants, and no line of enquiry seems likely to lead to any documents.

varieties of idealist thought evolved in response to these, all of this accompanied by a big increase in German influence. These were matters on which Maurice, Brown and their associates had little to contribute.

Amidst these changes, and not heedless of them, there emerged in Congregationalism one man who spoke out motivated by a prophetic and Christ-centred spirituality that Baldwin Brown had prefigured, clinging as Brown had done to the facts of the Gospel, his passion all the greater because of the popularity of liberal views that marginalized them. P.T. Forsyth was not particularly appreciated by his generation, nor particularly understood by the later generation that did appreciate him. Already in 1884 Forsyth feared that without Brown the radical wing of the denomination would leave their evangelicalism behind, provoking a period of conservative theological reaction.[115] His fears were not groundless, and his own efforts to remedy the situation proved ineffectual, but he did succeed in one area in which Brown failed, namely in writing works that would be read many years after his death. Baldwin Brown's continuing relevance is very largely connected to his part in moulding Forsyth. Forsyth's assessment of Brown's significance, that he was the greatest Independent since the seventeenth century,[116] was made soon after Brown's death and may now seem strange, but it says a great deal for what he meant to Forsyth himself.

---

[115] Forsyth, *Baldwin Brown*, 8-9.
[116] Brown, *In Memoriam*, 142.

CHAPTER 3

Robert William Dale (1829-95)

Introduction

Robert William Dale was born in London on 1 December 1829. His father was a dealer in hat trimmings; neither of his parents was well educated. They were members of Moorfields Tabernacle. Dale's childhood there coincided with the ministry of John Campbell, the celebrated Congregational editor and conservative controversialist. As several brothers died very young, and the only one that survived was ten years younger than Robert, he was the object of some very concentrated maternal affection. His mother's passionate desire that her son should become a minister must have influenced him powerfully during his childhood.[1]

Dale showed great ability at school, and became his schoolmaster's assistant in 1843. While occupying a similar post at Andover the following year, he went through a deep spiritual crisis that gave him some difficult months before suddenly being resolved in a conversion experience of Christ. He soon began to pray in public and teach in Sunday school, and in 1845 started preaching and contributing to Christian magazines.[2] That level of literary attainment did not satisfy him for long: the following year he brought out a book, *The Talents: or, Man's Nature, Power, and Responsibility*. Its precocious author was facing up to life with exceptional gifts allied to an archetypal evangelical seriousness: the amount of study that went into it indicates that Dale was very earnest in seeking to avoid the sin he set out to expose, namely man's guilt in not using his talents in God's service.

When Dale arrived at Spring Hill College, Birmingham in 1847 to train for the ministry, a fellow student described him as a thorough, hard-working student, whose thought was remarkably mature; his

---

[1] A.W.W. Dale, *The Life of R.W. Dale of Birmingham* (London: Hodder & Stoughton, 1899[2]), 1-4.
[2] *Ibid.*, 7, 13-19.

most salient characteristic was then, as later, his independence. Yet at the same time he was completely unconceited and a good companion.[3] John Angell James, minister of the Carr's Lane Church[4] in Birmingham and one of the most prominent Congregational ministers of the day,[5] immediately appreciated Dale's qualities. He began by according him more attention than the other students, and then gradually took steps to ensure that Dale joined him and then succeeded him as minister of Carr's Lane. Dale first supplied his pulpit in 1849. In his last year of studies, 1852-53, he preached for James once a month; after that he was engaged as assistant pastor, and in 1854 the church unanimously supported his ordination as co-pastor. This was not as smooth a process as the bare outline might lead one to suppose, for the big age difference between them led to some tension: Dale was unhappy with James's moderate stance on disestablishment, and there were also theological differences. James's kindness and sensitivity ensured that their working relationship survived these, and were also crucial in overturning Dale's initial vision for his ministry, which had been for further study in Germany, followed by the evangelism of the masses commencing with a small city congregation.[6]

It was not immediately apparent that Dale would spend all his life in this one church in Birmingham. James was an ideal colleague, but Dale did not find it easy to establish his own position in a church that had been moulded by one man for half a century. Even while he was still assistant he was given time off because of depression and ill-health, things that were to dog him at intervals all his life, and in 1856 James had to help him through a period during which he wondered whether he ought to be in the ministry at all. By most

---

[3] J.B. Paton, *The Reasonableness of the Evangelic Faith* (Nottingham: Arthur Johnson, 1895), 5-8.

[4] I use the spelling of the church's name current at least between Dale's ordination and memorial services, reflected in their published titles, rather than the more recent 'Carrs'. See 'Editor's Preface' in Clyde Binfield (ed.), 'The Cross and the City: Essays in Commemoration of Robert William Dale 1829-1895,' Supplement to the *Journal of the United Reformed Church History Society* Vol. 6 (Supplement no. 2), 1999, iii.

[5] 1785-1859. A typical member of the last generation of Congregational ministers to be deeply influenced by the Evangelical Revival, he was most widely known for his bestseller, *The Anxious Inquirer*, published in 1834.

[6] Dale, *The Life and Letters of John Angell James* (London: J. Nisbet, 1861), 457-65.

standards Dale was doing very well, but he was finding it difficult to live up to his own lofty ideal of ministerial earnestness, and was especially despondent about the lack of conversions through his ministry. Had it not been for forceful interventions by James and the church, Dale would have accepted invitations from other churches on two occasions. His position in Birmingham only finally became secure when the church united behind him in 1862.[7] Membership and congregations at Carr's Lane maintained buoyant levels throughout Dale's time there, despite this being a period in which many city centre churches were suffering from the exodus to the growing suburbs.

It was in great part as a political dissenter that Dale came to enjoy national prominence, whether in the ecclesiastical politics of disestablishment, as a leading supporter of Joseph Chamberlain in the municipal politics of Birmingham, or as a notable protagonist in the educational debates that were so important a feature of the Nonconformist politics of the period. He found time for foreign travel, including visits to Palestine and Australia; but his most significant journey was to Yale, where he was the first Englishman to deliver the Lyman Beecher lectures on preaching.[8] Recognition of his leading place in his own denomination came in 1869 when he was made chairman of the Congregational Union at the remarkably young age of thirty-nine. In spite of more or less withdrawing from denominational affairs and politics alike in his last years, largely because of the painful repercussions of his parting company with Gladstone on the Irish Home Rule question, Dale was offered the presidency of the first International Council of Congregational Churches, held in London in 1891, a clear sign that his denomination considered him its leading minister.[9]

It was during that year that Dale suffered a breakdown in health from which he never fully recovered, brought on initially by a bout of influenza. Thereafter his ministry was frequently interrupted and his workload of necessity reduced. He died on 13 March 1895, from heart failure following three weeks' critical illness.[10]

---

[7] Sermon by Dale in *The Jubilee Services of the Rev. John Angell James* (1855), 59-60; Dale, *John Angell James*, 471-2, 475-6, 478-81; A.W.W. Dale, *Life of R.W. Dale*, 45, 178-80, 675-6.

[8] *Ibid.*, 331-2. These were published as *Nine Lectures on Preaching* (London: Hodder & Stoughton, 1877).

[9] *Ibid.*, 230, 600-601.

[10] *Ibid.*, 602, 692; *Independent and Nonconformist*, 21 March 1895, supplement, 193.

Theology

As a boy Dale naturally accepted the teaching to which he was exposed week by week in church. This acquiescence was abruptly disturbed by a sermon that made him realize that nothing had come of this belief; the conclusion he drew was that he was not saved. Late in 1843, at the age of thirteen, he embarked on an anguished search that lasted months and was of profound significance for his entire subsequent Christian experience. Night after night when the house was quite he spent time in reading, thought and prayer. His textbook, John Angell James' celebrated *Anxious Inquirer*, led him to attempt to analyse the nature and content of genuine faith, an exercise that proved unfruitful.[11] The end of the quest came when his thoughts turned away from himself and his faith to the person of Christ: 'When we learnt that it was Christ – not merely the truth about Christ – that was to save us, it seemed a new Gospel. We turned from the truth to Him and were saved.'[12] This emphasis on the person of Jesus Christ was to remain pivotal to both his theology and his spirituality.

At first this was fitted into the Calvinism preached with a conviction that was already unusual by his minister, John Campbell. Though he was to turn away from this, Dale continued to believe that this phase had not been without its advantages: in 1880 he told Congregational ministerial students at Airedale College that at the age of fourteen he had known more than he did then, and that this systematic theology, though only partly true, had conveyed more spiritual and moral advantage than did contemporary despondency or indifference.[13] More than other English Congregationalists of his generation, Dale preserved the ideal of a theological system, and this, joined to his ability and application, made his efforts at theological reconstruction more valuable than theirs. It is no accident that the three most prominent Congregational theological leaders born in the 1830s and 1840s, A.M. Fairbairn, P.T. Forsyth and John Hunter, all came from the numerically weak Congregational

---

[11] Dale, *The Ordination Service of the Revd. R. W. Dale, M.A., to the Co-Pastorate of the Congregational Church Assembly in Carr's Lane Chapel, Birmingham* (1854), 31-2, *John Angell James*, 288, 299-301, and *The Epistle of James and Other Discourses* (London: Hodder & Stoughton, 1895), 205-6, 264-5. The preacher of the sermon that provoked the search was the Revd J. Sherman.

[12] Dale, *Epistle of James*, 206.

[13] Dale, *The Evangelical Revival and Other Sermons* (London: Hodder & Stoughton, 1880), 263-5.

churches of Scotland, where the decline of Calvinism was considerably slower than in England. It is an important paradox that it was those who were educated in Calvinism who were best equipped and motivated for the quest for something to take its place. Dale's first sermon, preached in the spring of 1845, was a defence of Calvinism; a year later he was avidly reading the works of Robert Hall, the great Particular Baptist preacher, whom he considered the most profound thinker he had yet come across.[14]

Publication of *The Talents* – a venture that Dale soon regretted – allows an unusual glimpse of a theological mind at such an early stage in its development. Two prominent features that can be ascribed to Campbell's influence, a harsh dogmatism and a florid style, were markedly absent in all his later writing, but the book also contained themes that were developed in later years, of which the uniting principle was his postmillennial hope that the day would come when all men would honour God on earth. Dale believed this final consummation would involve intellectual, political and moral change, and therefore that efforts should be directed against ignorance, tyranny and especially impiety.[15] Thus some of his most fundamental ideas predated the important formative years at Spring Hill College.

Dale left some clues as to the people and books, encountered before and during his studies, that contributed to the development of his thinking about these three kinds of change. F.D. Maurice never meant quite so much to him as to Baldwin Brown, but Dale did give him the main credit for showing many of his generation that the state was a divine institution, and consequently that political involvement was not worldly. Edward Miall, the editor of the *Nonconformist*, provided additional inspiration and dictated the political agenda.[16]

But the ethical and intellectual dimensions were deeper than the political, as is abundantly shown by two articles Dale wrote to mark the death of Thomas Carlyle.[17] He referred to the near panic that had

---

[14] A.W.W. Dale, *Life of R.W. Dale*, 18, 32-3.

[15] Dale, *The Talents: or, Man's Nature, Power, and Responsibility* (London: Aylott & Jones, 1846), 62, 67, 90.

[16] Dale, *Fellowship with Christ and Other Discourses Delivered on Special Occasions* (London: Hodder & Stoughton, 1891), 200-201; A.W.W. Dale, *Life of R.W. Dale*, 63.

[17] Dale, 'Thomas Carlyle', *Congregationalist*, 10 (1881), 208-17, 285-92. A.W.W. Dale and Mark Johnson both ignore this major influence, and Johnson aggravated the resulting distortion by inflating Miall's influence, especially through exaggerating its theological dimension

arisen among Nonconformists in the early 1850s because of the spell cast by Carlyle's genius and intensity on many of the younger preachers. 'He was more to us for a while than all our tutors; more to us than all the theologians and fathers of the church.'[18] Dale went on to say that though they had come to understand the incompleteness and mischievousness of some of his teaching, they were different to what they would have been had they not read *Sartor Resartus* and *Lectures on Heroes*. They were immeasurably indebted to him both for the substance and the method of their thought, and also for the intellectual exhilaration and moral earnestness of the years under his influence; in a real sense Carlyle had been the greatest preacher in England in the last half-century. These are strong words. Other influences were associated with that of Carlyle. Dale recalled that parts of Francis Newman's writings appealed to him, while he never forgot the thrill he experienced on reading the celebrated phrase of Emerson's, 'Trust thyself. Every heart vibrates to that iron string.' He remarked on Emerson's blend of stoicism and mysticism, and might have commented on the important place both of these had in his own thought and spirituality.[19] He himself had what he took to be the fundamental principles of transcendentalists and idealists, namely the moral freedom of man, the divine power of conscience and direct intuition of God.[20]

Dale was never the theological disciple of anyone: he read widely and was indebted to many people, but never even came close to throwing in his lot with a particular thinker. A fellow student wrote that the strongest impression he made on them from the first was one of strong and stately independence.[21] Nevertheless the re-examination of his theology that led him through dark struggles with doubt as a student was especially prompted and influenced by George Dawson, a young exponent of the transcendental philosophy, whose ministry Dale began to attend almost immediately after commencing his studies in Birmingham in 1847. Dawson

---

('The Dissolution of Dissent; an Accommodation, 1850-1918' (unpublished PhD dissertation, University of Toronto, 1982), 52).

[18] Dale, 'Carlyle', 210.

[19] Dale, 'Memoir', in Henry Rogers, *The Superhuman Origin of the Bible Inferred from Itself* (London: Hodder & Stoughton, 1893[8]), lxi, and *Epistle of James*, 245. Dale's writings contain numerous references to Epictetus and Marcus Aurelius; for an example of his mysticism, see *Evangelical Revival*, 210.

[20] Dale, 'George Dawson: Politician, Lecturer, and Preacher', *Nineteenth Century*, 2 (1877), 52.

[21] Paton, *Reasonableness*, 7-8.

was unusually radical for the period, going beyond a critique of Calvinism to challenge basic evangelical doctrines. Dale drew the line at the latter – he had a deep conviction that evangelicalism was fundamentally an expression of authentic Christianity, though in a new age it might require some radical reworking – but went along with the former: he accepted that there was much justice in Dawson's denunciation of moderate Calvinists for carrying on using the old language while abandoning its meaning.[22] The conceptual tools he used to separate the two categories were two parallel pairs of antitheses, between fact and theory, and substance and form; these were to remain an important part of his theological method. Fact and substance were revealed and eternal but theories and forms were temporary and required periodic reformulation.[23] Dale held that evangelicals should be grateful to Dawson for making them consider whether their traditional theological creed truly represented their spiritual faith; he believed that too many lost the truths themselves as well as untenable theological representations of them because they failed to distinguish revealed facts from human theories.[24]

The men who were supposed to be looking after Dale's education had a lesser influence on his theology. Indeed, John Angell James had none at all: he accorded Dale a personal interview upon hearing that the star student was drifting away from the evangelical faith, but his arguments, unlike his concern, made no impression on their object. Francis Watts, the theological tutor, was a fine though cautious exegete with a good knowledge of German scholarship in the field; he must have helped Dale develop his own very considerable exegetical skills. But his knowledge was inadequate in other areas, especially Old Testament criticism.[25] Theology at Spring Hill suffered because of the greater attractiveness of the philosophy classes of Henry Rogers, who was a much better teacher than Watts; long afterwards Dale wrote of his gratitude, affection and veneration for him.[26] He did not derive his own philosophy from Rogers, whose

---

[22] Dale, 'Dawson', 44, 47-8, 52-5; A.W.W. Dale, *Life of R.W. Dale,* 61. Dawson (1821-76) began as a Baptist minister but was by this time in charge of an independent 'Church of the Saviour'.

[23] The finest example of the method is in his major theological work, *The Atonement* (London: Hodder & Stoughton, 1878[7]); see ix, x, lxvii, 19.

[24] Dale, 'Dawson', 59-60.

[25] Dale, *John Angell James*, 458, 'The History of Spring Hill College', in *Mansfield College, Oxford: its Origin and Opening* (1890), 11, 13-14.

[26] Dale, 'Spring Hill College', 8-9, 12-13, and 'Memoir', lix-lxi. Rogers (1806-77) was best known as a talented contributor to the *Edinburgh*

thinking was of the previous generation, but Rogers helped him develop his intellect, as well as guiding the improvement in his style.

Dale's theology developed through the interaction between his Calvinist and evangelical heritage on the one hand, and the complex and powerful set of new Romantic influences chiefly associated with Thomas Carlyle on the other, within the context of developing critical scholarship and scientific knowledge. But there would remain at the very heart of it a christocentric spirituality rooted in the crisis and conversion he went through while in his teens.

* * *

'Whatever theologians may teach, I will do honour to moral excellence wherever I find it. I will not pervert the plain dictates of my conscience under the pressure of any theological system whatever.'[27] The theological system in question was Calvinism. In 1865, when Dale pronounced these words, he still felt its pressure sufficiently to warrant highlighting his rejection of it; fifteen years later he declared it dead, and thought there was no point in attacking it any more.[28] Calvinism is a minor theme in his published writings, most of which date from the period in which he no longer perceived it as a threat, but was a point of reference for all his thinking, whether in preserving some aspects or in reacting against others. The passage quoted above shows that the test to which he submitted it was that of conscience. Elsewhere he declared that Calvinism's theory of moral inability destroyed moral responsibility; that its dogma of imputed righteousness robbed final judgement of meaning; that its doctrine of perseverance took the edge off the New Testament's most urgent exhortation; that its eternal decrees rendered human effort insignificant; that its unqualified representation of God's sovereignty undid his moral character; and that, in sum, Calvinism destroyed the roots of religion and morality.[29]

Dale's justification of the magisterial role of conscience began with a set of presuppositions that he called acts of higher reason, contrasted with the logical understanding. The terminology was

---

Review and as the author of the very successful *Eclipse of Faith* (1852); he was later President of Lancashire Independent College (1858-69).

[27] Dale, *Discourses Delivered on Special Occasions* (London: Jackson, Walford & Hodder, 1866), 31.

[28] *Evangelical Revival*, 194-5.

[29] Dale, 'Mr. Matthew Arnold and the Nonconformists', *Contemporary Review*, 14 (1870), 546-50.

Coleridge's, and the outlook broadly Kantian. He held that they were universal and inevitable, and incapable of proof by the lower-ranking intellect. These fundamental beliefs were in man's moral freedom, the authority of the moral law, and the existence of God, the righteous administrator of the law. These intuitions he distinguished from, and elevated above, the realm of natural theology.[30] It was an ethical system in which God was accorded a judicial rather than legislative capacity.

Dale never attempted a systematic anthropology, contenting himself with loosely compiled references to various human faculties. Conscience was one of these – he rejected the theory that conscience is God's voice in humanity – and like other human faculties it developed gradually, and was subject to injury and decay.[31] He further recognized that though moral ideas were in a sense innate, ideals of virtue were largely socially determined. Yet though there was no direct revelation of the eternal law of righteousness (Dale's habitual term) man was nonetheless in possession of God's revelation in conscience.[32]

The authority structure of Dale's theology consisted of parallel ethical and spiritual elements, each of which had an external and an internal component: conscience gave internal testimony to the eternal law of righteousness, and God was known through the believer's direct experience of Christ. His urge to internalize authority was constant, but he never achieved a settled relationship between the ethical and spiritual elements.

The source of these difficulties lay in the way Dale conceived of the relationship between God and the law. In 1867 he considered whether the moral law was the expression of God's nature or will, as in classic Calvinism and the modified version of Grotius respectively, or something independent, necessary and eternal. Conscience dictated his answer, though he also acknowledged a debt to John Stuart Mill: moral distinctions could never be arbitrary, and God himself was only righteous because he was true to the eternal law, to

---

[30] Dale, *Christ and the Controversies of Christendom* (London: Hodder & Stoughton, 1869), 15, and *Christian Doctrine* (London: Hodder & Stoughton, 1894), 3-4, 87.

[31] Dale, 'The Positive Side of Modern Deism', *Eclectic Review*, new series vol. 3 (1858), 262-3.

[32] Dale, 'The Expiatory Theory of the Atonement', *BQR*, 46 (1867), 465-6, and 'The Idea of the Church in Relation to Modern Congregationalism', in *Ecclesia: a Second Series of Essays on Theological and Ecclesiastical Questions*, H.R. Reynolds (ed.) (London: Hodder & Stoughton, 1871), 363.

which he did homage.[33] When Dale returned to the subject in his 1875 Congregational lectures on the atonement his position remained substantially the same, though Dean Mansel had now replaced Calvinism as the butt of his criticisms: conscience spoke directly in the name of the eternal law, not needing to invoke God's authority before making its decisions. But he did recognize that his 1867 article appeared to set law over God, an idea from which he recoiled. He maintained that the eternal law had a certain priority, as its recognition by conscience was a necessary prelude to the awareness, through knowing God, that in him man was dealing with the same authority in personal form; and that the two operated as authorities in complementary spheres, that of the law being conscience and that of God being will.[34]

Never again did Dale imply that the law was above God, but he went on vacillating between recognizing them as distinct but equal and merging the two.[35] Amid this inconsistency there was a gradual shifting of the balance away from the law and toward God with the passing years. The most significant change came between 1875 and 1877, inspired by Dr Wace's *Christianity and Morality*, the Boyle Lectures of 1874-75, a book Dale recommended constantly, calling it 'in my judgement, the most valuable contribution to English theological thought that has been made for many a year'.[36] In the 1870s Dale became concerned at the growth of moral, subjective, theories of the atonement expounded by people who, like himself, took their stand on a directly perceived universal law. In Wace's work he found a theological argument that helped him respond to this by transferring his emphasis from the ethical to the spiritual side of his authority structure. Wace contended that righteousness was a relation between persons, and that men's relations to God must

---

[33] Dale, 'The Expiatory Theory', 484-7.

[34] Dale, *The Atonement*, 363-73. Gould argues that Dale believed God to be the creator of the law, but thoroughly misunderstands the two passages he cites in favour of his position – William Blair Gould, 'The Theological Contribution of Robert William Dale' (unpublished PhD dissertation, University of Edinburgh, 1955), 66; Dale, *The Ten Commandments* (London: Hodder & Stoughton, 1871), 20, *The Atonement*, 349-50.

[35] Thus God *is* 'the living law of righteousness', *The Epistle to the Ephesians* (London: Hodder & Stoughton, n.d.), 66; but compare *Christian Doctrine*, 156.

[36] Dale, *Preaching*, 211, and *Christian Doctrine*, 279-80. A leading Anglican evangelical, Wace was then Chaplain of Lincoln's Inn and Professor of Ecclesiastical History at King's College, London.

therefore be determined personally rather than metaphysically. The authority of an impersonal law could not create consciousness of sin and guilt, as distinct from awareness of transgression, and could not therefore prescribe an adequate response to the human predicament. Dale responded to Wace with a sharp change in emphasis: just two years after refusing to allow God to intervene between conscience and the law he declared that not even the law of righteousness must be allowed to come between the conscience and God.[37]

The way for the change of emphasis from law to God had been prepared by an experience in the 1860s that was second only to his conversion in its effect on his life and ministry. He recalled it many years later: 'I remember that when I discovered and knew that the Lord Jesus Christ is alive, I could think of nothing else and preach of nothing else for weeks.'[38] The revelation of law in conscience had started in the dominant position but this revelation of God in Christ began the process that ended with the positions being reversed. The common thread throughout was Dale's conviction that the Christian faith must rest on an internal authority rather than an external basis vulnerable to advancing knowledge: it was on Christ within the believer that he progressively laid an ever greater emphasis, not on the Jesus of the Bible.[39]

Dale believed this direct revelation to be not an esoteric doctrine but the foundation of all Christian life: 'For myself I believe that the religious life is originated and sustained in activity by the actual experience of the objective reality of the Divine righteousness and grace, and the power and glory of Christ as the Redeemer of men.'[40] He considered this direct contact between God and the soul the ultimate principle of Protestantism, and the prerogative of all Christians by the Holy Spirit's illumination.[41]

The pattern of the relationship between conscience and Christ showed a certain similarity to that between law and God. There was however an additional complication in the gradual transfer of emphasis from Christ in the Bible to Christ known in experience. In 1867 he stated that he based his theology on the final authority of Christ and those he commissioned. He added that this did not mean paralysing conscience: since it had received its own revelation it was

---

[37] Dale, *Preaching,* 211; compare *The Atonement,* 368.

[38] A.W.W. Dale, *Life of R.W. Dale,* 679.

[39] Dale, 'The Alleged Reaction in the Theology of Congregationalists', *Congregationalist,* 2 (1873), 59.

[40] A.W.W. Dale, *Life of R.W. Dale,* 679.

[41] Dale, *Protestantism: Its Ultimate Principle* (London: Hodder & Stoughton, 1874), 35-40, 77.

impossible to imagine a contradiction. The revelation of Christ went further, and it was necessary to receive it on bare authority first, trusting God's righteousness, although it could be expected that the moral condition of believers would develop so as to grasp it better.[42] The theology of atonement he then expounded rested quite as much on the authority of conscience as on the main drift of New Testament doctrine.

The next few years were ones in which Dale, like many others, sensed the imminence of a very considerable religious crisis, particularly for evangelicalism. He was concerned by anti-supernaturalist philosophy, radical biblical criticism and national materialism, but was still more worried by the condition of the Church, with the rapid growth of ritualism on the one hand and the theological confusion and spiritual decay of evangelicalism on the other.[43] He was becoming aware of the shortcomings of theology and religion in which spiritual experience had no prominent place, beginning to discern a contrast between a spiritual, God-centred, Christianity and its ethical, man-centred deformations. Inspired by his own momentous experience of the living Christ, he responded to this situation by calling for a return to the fundamentals of Christian spiritual experience in a prophetic style prefiguring that of twentieth century neo-orthodoxy:

> How is it that the dread of the Divine anger and the passionate longing for the divine Forgiveness have disappeared?
>
> ... The deepest reason of all seems to me to be this – in these last times we have broken with historical Christianity; ... we have invented a new kind of religion - which may claim the merit of originality; at least, there is originality in supposing that it is the religion of Christ. We have invented a religion without God.[44]

The effects this had on Dale's theological method can be observed when he returned to the atonement, his main field of systematic study, in 1875. He had not abandoned his belief that conscience could pronounce authoritatively on theological matters, but did criticize a very ethical religion in which the search for righteousness

---

[42] Dale, 'The Expiatory Theory', 465-7.
[43] Dale, 'Have We Forgotten Christ?', *Congregationalist,* 1 (1872), 705-6, and 'Prayer in Relation to Revival, *Congregationalist,* 3 (1874), 1.
[44] *Evangelical Revival,* 161.

was self-centred, God being looked to for inspiration and help but not submitted to and worshipped as an authority. The remedy for this was to be brought by the Holy Spirit, through preaching, awakening the ignorant conscience to the fact that transgression of the law was also sin against God, needing to be pardoned and not merely abandoned.[45]

The most complete statement of his later view of the relative positions of Christ and conscience was given in a sermon 'On Obeying Christ'.[46] Having condemned views that failed to acknowledge Christ's authority, he presented his own view:

> [Christ] speaks to us as an objective conscience – a conscience outside of us – with an authority to which we are bound to submit... Conscience touches God; God touches conscience. Whatever obedience I owe to the law which is revealed to conscience, I owe to God... Do you ask, "Why must a man obey God?" You can never have heard the voice of God if you ask that question. You may as well ask, "Why must a man obey conscience?" I must obey conscience because I *ought*; there is nothing more to be said. I must obey God because I *ought*; there is nothing more to be said.
>
> And in Christ God comes to me and claims my obedience... He is the Eternal Law of Righteousness incarnate.[47]

He defended this belief in the equality of Christ and conscience against the following argument for the supremacy of conscience: Christ himself appealed to conscience to recognize his claims; we cannot submit to him unless our consciences recognize his moral supremacy; if conscience is fit to judge on Christ's moral claims as a whole it must therefore be able to judge his teaching in detail and enforce only what it recognizes. Dale's answer was that in recognising Christ's moral authority conscience recognized its master and must then insist on obedience to him.[48] By this means he maintained a foothold in the

---

[45] Dale, *The Atonement*, 31-2, 349-50; compare *Evangelical Revival*, 164.
[46] Published in *Laws of Christ for Common Life* (London: Hodder & Stoughton, 1884), 273-88. The discussion in *The Living Christ and the Four Gospels* (London: Hodder & Stoughton, 1890), 47-9 reveals no changes.
[47] *Laws of Christ*, 281-3; emphasis Dale's. It may be observed that in calling Christ 'the Eternal Law of Righteousness incarnate' Dale is mixing his ethical and spiritual categories once more.
[48] Dale, *Laws of Christ*, 283.

evangelical tradition of external authority, even though he had participated to a considerable extent in the internalising of authority characteristic of liberalism.

But the foothold was insecure. In saying that Christ was to be obeyed as an 'objective conscience' Dale was evidently referring to pronouncements of the external Christ of the New Testament, supposing circumstances in which conscience was unable to judge. But this gave rise to a problem in the authority structure of his theology, for – as will now be shown – he had marginalized external authorities too much for his intellect to be prepared to recognize the authority of the Bible to the degree that his conscience recognized that of Christ, the complement without which the latter was somewhat hollow.

Dale had been brought up in a Protestantism preoccupied with an objective apologetic centred on the vindication of the biblical revelation by appeal to its miracles and fulfilled prophecies. The book which did most to lead him to abandon this position in favour of the internal authority of spiritual experience was Francis Newman's *The Soul: Its Sorrows and Its Aspirations,* which he probably read soon after its publication in 1849, especially a passage in which Newman contrasted the first Christians with the scholarly apparatus of modern apologists.[49]

Dale's popular lecture, *Protestantism: its Ultimate Principle,* included biblical authority among the principles whose pretensions to that title were discussed and then disallowed. There were two main lines to his argument, the first being to minimize Christian dependence on apostolic authority. The first part of the gospel, up to Romans 3:20, was authenticated by reason and conscience. Thereafter there was a sense in which the teaching must be accepted on apostolic authority, but this could be reduced to a minimum by various means: Christ himself had already taught these things; they were confirmed by the testimony of millions of Christians; the peace experienced through trusting Christ allowed one to dispense with all testimony; and there was little in the epistle lacking internal confirmation in the believer. He concluded that in practice the question of their authority was of little importance because Christ and the truth shone directly onto him through them.[50] His second line was to argue for a return to the reformers' position on biblical authority, in which the authority of the Bible was acknowledged because of a prior acceptance of its teaching and not vice versa.[51]

---

[49] Dale, *The Living Christ,* 272-4. See also 'Memoir', lx-lxi.

[50] Dale, *Protestantism,* 45-50.

[51] *Ibid.,* 60ff.

That lecture left the gospels out of consideration, but Dale concentrated on them in a later work, *The Living Christ and the Four Gospels* (1890), which showed that he was still thinking along much the same lines. Most of the lectures were given over to a popular presentation of the patristic evidence for the historical trustworthiness of the gospels, but this was preceded by his explanation why Christian faith continued despite contemporary science and criticism. That he restricted himself to the continuance of faith is significant: science and criticism made the commencement of faith even more difficult,[52] but it was a weakness of Dale's arguments about Christian experience that they could not be brought to bear on this different prior question. His answer was that '*Whatever may have been the original grounds of their faith, their faith* has been verified in their own personal experience'[53]. Though many Christians would proffer other explanations, Dale believed that in reality the continuance of their faith rested on experience of deliverance from sin and guilt, on consciousness of God in Christ, and on awareness of belonging to an eternal world.[54] Here Dale believed he had a firm foundation for faith, beyond the reach of science and criticism yet capable of bringing Christian assurance some way back into the territory in which these two rational disciplines did hold sway. For he held that the Christ known by faith could be recognized in the Jesus of the gospels; this authenticated the main lines of the four accounts, though the details and considerations of date and authorship remained outside this overlapping of the spiritual and rational domains.[55]

That same year a work appeared which contained an implicit challenge to Dale's doctrine of authority. In his *The Seat of Authority in Religion,* James Martineau agreed with Dale in centring this on a self-authenticating vision of God, but drew much more sceptical conclusions about the Bible and orthodox doctrine. Dale held Martineau's critical method responsible for the difference, criticising particular instances of Martineau's disposal of the gospel miracles by philosophical means and rejection of further large tracts, including eschatology and the kingdom in the Synoptics and the entire fourth gospel, through the illegitimate use of an ethical yardstick. He agreed with Martineau that the power and authority of the New Testament for the individual believer lay in the parts in which he found God and God found him; but he did not accept that

[52] Dale, *The Living Christ,* 9-10.

[53] *Ibid.,* 10. The emphasis is Dale's own.

[54] *Ibid.,* 10ff, 70-75.

[55] *Ibid.,* 20-23, 33ff, 51, 57, 75-7.

this gave any warrant for rejecting the rest. He argued that the development of moral discernment meant that other passages might later mediate spiritual revelation, and that one should respect the general experience of the Church, which covered the entire New Testament: one should not presume one's own spiritual experience to be on a par with that of the apostles or of many wise men who accepted the authenticity of recorded sayings of Christ.[56]

This was as far as Dale could go: spiritual authentication could seal acceptance of parts of the New Testament (though not down to historical detail, the province of criticism), but its absence was insufficient reason for rejecting other parts (though these could not be trusted without reservation either). Without internal spiritual verification there could be no certain identification of the words of the New Testament with God's truth, and therefore no grounds for implicit submission to Christ as presented there. Dale's recognition of Christ's authority as objective conscience was thus undermined by his inability to identify with confidence an objectively authoritative teaching.

Dale accorded the intellectual sphere a similar protection from spiritual interference as he gave spiritual experience from intellectual threats: 'As I want Science to be absolutely free from any control of Faith, so I want Criticism to be free from any entanglement with questions concerning the contents of the Christian Revelation. If I publish anything it will be an attempt to vindicate the autonomy of Science, Criticism, Faith.'[57] At face value, this involves the naïve assumption that the intellect can operate in a presuppositional vacuum; but on other occasions Dale showed that he did not really believe that. Thus he accepted that though theologians who did not know God in Christ might contribute to biblical studies, there would be defects in their work, defects that would become most serious in the higher regions, such as hermeneutics. In reply to the accusation that Christians approached the material with their minds made up he pointed out that the same thing could be said for others, citing Strauss on miracles and Baur on dating the New Testament.[58] In practice criticism and faith were not completely autonomous; Dale was inconsistent in maintaining that they were.

Dale was an interested and informed observer of the scientific and

---

[56] Dale, 'The Seat of Authority in Religion', *Contemporary Review* 58 (1890), 389-411.

[57] A.W.W. Dale, *Life of R.W. Dale,* 350; compare Dale, 'The Faith Once Delivered to the Saints', in *Mansfield College, Oxford,* 73-4.

[58] Dale, 'The Faith Once Delivered', 59, *Preaching,* 94f, and *The Living Christ,* 86-9.

critical debates of his time rather than a participant. The former did not present the same biblical problems to Dale as the latter: he felt that the revision necessitated by Darwinianism could be kept within the bounds of hermeneutics, for a revelation had to be given in contemporary thought forms.[59] But allowing the same substantial independence to biblical criticism obliged him to subject his views on biblical inspiration and authority to substantial revision. In this Dale, like most of his contemporaries, was dragged somewhat reluctantly along in the wake of scholarly opinion: whereas in the 1860s he believed that virtually all Gospel discrepancies were capable of harmonization and that the presence of errors in the Pentateuch had not yet been demonstrated, by the end of his life he had retreated to such an extent that he admitted that confidence in the Old Testament history would be rash, although he looked for a conservative revision such as had modified Baur on the New Testament. He remained more confident about the New Testament, believing that criticism would ultimately confirm conservative positions such as the Johannine authorship of the fourth Gospel.[60]

Dale wanted a way to guarantee the reliability of Scripture as a whole while admitting inaccuracy in minor details.[61] The solutions he turned to were conventional: distinguishing the revelation itself from its record or witness in the Bible, and referring to Scripture as containing rather than being the Word of God.[62] The infallibility of revelation was preserved, but the Bible was no longer able to bask in it. As the inroads of criticism deepened he developed a damage limitation programme, stressing the need to keep the two testaments apart, so that the New should not be mauled because of a misplaced solidarity with the Old, and even suggesting revision of the canon, citing 2 Peter, in order to deprive its assailants of an Achilles' heel at which to aim.[63] In his exegetical practice and preaching Dale did not abandon the simple evangelical appeal to the authority of the Bible, but employed it with a new care: he avoided as much as possible the thin ice of the Old Testament, and spread the weight of his appeal to the New Testament as broadly as possible, anxious not to place too much confidence in individual texts. He explained this approach

---

[59] Dale, *Discourses*, 197-8, and *The Jewish Temple and the Christian Church: A Series of Discourses on the Epistle to the Hebrews* (London: Hodder & Stoughton, 1896[10]), 21.

[60] Dale, *Discourses*, 199, *Jewish Temple*, 21, *Fellowship with Christ*, 276, *Christian Doctrine*, 290, and ' Seat of Authority', 411, 403.

[61] Dale, *Discourses*, 199.

[62] Dale, *Jewish Temple*, 17-21, *Preaching*, 290, and *Protestantism*, 73.

[63] 'The Bible – a Library, Not a Book', *Congregationalist* 2 (1873), 51-55.

and demonstrated it impressively in *The Atonement*.[64]

Dale was not unduly concerned by the retreat he believed necessary in the light of the problems posed by biblical criticism, for he believed that faith itself rested on the unassailable foundation of experience. But the impregnability of his foundation was illusory. He himself recognized a first problem: self-verifying experience was intermittent, wearing off and leaving doubts in its wake. He had a remedy, knowledge of the similar experiences of others,[65] but this was different in kind, external rather than internal; furthermore, it led on to a second problem, the plurality of religious experience. His answer to this was both straightforward and bold: he denied that any false idea was capable of verification in experience. A Catholic murderer who confessed to a priest could only experience release from guilt if the priest served merely as the channel for Christ's mercy and power; the religious experience of a Muslim could verify such true elements in his religion as the existence of one God, defender of the faithful and source of strength, courage and peace, but could tell him nothing of Mohammed.[66]

Two conclusions may be drawn. Firstly, the strength of Dale's argument from experience cannot, even on his own terms, be considered the measure of the forcefulness of his apologetic, for at crucial stages he was dependent on external authority, especially for the process of coming to faith. Secondly, Dale's simple appeal to the verification supplied by experience lacked the sort of sophistication required to impress a century that began with William James's *Varieties of Religious Experience*. Dale's attempt at rebuilding a basis for faith and theology might well compare very favourably with the efforts of most of his contemporaries, but does not stand out as having any lasting value.

* * *

To talk of systematic theology in nineteenth century England may appear a little venturesome. English Congregationalists and Baptists of the period were generally either Calvinists who believed in preserving a particular systematic theology, or they lacked interest in the concept altogether. Few were doing constructive theological work, fewer still in a systematic way.

Dale was unusual in expressing regret that there had been no great systematic theologians in evangelical Protestantism for two

---

[64] Pp. 20-25.
[65] Dale, *The Living Christ*, 24-9.
[66] *Ibid.*, 64-70.

centuries.[67] At the outset of his ministry he saw that the low ebb of theology resulted from a tendency to react against too great a preoccupation with 'dogma' by an equally one-sided concern for 'life'; and near its end he detected no improvement in the outlook.[68] He was all the more saddened by this because he thought he lived at a time when theological work was a particularly urgent requirement. It was a period of great intellectual change, and Dale believed that as a doctrinal system is an intellectual representation of the contents of the Christian faith, any change in the intellectual condition of humankind must be followed by theological changes of corresponding magnitude.[69] He had radical views as to the scale of the task: it must be no mere repair but a reconstruction, with new philosophical methods, new exegesis, and new theological systems – though he did not believe that any of the great evangelical doctrines would be rejected. He declared that the collapse of Protestant scholasticism some time earlier was bringing the theological movement that began with the Reformation to the end; that it was a great evil that no theological system had yet replaced the reformed one; and that systematic theological reconstruction would be a slow process: a generation could be satisfied with clear definition of one or two doctrines.[70]

Dale's own theological contribution was on the scale of his limited general expectations as to the rate at which the revision might progress. This is understandable: as the only minister of a large city church, with additional denominational, municipal and political commitments, he had plenty of other ways of occupying himself. Given his circumstances, he managed to fit in an impressive amount of theological (and other) reading.[71] He wrote a substantial biography of his predecessor John Angell James and a bulky history of Congregationalism (completed and edited by his son), but it took the invitation to give the Congregational Union lectures for 1875 to

---

[67] Dale, 'Expiatory Theory', 463; compare *Discourses*, 275-7.

[68] Dale, 'Modern Deism', 255; A.W.W. Dale, *Life of R.W. Dale*, 624.

[69] Dale, *Evangelical Revival*, 265.

[70] Dale, 'Expiatory Theory', 463-5, 'On Some Present Aspects of Theological Thought among Congregationalists', *Congregationalist*, 6 (1877), 2-3, *Evangelical Revival*, 18-20, and *Fellowship with Christ*, 263-5.

[71] Dale, *Preaching*, chs. 3 and 4, especially p. 112. I appreciate the stimulus provided by Donald W. Norwood in improving this paragraph ('Dale: The Pastor and Church Meeting', in Clyde Binfield (ed.), 'The Cross and the City: Essays in Commemoration of Robert William Dale 1829-1895', Supplement to the *Journal of the United Reformed Church History Society* Vol. 6 (Supplement no. 2), 1999, 62.)

draw out of him his one major theological work. The diffidence he expressed in *The Atonement* as to its value was not simply conventional: the book begins with a description several pages long of theological problems requiring elucidation before more progress could be made in the understanding of atonement.[72] With regard to systematic theology Dale walked by faith rather than by sight.

Dale believed theological reconstruction necessary because of philosophical changes – and there he immediately ran into severe problems. The strong romantic tide of the 1840s, in which his own philosophy was grounded, was soon on the ebb, to be succeeded by a powerful empiricist and materialist surge. It meant that his theology for a new age was at many points in sharp collision with some of that age's most characteristic thinking. He was most troubled by the determinist threat to moral freedom. At the end of his life he said that the idea of moral freedom had been in retreat for thirty to forty years, endangering the sense of personal responsibility; the aggressor was scientific imperialism, which he defined as philosophies illegitimately attempting to carry the authority of physical forces beyond the material universe.[73] Dale was alarmed by the penetration achieved by such thinking into the ranks of the Congregational ministry by the late 1870s, identifying it as one of the many tendencies chaotically filling the vacuum left by Calvinism.[74] In his later years a new theme, social sin, arose to increase the pressure on moral freedom and responsibility; to Dale it was a dangerous half-truth.[75]

Dale organized his defence around a clear separation of the human soul from the physical universe: the soul was free for, unlike natural laws, moral laws could be disobeyed.[76] In his later writings Dale gave ground, allowing considerable influence to environment and especially heredity, but without contemplating concessions that would compromise human freedom and responsibility.[77]

Alongside his stand in favour of human freedom, Dale also had something to say about the freedom of God. Indeed, believing God to be the source of personality, of which freedom is a property, he could say that human freedom was an imperfect symbol of God's.[78]

---

72 Dale, *The Atonement*, 5-10.

73 Dale, *Epistle of James*, 245-6. An early version of this protest can be found in *Discourses*, 255-6.

74 Dale, 'Theological Thought among Congregationalists', 2-5.

75 Dale, *Fellowship with Christ*, 253.

76 Dale, *Discourses*, 290-93.

77 Dale, *Christian Doctrine*, 203-8, and *Epistle of James*, 252ff.

78 Dale, *Fellowship with Christ*, 143.

His main emphasis was on God as active, and not a programmed element in a mechanistic spiritual system: he answers prayer, he accepts worship, he reveals himself, all as he wills.[79] He did not, however, have anything a Calvinist would recognize as a doctrine of election, teaching that one becomes elect by turning to Christ and thus aligning oneself with God's will.[80]

The question that follows on from that of the freedom of God and humanity is the use to which this freedom is to be put. Evangelical theology traditionally supplied the simple answer 'salvation', understanding this to be forgiveness of sin and eternal life, obtained through the substitutionary atonement Christ made in dying on the cross. In the 1850s Dale was already demonstrating independence from this tradition by placing greater emphasis on the person than on the work of Christ.[81]

Dale's use of two theological words, 'incarnation' and 'grace', marks his development of the relationship between Christ and humanity in writings of the early 1870s. Both were assigned a very high place. He broke with evangelical tradition by calling the incarnation the supreme fact in the history of the world, and 'the most vital doctrine of the Christian Faith',[82] thereby relegating the atonement to second place. This was because Dale was looking beyond the mere fact of the Christian hope of eternal life to the nature of that life: through Christ it was possible for people to receive God's life. The atonement brought righteousness, which was a great thing, but the incarnation contained the promise of sonship, which was a greater thing. He concluded that the ultimate root of the Church is in the incarnation. Grace differed from incarnation both in having a major place in Dale's theological heritage and in not being a fashionable theological term in the late nineteenth century. He was not altogether successful in fighting this neglect, but grace was nevertheless the word he turned to in order to do justice to the magnitude of God's act in raising humanity from the greatest depths to the high status of children of God.[83]

The most significant period of Dale's mature theological

---

[79] *Ibid.*, 142-4. Beginning with Matthew 11:27, he made the point even more forcefully with respect to Christ (*Ibid.*, 187-91).

[80] Dale, *Ephesians*, 29-32, 40-41.

[81] Dale, 'Modern Deism', 254.

[82] A.W.W. Dale, *Life of R.W. Dale,* 327; also Dale, 'The Idea of the Church', 355, 406-7.

[83] Dale, 'The Church the Fullness of Him that Filleth All in All', *Congregationalist,* 1 (1872), 459-60, and *Ephesians*, 177; A.W.W. Dale, *Life of R.W. Dale,* 636.

development occurred in the mid-1870s. It was at this time that he gained for himself an important degree of relief from the problems associated with his assertion of the independence of the 'Eternal Law of Righteousness', thanks largely to Henry Wace's idea that righteousness is fundamentally personal rather than metaphysical. But another important change, which first became explicit in *The Atonement* in 1875, slightly preceded and quite possibly prepared the way for the other. Here he introduced the subject of Christ's relation to humanity as a complement to an earlier line of thought on the relation of Christ to the law. His purpose was to vindicate the idea of expiation by showing that there was something in Christ's relation to humanity that made the atonement possible without compromising God's righteousness. It is interesting that he mentioned F.D. Maurice as the pioneer of recent English thought on Christ as head and representative of humankind, for there is more than a hint of Maurice's influence in the way he did not pause at the incarnation but turned directly to 'the original and ideal relation of the Lord Jesus Christ to the human race'[84] in order to discover that 'the Lord Jesus Christ is in very truth, by the original law of the universe, the Representative of mankind'[85]. He looked at the New Testament evidence for this idea, especially at passages depicting Christ not only as the creator and sustainer but also as the ground and goal of the universe, and at the language of being in Christ. He summed up the results as two laws: firstly that human spiritual life is derived from Christ, being a revelation of his life; and secondly that 'our own relation to the Father is determined by the relation of Christ to the Father. By no fictitious imputation or technical transfer, but by virtue of a real union between the life of Christ and our own life, His relation to the Father becomes ours.'[86]

Dale's thought developed further in later years, with Westcott's influence supplementing that of Maurice. Having come to believe that it was God's eternal purpose that humanity should be in Christ, he rejected the common evangelical position that the incarnation was an afterthought, contingent on sin, which meant that our life is in Christ only because we ruined our own life by rebelling against

---

[84] Dale, *The Atonement,* 402. The Maurician note comes across more clearly in a reply to criticisms of *The Atonement* in which he stated his belief that all Christ's relations to men are rooted in the eternal relations within the Trinity, which are not changed but only manifested in the historical Christian revelation – 'Unitarian Criticism on the Congregational Union Lecture for 1875', *Congregationalist,* 5 (1876), 286.

[85] Dale, *The Atonement,* 433.

[86] *Ibid.,* 420.

God. Thus he arrived at the Scotist conclusion that the incarnation would have happened even had there been no sin: the presence of sin did however make its redemptive aspect necessary.[87] He also followed his Anglican mentors in assimilating his anthropology into a Trinitarian doctrine of God, to the extent of making Christ incomplete without humanity:

> If on the one side of His nature He is eternally one with God, on the other side of His nature He is eternally one with us; and fellowship with us in the perfection of our righteousness and the perfection of our blessedness, is as necessary to the heavenly glory of Christ as His fellowship with the Father Himself.[88]

But he differed from Westcott and especially Maurice in binding reality more firmly to the existential than to the ideal: for Dale the human experience of sin and alienation from God are destructive of our fundamental relations rather than simply preventing us from enjoying them, and consequently our relationship with Christ needs to be based on reliance on his sufferings for deliverance from guilt.[89] The atonement was more important to Dale than to Maurice and Wescott; indeed in practical if not in conceptual terms he considered it the first truth of the Gospel.[90]

All Dale's writings on the atonement were aimed at Trinitarians who acknowledged biblical authority but were adopting moral and subjective views of the atonement. He was unsure how many Congregationalists came into this category, for the changes taking place were insidious, attended by hardly any public debate. He was afraid that justification by faith was being replaced by a doctrine of justification by inherent righteousness and works, and that the

---

[87] Dale, *The Old Evangelicalism and the New* (London: Hodder & Stoughton, 1889), 43-6, and *Fellowship with Christ*, 5. There is considerable circumstantial evidence that Dale derived his Scotist view of the incarnation from Westcott: the sermon in which it is introduced was preached only months after he read appreciatively Westcott's *The Epistle of St. John* (1883), which contained (pp. 271-315) an essay on the subject (see A. W. W. Dale, *Life of R.W. Dale*, 523-5).

[88] Dale, *Christ and the Future Life*, (London: Hodder & Stoughton, 1897[3]), 80-81. See also *Fellowship with Christ*, 158-60.

[89] Dale, 'Maurice on the Gospel of St. John', *Eclectic Review*, new series 2 (1857), 51. Dale never went back on this early critique of Maurice. See also 'The Moral View of the Atonement', *BQR*, 44 (1866), 410.

[90] Dale, *The Old Evangelicalism and the New*, 51.

Reformation battle might have to be fought all over again.[91]

In 1875 Dale identified what he took to be the main reason for the rejection of objective atonement: people found it hard to believe that God could be angry with sinners as a result of transferring their own tolerance for sin to God. The remedy was a greater sense of the greatness and authority of God, of the awfulness of sin as committed against him.[92] During the Leicester Conference Controversy in 1878 Dale took this a step further, arguing that whereas his contemporaries thought they believed in a merciful God, in fact the smaller his resentment against sin the smaller his mercy became, and where there was no resentment there was no mercy: their God was not more merciful but less righteous, and therefore no God at all. Humanity, he concluded, had taken first place in this religion, leaving God only a secondary place.[93]

Analysing a theological trend, labelling it as heretical, and prophesying against it were easier than presenting a well argued alternative theology, a task that no-one had yet done in a way that satisfied Dale. His conscience had reacted differently to the two main elements in the traditional evangelical doctrine. It had no time for penal substitution, for it was puzzled to see how the righteous law could be honoured while an innocent was punished so that the guilty might be cleared; but it endorsed the demand that God punish sin, which was a crime deserving retribution rather than a disease to be cured, and incapable of cancellation by subsequent righteousness.[94] It is likely that it was because Dale felt the attractiveness of unconditional forgiveness that he always attached great importance to the idea that God was the administrator of the law, and thus differently placed from any human being, using this to differentiate his forgiveness from the human variety, and justify the need for atonement.[95]

Dale first expounded his theory of the atonement in 1867. He began by suggesting that the moral significance of divine retribution

---

91 Dale, *The Atonement*, xiv-xvii, 'Moral View', 450-52, and *The Old Evangelicalism and the New*, 52-5.

92 *The Atonement*, 338-9, and 'Theological Thought among Congregationalists', 6-9.

93 Dale, *Evangelical Revival*, 164-9.

94 Dale, 'Expiatory Theory', 502, and 'Moral View', 425. McLeod Campbell's *The Nature of the Atonement* (London: Macmillan, 1856) had been a notable previous attempt to preserve objective atonement while rejecting substitution, but Dale did not think his theory of vicarious confession adequate (*The Atonement*, 424-5).

95 Dale, *Christian Doctrine*, 236-48.

is to be measured by God's great love, which makes the imposition of the punishment so costly to him. He went on to say that the cost to both the Father and the Son of the Son's voluntarily suffering the penalties of sin[96] instead of inflicting them is even greater, and so of greater moral significance. Thus the principle of retribution received even more sublime recognition than would have been accorded by its application.[97] Though later overshadowed by other elements, this always remained a vital part of Dale's theology of atonement, the vindication of the righteousness of the whole proceeding. Yet it is fatally flawed, involving a confusion between the moral significance of the act of punishing and that of the punishment itself: the moral significance of divine retribution must lie pre-eminently in its justice, and it would not be possible for the injustice of its omission, however much more costly the substituted gesture, to accord the law greater recognition than would the justice of its execution.

The 'greater recognition' argument was the last of the four points under which Dale summarized the developed form of his theory expounded in *The Atonement*, and the only one not dependent on Christ's eternal relationship to man.[98] The focus of the first point is on acknowledgement of the righteousness of the law. Christ's action here is two-fold: firstly (as in McLeod Campbell's theory), he acknowledged the righteousness of sin's penalty; but secondly (going beyond Campbell), Jesus actually submitted to that penalty, God-forsakenness and death. This action of Christ's *can* relate to us

---

[96] In Dale's mind Christ's voluntary suffering of the penalty of sin was quite different from his being the object of punishment: he held that Christ suffered the *penalty* of sin, which was God-forsakenness and death, but not as a *punishment*, which is the judicial infliction of a penalty. R.C. Moberly's failure to pick up this nuance is one of the problems that largely invalidate his influential assessment of Dale's theory (*Atonement and Personality* (London: John Murray, 1913), 391-2). Worse, others have perpetuated this error, including James M. Gordon, *Evangelical Spirituality: From the Wesleys to John Stott* (London: SPCK, 1991), 153, and Dale A. Johnson, *The Changing Shape of English Nonconformity, 1825-1925* (New York/Oxford: OUP, 1999), 154. Dale was not however entirely innocent, for this point was not made nearly as clearly in *The Atonement* as in 'The Expiatory Theory'.

[97] Dale, 'Expiatory Theory', 499-502; compare *The Atonement*, 385-95, lxv-lxvi, and *Christian Doctrine*, 261-5.

[98] The following summary of the remaining three points in Dale's argument is derived from the form in which I presented them in my article on Dale in Timothy T. Larsen (ed.), *Biographical Dictionary of Evangelicals* (Leicester: IVP, 2003), 177, and is used with permission.

because of the original and ideal relationship between Christ and humanity; Christ is the root of humanity, and his life is in us when we trust and submit to him. It is that underlying fact that made incarnation possible. For this thinking Dale's principal debt is to F.D. Maurice. Christ's action *does* relate to us when we ask God to accept both his attitude and his act as our own homage to the righteousness of the law.

In his second point Dale's focus is on the reality of reconciliation between God and humanity, or, in his language, the retention or recovery of the original and ideal relationship that was spoilt by sin. Our problem is that sin has so changed our perspective that we cannot see how Christ's relationship to the Father can have any relevance to our own situation of alienation. But Christ solves this problem by putting himself right where sin had brought us in relation to God, thereby enabling us to see that we can approach God and retain or recover our relationship with him. This point is, therefore, a version of the subjective theory of atonement, which Dale considered inadequate on its own.

The third point is concerned with the righteousness of humanity, for Dale was convinced that genuine righteousness, not just a righteous status, had to be the outcome of atonement. The death of Christ involves the actual destruction of sin in those who through faith recover their union with him. This comes about because of the mystical relationship with him that is discussed in the first point.[99]

Dale admitted that he did not have a complete theory,[100] and his points were not cemented into a single argument. Their assembly to some extent compensated for their individual weakness, but perhaps more by way of disguising than alleviating it. Furthermore, the unifying focus on the relationship between Christ and man is blurred: there is the clarity neither of the Maurician eternal ideal nor of a coherent exposition of its new creation through death and resurrection.

In later years Dale became all the more convinced that the key to understanding the atonement lay in the mystical relation between Christ and humanity, and that this meant that its objective aspect should be approached through the subjective.[101] He developed a growing spiritual vision of the results and something of the process of objective atonement that outstripped his power to explain theoretically. This can be seen in his description of his new perception of justification as something beyond the forgiveness with which

[99] Dale, *The Atonement*, lvi-lxvii.
[100] *Ibid.*, 432.
[101] A.W.W Dale, *Life of R.W. Dale*, 524.

he had dealt exclusively at the time of the lectures:

> Of late it has come to me with such clearness and force that I feel that I never knew it before; but I cannot put it; what I say seems to miss the best part of what I have seen… I wonder whether we shall soon get a statement of Justification by Faith that will be intellectually satisfactory.[102]

He made prominent use of a new word borrowed from Westcott, solidarity,[103] especially in a last major look at the atonement in *Christian Doctrine*, in which he also attempted to employ a new approach. He believed that failure had resulted from conceiving of the atonement as a mystery (as he himself had previously done) whereas it should be looked upon in addition as a glorious revelation.[104]

In spite of new language and the power of positive thinking there were no new results. 'Solidarity' was a useful label for the uniquely close relationship between Christ and humanity in which the explanation of the atonement had to be hidden, but Dale was still relying on the cumulative effect of several arguments that reached the threshold of that solidarity from different directions, yet without achieving the unity that would come from penetrating the mystery. His progress in spiritual understanding was not matched by that of his intellect.

However, Dale's attempt to construct a theory was not his best work on the atonement. He put forward some very cogent criticisms of subjective views of the atonement, especially those of Horace Bushnell and John Young, in *The Moral View of the Atonement*. But his finest achievement was the very perceptive survey of atonement in the New Testament which took up half of the lectures in *The Atonement*. He went way beyond the use of standard proof texts that had satisfied so many of his predecessors to build up a powerful case for objective atonement. One commentator considered that all theories of the Ritschlian school would have to reckon with Dale's establishment of the place of expiatory sacrifice in the primitive church if they wanted to establish a connection with New Testament religion.[105]

---

[102] *Ibid.*, 536; see also p. 526.

[103] *Ibid.*, 525.

[104] *Christian Doctrine*, 256.

[105] R.S. Franks, *A History of the Doctrine of the Work of Christ*, ii, 240, quoted in L.H. Hough, 'R. W. Dale'. *CQ*, 7 (1929), 419.

Three themes that follow on from the atonement will conclude this survey of Dale's theology: the current standing before God of humankind; the nature of the church; and what awaits us after death.

Views of the standing of humankind following the atonement can normally be divided into two groups, according to whether the onus is on 'opting in' or 'opting out' of salvation. Evangelicals had traditionally been of the former persuasion: it was through conversion that they gained an interest in Christ. Dale had no intention of rejecting this inheritance and took up a stand against some threats that he perceived to it: in 1871 he condemned the notion of child membership of churches on the ground that only those possessing the divine life should be members.[106] But in typical fashion he tried to combine elements from both old and new views. In 1864 he said that the relationship of humanity to God was now changed, resting on the atonement, but men must come to God in faith to be regenerated by the Holy Spirit in order to complete that work.[107] Twenty years later Dale expounded baptism as a sacrament for all infants, affirming that all are Christ's subjects, loved and redeemed by him, and assured of his protection until they inherit his glory – provided they did not resist his authority and grace.[108] But in practice those who did not at any time resist Christ were the exceptional cases: most, having 'opted out' at some stage, needed to turn to Christ again. It is then that regeneration occurred as the Holy Spirit entered in.[109] Dale often used the phrase 'retain or recover' when referring to relationship with Christ so as to keep both possibilities in view.

The tension that resulted from mixing the two streams of thought shows up in Dale's treatment of fatherhood and sonship. Although these were pivotal terms in much contemporary theology, he paid them little attention before the 1890s,[110] at which late stage he realized that he had been guilty of using both words rather loosely.[111] And yet the results of his mature reflection can hardly be described as taut. He agreed with Baldwin Brown in insisting on the

---

106 Dale, 'Idea of the Church', 375-8.

107 Dale, *Discourses*, 150-51.

108 Dale, *A Manual of Congregational Principles* (1884), 126-8.

109 Dale, 'The New Birth', *Congregationalist*, 1 (1872), 327-30.

110 An 1891 letter in A.W.W. Dale, *Life of R.W. Dale*, p. 654 shows that Dale himself was aware of this. I have only noted brief references to fatherhood in Dale, 'Congregationalism', *BQR* 73 (1881), 1-9, *Ephesians*, 45ff, and *Laws of Christ*, 25.

111 A.W.W. Dale, *Life of R.W. Dale*, 654.

universal fatherhood of God, but quarrelled with the inference that all people are therefore God's children. He drew on several arguments in an attempt to consolidate this position: the danger of arguing analogically from the human to the divine; the New Testament's restriction of sonship to those who have faith in Christ; the perilous complacency in which people rebellious against God would be left by the preaching of universal sonship; and, conversely, the disturbance or destruction of the grounds for faith that would result from the preaching of limited fatherhood. Above all he once more indicated his concern for reality as opposed to imputation by stressing that holiness (as an ethical quality) must be a feature of sonship, as this involves sharing in God's holy life.[112] Universal fatherhood dovetailed with universal redemption, as expounded in his theology of baptism, and limited sonship suited his evangelical assessment of the lostness of the generality of people; but, in spite of Dale's arguments, their cohabitation was uneasy.

Dale was more unequivocally evangelical in his doctrine of the Church. His exposition of Congregational ecclesiology was exceptionally lucid and powerful, and all the more outstanding in view of contemporary Nonconformist neglect of the subject. He believed that the main vocation of Congregationalism – and its justification – lay in its embodiment of and witness to the true idea of the Church. Unlike most of his contemporaries he did not consider a demonstration of its apostolicity to be of itself an adequate vindication of the polity: its permanent authority must depend on its being shown to give the highest and most natural expression to the central truths of Christianity:

> The Congregational polity has its roots in a very definite religious faith. It cannot be justified where that faith is surrendered. To perpetuate the polity when the faith is lost is an impossible task. The infinite significance of conversion, of faith in Christ, of the remission of sins, of regeneration, is the real foundation on which Congregationalism is built.[113]

The consequent restriction of church membership to those who had undergone this transformation was something he held in common with all evangelicals, but Dale went beyond the pragmatism with

---

[112] Dale, *Fellowship with Christ*, 355-7, and *Epistle of James*, 227-44; see also A.W.W. Dale, *Life of R.W. Dale*, 654-5.

[113] Dale, 'Congregationalism', *BQR*, 11; see also 'The Idea of the Church', 412, and *Manual*, 4-8.

which most were satisfied thereafter. He believed that a particular church was constituted by the presence of Christ among Christians regularly meeting with each other and with him. The founder was therefore Christ, and it was wrong to conceive of churches as voluntary societies. A church that ceased to restrict membership to people who were in Christ abandoned its constitution and forfeited its status, and a Christian society that added any further qualifications for membership was a sect and not a church in the highest sense. Thus a credal basis of communion was by its very nature inadmissible: no limitations could be valid that excluded anyone in Christ.[114]

A second guiding principle followed: because all members are in Christ, all are directly responsible to him for maintaining his authority in the Church. As the church is Christ's body its acts are ideally his, locally as much as universally.[115] Satisfied that both principles were firmly rooted in the New Testament, Dale defended them against the charge of impracticality to which the second was especially vulnerable:

> We have been often told that it is impossible to draw into the membership of the Church all those in whom the life of God is present, and impossible to exclude those from whom it is absent. We admit the impossibility... Divine ideals have never yet been realized in the life of either individual saints or of societies. For us, and in this world, the Divine is always the impossible. Give me a law for individual conduct which requires a perfection that is within my reach, and I am sure that the law does not represent the Divine thought... Give me a Church polity which is what men call practical – a polity which in its completeness can be realized – and I am sure that is something different from the ideal polity of that Divine society whose Builder and Maker is God.
>
> The Church – this is the Congregational ideal – is a society larger or smaller, consisting of those who have received the Divine life; and who, with whatever inconstancy and whatever failures are endeavouring to live in the power of it... The responsibilities and the corresponding powers attributed to the commonalty of Christian people are directly related to the assumption that they

---

114 Dale, 'The Idea of the Church', 376, 396-7, 410, *Manual*, 49-50, 205, and *History of English Congregationalism*, A.W.W. Dale (ed.) (London: Hodder & Stoughton, 1907), 274.

115 Dale, 'The Idea of the Church' 399-400, and *Manual*, 51-64.

> have received the life that dwells in Christ, and that they are one with Him. When they are gathered together in His name ... Christ Himself is in the midst of them ... so that their prayers are His and their decisions His rather than theirs. If the ideal were realized, what things soever they bind on earth would be bound in Heaven; and what things soever they loose on earth would be loosed in Heaven; and whatever they agreed to ask, would be done for them of the Father. All this would be true if the ideal were realized. It is actually true in the *measure* in which the ideal is realized.[116]

Dale's third principle, the independence of the local church, was inferred from the second: as the entire membership of each church participated in Christ's authority they could not be held accountable to any external human authority.[117]

In his eschatology Dale tried to maintain the sharp separation between Church and world that was characteristic of his ecclesiology. However, his views were not static. After ruling out the doctrine of the annihilation of the impenitent for many years because of his belief in the immortality of the soul he underwent a gradual change of mind, through study of the Bible and his friendship with Edward White, its main Congregational proponent, and eventually espoused it publicly in the Congregational Union in May 1874. One advantage it had for him over everlasting punishment was that it opened up a less appalling prospect without compromising the definitiveness of the final judgement. But of even greater importance was the reinforcement it brought to the threatened evangelical doctrine of regeneration. It was probably also a significant factor in his new thinking at this time on the relationship of humanity to Christ.[118]

Conditional immortality thrived on the links it forged with Darwinian evolution, but Dale went much further in developing a deeply evolutionist eschatological vision:

> We have come to think of the work of creation as unfinished, and of ourselves as spectators of the mystery. The ages are as yet in the

[116] Dale, *Fellowship with Christ*, 359-60; emphasis Dale's.

[117] Dale, *Manual*, 69.

[118] Dale, *The Talents*, 120; A.W.W. Dale, *Life of R.W. Dale*, 310-13; F.A. Freer, *Edward White, His Life and Work* (London: Elliot Stock, 1902), 348, 354; *Evangelical Revival*, 166. The development of the doctrine in Victorian England is discussed by Geoffrey Rowell in *Hell and the Victorians* (Oxford: Clarendon, 1974), ch.8.

> remote future in which the universe will reach that consummate perfection to which it was destined by the forces which have determined its development and history. Perhaps that perfection may never be actually achieved, but the mighty movement which in the past has struggled forward through storm and conflict and suffering, may some day pass into a peaceful progress towards an ideal glory, a progress to be prolonged through eternity.
>
> God, too, has His unrealized ideals; He, too, is in pursuit of an unachieved perfection; He is thwarted, hindered, baffled by we know not what hostile powers; but ... the golden years will come when the eternal purposes of His righteousness and His love will be fulfilled. In this perpetual effort of God to reach a perfection that still lies far before Him, we may find grounds for faith in His sympathy with ourselves in the pursuit of an ideal righteousness.[119]

Dale was so happy with the dynamic idea of progress that 'a peaceful progress' seemed preferable to 'consummate perfection'. Here there is no hint of any climactic eschatological event, nor of a radical contrast between time and eternity, the life on earth and life after death. He had taken up ground that was proving fertile for theologies with a universalist tendency, but had no support to offer to his own belief in a definitive last judgement. It left him with nothing stronger to say on the possibility of a renewed opportunity to repent after death than that there were no sure grounds for it that he could discover, and that it would therefore be unwise to count on it.[120]

This is yet another example of a recurring pattern in Dale's theology. It contains many elements drawn from the old evangelical theology; it also embraces versions of a number of alternatives currently under development. But there is rarely more than a glimpse of an elusive synthesis. For the most part he either leant more toward his evangelical heritage and heart or expended considerable ingenuity in persuading alien ideas to engage in uneasy cohabitation. Spurgeon, aware of this deep-seated tension, commented on it in his own inimitable style from his side of the fence that Dale was uncomfortably straddling: 'He is too gracious ever to become a success as a heretic.'[121] Dale's theology was a noble

---

[119] Dale, *Fellowship with Christ*, 184-7.
[120] *Ibid.*, 26.
[121] *ST*, 13 (1877), 280.

effort but it was not a way forward.

Influence

Even as a seventeen-year-old starting at college Dale stood out from the crowd. A fellow student remembered the wonder and admiration with which they met the new arrival, whose reputation as a preacher had preceded him. John Angell James endorsed that feeling by singling him out at an early stage and grooming him to be his eventual successor at Carr's Lane – which sufficed to mark him as a man to be watched in the denomination.[122]

But three more qualifications were necessary in order to attain leadership status: a successful ministry; acceptance in the peer group of the leading ministers of his generation who were destined to comprise Congregationalism's informal episcopacy; and a significant contribution to denominational affairs. None of these presented any difficulty to Dale in the early 1860s, the proof being his accession to the chair of the Congregational Union in 1869.[123]

The first two qualifications went together, for their success was one of the main things that brought up and coming leaders together in the Congregational Union. It was a time of unusual opportunity for younger ministers: the generation that had founded the Congregational Union thirty years earlier was fast dying out, and there were few influential ministers in the intermediate age group. Dale was the youngest of a compact group of successful ministers in their thirties or forties who took over the reins at this time. A particular friend of his among them was Henry Allon, the man most at the hub of the network, constantly entertaining, bringing people together; already one of Dale's closest friends in 1864, their intimacy continued until Allon's death in 1892, an event that affected Dale very deeply.[124] He was closest of all to James Guinness Rogers, whose congregation at Grafton Square, Clapham, probably had the highest social standing of any in the denomination.[125]

Dale's most conspicuous early contribution to denominational affairs was in the field of religious politics, through a lecture commemorating the bicentenary of the great ejection of 1662.

[122] Paton, *Reasonableness*, 5; Dale, *John Angell James*, 449-84.

[123] A.W.W. Dale, *Life of R.W. Dale*, 230.

[124] *Ibid.*,201-2, 627-8. Allon was minister of Union Chapel, Islington, which was rebuilt in imposing style to house his large congregation.

[125] David Bebbington, *The Nonconformist Conscience: Chapel and Politics, 1870-1914* (London: Allen & Unwin, 1982), 87. For their relationship see Rogers' account in A.W.W. Dale, 723-5.

Delivered to a packed audience in Birmingham Town Hall, it created considerable controversy, provoked a number of published replies, and led to a variety of other speaking engagements. It was this lecture, as he himself saw later, that 'fairly launched' him on his public career.[126] An important feature of the episode was the exposure this gave him in Church of England as well as Nonconformist circles, something greatly enhanced by his prominence in the debate over the 1870 Education Bill.[127] These and other political activities helped make Dale one of the few Nonconformist ministers to emerge from general anonymity as a nationally known figure. This was to be a factor in his theological influence, especially within the Church of England.

* * *

Dale's congregation is the best place at which to start an assessment of the means of theological influence of which he disposed and what he made of them: it was at the heart of his activities, the beneficiary of the greatest investment of his time and energy. He described it as containing few manufacturers and professional people, but many retailers and their employees, and still more working people; they were interested in public affairs and contemporary theological debates but were not very educated.[128] He frequently subjected his preaching to self-critical analysis – he was deeply concerned by a lack of conversions from the very outset of his ministry. Analysing the same problem much later he thought that he tended to be too concerned for truth and too little for people. He also felt that he had erred in adopting a rather austere approach, owing to his dread of popularity seeking. He tried to be practical – his ethical preaching has been singled out for special praise – but his was never a 'popular' ministry. One difficulty was an unnatural pulpit manner that became more pronounced with the passing years. [129] His appeal

---

126 A.W.W. Dale, *Life of R.W. Dale,* 166, 175, 186. It was published as *Churchmen and Dissenters: Their Mutual Relations as Affected by the Celebration of the Bicentenary of St. Bartholomew's Day, 1662* (Birmingham, 1862).

127 A.W.W. Dale, *Life of R.W. Dale,* 266ff.

128 Dale, *The Ten Commandments*, v, and *The Living Christ*, vii-viii.

129 Dale, *John Angell James*, 478-9; A.W.W. Dale, *Life of R.W. Dale,* 590-91; *Ordination Services of Dale*, 37; Paton, *Reasonableness,* 15; Horton Davies, *Worship and Theology in England from Newman to Martineau*, 1850-1900 (Princeton: Princeton University Press, 1962), 324; Albert Peel and J.A. Marriott, *Robert Forman Horton* (London: G. Allen & Unwin, 1937), 137.

was mainly to the serious and the intelligent.

The same applies to the broader public he reached through his publications, the vast majority of which were originally sermons addressed to his or other congregations, and only altered in minor respects. His contributions to the *Congregationalist*, of which he was the first editor, were in a different category; through them he made a serious effort to influence developments in Congregationalism at a time – the 1870s – when he was particularly conscious of living in a period of religious and theological crisis. He addressed current issues, concentrating on ecclesiology, theology and preaching, and pleading for a revival. But the magazine was too serious to have a very broad appeal, and the small size of its constituency eventually led to its demise.[130] Its impact was too diffuse for historical measurement.

Of all Dale's writings *The Atonement* had by far the most impact. At the time of his death the rate of sale was on the increase, with the seventeenth edition in twenty years about to appear. In 1877 it was recommended summer reading for the Baptist students of Regent's Park College; but it was also widely used in Anglican theological colleges, having been received enthusiastically by both *The Record* and Liddon. It was an Anglican who said that 'there is probably no book on the subject more widely known amongst churchmen than the lectures of the late Dr Dale'.[131] There were translations into French and German (and partially into Japanese!), and favourable notices in a couple of German periodicals. Perhaps no other work of nineteenth century Nonconformist theology enjoyed such breadth of appeal: very complimentary letters arrived even from Newman and Gladstone.

Not many Nonconformists could claim a personal association with names such as these: Dale's circle of friends and acquaintances was unusually diverse and distinguished. This had much to do with his personal qualities, which drew high praise from all sides. After

---

130 A.W.W. Dale, *Life of R.W. Dale*, 305-6; see 756-7 for a list of his articles. *The Congregationalist* was started in 1872.

131 R.C. Moberly, *Atonement*, 382; compare p. 139. Other references in the paragraph are to *Independent and Nonconformist*, 21 March 1895, 196; Ernest A. Payne, 'The Development of Nonconformist Theological Education in the Nineteenth Century, with Special Reference to Regent's Park College', in *Studies in History and Religion*, Payne (ed.) (London: Lutterworth Press, 1942), 248; A.W.W. Dale, *Life of R.W. Dale*, 324-5; Birmingham University Library, Letters to R.W. Dale, Henry Wace to Dale, 13 October 1880, and W.E. Gladstone to Dale, 20 May 1875.

his death two of his closest friends said that they had never heard him utter an ungenerous word, and had never known him descend to personalities even in the most highly charged political meetings. After generosity, sympathy was perhaps the quality most appreciated in him. Guinness Rogers summed up the impression Dale made on those who knew him: 'The transparent simplicity, the unfeigned humility, the strong faith, the generous estimate of other men, the intense anxiety to be loyal to truth and right, the glowing warmth of heart – all spoke a man who had been much with Christ and learned of Him.'[132]

* * *

In the special circumstances of the eulogistic period immediately after Dale's death an Anglican said that 'no witness for Christian faith and Christian life in our day has surpassed in power and influence that of Robert William Dale... His writings have had a profound influence, not only upon the Nonconformists among his contemporaries, but on the thoughtful and well-read members of our own communion.'[133] Over a century later these words appear somewhat bold. The persistence of a man's influence is an important aspect of it, and the list of twentieth century publications on or by Dale is on the slight side. Until the appearance of a volumes of essays to mark the centenary of his death,[134] a sign that Dale is taking his rightful place in the increasing study of nineteenth century Nonconformist history, there had been just a few introductory sketches, and the only works of his to be reissued after the First World War were *A Manual of Congregational Principles* in 1920[135] and his popular lecture *Protestantism: Its Ultimate Principle* in 1928.

Dale bequeathed no theological school, and nor did he leave behind him a group of disciples. His theology, more a mixture than a synthesis of old and new elements, lacked a strong unifying theme

---

[132] A.W.W. Dale, *Life of R.W. Dale,* 745. Other references are to A.M. Fairbairn and J. Guinness Rogers, in *Memorial Services,* 12, 28; Birmingham University Library, Letters to R.W. Dale, Wace to Dale, 31 March 1876.

[133] Archdeacon Sinclair, quoted in *Independent and Nonconformist,* 21 March 1895, 187.

[134] Clyde Binfield (ed.), 'The Cross and the City: Essays in Commemoration of Robert William Dale 1829-1895', Supplement to the *Journal of the United Reformed Church Historical Society* 6 Supplement no. 2 (1999).

[135] Alan Argent, 'Dale and Congregationalism' in Binfield (ed.), 'The Cross and the City', 37-8.

to act as a handle by which contemporaries and posterity could grasp it. A friend did try to identify one – 'the essential relation of humanity to the Eternal Son of God'[136] – and on this basis count Dale the chief revivifier of evangelicalism; but this idea does not appear to have been widely accessible and inspirational, and Paton's bold claim cannot be upheld.

Instead it was A.M. Fairbairn's theology of the fatherhood of God that most influenced the direction taken by early twentieth century Congregational theology. It is therefore of interest that it was through reading Dale's 1866 *Discourses Delivered on Special Occasions* that the young Scottish minister 'felt as if the scales fell from his eyes, and he saw the word he had tried to preach become a larger and roomier thing than he had ever dreamed of it being'.[137] However in subsequent years Dale's theology only had a minor place in the development of Fairbairn's quite different corpus of ideas.

It did not take the twentieth century long to develop a low view of its predecessor. A quarter of a century after Dale's death, a preacher at his Carr's Lane Church first showed how Dale had failed to transcend the limitations of his age before suggesting with mingled boldness and condescension that Dale might even have something to say to his day.[138] If such things were taking place within his own denomination, it is not surprising that his reputation was equally transient in the Church of England. There his influence had been partly through friends and acquaintances, such as Westcott who recommended Dale's *Ephesians* to his son,[139] but it was pre-eminently through one book, *The Atonement*. This stood firm for a generation in part because such a non-systematic period had thrown up little competition and in part because of its biblical and historical, as distinct from systematic, strength.[140] When another major work on

---

136 Paton, *Reasonableness*, 10; see also p. 9.

137 Fairbairn, in *Memorial Services*, 15. A close relationship between the two men developed through their collaboration on the Mansfield College project; A.W.W. Dale wrote (p. 494) that his father considered this, next to his pastorate, the most important work of his life; but Fairbairn's influence at Mansfield was unquestionably much the greater.

138 L.H. Hough, *Dr. Dale after Twenty-five Years* (Birmingham: Cornish Bros., 1922), 13-15.

139 Arthur Westcott, *Life and Letters of Brooke Foss Westcott*, 2 vols. (London: Macmillan & Co., 1903), II, 305. I am indebted to Dr Geoffrey Rowell for this reference.

140 Colin Gunton was considerably more enthusiastic about Dale's grasp of the history of the doctrine than his constructive efforts, which

the atonement did arrive, R.C. Moberly's *Atonement and Personality* in 1901, as well as taking some of Dale's thinking a stage further it included an unduly negative assessment of Dale's book that must have speeded its fall into disuse.[141]

More recent writers have tended to echo the tributes paid him by contemporaries. According to J.K. Mozley, 'Dale was a great Christian teacher and a great Christian man, one of the greatest of his century'.[142] John Grant considered him 'the outstanding Nonconformist theologian of the time'.[143] And while R. Tudor Jones made him share that theological accolade with Fairbairn, he did affirm that 'taken all in all Dale was the most remarkable Congregationalist of the nineteenth century'.[144]

'Taken all in all' is the key phrase. Fairbairn had also used it: 'Of all the men it has been my privilege to know, he was, taken all in all, the largest.'[145] Another who conveyed its sense was Guinness Rogers, who drew attention to a wide variety of gifts – theologian, administrator, preacher, orator, committee man, counsellor – to illustrate Dale's 'remarkable allroundness'.[146] As an all-rounder his impact was broad rather than deep, and only deep impact can be lasting. With the benefit of a hindsight Rogers could not possess, Binfield ends his own list of Dale's many roles with an appropriate backward step: 'Here was a historian, a theologian, a citizen and man of affairs, an educationist, a pastor, a preacher, and a Congregationalist. He was grand, even outstanding, as each. He was formative in each. And yet in none was he original.'[147]

So though Dale was a notable theologian, he was many other

---

perhaps informed his hesitant overall judgement that Dale's is 'a major, perhaps great, book on the atonement'. 'The Cross and the City: R.W. Dale and the Doctrine of the Atonement', in 'The Cross and the City', 1.

141 That very year W.F. Adeney recorded that *Atonement* was continuing to sell at a thousand copies a year. Dale A. Johnson, *The Changing Shape of English Nonconformity, 1825-1925* (New York/Oxford: OUP, 1999), 216, note 93, citing Adeney, *A Century's Progress in Religious Life and Thought* (London: James Clarke, 1901), 146.

142 'R. W. Dale, 1829-1895', in *Great Christians*, R.S. Forman (ed.) (London: Ivor Nicholson & Watson, 1933), 172.

143 *Free Churchmanship in England 1870-1940, with Special Reference to Congregationalism* (London: Independent Press, [1955]), 69.

144 *Congregationalism in England*, 1662-1962 (London: Independent Press, 1962), 266.

145 Fairbairn, *Memorial Services*, 12.

146 *Independent and Nonconformist*, 21 March 1895, 177.

147 Clyde Binfield, 'Dale and Politics', in 'The Cross and the City', 91.

things beside; and it was their combination rather than any particular one of them that constituted his greatness.[148] In his theology Dale engaged valiantly with the difficult problems of the century but failed to blaze a trail through them: never thus succeeding in becoming a theological leader, he never gained much of a following. William Robertson Nicoll wrote that 'he passed away in the full height of an influence that was never so intense and pervasive as in the closing period of his life';[149] but it was a personal influence that can only re-echo faintly beyond its immediate recipients, not the influence of new ideas able to arrogate a permanent place for themselves in the church's library of resources.

---

148 In keeping with this, only one of the ten centenary essays, by Colin Gunton on Dale's doctrine of atonement, is primarily theological in focus.

149 *Princes of the Church* (London: Hodder & Stoughton, 1921), 74.

CHAPTER 4

The Leicester Conference Controversy (1877-78)

Introduction

In May 1877 a preliminary meeting resolved to call 'a public conference open to all who value spiritual religion, and who are in sympathy with the principle that religious communion is not dependent on agreement on theological, critical or historical opinion.'[1] The Leicester Conference on Religious Communion took place on 16 October 1877 in the Wycliffe Congregational Church, Leicester, during the week in which the Congregational Union was holding its autumn meetings there. Almost all of the participants were Congregationalists,[2] and the upshot was what Mark Johnson rightly termed the keenest Congregational theological controversy of the century.[3]

The circumstances that proved auspicious both for the conference and the controversy had been in the process of developing over a number of years. James Baldwin Brown had a good sense of history, which helped him become no mean analyst of contemporary trends. In 1871 he discussed the way in which the growing accent on spiritual life, a reaction against what was felt to be an over-concentration on a narrowly defined intellectual orthodoxy, affected conceptions of religious communion:

> I imagine that no thoughtful observer of the progress of opinion can have failed to note that, during the last generation, ecclesiastical and theological ideas have steadily declined as a basis of fellowship and co-operation, while spiritual ideas have taken their

[1] The text of a circular letter advertising the conference, reconstructed from quotations containing minor discrepancies.

[2] Thomas Gasquoine, in *Public Conference on the Terms of Religious Communion*, 10.

[3] Mark Johnson, *The Dissolution of Dissent, 1850-1918* (New York: Garland, 1987), 63.

> place. Men are increasingly drawn together by that which belongs to the sphere of the sympathies, and those beliefs which mould the life; while they attach less and less importance to merely intellectual agreement with regard to the propositions in which they express their judgement about forms of truth. ... It is felt now that there may be a true spiritual oneness – oneness of interior conviction, aim, hope, and work – beneath very diverse intellectual conceptions of the deep things of God.[4]

This is very close to the position taken up by the promotors of the Leicester Conference, showing that the idea they propounded was circulating and gaining acceptance in the preceding years.

The way for a bid to revise the terms of religious communion in the Congregational Union was being prepared by a new sort of language in Assembly, and especially from its chair. The new generation that inherited its leadership in the 1860s exulted in the freedom of the denomination from creeds and ecclesiastical authority, and joined in the chorus of voices extolling life at the expense of dogma. One notable sample of such language was cited by supporters of the Leicester movement in their defence:

> We are free, without a binding formulary, for the 'declaration' which still figures in our Year-book (from which, as its presence there is misleading, it might as well be omitted) binds no one; we have no subscription and no test; and yet I venture to say that there is no body of ministers among whom there is more essential unity of faith. We may well, then, let liberty have its perfect work among us... And if our theology has been undergoing a silent revolution; if we see that certain things have been supposed to belong to the essence of the Gospel which we have learned are, at best, but secondary questions; if we feel that some of our modes, and even some of our opinions need modification, let us be free and bold enough to follow truth openly wherever it leads. Let us be careful how to deal with differences of opinion, how we make men offenders for words, how we call the good evil when associated with what we call heterodoxy, and the evil good when sanctified by the flavour of sound doctrine.[5]

---

[4] Brown, *First Principles of Ecclesiastical Truth: Essays on the Church and Society* (London: Hodder & Stoughton, 1871), 336.

[5] James Guinness Rogers, 1874 Chairman's address, quoted in Thomas Stephenson, *CW*, 16 November 1877, 824-5. In 1870 Rogers had regretted

A major misunderstanding arose between the denominational leadership and the promoters of the Leicester Conference on this subject. The former allowed themselves such indulgent language because their confidence in the basic theological unity of their denomination was unbounded. The founding fathers of the Congregational Union had rejoiced in this, contrasting as it did with the party divisions of the Church of England and the schisms of Methodism; their successors rejoiced all the more, gaining confidence after successfully weathering the Rivulet Controversy and introducing theologies free of many of the aspects of Calvinism that the Victorians found painful. These hardly received dogmatic expression because of the strong anti-dogmatic tendency of the day and also because of a weakness of construction that could only thrive in association with vagueness; but the parameters were nevertheless widely understood, by the leaders at least, for the increased comprehension did have limits. Yet as limits were not popular things and a need to expatiate on them was not felt, speeches like that cited above made no allusion to them. The Leicester convenors took the rhetoric at face value and tripped over the unspoken limits rather badly. It is not easy to decide whether the misunderstanding was in part wilful; but an element of genuine surprise at the strength of the hostile reaction was undeniably present. They certainly believed that the outlook for the conference was more propitious than it turned out to be.

The two main factors in the background of the Leicester Conference movement were therefore the development of new attitudes to religious communion among the more radical liberals, and a partial liberalisation in the Congregational Union which led them to believe that the moment was opportune for a pressure group to press for more.

The conservative reaction that interpreted the Leicester initiative as a challenge and set about turning it into a major controversy was another product of the previous two decades. The presence of radical liberals in the denomination and that of others of less radical views consorting with them did not pass unnoticed, the result being growing uneasiness among the more conservative. An instance of the sort of incident that fuelled this, which took place shortly before the Leicester Conference, was the presence of Baldwin Brown and Thomas Gasquoine (one of the Leicester Conference's leading lights)

---

that Congregationalists had not altogether escaped the idea 'that agreement in doctrinal views is essential to unity of spirit' ('The Congregationalism of the Future', in H.R. Reynolds (ed.), *Ecclesia* (London: Hodder & Stoughton, 1870), 510).

at the opening of a Free Christian Church[6] in Whitchurch, Brown being among the speakers. The man who drew this to public attention made veiled allusion to another significant factor, the taunts of the evangelical party in the Church of England:

> I am afraid, unless some explanation is given of their presence on the occasion, especially by Mr. Brown as chairman-elect, it will afford additional ground for the charges of our opponents and the fears of some of own friends, that an incipient Socinianism is slowly progressing among our ministers and churches, which will be fatal to their spiritual life, and paralyse all earnest efforts for the evangelisation of the world.[7]

Feeling was sufficiently strong to defeat all attempts to play down and ignore the outburst of concern that occurred both at Leicester and subsequently.

History

The genesis of the Leicester Conference on Religious Communion lay in a discussion between Thomas Gasquoine and W. Carey Walters early in 1877, at which the former, who regretted the tendency of the 'broader men' to stand aloof from the Congregational Union, said that he thought it would be good for them to get together specially during its meetings. Walters suggested they do so in Leicester in October, and that they invite James Allanson Picton, who was at one and the same time the most senior, most widely known, and most theologically radical of their number.[8] The main milestone on the road from there to Leicester was an informal meeting at which some fifty people were present, held during the Congregational Union meetings in May.[9] An

[6] Free Christian Churches were not supposed to adopt any particular theological stance, but in practice were very close to the newer spiritual wing of Unitarianism.

[7] H. Sturt, in *EI*, 4 October 1877, 1054; for other comments see *Congregationalist*, 7 (1878), 328; *EI*, 15 November 1877, 1258.

[8] Mark Johnson has delineated this in 'Thomas Gasquoine and the Origins of the Leicester Conference', *JURCHS*, 2 (1982), 340-52, using a document written by Gasquoine held by Dr Williams' Library; see also Gasquoine in *BW*, 10 March 1907, 534.

[9] *Leicester Chronicle and Leicestershire Mercury*, 20 October 1877, 7; *CW*, 23 October 1877, special extra number, 5.

organizing committee was appointed, with a Leicester minister, Joseph Wood, as its secretary, and a membership that reflected the diversity of the movement's constituency both in theology and in denominational affiliation.[10]

It was the publicity which they organized that eventually brought the Leicester Conference to the attention of the Congregational Union and the press. The first means used was a circular letter that summarized the results of the London meeting and announced the Leicester Conference, closing with the statement of its platform on religious communion that has been quoted in the introductory paragraph of this chapter. This was only sent to people who, it was felt, would be in sympathy with the aim of the conference, not to all Congregational Union delegates as has been wrongly suggested.[11] This must to some extent have been supplemented by word of mouth: when a fellow member of the local committee organizing the Union's meetings criticized Wood for not informing them about the conference, the latter said he had talked of it with more than one local minister and many members of different churches.[12] As with the circular, oral publicity was evidently restricted to people known to be sympathetic.

This policy must have succeeded, for there was no official or press reaction until the appearance of a press advertisement, the final publicity method, in the fortnight prior to the Leicester Assembly. It announced that 'a public conference of those who feel that agreement in theological opinion can no longer be held to be essential to Religious Communion, will take place on Tuesday evening, October 16th 1877, in the Wycliffe Congregational Church, Leicester'.[13] These words soon became even more notorious than those of the circular – the appearance of the words 'no longer' bore menacing overtones of change. It was as a result of this final stage in the publicity that the Leicester Conference became a highly charged confrontation in which opponents of the platform were in the majority rather than the congenial meeting of like-minded people its convenors had intended.

---

[10] *CW*, 15 May 1878, special May Meeting number, 10; *EI*, 8 November 1877, 1232.

[11] John W. Grant, *Free Churchmanship in England 1870-1940* (London: Independent Press, 1955), 90. Henry Allon said he had not had an opportunity to see the circular before arriving at the conference (*CW*, 23 October 1877, special extra number, 9) and a journalist believed this to be true for the majority of those present (*EI*, 25 October 1877, 1145).

[12] *EI*, 14 February 1878, 154-5; 21 February 1878, 177.

[13] *Nonconformist*, 3 October 1877, 996.

One convenor of the Leicester Conference declared that at the meeting at which it was planned the Congregational Union was not thought of from first to last, an extraordinary claim in view of the fact that Gasquione's original vision of it as a fringe meeting during the Union Assembly was maintained throughout.[14] When Alexander Hannay, Secretary of the Union, heard about the Conference he had no difficulty in connecting it with the Union, and involved himself in two moves against the Conference before it took place. Firstly there was an attempt to get it called off, by bringing pressure to bear privately on Wilks and possibly other leaders.[15] When this failed Hannay published an advertisement in the press which ended speculation on the subject by declaring that the conference being advertised was not under the auspices of the Congregational Union.[16]

The conference was given a poor start by the introductory remarks from the chairman, Mark Wilks, a Congregational minister from Holloway: his outline of three questions they were to consider that evening – science and the Bible, private judgement, and the future of the movement – bore no relation to the papers presented next, let alone to the ensuing discussion. James Allanson Picton paraded his pantheism without embarrassment in addressing his subject, 'Some Relations of Theology to Religion'; his conclusion was that quite different theologies were equally useful aides to the religious life, and there should therefore be no discrimination between them. The second paper, read by Thomas Gasquoine, was an inferior production impatiently endured by an audience that was eager for the promised discussion.[17] All semblance of order was soon lost when Picton was asked to define his phrase 'the divine totality of being', and Professor Simon of Spring Hill College had to help the Chairman regain control and make a genuine debate possible, though considerably restricted by the limited time available.

Simon and Henry Allon, the leading opponents of the platform, both complained that the papers were abstruse, and were apparently

---

[14] William Dorling, in *CW*, 15 May 1878, special May Meeting number, 3; Gasquoine, in *Public Conference on the Terms of Religious Communion*, 8.

[15] *CW*, 23 October 1877, special extra number, 5. Compare *Congregationalist*, 6 (December 1877), 713-14; *CW*, 15 May 1878, special May Meeting number, 4.

[16] 'Onlooker', *The Theological Chaos and the 'Congregational' Crisis* (London: n.p., 1878), 4; *Leicester Chronicle and Leicestershire Mercury*, 13 October 1877, 9; *Nonconformist*, 24 October 1877, 1066.

[17] The summary of the conference is largely drawn from the verbatim account in *CW*, 23 October 1877, special extra number, 5-10.

disconcerted that they could see no obvious line for a counter-attack. Like the other three champions of a theological basis of communion, they both ended up by requesting definitions of the terms used in the circular summoning the conference, especially the phrase 'religious communion'. The response of the convenors was less than enthusiastic: both Picton and Wood said that the words were used in their ordinary sense; Picton added that the request was scarcely in place, and Wood was applauded for contending 'that the passion for definition has been one of the greatest curses of the Church'.[18] But the other speaker in favour of the platform, John Page Hopps, a Leicester Unitarian, did offer some definitions in a powerful speech that showed that he had not given way to the hard, tense atmosphere that impoverished the meagre discussion. Amid all its disappointments the one achievement of the Leicester Conference was to make clear the moralistic emphasis that was the common feature of the variety of theologies represented in the movement. Wood said that all that was essential for religious communion was a good life; Page Hopps agreed, adding that God accepted good and truth-seeking people, not those with the right opinions.

* * *

Opinions as to the extent to which the Leicester Conference became the subject of interest and concern in the denomination differed substantially. In May 1878 James Brown of Lewisham wrote that he worked closely with three Congregational churches and travelled constantly, but never heard anyone talk about the Conference until shortly before the recent Union Assembly, while in the same month Enoch Mellor said 'I have never been in any town since the Leicester Conference in which I have not met with great uneasiness'.[19] The evidence suggests that Mellor's experience was the more representative.

Letters to the religious press are a useful indicator of reactions, and were important at the time in presenting the issues to the Christian public and in keeping them alive. Correspondence in *The Christian World* and *The English Independent* did not flag in the entire period of seven months separating the Leicester and London assemblies. In one issue the editor of *The Christian World* added at the end of several columns of letters that he could have filled twenty

---

[18] *CW*, 23 October 1877, special extra number, 9.

[19] *CW*, 8 May 1878, special May Meeting number, 11; also 17 May 1878, 399 (Brown).

more.[20] Unfortunately the quality of the correspondence did not match the quantity. But the latter was enough to induce a writer in *The Congregationalist* to conclude that 'there is an agitation abroad among the Churches which is unusual both for its extent and its intensity'.[21]

Perhaps the clearest index of the amount of denominational interest in the controversy is the importance accorded it at the May 1878 Congregational Union Assembly, held in the spacious Union Chapel, Islington. Attendance on the second day of the debate about the Leicester Conference was considered greater than ever before:[22]

> The great debate which occupied nearly the whole of the time of the Congregational Union at its recent meetings, created a far deeper and more intense interest than any other discussion which has taken place in the Union for many years.[23]

> It will long be remembered that the chapel was crowded everywhere, that the people sat or stood for hours, that the one topic anticipated and discussed was that of the basis of 'Religious Communion' as suggested at Leicester, and that there were a passion and enthusiasm, an eagerness and earnestness which, so far as our experience goes, were perfectly unique.[24]

The issues were sufficiently important to attract attention well beyond the confines of the denomination, a fact of some importance, for Congregationalists were sensitive to their image in the wider Church. The Baptists were, as usual, most closely concerned by the fortunes of their sister denomination, and many were present at the crucial May debates.[25] The orthodox in all denominations naturally condemned the views held by the convenors of the Leicester Conference, but thereafter three different attitudes can be discerned. In some the dominant response was the expression of confidence that the Congregationalists were basically quite sound; in others

---

[20] 1 February 1878, 85.

[21] *Congregationalist*, 6 (December 1877), 707.

[22] *Nonconformist,* 15 May 1878, 501.

[23] *Congregationalist*, 7 (June 1878), 326.

[24] *EI*, 17 May 1878, 498.

[25] They caused some concern by getting in amongst the representative members of the Union. Hannay explained that the barricades had been forced, initially by the ladies, but that they had since been strengthened. *CW*, 10 May 1877, 377; 15 May 1878, special May Meeting number, 1.

concern at the situation and pleas for decisive action were to the fore.[26] The third attitude, found mainly where least love was lost – in the Church of England and especially in its evangelical party – was one of unashamed glee at the discomfiture of a rival.[27] Enoch Mellor expressed himself strongly on the subject early in his speech opening the debate at the May Assembly:

> [The Leicester Conference] has also awakened, I will call it a malicious triumph in the minds of many who have been disposed to say that they see in this conference another illustration and proof of the invincible and inveterate tendency of all free religious organizations to swerve from the limits of evangelical faith.[28]

As would later be the case in the Downgrade Controversy, Anglican exploitation of Nonconformist difficulties over liberal theology, arising from a context of sharp rivalry, played a major role in persuading denominational leaders to make a gesture to vindicate their orthodoxy. Anglicans, especially the evangelical party, were always on the lookout for something tangible with which to retort to the barbed Congregationalist boast of freedom and unity in orthodoxy.

With about seventy-five members, the Congregational Union Committee could act as quite an effective sponge, soaking up this mixture of responses from the various sources. It was made up of ministers and laymen of differing viewpoints, including in William Dorling a member of the Leicester Conference Committee. If any riposte to that conference was to be made, the responsibility for

---

[26] *The Watchman* and *The Methodist Recorder* were examples of each view, quoted in *EI*, 22 November 1877, 1294, and 6 December 1877, 1339.

[27] This 'sectarian spite' was fully reciprocated by Nonconformists. A piece in *The Christian World* entitled 'A Specimen of Brainless Journalism' illustrates the nature of relations between the two groups: 'It is pretty generally known that there is such a paper as "The Record", though its readers, even in Episcopal circles, are now so few as to make its continued existence a surprise. For many years past its special aversion has been Intellect. All Thinking on religious subjects is its avowed abomination. It hates mental activity, in the sphere of Christianity, even more than it hates dissent, - and that is saying a good deal. Rarely a number comes out without its columns supplying specimens of the most pitiable weakness, and sectarian spite; but of late it has quite out-done itself in both these qualities.' (7 June 1878, 474).

[28] *CW*, 8 May 1878, special May Meeting number, 11.

initiating it lay in the hands of the committee, which was responsible for preparing the programme for the Union's annual conference. At its meeting on 4 December 1877 a special committee made up of twenty-seven of its members was set up at the instigation of Guinness Rogers, to discuss what action, if any, to take in response to the Leicester Conference. Rogers himself, Baldwin Brown, Dale, and Dorling were among its members. Brown was absent from its initial meeting on 4 January 1878, when Rogers' motion, that in view of prevailing uneasiness the Union be called upon to reaffirm its constitutional aim 'to uphold and extend evangelical religion' was carried by fifteen votes to six.[29] There ensued 'several lengthy sittings'[30] involving the full committee as well as the special committee before the text of a resolution to be put before the Assembly was publicly released in April 1878. In the early stages of this process few wanted to go further than this and formulate evangelical doctrines,[31] but they changed their minds, as a member of the special committee explained:

> The more we entered into the facts of the case, the more fully we were informed from the country, from reliable sources, of the state of feeling among the ministers and the churches; the more we looked at the nature of the conflict between the two camps, if I might speak of it so, the more we felt that nothing less than this distinct testimony, which is in no way authoritatively or ecclesiastically binding, would, in our view, meet your desire, or, at any rate, satisfy ours.[32]

Several conclusions follow: that there was a strong and persistent antagonism to the Leicester Conference within the denomination; that if anything the pressure was from the bottom upwards rather than being orchestrated by the leadership; and that the issues raised by the Conference took on greater importance the more they were considered. These are further illustrated by the editorial line of *The English Independent,* which was very close to the position of the leaders. At the beginning of 1878 it had included the Leicester Conference very much in the retrospect part of its 'Retrospect and Prospect' article. Its message was that the Congregational Union had

---

[29] *CY,* 1879, 38-39; Johnson, *Dissolution of Dissent,* 94.
[30] *EI,* 4 April 1878, 316.
[31] *CW,* 25 January 1878, 66, apparently using information supplied by committee members.
[32] *CW,* 15 May 1878, special May Meeting number, 2.

promptly and successfully vindicated itself against the Leicester Conference: 'As it is, every one now knows that association with Congregationalism implies on the part of ministers and churches a firm adherence to the fundamental facts and doctrines of Evangelical Christianity'.[33] Those words would not have appeared a few weeks later.

The resolution submitted by the sub-committee was adopted by the Union Committee with slight alterations on 5 March 1878, by a convincing majority of fifty votes to four.[34] The text read as follows:

> That, in view of the uneasiness produced in the churches of the Congregational Order by the proceedings of the recent Conference at Leicester on the terms of Religious Communion, the Assembly feels called upon to re-affirm that the primary object of the Congregational Union is, according to the terms of its own constitution, to uphold and extend Evangelical Religion.
>
> That the Assembly appeals to the history of the Congregational churches generally, as evidence that Congregationalists have always regarded the acceptance of the Facts and Doctrines of the Evangelical Faith revealed in the Holy Scriptures of the Old and New Testaments as an essential condition of Religious Communion in Congregational churches, and that among these have always been included the Incarnation, the Atoning Sacrifice of the Lord Jesus Christ, His Resurrection, His Ascension and Mediatorial Reign, and the work of the Holy Spirit in the renewal of men.
>
> That the Congregational Union was established on the basis of these Facts and Doctrines is, in the judgement of the Assembly, made evident by the Declaration of Faith and Order adopted at the Annual Meeting in 1833; and the Assembly believes that the churches represented in the Union uphold these Facts and Doctrines in their integrity to this day.[35]

---

33 3 January 1878, 2.

34 *CY*, 1879, 39; Johnson, *Dissolution of Dissent*, 94; *CW*, 15 May 1878, special May Meeting number, 3.

35 *CY*, 1879, 44-5.

* * *

The sense of anticipation aroused by the forthcoming debate on this resolution was heightened by the fact that it was to coincide with Baldwin Brown's chairmanship of the Union, itself a matter of considerable interest. It was felt that the chairman's address of the morning of 7 May would in some way be connected to the great debate scheduled for the afternoon;[36] but the degree and nature of the connection surprised and shocked. Brown started uncontroversially, but in the middle of his address he commented directly and bluntly on the imminent debate: 'A course of action is proposed for adoption by this Union, from the policy of which I dissent utterly.'[37] After briefly explaining and excusing himself for what was widely seen as a transgression of the unwritten laws of chairmanship,[38] he mustered a considerable number of arguments in support of his contention.

The debate was spread over two days, Tuesday 7 and Friday 10 May, but only occupied six or seven hours; the atmosphere was tense, and speakers favouring the Leicester Conference had difficulty in getting a hearing: Congregationalists were scarcely justified in congratulating themselves on the tone of the debate.[39] The victory of the resolution was never in doubt, but the denominational leaders understandably attached great importance to obtaining an overwhelming vote in its favour, which meant that much was at stake in the debate. Its early stages were not auspicious for them. Brown's powerful speech had given their opponents a standing start, and they pressed home that advantage by exploiting two attractive arguments: that the resolution was a thinly disguised creed, and that the evangelicalism of the Congregational Union was too evident to require vindication. The leaders were not helped by some of their own speakers, commencing with Dr Enoch Mellor, who moved the resolutions in a rather hesitant speech, evidently

---

[36] *Nonconformist*, 9 May 1878, 469.

[37] *CY*, 1879, 70.

[38] Alexander Raleigh, *CW*, 15 May 1878, special May Meeting number, 1; *BQR*, 68 (July 1878), 193-4; *Congregationalist*, 7 (June 1878), 329-30. Compare Brown's more conventionally correct chairmanship in a not dissimilar situation on the London Board of Congregational Ministers – Brown, *The Doctrine of Annihilation in the Light of the Gospel of Love* (London: Henry S. King, 1875), v.

[39] As did e.g. *Congregationalist*, 7 (July 1878), 193; *EI*, 17 May 1878, 488. See also *CW*, 10 May 1878, 376.

taken aback by Brown's comments.[40]

Potentially the most serious menace of all was posed by an amendment tabled by Joseph Parker of the City Temple, Congregationalism's most colourful preacher, which threatened to divide the anti-Leicester vote:

> That whilst this Assembly views hopefully every honourable effort to extend the terms of personal Religious Communion, it is of opinion that theological and co-operative fellowship, as between churches and any of their organized forms, can be made complete and useful only by the acceptance of a common doctrinal basis, and therefore that the Assembly solemnly re-affirms its adhesion to those Evangelical Doctrines which the Congregational Union has maintained throughout the whole period of its existence.[41]

Parker argued that this affirmed evangelical faith just as much as the resolution, but was preferable in that it avoided a creed-like list of doctrines, it made no specific reference to the Leicester Conference, and it showed some charity. Two speakers furthered his cause, one of them unintentionally. Eustace Conder, the last speaker on Tuesday, spoke strongly against the Leicester Conference but said that he did not mind whether the resolution or the amendment was passed; Alexander Raleigh, who resumed the debate on Friday, did not help matters with his frank admission that something like Parker's amendment had at one time seemed sufficient to the committee. Dale set about countering the amendment: he confessed himself surprised at Conder and Raleigh, and drew attention to its opening clause, which he maintained gave a quasi-sanction to the Leicester Conference; he concluded that no resolution at all would be preferable to that. His speech yielded an unanticipated bonus: Mark Wilks, the chairman of the Leicester Conference, declared that after hearing Dale he now believed that if a resolution must be passed, it should be the amendment. Such advice from such a source was bound to dissuade several evangelicals from voting for Parker for every liberal it persuaded to do so: Dale's 'hear, hear' was loud enough for *The Christian World's* shorthand writer to note down.

---

40 *Nonconformist*, 9 May 1878, 469. The main source for the debate is the verbatim account in *CW*, 8 May 1878, special May Meeting number, 11-13, and 15 May 1878, special May Meeting number, 1-7. The most suggestive analysis of the debate is that of *The Congregationalist*, 7 (June 1878), 326-7.

41 *CY*, 1878, 45.

Guinness Rogers, like Dale a man experienced in political debate, drove home the advantage.

The denominational establishment was thus able to face the vote with greater confidence. Counting the hands in the different corners of a very large chapel was not easy, and there was a degree of variation in the estimates. Parker's amendment received about sixty votes; the resolution was carried by roughly a thousand votes to twenty-five.[42] No one was able to find such a majority unconvincing.

If the correspondence columns are anything to go by, the excitement receded fast. *The Christian World* was the only newspaper to carry a significant body of correspondence after the Assembly, mainly from frustrated supporters of the minority. One writer who gallantly held himself back until 22 June in order to allow sufficient time to pass to renew the discussion in a calm spirit, discovered that the excitement had waned all too much – only one reply to his letter was ever published.[43]

There was a brief period of felicitation, self-congratulation and optimism in which evangelicals from outside the denomination shared, as is illustrated by comments Spurgeon felt inspired to make:

> A few noisy individuals, for ever clashing the 'high-sounding cymbals' of their pretended thoughtfulness and culture, have led many to fear that Congregationalism would ultimately become another name for a lawless, creedless scepticism, but those fears are groundless; the sons of the Puritans are aroused, and have avowed the faith once delivered unto the saints. ... It was high time that something was done, and now that it is done we thank God and take courage, and feel that the Congregational Union has made a new departure, and will henceforth no longer be a place where Pantheists and Socinians will dare to say that they find themselves at home.[44]

Such language reinforced impressions liberals gathered from the debate, at which some of the speakers had been abetted by much of the audience in their efforts to maximize the pressure the resolution could be made to bring to bear. Their early assessments therefore tended to be angry and fearful, but when it became clear that no

---

[42] Based on varying estimates in *CW*, *Nonconformist*, *Congregationalist*, *Evangelical Magazine*, and *Leicester Chronicle and Leicestershire Mercury*.
[43] *CW*, 28 June 1878, 539; 12 July 1878, 574.
[44] *ST*, 14 (1878), 316-17.

action was to be taken against them this was succeeded by a tendency to dismiss the threats as posturing. Baldwin Brown's own postscript on the controversy adopted this line: in his autumnal address from the chair he said that he had come to see that the resolution was not to be used as a basis for action, and that it was a way of relieving feelings rather than a new policy of doctrinal definition. Guinness Rogers' reply was revealingly conciliatory, calling for the maintenance of peace and emphasizing the points on which Brown and those responsible for the resolution were agreed.[45] Critics had been silenced, and the uneasy had been reassured by the resounding victory of the resolution, and the matter might end there. Liberals showed some short-lived caution, but did not gratify their opponents by do anything so drastic as leaving the Union.

The Leicester movement itself continued for a while, turning itself into the Association for Promoting Religious Communion. It held conferences and devotional meetings during the Congregational meetings in May 1879, but there was no sign of it left by May 1880. The initial public interest it had aroused subsided rapidly. *The Christian World* carried a verbatim account of the 1878 conference but only gave a summary of that of 1879.[46] Many years later the movement's co-instigator, Thomas Gasquoine, wrote that the Association ended because its work of widening horizons and promoting a simpler brotherhood was done, and repeating the conference endlessly would have been boring.[47] While the first reason sounds presumptuous the second is very plausible. And, remarkably in view of its scale and intensity, the controversy itself soon followed the movement that triggered it into oblivion: as early as 1891 Charles Miall was already writing that 'the recollections of that remarkable episode are fading into the distance'.[48] To understand the reasons for this eclipse it is necessary to turn to the theological debate.

Issues

It was natural that a plan to redraw the patterns of religious association should bring theological change into the realm of public controversy. Religious communion is the point at which the thought

45 *CY*, 1879, 82; *CW*, 18 October 1878, special extra number, iii, 5.

46 *CW*, 15 May 1878, special May Meeting number, 7-11; 16 May 1879, 309.

47 *BW*, 14 March 1907, 634.

48 Herbert S. Skeats and Charles S. Miall, *History of the Free Churches of England 1688-1891* (London: Alexander & Shepheard,1891), 656-7.

movements of theology impinge on the visible practicalities of church life about which people tend to feel deeply. The conference on religious communion was not misnamed: this was the central issue of the controversy. Mark Johnson's alternative thesis, that 'Although the language of the controversy was purely theological, the central issue was the political one of unity,'[49] is a misguided attempt to fit the controversy into his socio-political explanation of nonconformist decline through opting for full participation in the life of the nation, with a consequent loss of identity and purpose. Quite apart from the weakness of his thesis statement – for even to a highly political dissenter such as Guinness Rogers unity was a theological and religious issue before it was a political one – the only evidence he can offer is circumstantial: the coincidence between the Leicester Conference debacle and a major disestablishment campaign that required nonconformist unity, and the prominence of Guinness Rogers in both. He does not present any evidence from the multitude of available published letters and reports of speeches of the political link having been made explicit.[50] In fact, nonconformist political unity was unaffected by its internal theological differences, and the main 'outside' bearing of the controversy was on the reputation of the Congregational polity; the difficulty here was that freedom was quite as important a component of this as orthodoxy, and the Leicester Conference made it exceedingly awkward to rescue both more or less intact.

The definition of 'religious communion' was one of the main themes of the debate at the Leicester Conference itself and also of the ensuing newspaper correspondence. Conflicting answers were put forward, sometimes from the same source: at the conference Joseph Wood said that religious communion meant 'the possibility of joining in common acts of worship',[51] but later defined it as 'friendly intercourse between men who are interested in religion – who feel its claims, own its authority, and desire its triumph'.[52] P.T. Forsyth said he took Christian communion to mean the communion service, a much narrower definition. A correspondent in *The Christian World* pointed out the confusion and made a laudable plea for clarity, saying that he could agree or disagree with the Leicester platform depending on how it was defined.[53] But the debate moved away to

---

[49] *Dissolution of Dissent*, 63.

[50] *Ibid.*, 94-102.

[51] *CW*, 23 October 1877, special extra number, 9.

[52] *EI*, 1 November 1877, 1216.

[53] *EI*, 1 November 1877, 1202; Eric Lawrence, in *CW*, 23 November 1877, 848.

other issues and he never received an answer. The wider aspects of religious communion were left behind in favour of a narrower focus on the simpler matter of the basis of membership in the Congregational Union. It was in the Union's interest to turn a complex debate into a stand on a simplified issue which would be acceptable to a vast majority of simple Congregationalists – after which the whole question could simply be dropped. However one definition of religious communion does stand out from the rest: S. Lambrick of Leicester defined it as 'mutual intercourse or interchange in the performance of those duties which we owe to God; union of faith, fellowship in worship'.[54]

Like all the others, Lambrick then proceeded to discuss the main issue, the basis of religious communion. This broad question is best considered from two different angles: firstly a theological one, the doctrinal basis of communion; and secondly an ecclesiastical one, how a basis of communion could operate under the Congregational polity.

Theological

Though silent on what was to be the basis of religious communion the Leicester Conference circular was explicit on what it was *not* to be – agreement in theological, critical or historical opinion. It might therefore appear inappropriate to include its supporters in a discussion of the theological basis of communion. However they did have a basis of communion, succinctly expressed by Page Hopps at the conference: 'If God holds communion with me, spirit to spirit, I ask my brother man whether he will hold communion with me, too.'[55] The Leicester Unitarian then brought this thought into contact with their principle about religious communion being independent of theological considerations, drawing the conclusion that acceptance with God was not a matter of having the right opinions. After the conference Joseph Wood again came out with an account of the basis of acceptance with God and therefore of religious communion which differed from the one he expressed in it. His earlier suggestion was that a good life was the one essential for religious communion, his later one that the one condition of religious communion was religion.[56] What they appear to have failed to understand is that these 'non-theological' terms of religious communion were in fact established in a thoroughly theological

[54] *Leicester Chronicle and Leicestershire Mercury*, 10 November 1877, 10.

[55] *CW*, 23 October 1877, special extra number, 9.

[56] *CW*, 23 October 1877, special extra number, 9; 2 November 1877, 785.

way, for the grounds of acceptance by God cannot but be a theological question.

One of the leaders of the movement did not even observe their basic principle: both at the conference and afterwards Mark Wilks stated that the movement aimed to discover what limits those unhappy with orthodoxy as a basis of communion would be prepared to accept, asking whether miracles, the incarnation and the resurrection of Christ should be considered open questions in the free churches.[57]

There was however a level on which they could present a united approach to the basis of religious communion, namely in asserting religion as against theology, and life as against dogma. James Martineau put this opposition forcefully in the course of a simultaneous Unitarian debate along very similar lines:

> In short, the choice has to be made. You may devote a Church to the enduring life of religion, which persists through changing theologies; or to a given theology, with such religion as in its day it can manage to hold. But you cannot combine both methods; since the trustful piety of the former consists in renouncing the comfortable securities of the latter. My own allegiance is unreservedly given to the former.[58]

Wilks stressed the moral nature of the religious life that was to be the basis of their communion. This was an absolute, for the time had not yet come when moral relativity would begin to appear alongside the theological relativity they felt deeply:

> What is the number of members of our free churches, lay and ministerial, who are prepared to say spiritual life is independent of creed, of doctrine, of metaphysical and theological dogmas – not indeed, of course, of moral dogmas and doctrines, but that all creeds except those that have respect to conduct are non-essential to the maintenance and sustenance of spiritual life? ... We ask for a conference among those who already profess independence of theological creed, who already assert that religion is a life, and not a matter of belief or of doctrine.[59]

---

[57] *CW*, 23 October 1877, special extra number, 6; 23 November 1877, 848.

[58] *CW*, 25 January 1878, 66; the debate was over the rights and wrongs of fellowship with theists.

[59] He was speaking at the Leicester Conference: *CW*, 23 October 1878,

Opponents of the Leicester Conference were aware of the appeal of this vision of a broader Christian sympathy, extending beyond theological agreement. One of the two main thrusts of their reply to the Religious Communion thesis was therefore an endeavour to expose fallacies in its fashionable stand on life as against dogma. It was urged that it was wrong to separate the two, contrasting one favourably with the other, for in order to live it was necessary to have truths to embody.[60]

A member of the Leicester Conference Committee conceded the point: conviction did to a great extent determine character.[61] Wilks' assertion that spiritual life was independent of doctrine was a difficult position to defend, and some at least of the movement's supporters found it untenable. John Kennedy exploited this breach in the Religious Communion movement's position: he pointed out that the spiritual life produced by or associated with different theologies differed as much as these theologies, citing the cases of Islam and Christianity.[62] The advantage in the debate clearly lay on the orthodox side: they were able to expose the naiveté with which the Religious Communion movement supposed evangelical morality and spirituality could be produced and sustained in association with any theological system. That fallacy was possible because of the common tendency of the age to assume that an absolute neo-Christian ethic was enthroned in the conscience, unaffected by the vagaries of philosophy and theology. However, their opponents were too much affected by the same assumption to be able to press home the advantage.

The other main way in which the orthodox criticized the Leicester Conference movement was by saying that its talk of 'religious' rather than 'Christian' communion showed that it was broader than Christianity itself. Attention was concentrated on Picton, whose views were the most extreme. It was noted that a book of his put Christianity on a level with other world religions.[63] The Victorian public were less enchanted by this than they were by the movement's emphasis on life.

But these criticisms made up only a small proportion of the evangelical theological reaction. Their main efforts were directed

---

special extra number, 6.

60 *CW*, 8 May 1878, special May Meeting number, 12; 23 October 1877, special extra number, 9; *BQR*, 68 (July 1878), 206.

61 William Miall, in *CW*, 1 February 1878, 84.

62 John Kennedy, *The People Called Independents: With Relation to their Doctrinal History and Beliefs* (London: John Snow & Co., 1878), 53-4.

63 *CW*, 2 November 1877, 785.

toward patching up their own position by proclaiming what doctrines they considered fundamental. The three main points, incarnation, atonement, and resurrection, were prominent in the Congregational Union resolution. Unitarianism was excluded from this basis of communion, so was a purely moralistic view of salvation and so too was rationalist denial of the supernatural.[64]

Thus far the opposition were united and emphatic, but this was all dissipated when they came to the question of the relation between their platform and the basis of acceptance by God. A bold 'lay Congregationalist' adopted an exposed position with the following categorical statement:

> Here, then, is a testing-point for true Christian communion. Those who do not believe in the Divinity, the Atonement, and Resurrection of the Lord Jesus Christ are not Christians, in spite of all pretty speeches and delusive compromises, for they practically 'deny the Lord that bought them', as well as deny that 'Jesus Christ, the everlasting Son of the Father, is come in the flesh,' both prophetically indicated as heresies that should abound in the 'latter days'.[65]

However this was rare; most displayed a coyness on the subject similar to that of the Leicester movement, concealing similar uncertainty and disagreement. More typical was Lambrick's opinion that he did not think Unitarians would be punished for their unbelief, at least not in the gross way thought of in the past.[66]

Though rather unsuccessful in their attempts to justify their basis of fellowship, opponents of the Leicester Conference were able to point out a major flaw in its thesis on religious communion. Joseph Wood unconsciously revealed it when he stated flatly that neither belief in the Trinity and the resurrection of Christ, nor the opinion that such beliefs were essential for the religious life, was essential for religious communion.[67] This is illogical: anyone who considered the above-mentioned beliefs essential to religious life would refuse religious communion with those who denied them, in the same way that Wood would deny communion to a notorious criminal, however fervently the latter believed religious communion should

[64] *Leicester Chronicle*, 15 December 1877, 4; *CW*, 8 February 1878, 105; *CW*, 30 November 1877, 861; *Congregationalist*, 7 (June 1878), 326.

[65] *EI*, 8 November 1877, 1234.

[66] *Leicester Chronicle*, 10 November 1877, 10.

[67] *CW*, 23 October 1877, special extra number, 9.

be independent of moral opinions. This point was made by several orthodox writers,[68] but the best version, quoted approvingly by opponents of the Leicester movement, was that of the *Unitarian Inquirer*:

> The whole popular conception of what Christianity is, and the grounds of Christian obligation, must be radically changed before there can be genuine cordial communion between the Trinitarian and Unitarian churches. We are also convinced that nothing but harm would arise from a constrained, artificial communion... There can be no real union between those who believe that orthodoxy in any form is essential to salvation or even to the Christian name, and those who believe that the life and essence of Christianity are independent of mere dogmatic opinions. The dogmas referred to above are either tremendous realities or they are not. If they are true there can be no indifference about them; they constitute the very heart of the Gospel... We agree with the orthodox critics that there is an unreality about the whole movement, and sooner or later there must be a separation between widely diverging tendencies of thought... The theological atmosphere would be cleared if we all had more of the courage as well as the logic of our convictions, and cultivated friendly relations with each other, without striving to maintain a union which has ceased to be either practicable or desirable.[69]

The Leicester movement had in effect suggested that their thesis on religious communion could be the means to break down the dividing wall between Unitarianism and evangelicalism; it is not surprising that the message came back from both sides that that could not happen without a fundamental change in the nature of evangelical theology. Conservatives like Spurgeon would have none of it:

> After having denied the faith, and plunged their daggers into the heart of vital doctrines as best they can, they still claim to be ministers of the gospel, and ask to be received into union on the ground of some peculiar inward virtue which exists in them apart

---

68 E.g. Lambrick, in *Leicester Chronicle,* 10 November 1877, 10; Robert Bruce, in *EI*, 15 November 1877, 1255; *Congregationalist,* 6 (December 1877), 714.

69 Quoted in *EI*, 6 December 1877, 1339-40.

from all doctrinal belief.[70]

Up to this point the discussion might leave the impression that the controversy was a confrontation between conservatives and the radical leaders of the Religious Communion movement. This was what the Union committee wanted it to appear: the easiest way to repudiate the religious communion thesis was to concentrate attention on its most radical proponents, not a difficult task as these were its most prominent men. Unitarianism was an adequate target for their purposes, but Picton's pantheism was even more attractive, especially as Picton was not shy of parading it, both in his paper at the Leicester Conference and afterwards.[71] Though several supporters of the Conference told him that his paper was not suited to the occasion, for a while Picton was not unhappy with the attention focused on him, arguing that if his extreme case proved acceptable them all others would be decided with it. However it was not long before he joined Wilks in pleading that the debate be shifted from the rights and wrongs of particular theologians back to the religious communion principle itself.[72] The appeal fell on deaf ears, and the orthodox succeeded in accentuating the degree of polarization. The reality was different: the theological gap between orthodox supporters of the Leicester Conference and its most liberal opponents was minimal, as will be seen by analysing mediating positions. What is more, it was agreed on all sides that the majority of supporters of the religious communion movement had not rejected the christological doctrines of the Congregational Union's resolution.[73] Theological differences between opponents of the Conference were less obvious but can nevertheless be discerned.

The middle ground can be studied by comparing the views of P.T. Forsyth, a man on the orthodox wing of the Religious Communion movement, with those of Baldwin Brown, the most sympathetic of its main opponents. Their importance as theologians and their close personal relationship[74] add further interest to the study.

Forsyth's stance on Religious Communion can be studied at two

---

[70] *ST*, 14 (1878), 99-100.

[71] 'Of course I am a Pantheist – but, mark! of the spiritual, not of the materialistic school.' Picton, in *EI*, 22 November 1877, 1282.

[72] *EI*, 8 November 1877, 1231; Picton, in *CW*, 9 November 1877, 804; *EI*, 22 November 1877, 1282; Wilks, in *CW*, 23 November 1877, 848.

[73] Wilks, in *CW*, 15 May 1878, special May Meeting number, 4; *EI*, 1 November 1877, 1194; Brown, 'The Perfect Law of Liberty', in *CY*, 1879, 90.

[74] See pp. 40-41, above.

points, in two letters to *The English Independent* in November 1877, and in a paper entitled 'A Larger Comprehension the Remedy for the Decay of Theology' read at the London Religious Communion conference of May 1878.[75] The November letters were characteristic of the Religious Communion movement in clearly separating theology and religion and allowing the latter to determine the limits of communion. Forsyth wrote that the facts of Christianity were only useful so far as they helped realize the Christian character; people rejecting the facts should not be excluded so long as they maintained the character, even though their position be illogical. At this early stage in his career Forsyth's views and emphases were still volatile, and those of May were manifestly different from those of November. The most obvious change was a complete about turn on ecumenism. He began his November correspondence with a visionary passage about the Church of the Future, which would include all God's family, and for the formation of which Congregationalism was the most hopeful sect, provided it did not sacrifice its freedom and comprehension. But in May he said he did not believe in a universal church, but that the different sects should continue with their particular ecclesiastical views and theologies, while maintaining communion beyond them, their curse being not their separation but isolation.

It is therefore wise to analyse the message of his paper independently of that of the letters in other respects too. The very different starting point he adopted is instructive – he had not shown the same concern to broadcast his orthodoxy in November:

> For my own part, I stand here to assert the right of a Christian minister of evangelical views to hold and express without prejudice to his ministerial reputation whatever ideas as to ecclesiastical comprehension may command themselves to his mind... I stand here as a believer in the Incarnation; as a believer in the Atonement, of the more recent school; with a terrible inward evidence of sin, and a splendid inward witness of Redemption; as a believer in the Christian miracles; above all, as one who from time to time has felt the supreme and unspeakable communion of Him from whom the whole family in heaven and on earth is

[75] *EI*, 1 November 1877, 1202-3, and 8 November 1877, 1230-32; *CW*, 15 May 1878, special May Meeting number, 7-8. The letters are published in an appendix to W.L. Bradley, *P. T. Forsyth: the Man and his Work* (London: Independent Press, 1952).

named.[76]

The language with which he affirmed support for the movement was also significantly different:

> I think there is no faith and hope in God except by the operation of the Incarnation. But I know too little about the mystery of that truth to cut myself off from those who, having the faith and hope which are the end, stumble about the steps of the process in our actual experience of the means.[77]

The end was now referred to as faith and hope rather than character, and though the great christological doctrines were still means they were no longer treated as of peripheral interest.

In November the excitement and enthusiasm of Leicester were still at their height and he expressed himself as radically as he could; later there were calmer moments during which some influence may have been brought to bear on him. The 'church of the future' question provides a clue: the new view has Baldwin Brown's signature written all over it.[78] There is no clear-cut evidence for this, although it is known that Forsyth consulted with Brown by post on the subject of religious communion involving Unitarians.[79]

Yet despite the more evangelical emphasis in his paper Forsyth's basis of communion was not changed. The saving faith which bound men to God was to be a sufficient bond between men, unsupplemented by 'essential truths', for 'the saving essence and sufficient bond of Christianity cannot be anything requiring for its proof an intellectual process more or less severe'.[80]

Brown agreed with Forsyth that there could be no faith and hope in God apart from the operation of the Incarnation, and that the power of the great Christological doctrines operated more widely than they were recognized.[81] He also opposed the Union policy of

---

[76] *CW*, 15 May 1878, special May Meeting number, 7.

[77] *CW*, 15 May 1878, special May Meeting number, 8.

[78] See Brown, *Misread Passages of Scripture,* second series (London: Hodder & Stoughton, 1871), chapter 1.

[79] The fact that the matter was discussed by letter would place it in all probability in Forsyth's Shipley period in the late 1870s. Forsyth, in Elizabeth Baldwin Brown (ed.) *In Memoriam: James Baldwin Brown* (London: J Clarke & Co., 1884), 140.

[80] *CW*, 15 May 1878, special May Meeting number, 7.

[81] 'The Basis of Communion', a lecture reported in *Nonconformist,* 19

drawing a theological line beyond which there was to be no communion, in part because he believed that spiritual life survived outside such limits:

> Mr. Picton touched all hearts when he addressed us in May. I am not afraid to say that there was something in the temper and spirit, the yearning and inspiration, which he manifested, with which I would not have dared to feel myself out of sympathy, lest I should be fatally out of sympathy with my Lord. I believe that, in ways which we know not, that spirit is fed from a Christian fountain, and that if we do not embitter their hearts by forcible repulsion, these brethren will find, and soon, that there is but one power which can kindle that spirit and nurse that devotion – the Gospel of 'God manifest in the flesh'.[82]

Yet he parted company with Forsyth on the central issue of the controversy, the basis of communion, holding that there could be enduring communion only on the basis of the historical gospel:

> I hold, as you know, that [the Leicester Conference's] fundamental principle, that we can dispense with doctrinal belief in the edifying and confederating of souls and churches, is a dire, a fatal delusion.[83]

> The Gospel is not a noble and beautiful speculation about God, about life, about duty; the Gospel is the tale of what the God who made the world has in His own living person done and suffered for the world. Here is the firm, strong, basis of Christian communion. A communion which has feeble hold on the truth which God has given to unite and compact mankind, has in it the principle of decay and the prophecy of dissolution, and can only in the end mock the hopes of all longing hearts.[84]

Therein lay the difference between them: Forsyth saw that the power of the Gospel was present in some who denied its source, but Brown argued that this was a diluted power, doomed to extinction unless the contact with its source could be re-established, and that in order

---

December 1877, 1267.

[82] Brown, 'The Perfect Law of Liberty', 85.

[83] *Ibid.*, 89.

[84] Brown, 'Our Theology in Relation to the Intellectual Movement of our Times', in *CY* (1879), 70.

to last, a basis of communion must recognize the evangelical source of life and power. Brown depicted this as a difference in experience and vision between an older and a younger man:

> Those who have known [Forsyth] as I have, through many years and in trying times, will sustain my witness that he is an earnest, high-minded, and faithful man, with his heart set on the work of the ministry. But he is also, I should say – I hope he will forgive me; the world has held many noble men of that type – one easily fascinated by, and led after, impracticable ideals. I think that through generous sympathies, which I for one heartily appreciate, he is being drawn in the direction now.[85]

To see the Religious Communion controversy as a clash of two parties is an over-simplification: the spectrum of theological opinion was too complex for such a neat division.

Ecclesiastical

All Congregationalists were in agreement that the basis of their polity was the principle from which they drew both their name and their distinctiveness: the dependence of the local church on God alone, giving it the right to decide on its theology and organization without having to defer to any human authority. However, they were not always convinced that they were all abiding by this principle, or had correctly understood its implications. In consequence excursions back into Congregational theory and history were a feature of the controversy. John Kennedy led the way with his pamphlet *The People Called Independents: with Relation to their Doctrinal History and Beliefs*, the only substantial piece of work of any kind to be produced in connection with the controversy.

Kennedy drew particular attention to the Savoy Declaration and Synod of 1658. The former was the Westminster Confession modified to suit a Congregational polity, and true to Congregational principles it was expressly a declaration, and not an enforceable creed. Throughout denominational history Kennedy found this example followed, right down to the 1833 Declaration of Faith and Order published by the Congregational Union: doctrine was expressed in non-authoritative but firmly orthodox and broadly representative declarations.[86] Kennedy also looked to the Puritan

[85] In *EI*, 22 November 1877, 1293.

[86] Kennedy, *People Called Independents*, 8-10. See Appendix 1 for the 1833

period to indicate the authentic Congregational approach to the question of fellowship between churches, finding it in the Savoy Synod's provision for renunciation of communion with heretical or immoral churches. He concluded that

> The right to separate is involved in the right to unite. And if the union is based on understood principles, these being violated the right to separate comes into force. ... Moreover this right is exercised perpetually among us. Let a church invite or retain a morally unworthy man for its pastor, and the Association to which it belongs, declines or renounces communion with it. And nothing more than this is required, when a minister ceases to 'hold the truth as it is in Jesus'.[87]

He gave more evidence to demonstrate that this had been implemented down the years, in particular during the problem with Arianism in the eighteenth century. Finally, he sought to show that after a period of laxity there had been recent moves back to traditional ways.

The Congregational Union's brief history had been relatively untroubled. Its founders had been able to make a declaration that was both evangelical and broadly representative. There had been a difficult interlude in the 1850s and early 1860s when younger ministers dropped Calvinism and explored broader interpretations of evangelicalism. By the 1870s these men were in charge, rejoicing in a greater freedom that had apparently not compromised their unity. But then came the Leicester Conference with its radical thesis that went beyond the bounds of the evangelicalism that had been the basis of earlier Congregational communion. It presented the Union with a difficult choice: was it to sacrifice its ability to comprehend all Congregationalists within itself, or was it to sacrifice its distinctively evangelical stance? It no longer seemed possible to preserve both.

One question that had to be answered was: how fundamental to Congregationalism was its evangelicalism? Were there any limits to Congregational theological development, and if so what was their basis? *The Christian World* acted as the liberal champion, taking upon itself the task of replying to Kennedy. Its main argument was based on the saying of John Robinson, so often repeated that it could be called a Congregational principle, that there was more light to break forth from the Word of God. The recognition that allowance must be

---

declaration.

[87] *Ibid.*, 59; see also p. 58. The rest of the paragraph draws on pp. 22-31.

made for theological development was deeply embedded in Congregationalism, in a way impossible to churches that required subscription to creeds. Refusal to impose creeds not only meant that a church could not bind its fellow churches, but also that it could not bind its own future.[88] Kennedy replied that according to this principle more light was to come from God's Word, which was therefore seen as the authoritative source of Christian doctrine, whereas the Leicester group associated themselves with people who did not consider God's Word to be the standard of truth.[89]

A better liberal argument was based on the fact that there had been theological development throughout the denomination:

> With regard to the Doctrines of the Fall, of Original Sin, of Election, of God, of the nature of the Inspiration of the Bible, of the Fatherhood of God, of the nature of the Atonement, of the Immortality of the Soul, and of the Destiny of the Wicked, will Dr. Kennedy for a moment contend that the Independency of to-day is doctrinally at one with the Independency of the divines who took part in the Westminster Assembly?[90]

Different people had taken this development to different lengths, but who was to decide on the limits of acceptable development, and on what basis?[91]

One suggested answer was that interpretations might change but the great evangelical facts must be maintained,[92] but rather than try to build up a case for evangelicalism being of the essence of the Congregational polity the orthodox tended to plump for an easier task in arguing that it was fundamental to the Congregational Union. The resolution itself reminded the denomination 'that the primary object of the Congregational Union is, according to the terms of its own constitution, to uphold and extend Evangelical Religion',[93] and it was urged that the presence of the words 'no longer' in the advertisement for the Leicester Conference showed that the Religious Communion movement recognized this to be so.[94] Supporters of the movement were unable to deny this but still found

---

[88] 5 April 1878, p. 271.

[89] Kennedy, *People Called Independents,* 13.

[90] *CW,* 5 April 1878, 271.

[91] *Ibid.,* 271; see also 18 January 1878, 45.

[92] E.g. *EI,* 4 April 1878, 317.

[93] *CY,* 1879, 44.

[94] *Congregationalist,* 6 (December 1877), 711, 716-17.

a telling rejoinder: they said that such talk was new to them. They had been encouraged to stay in the Union by addresses denouncing creeds and revelling in freedom and unity, themes so prevalent during the past fifteen years:

> We have talked – I am afraid sometimes talked blatantly – about our freedom from the fetters imposed by creeds, confessions, and formularies; and yet now, when some of our number, in an unusual manner, assert that freedom, we find an article in the English Independent flourishing in our faces *an unwritten creed* – to which it appears we are pledged by honesty and honour; and persons who will not abide by it are imperatively told that 'the sooner they leave *our* pulpits the better'. We may shortly reply, that if this be the case, the sooner this unwritten creed is written out the better for all parties to the compact.[95]

The Congregational leaders had created an atmosphere in the Union which encouraged those who had abandoned evangelical belief to think that they were still welcome. Though Picton's theological wanderings were well known to them – to mention only the most prominent case – they saw fit to alter their language only when embarrassed by the open challenge posed by the Leicester Conference; by that time the damage was done. The evangelicalism of the Union was unimpeachable in theory, but had become compromised in practice.

Opponents of the resolution used a variety of other arguments. Both Picton and Brown said that it would do harm to people struggling with doubts, whose need was for help rather than discouragement, fellowship rather than ostracism:

> But if you put your seal to such resolutions as this, then you do more than merely affirm what nobody doubts – that the Congregational Union is Evangelical in sentiment, but you also cast a forbidding shadow upon the path of many suffering and struggling souls who fear to give up their living faith, but who cannot reconcile their scientific instruction or their historical knowledge with the external framework in which that living faith has been embodied.[96]

---

[95] Thomas Stephenson, in *CW*, 16 November 1877, 824-5; also Picton, in *CW*, 8 May 1878, special May Meeting number, 13.
[96] Picton, in *CW*, 8 May 1878, special May Meeting number, 13; compare

But the intentions of the two men were not as similar as their language. Whereas Brown was interested in helping doubters regain the orthodox theology they had lost or were losing, Picton's aim was to help people preserve a spiritual religion in spite of having felt constrained to abandon orthodox theology. Several opponents of the Leicester Conference distinguished between two categories, advocating tenderness toward seekers and questioners but firmness with regard to people who were hardened and confirmed in denial of the faith.[97]

A more widespread argument of great contemporary appeal to Congregationalists was the contrasting of spirit, truth and life with the mere letter of the resolution. The Congregational polity is incompatible with a belief that a human intermediary power is required to supervise and safeguard the orthodoxy of local churches. It was argued that if churches were unable to preserve the orthodoxy of their minister, then belief in the superintendence of each church by Christ is compromised, and the independent polity must be abandoned.[98] This was Brown's manifesto: 'I believe in the Independency that seeks to keep the truth in the Church and the Church in the statutes of life, by the light of the Scripture and the grace of the Spirit alone'.[99]

No one controverted this point for the simple reason that everyone agreed with it. The Leicester Conference did not cause the majority to reject ideas and emphases they had proclaimed as eagerly as those who now stood against them. What it did do was cause them to regret the imbalance and misunderstanding that resulted from their neglect of another idea, the evangelical basis of communion. The resolution, and indeed the controversy, was about the basis of communion, and not about how to preserve orthodoxy in the churches. Only one contributor to the debate even ventured to suggest that the resolutions might point the minds of ordinary people (but not the educated) in the right direction if passed virtually unanimously.[100] The question of what would be best for doubters was also a side issue for the orthodox, which they addressed only in reply to their opponents' arguments.

The irrelevance of the appeal to faith in the Holy Spirit and to the

---

Brown in 'The Perfect Law of Liberty', 85, 90.

97 Simon, in *CW*, 23 October 1877, special extra number, 8; Kennedy, *People Called Independents*, 55-6; Rogers, in *CW*, 15 May 1878, special May Meeting number, 5.

98 *CW*, 5 April 1878, 271.

99 Brown, 'The Perfect Law of Liberty', 81.

100 Edward White, in *CW*, 15 May 1878, special May Meeting number, 6.

power of truth to prevail against falsehood to the basis of religious communion, the main theme of the debate, is demonstrated by the use of it made by *The Christian World*. It agreed with Kennedy's contention that the moral character of ministers was a proper concern for fellow-ministers in deciding whether to recognize them, but maintained that belief in Christ's superintendence implied that they should not concern themselves with theological criteria for recognition.[101] The apparent implication is that while Christ can be trusted to look after the theology of his Church, he is in need of a little help in preserving its morals. The theological basis of such a division of labour is shrouded in mystery. The orthodox Congregational view was that Christ was to be trusted for all aspects of the preservation of his Church – no outsider had the right to interfere in the internal affairs of a church – but that at the same time other churches were to take both the moral and theological standing of a church into account when deciding whether to have communion with it. *The Christian World's* argument does not amount to anything more than the platform of the Leicester Conference, that theology should not be a barrier to religious communion because it was a matter of secondary importance.

Opponents of the Union resolution reached closer to the heart of the question when they expressed the feeling that it was unprecedented as well as objectionable. However they found it hard to reply to the conservative claim that the resolution was a declaration no more authoritative, and rather less strict and complete, than previous ones.[102] Joseph Wood began his speech in the debate on the resolution by saying that if it were just a statement of facts it might be allowed to pass, but that all the speeches showed that it was an instrument of pressure, aimed at narrowing the basis of Congregational fellowship. The applause which met this statement was confirmation of his interpretation.[103] At an earlier stage in the controversy he had used a stronger term, persecution.[104] There was no denying the existence of this pressure. The 1833 Declaration was explicitly intended to inform the general public about Congregational beliefs,[105] which placed it in the tradition of the Savoy Declaration of 1658. This was of course still part of the aim of the 1878 resolution, but its primary aim, to affirm a contested basis

---

[101] 5 April 1878, 271.

[102] Kennedy, *People Called Independents*, 58.

[103] *CW*, 15 May 1878, special May Meeting number, 6.

[104] *EI*, 1 November 1877, 1216. So had Forsyth – ibid., 1203.

[105] Dale, *History of English Congregationalism*, edited and completed by A.W.W. Dale (London: Hodder & Stoughton, 1907), 700.

of communion, was new.

The response of supporters of the resolution was not to attempt to deny the obvious – that it exerted pressure – but to maintain that the Leicester Conference exerted a corresponding pressure: 'If the brethren connected with the Leicester Conference are so afraid of being pained, what right had they to take an action which has been pain and anguish and distress to hundreds and thousands in our churches?'[106] The argument disallowing a statement of its faith by the Assembly on the grounds of the pressure this exerted on those who dissented from that faith[107] could be turned on its head:

> There seems really no limit to the unwarrantable demands made upon us on behalf of liberty. There are men who seem to think themselves justified in trampling upon the rights and liberties of others, under this ever-ready plea that they must assert their freedom. We should be sorry to say that there is consciously any such purpose here, but this is the practical issue. The liberty of those who cling to the old faith is essentially narrowed if they are told that they cannot lay down the terms of their association, so as to make it a Christian body, without becoming persecutors of those who reject the Christian doctrines, and yet may wish to join them.[108]

This was a very important argument for the orthodox position, and the failure of the liberals to appreciate it and evaluate its significance was pivotal to the outcome of the controversy. The pressure exerted upon themselves was obvious to all, but in order to understand its counterpart on the conservative side it was necessary to have a sympathetic insight onto the conservative theological position that the liberals did not have.

That judgement is borne out by the alternative basis of communion they proposed. This was that instead of attempting to draw the boundaries of religious communion through resolutions, with all their shortcomings and artificiality, they should let the lines draw themselves naturally. James Martineau summarized the theory behind this very well:

> 'But must you not draw the line somewhere? Is Christianity itself

---

[106] Rogers, in *CW*, 15 May 1878, special May Meeting number, 4. He added that the Leicester Conference had started the process.
[107] Brown, 'The Perfect Law of Liberty', 88.
[108] *Congregationalist*, 6 (December 1877), 712-13.

> to be an open question?' I reply, if you leave scope for the natural play of religious sympathies, the line will always draw itself somewhere; and the predominant type of worship and spiritual culture will hold some persons within, and leave others without, its range of attraction. But that any prior definition of ours can meet the exigencies of religious society more than this spontaneous adjustment, I can see no reason to think. Time will disclose, far better than we can foresee, the direction, by no means constant, for the dividing line to take.[109]

Picton urged this in the Union debate, where his mention of the 'selective action of spiritual affinities'[110] was met with laughter – evidently a considerable number of delegates had never heard of such things before, and were not disposed to take them seriously. Fortunately others were prepared to consider this point with the seriousness it deserved.

So far from being a new idea, spiritual affinities had been fundamental to Congregational religious communion from time immemorial. No one said this in as many words, but some indicated that they understood this in language such as the following:

> We have no love for excommunication, we have hitherto left men to the dictation of their own consciences. It has been ordinarily sufficient to assert the standards of our belief in various ways, and to let the operation of men's thought and spiritual susceptibility judge accordingly.[111]

Both Dale and Kennedy spoke of mutual confidence as the bond that held Congregationalists together, the former adding that it was a confidence in the great facts and doctrines of the evangelical faith, while the latter went on to say that in practice cases of Congregational ministers not leaving that fellowship after developing Unitarian views were scarcely known.[112] Spiritual affinities in alignment with a theological basis had successfully defined the line between Congregationalists and Unitarians over a considerable period.

It is essential that there be agreement on both sides for an

---

[109] *CW*, 25 January 1878, 66.

[110] *CW*, 8 May 1878, special May Meeting number, 13.

[111] *EI*, 17 May 1878, 499.

[112] Dale, in *CW*, 15 May 1878, special May Meeting number, 2-3; Kennedy, *People Called Independents*, 57.

informal arrangement of this kind to work. The Religious Communion controversy with its pressure and sense of persecution was itself the product of the breakdown of the old system of spiritual affinities, caused by a new factor which did not fit in with it, namely religious communion without a theological basis. It is ironic that Picton could talk of establishing religious communion on spiritual affinities while leading the initiative which sabotaged the operation of that very principle. What he in fact wanted to do was to see communion on the basis of a new religious consensus substituted for communion on the basis of the old theological one. He did not appreciate that the spiritual affinity he felt toward members of the Congregational Union was in many cases not reciprocated; as one speaker in the debate put it, by making room for Picton on one side they would drive away others on the other side.[113] The Religious Communion movement did not face up to the implications of their platform: the radical change in the nature of the basis of communion they proposed was unacceptable to the majority in the Union.

As the natural operation of spiritual affinities had broken down, Dale could reasonably describe the resolution as a declaration of the spiritual affinities of the majority, which needed to be made clear in order to be allowed to operate.[114] Conservatives hoped that this point might be made sufficiently clear by the resolution for the Religious Communion movement to withdraw its challenge to the sway of the old affinities that still held the loyalty of the great majority. In justice to Picton it should be added that such a clarification was overdue: the talk of freedom of the past fifteen years, together with the liberalization of the old Calvinist orthodoxy, had created conditions in which he and others similarly placed were genuinely able to sense no breakdown in spiritual affinity while their theology changed radically.

The question which exercised nearly everyone concerning the resolution, and the focus of the sharpest debate, was whether or not it amounted to a creed. Congregationalists were thoroughly allergic to creeds, and the suspected sighting of one in their Union Assembly could not fail to arouse them. An argument levelled at the resolution was that representative assemblies should not lay down credal standards for the churches. Supporters of the Union denied that they were doing this. Dale argued that the Union was a voluntary society, and no one ceased to be truly Congregationalist by withdrawing from it because he was no longer in agreement with its basis; and

---

[113] Herber Evans, in *CW*, 15 May 1878, special May Meeting number, 5.
[114] *CW*, 15 May 1878, special May Meeting number, 3.

someone else found a precedent in a theological resolution passed by the Union in 1843.[115] In the course of the debate Kennedy asked, 'Has it come to this, that of all the voluntary societies in the world the Congregational Union is the one which has no right to say for itself and for others who shall be, and who shall not be, members of its fellowship?'[116] They could justly deny that they were imposing a standard of belief on the churches, but the argument they used for that purpose indicated that they were laying down a standard of belief for the Union; and, in spite of Kennedy's denials,[117] the latter was just as much a creed as the former, only an organizational rather than a denominational one. Moreover, the distinction between the denomination and the Union was fading rapidly, further eroding the force of Dale's and Kennedy's argument. Congregational churches not in membership of the Union were already exceptional; the official *Congregational Yearbook* list of ministers was very influential, and in parts of the country membership of a County Association was necessary for inclusion in it; and the Church Aid and Home Missionary Society, whose constitution was agreed in 1877, was about to add considerable financial incentives to Union membership.[118]

Kennedy's historical study in *The People Called Independents* had two main conclusions: that creeds were foreign to the Congregational tradition, and that Congregational communion had been maintained on an evangelical basis by the exercise of a right to renounce communion. But renunciation of communion on theological grounds can only be through the application of some doctrinal standard. An 'unwritten creed' sufficed so long as a consensus on the theological limits of fellowship was maintained, and the tension inherent in the tradition was concealed. But when this was contested it became impossible to renounce communion without formulating a doctrinal basis – which amounted to supplying the Congregational Union with a creed.

More light can be shed on the inconsistency of Kennedy's position by looking at what he had to say about excommunication. He put

[115] Dale, in *CW*, 15 May 1878, special May Meeting number, 3; J.K. Phillip, in *EI*, 30 May 1878, 576.

[116] *CW*, 15 May 1878, special May Meeting number, 4. See also Eustace Conder, in *EI*, 19 May 1878, 461.

[117] *EI*, 21 November 1878, 1285.

[118] Its constitution had been agreed in 1877 – Albert Peel, *These Hundred Years, 1831-1931: A History of the Congregational Union in England and Wales* (London: Congregational Union of England and Wales, 1931), 306-7.

himself at an immediate disadvantage by the mere fact of using a word whose connotations were about as negative as those of 'creed' to contemporary Congregationalists. He came out with his 'voluntary society' argument in answer to criticisms made by Baldwin Brown, saying that Brown himself excommunicated or did not admit to communion people who denied the Lord, although he did not use the word. He also defended excommunication on theological grounds by associating it with the uncontroversial practice of excommunicating on moral grounds.[119] But it is difficult to see how there can be excommunication from an organized body such as the Congregational Union on theological grounds without a creed: Kennedy could not really have one without the other

Though he baulked at creeds, by grasping the nettle of excommunication Kennedy went further toward applying the 'voluntary society' theory than most champions of the Union's resolution. Another commentator was more cautious:

> But should circumstances render it imperative for the Congregational Union to exercise the extreme right which must belong to it, in common with all other bodies, of withdrawing the privileges of membership from some who have distinctly violated the conditions of membership, there would be nothing in this which could fairly expose it to a charge of persecution.[120]

Evidently feeling that this was a very daring statement, he endeavoured to cover himself by saying that no one was hinting that this right would be exercised and stressing that he did not think such circumstances remotely likely.

Even this was too much for many supporters of the resolution, among whom there was no consensus for any further measures, should it not succeed in re-establishing the old informal spiritual affinities. *The English Independent,* though on the side of the leadership, found the idea of excommunication 'as repulsive as it is unfamiliar';[121] and *The Congregationalist* expressed satisfaction that Baldwin Brown was discovering more unity against creed-making and excommunication than he had previously thought existed.[122] It is significant that both these statements were made near the end of 1878 when the Union's leadership was actively trying to damp down

---

[119] *CW*, 15 May 1878, special May Meeting number, 4; Kennedy, 59.

[120] *BQR*, 68 (July 1878), 204-5.

[121] 17 October 1878, 1097.

[122] Vol. 7 (November 1878), 665.

further debate. The resolution was as far as they were prepared to go in response to the Leicester Conference, and when its supporters decided not to resign they had no cards left to play and felt their wisest course of action would be to end the game promptly. In the main the Leicester Conference convenors were willing to adopt a lower profile, which meant that at least the Union leadership was spared embarrassment.

The Congregational Union of the 1870s was not therefore quite like the voluntary societies to which Kennedy and Dale compared it. Unable to have formal rules, it had to work on trust and mutual understanding as to what was and what was not acceptable to members. It could not even exclude members in breach of that trust, for that could only be done by drawing up rules – which it could not do; the most the majority could therefore do was indicate to those they considered out of line what views they believed to be compatible with membership.

Congregationalism did not lay down credal standards for churches, but it had always had credal standards, albeit informal and flexible ones, for communion between churches. When these became controversial they were presented with the unwelcome alternatives of either sacrificing the informality and flexibility by committing a creed to writing, or accepting the broadest of the various bases of communion currently contemplated. One solution would have led to grievance on the liberal wing, the other to dissatisfaction on the conservative side; in either case they could hardly have avoided resignations. Instead they managed to find a middle way, passing a declaration that acted as a warning shot across liberal bows, but which was not used as a basis for any kind of action, and certainly not excommunication. The Leicester Conference movement was exposed as a small and unrepresentative minority position in the denomination, and the vanguard of theological change adopted a lower profile until the New Theology controversy of 1907 brought the same issues to the fore once more. The twentieth century saw the conservatives losing the compromise. For many years diminishing and defensive, they seeped out of a Union that seemed increasingly alien. There could be no solution to the basic problem: a basis of communion broad enough to include all versions of Christian belief excludes those who consider some of these versions not properly Christian at all.

II

THE BAPTISTS

CHAPTER 5

Charles Haddon Spurgeon (1834-92)

Introduction

There can hardly be a religious figure in nineteenth century Britain whose life has been the subject of more biographical publications than C.H. Spurgeon's, and yet much about him has continued to elude the understanding of admirers and critics alike. The basic facts are common knowledge, but insight into Spurgeon's character and thought has remained fairly superficial.[1] Accordingly, the biographical outline is here kept to a minimum, and is concentrated on the experiences and traits of character that most moulded Spurgeon the theologian and minister.

Charles Haddon Spurgeon was born on 19 June 1834 in Kelvedon, Essex. Between the ages of one and six he lived in Stambourne with his grandparents James and Sarah Spurgeon, whose influence on the precocious child, extended by later visits, was considerable. James Spurgeon was a Congregational minister, and a representative of an

---

[1] In 1917 William Robertson Nicoll wrote that 'most of his old students who have written about him have failed entirely to do justice to the deeper and finer element in his mind and culture' (T.H. Darlow, *William Robertson Nicoll: Life and Letters* (London: Hodder & Stoughton, 1925), 403) – a criticism which is not invalidated by W.Y. Fullerton's *C.H. Spurgeon: A Biography* (London: Williams & Norgate, 1920) and J.C. Carlile's *C.H. Spurgeon, An Interpretative Biography* (London: Religious Tract Society, 1933). More recently W. Charles Johnson has said that 'we still await an adequate record and assessment of the man' (*Encounter in London: The Story of the London Baptist Association*, 1865-1965 (London: Carey Kingsgate Press, 1965), 19). We still wait. The main primary sources used have been *The Sword and the Trowel*, the magazine Spurgeon founded and edited, and a cross section of the published sermons; some material is derived from the other major source available, namely the large collection of newspaper cuttings and other documents in Spurgeon's College.

older tradition of Dissent. To talk, as many do, of a 'Puritan atmosphere' may be somewhat bold, but he read the Puritans extensively and certainly had considerably more in common with the Puritan period than with the kind of Congregationalism that became prevalent in the later nineteenth century.

By the time Charles returned to his parents John and Eliza they had moved to Colchester, where his father worked as a clerk in a coal merchant's office while ministering to a Congregational church in a nearby village in his spare time. But it was his mother who was most active in the religious life of the home. Spurgeon later expressed gratitude for the Sunday evenings she spent with her children, explaining the Bible and pleading with them to seek the Lord before closing with prayer.[2] It is easy to understand the reasons for the young Spurgeon's deep sense of sin, his preoccupation with the need for conversion, and his high idea of the calling to be a minister.

On several occasions Spurgeon mentioned a period of five years prior to his conversion, between the ages of ten and fifteen, during which he was under conviction of sin. It was a time of deep unhappiness that he compared unfavourably even to the periods of severe pain he later experienced.[3] He was motivated in his search for Christ by the fear that he could not otherwise escape the sins into which he had seen others fall, a prospect that horrified him, and by the belief that Christ could keep him from sin. But he was so conscious of his sinfulness that he did not believe that Christ would pardon him. Other obstacles were the difficulty he had in understanding the righteousness of atonement – how God could be just and yet put away man's sin – and the fear that he did not feel his sinfulness sufficiently to come to Christ. In later years he found the variety and intensity of these problems of great help in evangelism.[4]

---

[2] **No. 581**, in Spurgeon, *Metropolitan Tabernacle Pulpit*, 10 (1864), p. 418. Numbers in bold type identify sermons in the weekly published series, whether read in the consecutively numbered *New Park Street and Metropolitan Tabernacle Pulpits* (both hereafter cited as *Pulpit*) or in other editions. Susannah Spurgeon and Joseph Harrald (eds.), *C.H. Spurgeon Autobiography*, revised ed., 2 vols. (London: Banner of Truth, 1962, 1973), I, 43-4. The basic facts of Spurgeon's life are generally accessible in Arnold Dallimore, *Spurgeon* (Edinburgh: Banner of Truth, 1985).

[3] *Spurgeon Autobiography*, I, 58, 60.

[4] **No. 1056**, in *Christ's Relation to his People* (London: Passmore & Alabaster, 1904), 261; **no. 1243**, in *The Messiah: Sermons on our Lord's Names, Title and Attributes* (London: Passmore & Alabaster, 1898), 27; **no. 1889**, in *Pulpit*, 32 (1886), 141; Spurgeon, *Faith; What It Is, and What It Leads To,*

The exhilaration and decisiveness of his conversion were on the same scale as the dark struggles that had preceded it. In January 1850 he happened upon a Primitive Methodist chapel where a man of distinctly limited abilities occupied the pulpit.[5] Having rapidly reached the end of his material, the preacher singled out the troubled young stranger in the tiny congregation:

> Then, lifting up his hands, he shouted, as only a Primitive Methodist could do, 'Young man, look to Jesus Christ. Look! Look! Look! You have nothin' to do but to look and live.' I saw at once the way of salvation. ...
>
> ... I can testify that the joy of that day was utterly undescribable. ... Many days of Christian experience have passed since then, but there has never been one which has had the full exhilaration, the sparkling delight which that first day had.[6]

Spurgeon lost no time in channelling this rush of spiritual life into practical Christian commitment and work. By February 1850 he was distributing tracts, in April he was admitted to church membership, in May he was baptized by immersion (in accordance with convictions arrived at before his conversion) and began teaching a Sunday school class, and by June he was visiting seventy people regularly on Saturdays to converse on spiritual things. He started lay preaching soon after moving to Cambridge in September 1850, and began his first ministry a year later in the nearby village of Waterbeach when only seventeen. His success was immediate and immense: even as a Sunday school teacher he attracted adults to his class, while during his two years at Waterbeach the congregation grew from forty to more than four hundred and the character of the

---

new ed. (London: Passmore & Alabaster, 1903), 27; *Spurgeon Autobiography*, I, 53-4.

[5] For discussion of the details of this event, see Mike Nicholls, *C.H. Spurgeon the Pastor Evangelist* (Didcot: Baptist Historical Society, 1992), 3-5. To head off possible misunderstanding, it should be noted that the surprising similarity at a number of points between Nicholls' language and my own (compare, e.g., Nicholls, 49-50 with pp. 128-31 below) holds good for my 1988 Oxford D.Phil. dissertation ('Baptists, Congregationalists, and Theological Change: Some Late Nineteenth Century Leaders and Controversies') as well as the present work.

[6] *Spurgeon Autobiography*, I, 88-9.

entire village was altered.[7]

These activities coincided with the last stages of a varied education, in which Spurgeon worked as an assistant teacher at schools at Newmarket and then Cambridge in exchange for board and lodging and help with his own education. Though fragmented, it amounted to a reasonable middle class education.[8] He considered undertaking theological training at Regent's Park College, but believed that he was called to renounce this prospect and continue in his ministry.[9]

Spurgeon's career began to veer from the unusual to the exceptional in January 1854 when he received a call to the pastorate of one of London's most venerable Baptist churches, with a large building in New Park Street, Southwark, but a depleted congregation. His preaching rapidly drew greater crowds than had been seen since the time of Whitefield, and attracted more press comment (at first mainly hostile) than any minister since Edward Irving. The story is customarily related as a succession of full buildings: New Park Street both before and after extension, Exeter Hall and the even larger Surrey Gardens Music Hall, and finally the Metropolitan Tabernacle in Newington, opened in 1861 and filled by more than five thousand people Sunday by Sunday throughout Spurgeon's ministry.

But there was one dramatic interruption in this progress, an episode whose importance in Spurgeon's spiritual experience was second only to that of his conversion. On 19 October 1856 during his first service in the Music Hall there were unwarranted cries of 'Fire!', and seven died and twenty-eight were injured in the ensuing panic. He later said that he thought few had passed through such horror as he knew in the following days, and that he did not think he could have survived a second experience of the kind; [10] in its wake he believed himself near to insanity and dared not look up to God, finding his attempts at prayer led merely to terror. Then

> On a sudden the name of Jesus flashed through my mind. The person of Christ seemed visible to me. I stood still. The burning lava of my soul was cooled. My agonies were hushed. I bowed

---

[7] *Ibid.*, I, 112-19, 125, 158, 178, 182ff., 194; Dallimore, *Spurgeon*, 31-5.

[8] Spurgeon called it the best education possible (G. Holden Pike, *James Archer Spurgeon, D.D., LL.D., Preacher, Philanthropist, and Co-Pastor with C.H. Spurgeon at the Metropolitan Tabernacle* [London, 1892], 23).

[9] *Spurgeon Autobiography*, I, 207-8.

[10] Spurgeon, *Lectures to my Students*, first series, (London: Passmore & Alabaster, 1875), 175; *Spurgeon Autobiography*, I, 448.

> myself there, and the garden that had seemed a Gethsemane became to me a Paradise.[11]

> Never since the day of my conversion had I known so much of his infinite excellence, never had my spirit leaped with such unutterable delight.[12]

This experience compassed the extremes of Spurgeon's spiritual and emotional life: a vivid communion with Christ that led Robertson Nicoll to class him with Bunyan as the greatest of English evangelical mystics, and a singular proneness to severe depression.[13] His own analysis of this cycle perceptively linked it to the effectiveness of his ministry. Sermons that moved audiences were not only costly in preparation and emotionally wearing in delivery, but continued to thrill him irresistibly for hours and even days, only to be followed by a reaction whose depths often equalled the preceding heights.[14]

Spurgeon did not believe in pacing himself: 'I believe that a Christian man is generally right when he is doing more than he can; and when he goes still further beyond that point, he will be even more nearly right.'[15] Many bouts of depression were provoked by the extreme pressure of his work schedule and the burden of his many responsibilities, not least the financial ones:

> The pastorate of a church of four thousand members, the direction of all its agencies, the care of many churches, arising from our College work; the selection, education, and guidance in their settlements of the students, the oversight of the Orphanage, the editing of a magazine, the production of numerous volumes, the publication of a weekly sermon, an immense correspondence, a fair share in public and denominational action, and many other labours, besides the incessant preaching of the word, give us a right to ask of our friends, that we be not allowed to have one

---

11 **No. 214**, in *The Messiah*, 121.

12 Spurgeon, *The Saint and his Saviour: the Progress of the Soul in the Knowledge of Jesus* (London: Hodder & Stoughton, 1889), 266.

13 Darlow, *Robertson Nicoll*, 402; Spurgeon, 'A Sermon and a Reminiscence', *ST*, 9 (1873), 124.

14 Spurgeon, 'Be Not Discouraged'. *ST*, 15 (1879), 571.

15 Spurgeon, *An All-round Ministry* (London: Passmore & Alabaster, 1900), 30.

anxious thought about the funds needful for our enterprises.[16]

In spite of strain and depression Spurgeon exhibited great staying power, confounding the prophets who thought his career would continue to mirror that of Irving. Whatever the index taken – congregation or church membership, sermon and magazine sales or the income that supported his numerous activities – far from sagging, the extraordinary levels reached in the early years were steadily consolidated as the decades passed.

Nothing did more to amplify the cycle of ecstasy and despondency than the ill-health that dogged him for most of his ministry. The kidney trouble he began to have in his early twenties developed into chronic Bright's disease; and he was afflicted by rheumatic gout for prolonged periods after 1867.[17] Despondency was a normal reaction, but there was a compensatory counter-reaction: 'We have suffered, and can testify that there is a point where suffering and pain are the vestibule of bliss. When they bring men as near to Jesus as they carried us, they are not angels in disguise, but seraphs all unveiled.'[18] Suffering effected this by facilitating entry into the state in which Spurgeon found his greatest joy, 'a condition of conscious dependence upon God. ... It is inexpressibly delightful to lie passive in the hand of love, to die into the life of Christ.'[19] Preaching at such a time heightened the experience still further: 'I love to preach in such a mood, not as though *I* was about to preach at all, but hoping that the Holy Spirit will speak through me.'[20]

Suffering also had various negative effects on Spurgeon. Perhaps the most significant of these is illustrated by an excerpt from an address given in great weakness after severe illness: 'Very soon, "advanced thought" will only be mentioned by servant girls and young Independent ministers. It has gradually declined till it may now be carried off with the slops. There is nothing in the whole bag of tricks.'[21] Here his mood was defiant, a mixture of an exaggerated optimism, with which he reacted against the pessimism to which suffering inclined him, and a relaxation of the self-censorship his

---

16 *ST*, 6 (1870), 143; compare 5 (1869), 479, 481.

17 P.S. Kruppa, *Charles Haddon Spurgeon: A Preacher's Progress* (New York: Garland, 1982), 34, 458-9; Spurgeon, 'The Editor's Illness', *ST*, 3 (1867), 536-7.

18 *ST*, 6 (1870), 139. One of many similar passages can be found in *ST*, 7 (1871), iii.

19 Spurgeon, *An All-round Ministry*, 190.

20 *Ibid.*, 191.

21 *Ibid.*, 238.

very creative imagination required. The latter in particular was an important factor in the Downgrade Controversy.

Spurgeon's character contained other contrasts too. Thus he was capable of great tenderness, but in some circumstances could display considerable severity too.[22] There was also constant warfare between a propensity to vanity and a profoundly spiritual humility. As early as 1856 it was apparent that the latter was prevailing,[23] and his humility featured prominently in many tributes to him.[24] Some would question this judgement of a man who spoke so much about himself; but he did so out of a humility too genuine to want to nurture its own reputation, always with the intention of celebrating God's work.

Spurgeon's illnesses and heavy workload aged him prematurely. At the age of forty-five he was already regretting the loss of 'the elasticity of spirit, the dash, the courage, the hopefulness of days gone by'.[25] The unsuccessful outcome of the Downgrade Controversy of 1887-88 cast a shadow over the last years of his life: he lacked the resilience to recover. In the summer of 1891 he was incapacitated by what proved to be his final illness; he died peacefully in his winter quarters at Mentone in the south of France on 31 January 1892.

---

[22] James Douglas drew attention to this in his perceptive analysis of Spurgeon, *The Prince of Preachers: A Sketch, a Portraiture, and a Tribute* (London: Morgan & Scott, [1893]), 79. Spurgeon's own comments on these two qualities can be found in *Spurgeon Autobiography*, I, 44-5.

[23] 'Constitutionally he has in him no small amount of self-esteem, but so far from growing with his daily extending frame, he appears to be more humble and more subdued than when he first burst on our astonished gaze.' James Grant in *Morning Advertiser*, 18 February 1856, quoted in *Spurgeon Autobiography*, I, 352. The earliest stages of the conflict were recorded in Spurgeon's diary (*Autobiography*, I, 125-43). For its later history see *Lectures to my Students*, second series (London: Passmore & Alabaster, 1877), 174.

[24] 'I know nothing more beautiful, as there was nothing more winning and powerful, in our brother's work, than his utter self-forgetfulness.' Alexander McLaren, quoted in [W.Y. Fullerton (ed.)], *From the Pulpit to the Palm Branch: a Memorial of C.H. Spurgeon*, (London: Passmore & Alabaster, 1892), 126. Compare an entry in the Earl of Shaftesbury's diary, quoted in William Williams, *Personal Reminiscences of Charles Haddon Spurgeon* (London: Religious Tract Society, 1895[2]), 73-4.

[25] Spurgeon, *An All-round Ministry*, 139.

Theology

'Charles Haddon Spurgeon always claimed to be a Calvinist ... but his intense zeal for the conversion of souls led him to step outside the bounds of the creed he had inherited.'[26] This comment is representative of the attitude to Spurgeon's theology of historians sympathetic to the man but not to his Calvinism. It is inaccurate in two important respects: Spurgeon's Calvinism was consciously adopted, and not merely inherited; and whatever tension there was lay within his particular brand of Calvinism, rather than taking the form of a contradiction between theology and practice. It is the conviction of the present writer that, in spite of all its problems, Spurgeon's theology was both deeper and richer than the non-Calvinists among the commentators have realized, and more original and contemporary than the Calvinists have supposed. The paradoxical notion of a full-blooded, three-dimensional man drawing on an old cardboard cut-out set of borrowed ideas may be discarded.

The refutation of the second of these inaccuracies must be a prolonged affair, but the first may be exposed at the outset. It was not till some months after his conversion that Spurgeon became a Calvinist. The account he gave eight years later may have dramatized that change by focusing on a single train of thought, but there is no reason to doubt its substantial accuracy:

> Well can I remember the manner in which I learned the doctrines of grace in a single instant. Born, as all of us are by nature, an Arminian, I still believed the old things I had heard continually from the pulpit, and did not see the grace of God. I remember sitting one day in the house of God and hearing a sermon as dry as possible, and as worthless as all such sermons are, when a thought struck my mind – how came I to be converted? I prayed, thought I. Then I thought how came I to pray? I was induced to pray by reading the Scriptures. How came I to read the Scriptures? Why – I did read them; and what led me to that? And then, in a moment, I saw that God was at the bottom of all, and that he was the author of faith. And then the whole doctrine opened up to me, from which I have not departed.[27]

---

[26] A.C. Underwood, *A History of the English Baptists* (London: Carey Kingsgate, 1947), 203-4.

[27] **No. 50**, in *Twelve Sermons on the Holy Spirit* (1937), 36. This is one refutation among many of the unfounded claim that Spurgeon was

Some interpreters have attempted to buttress the conventional contrast between the depth of the man and the supposed shallowness of his theology by suggesting that his intellect was feeble in comparison with the strength of other qualities. Others have emphasized the intellectual consequences of Spurgeon's lack of a formal theological education. Neither approach is sound or helpful in advancing understanding of the limitations of his thought. There are testimonies to the power of Spurgeon's intellect from unimpeachable sources.[28] He was familiar with Greek and Hebrew;[29] his speed and retention in reading were extraordinary,[30] and helped him acquire an exceptional knowledge of several branches of Christian literature, notably the works of Calvin and the Puritans, biblical commentaries, and homiletics.[31]

Although Spurgeon's reading was vast, it was nonetheless selective, neglecting some important subjects. He was reluctant to read anything he regarded as heretical, confessing that when he did do so it was as an unwelcome duty, performed in the belief that he could help refute the error or keep people from falling into it.[32] This criterion more or less wrote off the entire field of biblical criticism so far as he was concerned.[33] Philosophy did not fare much better: near the end of his life he said that its history was 'absolutely identical with the history of fools, except where it diverges into madness'.[34]

---

brought up surrounded by a time-warped Calvinist Congregationalism.

28 'His intellectual qualities were of the supremest kind. I have met many great men, but never one so swift in perception, so rapid in seizing on the prime element in every cause, so prompt in discussion.' Dr Richard Glover, quoted in Fullerton, *Spurgeon*, 270.

29 *Spurgeon Autobiography*, II, 346.

30 Spurgeon could read five or six books in a session and afterwards quote extensively with great accuracy (*ibid.*, 2, 345-6).

31 *Ibid.*, 1, 531; *Commenting and Commentaries* (London: Passmore & Alabaster, 1876), vi, 33 (for which he consulted more than three thousand commentaries); *Lectures to My Students*, second series, (London: Passmore & Alabaster, 1877), chs. 6, 7.

32 **No. 1004**, in *Twelve Sermons on the Passion and Death of Christ* (Grand Rapids, 1971), 75.

33 He admitted never having read Graf, Kuenen, and Wellhausen, and having no intention to do so (*ST*, 21 (1885), 371).

34 *The Greatest Fight in the World* (London: Passmore & Alabaster, 1892), 30. He nonetheless allowed the philosophy of the Scottish common sense school to be taught in his Pastors' College (David Bebbington, 'Spurgeon and British Evangelical Theological Education', in D.G. Hart and R. Albert Mohler, Jr. (eds), *Theological Education in the Evangelical*

The key to understanding both the selectivity of Spurgeon's reading and the gulf separating his theology from those of most leaders of thought in his generation lies not so much in his lack of a formal theological education as in the nature of the authority structure underlying his theology. Whereas others allowed reason and conscience to dictate the parameters of their theologies, he had insufficient confidence in these to follow their example.

Spurgeon had too much respect for the philosophy of the English empirical school to decry reason.[35] He accepted their natural theology, holding that order and design in the universe were such decisive evidence that one must be either weak-minded or wicked not to see something of God in them.[36] He went further, arguing that the authenticity of Scripture could also be proved, yet only to conclude that 'you will doubt in the teeth of argument ... as long as your heart does not love the truth; your head may be convinced, but your heart will always supply enough atheism to keep your head at work.'.[37] Reason was capable of much, but sinful man overruled his reason, and so must be reached by spiritual rather than rational means. This tension between reason's great theoretical competence and its small practical value can be observed unresolved in Spurgeon's attitude to rational apologetics. At one moment he considered that 'defending the outworks' of Christianity had a useful supplementary role, while at another he declared that it was misplaced effort, neither beginning nor strengthening faith.[38] In practice Spurgeon accorded apologetics very little attention, preferring to concentrate on biblical theology and preaching the gospel.[39] In these areas he accorded reason less competence than his philosophical presuppositions had conceded it in natural theology: his early practice of supplementing exegesis with rational philosophical arguments was virtually abandoned by 1860.[40]

Tradition [Grand Rapids: Baker, 1996], 222-3).

[35] His ridicule of philosophy was not uniform; his worst strictures were reserved for German idealists (*ST*, 14 (1878), 357) but he actually recommended Bacon, Newton and Locke (Williams, 193).

[36] *ST*, 6 (1870), 316.

[37] **No. 679**, in *The Messiah*, 696.

[38] *ST*, 7 (1871) 46; 9 (1878), 283. Compare his ambivalent attitude to Butler and Paley: *ST*, 14 (1878), 462; **no. 1106**, in *Twelve Sermons on the Resurrection* (Grand Rapids, 1968), 100.

[39] *ST*, 20 (1884), 641.

[40] **No.1** is an outstanding example of the early metaphysical manner (in William Robertson Nicoll (ed.), *C.H. Spurgeon: Sermons*, (London: Thomas Nelson, 1910), 15ff).

Spurgeon emphasized the depravity of the conscience of the natural man, teaching that it never brought such self-abhorrence and renunciation as to lead anyone to Christ; instead it was easily satisfied with reformation.[41] Only when awakened by the Holy Spirit did conscience react properly to sin, demanding recompense to God for it, and finding that nowhere but in Christ.[42] At this point Spurgeon's conscience insisted on substitutionary atonement as vehemently and imperiously as Baldwin Brown's rejected it: 'I cannot help holding that there must be an atonement before there can be pardon, because my conscience demands it, and my peace depends on it. The little court within my own heart is not satisfied unless some retribution be exacted for dishonour done to God.'[43] This commanding role continued in his life as a Christian: with a placid conscience witnessing to God's approbation he felt he could afford to be indifferent to human opinions.[44]

His belief in the bankruptcy of reason and conscience in the natural man emerged from his boyhood experience, during which both had been furiously but ineffectively at work. His understanding of the way out of the impasse was just as profoundly influenced by the suddenness and intensity of his conversion, which was in essence not an intellectual breakthrough but an experience of forgiveness and love upon which he subsequently reflected rationally. His fundamental conviction was that it had not been his own work but that of the Holy Spirit: the loving initiative lay with God.[45]

Spurgeon's basic approach to authority was an experiential one inspired by his conversion:

> But let me say to you if you want to know God you must know Christ; if you want to be sure of the truth of the Bible you must believe Jesus; and I warrant you that when you have looked up and seen incarnate God bearing your sins; when you have thrown yourself flat upon the Rock of Ages, and have felt the inward joy and peace which flow from believing in God, you will have heard an Amen to that old book, and an Amen to the existence of God, and an Amen to the gospel, which Satan himself can never remove

---

41 *Pulpit,* 4 (1858), 140, quoted in H.F. Colquitt, 'The Soteriology of Charles Haddon Spurgeon Revealed in his Sermons and Controversial Writings' (Edinburgh DPhil diss., 1951), 43; *Saint and Saviour*, 44.

42 *Pulpit,* 4 (1858), 140, quoted in Colquitt, 43; Spurgeon, *An All-round Ministry*, 376.

43 Spurgeon, *Lectures,* second series, 47.

44 *Ibid.*, 169.

45 **No. 986**, in *The Messiah*, 478.

from your remembrance.[46]

At times, however, he argued the exact opposite, that 'we accept the Gospel because it is in Holy Scripture, and because we receive Holy Scripture as spoken of God. I think it is ours to believe the Bible before we have any proof of it; without going into detail as to this or that, it is for us, without proof even, to take it as God's Word.'[47] The context of this quotation indicates that his underlying concern was to exclude human judgement as far as possible, for fear that its decision to accept the authority of the Bible would imply its own superior authority. He had failed to appreciate that the mind must accept an authority before it can become operative, a decision that is always taken on certain grounds, be they rational or otherwise. Spurgeon confessed his own deficiency in philosophy,[48] a discipline that was alien to the customary spiritual orientation of his mind;[49] it is a safe rule that the more existential the statement, the more directly it proceeded from the heart of his thinking. His more metaphysical statements tend to be peripheral rationalisations of inferior authenticity as well as quality.

At heart Spurgeon shared the more experiential approach to authority in religion characteristic of his generation,[50] but differed markedly from many contemporaries in the extent to which he refused to allow this to lead to any relativizing of the authority of the Bible: whereas to them the Bible was the vehicle for introducing authoritative Christian experience, to Spurgeon it remained central as the medium of that experience. He described it thus:

> When I take down the Bible I find it knows more about me than I know about myself. I find it condemns me, and I have to admit that I ought to be condemned. ... And that same Book will some-

---

[46] **No. 679**, in *The Messiah*, 696-7.

[47] 'The Foundations of our Faith: Evidence, and Experience', *Word and Work*, 30 March 1888, in Spurgeon's College, Spurgeon Scrapbooks (see bibliographical note in ch. 7 note 17).

[48] *ST*, 17 (1881), 283.

[49] This is encapsulated in the following; 'Take Christ into your very soul – into your *heart's* belief as well as into your mind's belief. Mental beliefs shift and change: the inward soul's belief never alters. I reckon that we know nothing rightly till we have absorbed it, and made it part and parcel of ourselves.' **No. 1460**, in *The Messiah*, 546.

[50] Evident in his warm welcome of Dale's *Protestantism: its Ultimate Principle* (*ST*, 10 (1874), 488).

> times thrill me with an intense delight. It is the master of my being; it answers to every chord within my nature; ... I know it is true, or else I do not exist. I am myself a fiction, or else that Book records facts in what it teaches.[51]

His response was a submission to the Bible commensurate with his sense of its superiority: 'The Bible ... is still the infallible revelation of God. It is a main part of our religion humbly to accept what God has revealed. Perhaps the highest form of adoration possible, on this side the veil, is the bowing of our entire mental and spiritual being before the revealed mind of God.'[52] The final stage was theological expression appropriate to his spiritual response: 'As the Christ reveals God, so this Book reveals Christ, and therefore it partakes, as the Word of God, in all the attributes of the Incarnate Word; and we may say many of the same things of the written Word as of the embodied Word; in fact, they are now so linked together that it would be impossible to divide them.'[53]

So profoundly did Spurgeon identify the Bible with God that he could declare 'I would as soon dream of blaspheming my Maker as of questioning the infallibility of his word.'[54] The idea of infallibility, by which he meant some accessible fundamental authority that was not to be questioned, was psychologically very important to him: 'When the Bible is fully accepted as God's own revelation of himself, the mind has come to a quiet anchorage; and this is no small gain. A safe resting-place is an urgent need of the soul.'[55] This reinforced Spurgeon's implacable opposition to liberal denials of biblical infallibility:

> If I did not believe in the infallibility of the Book, I would rather be without it. If I am to judge the Book, it is no judge of me. If I am to ... lay *this* aside and only accept *that*, according to my own judgement, then I have no guide whatever, unless I have conceit enough to trust to my own heart. The new theory denies infallibility to the words of God, but practically imputes it to the judge-

---

[51] Quoted in G. Holden Pike, *The Life and Work of Charles Haddon Spurgeon*, 3 vols (London: Cassell & Co., [1892-93]), III, 147.

[52] Spurgeon, *An All-round Ministry*, 189.

[53] Quoted in *Word and Work*, 2 March 1888, in SS, DG4a, 1.

[54] Spurgeon, *Lectures*, second series, 41.

[55] Spurgeon, *The Clue of the Maze* (Pasadena, n.d.), 76-7. Compare *ST*, 20 (1884), 114; 24 (1888), 207. On one occasion he said he believed infallibility was essential in any religion (*ST*. 24 (1888), 260).

ment of men; at least, this is all the infallibility they can get at.[56]

This much was conventional conservative thinking, but Spurgeon then parted company from those who inconsistently placed implicit confidence in reason when they went on to hermeneutics and biblical theology. His belief in the infallibility of the Bible was grounded in spiritual experience, and it was of very practical relevance to the method he followed in his biblical theology that it should be as 'opened up to our minds by the Holy Spirit'.[57]

* * *

Spurgeon never lost sight of the gulf between God's wisdom and the finite mind of man. On one occasion he said that if he understood the entire Bible he would not believe that it came from God.[58] By 1860 he had come to believe that to attempt to fashion a systematic creed was to embark on a rationalist enterprise doomed to failure: 'It is time that the systems were broken up, and that there was sufficient grace in all our hearts to believe everything taught in God's Word ... If it is not in the Word, away with it! away with it! but if it be in the Word, agreeable or disagreeable, systematic or disorderly, I believe it.'[59] Harmonizing, logic and speculation also attracted his condemnation as basic hermeneutical principles; his own study convinced him that they could only encompass some parts of the Bible's teaching, and must inevitably lead to disbelief of others. The principle that should replace them was faith, which according to Spurgeon simply accepted everything in the Bible, taking its contradictions as apparent rather than real, and even sensing the underlying harmony, though it could not expound it. To reach toward that, and to attain the 'practical truth' through which God blessed his people, it was important to set 'relative truths' side by side, and to make sure they were not allowed to qualify and deform one another.[60] His remarkable series of published sermons

---

[56] **No. 2084**, in *Pulpit*, 35 (1889), 257.

[57] *ST*, 24 (1888), 260.

[58] 'Foundations of Faith', Spurgeon's College, Spurgeon Scrapbooks.

[59] **No. 303**, in *Twelve Sermons on Holiness* (1937), 7. 'Angels may, perhaps, be systematic divines; for men it should be enough to follow the word of God, let its teachings wind as they may.' *ST*, 4 (1868), 102.

[60] These terms are found in *Pulpit*, 30 (1884), 472-3, quoted in Colquitt, 'Soteriology of Spurgeon', 147. This analysis is built largely on this and three other important passages: *Pulpit*, 10 (1864), 231, quoted in Colquitt, 'Soteriology of Spurgeon', 133; *ST*, 5 (1869), 246; and Spurgeon,

constitute his demonstration of this method; most of them were straightforward expositions of a wide variety of texts aiming to cover all aspects of the Bible, whether they individually leant to one or another of the emphases he sought to balance, namely the practical (or ethical), the experiential, and the doctrinal. H.F. Colquitt chose an excellent quotation for the conclusion of his study of Spurgeon's theology: 'I like to read my Bible so as never to have to blink when I approach a text. I like to have a theology which enables me to read it right through from beginning to end, and to say, "I am as pleased with that text as I am with the other."'[61]

Spurgeon developed this method himself in the 1850s – in a paradoxical way independence and originality were qualities he valued highly and sought to display.[62] Thus while believing that 'there is nothing new in theology save that which is false'[63] he was determined right from his conversion not to follow anyone but to work out for himself the meaning of God's revelation by studying the Bible with the help of the Holy Spirit.[64] Acknowledgements of theological indebtedness are rare in his writings, the odd exceptions showing that he had no aversion to making them where appropriate. A.A. and Charles Hodge of Princeton were the theologians of his century of whom he thought most highly,[65] but this was rather because his own understanding of the Bible so nearly coincided with theirs, than because he chose to adopt their views.

But in the early 1850s Spurgeon's independence of thought had yet to be established. His adoption of Calvinism soon after his conversion was linked to his contact with Mary King, his Newmarket school's devout Calvinist cook: hers was possibly the greatest personal influence on Spurgeon's theology.[66] The writings that most influenced him were those of Calvin and the Puritans, among whom John Owen was his favourite.[67]

Spurgeon said he thought a man happy who was so well taught at

---

An All-round Ministry, 31.

[61] *Pulpit*, 10 (1864), 237, quoted in Colquitt, 'Soteriology of Spurgeon', 278.

[62] See *ST*, 2 (1866), 282; 9 (1873), 284.

[63] *Saint and Saviour*, 71. While this is an early statement it was echoed rather than qualified later.

[64] **No. 1531**, in *Twelve Sermons on Decision* (Grand Rapids, 1971), 63.

[65] *ST*, 15 (1879), 339; *Commenting and Commentaries*, 178.

[66] 'I do believe I learnt more from her than I should have learnt from any six doctors of divinity of the sort we have nowadays.' *Spurgeon Autobiography*, I, 39.

[67] Douglas, 188.

the start that he never had to recant a doctrine or mourn an important omission; and when revising his first published sermons over thirty years after delivering them he boasted that though he might alter some expressions there was no need to change any doctrine.[68] His record on omissions was not quite so spotless: his inclination to issue a free invitation was for a while fettered by an idea then common among Calvinist Baptists, following Richard Baxter and other Puritans, that only sinners who displayed some evidence that the Holy Spirit was convicting them should be invited to believe. Although his theology remained fundamentally Calvinistic, by the end of the 1850s it was of a lower variety than in his earliest preaching.[69] In 1874, when Dale called him the only Calvinist among the current leaders of Nonconformity, he did not object to the name, but he distanced himself from 'pure and simple' Calvinism in favour of what he termed Calvin's own Calvinism, by which he meant one that acknowledged that God's truth was wider than both Calvinism and Arminianism, including some of the truth of each.[70]

A misapprehension Spurgeon was at pains to correct was the idea that his Calvinism was an intellectual imprisonment that he would gladly escape if only he could find a way; on the contrary, he insisted that it was a source of joy and peace.[71] Although his theology ran against the trend of his day he shared in the general urge to find a theology in which heart and intellect need have no complaints about each other. The following examination of Spurgeon's theology accounts for the divergence by showing that his heart's concerns were not the same as others'.

* * *

At the very foundation of Spurgeon's theology lay a desire to demonstrate the vastness of the Christian faith by exploring both the heights of God's holiness and greatness and the depths of human sinfulness and abjectness in our state of rebellion, so in consequence

---

[68] Spurgeon, *Lectures*, first series, 82; *Spurgeon Autobiography*, I, 396.

[69] **No. 279**, in Nicoll (ed.), *Sermons*, 58; *ST*, 8 (1872), 209; Spurgeon, *Faith*, 23-5. There is an example of his early higher Calvinistic dismissal of free will in **no. 30**, in *The Holy Spirit*, 24. There is already a general appeal in *Election* (**nos. 41-42**) (Welwyn: Evangelical Press, 1978), 24-6.

[70] *ST*, 10 (1874), 51-3. Dale's comment was in an article in *The Daily Telegraph*, reprinted in *Christianity in Britain: an Outline of its Rise, Progress, and Present Conditions* (London: Hodder & Stoughton, 1874), 136-7.

[71] Spurgeon, *An All-round Ministry*, 376-7.

magnifying the grace of God that reconciled the two. In his mature thought the latter two dimensions became as necessary as the first, as he felt his way toward a dialectic in which sin was a precondition of union with God in Christ through atonement:

> It was not, as some have tried to represent it, that Jehovah made a mistake by creating men who fell into sin, and that then he adopted an expedient by which he restored them; but the whole scheme of redemption is all part of the great eternal system and plan matured in the divine mind, that by redeeming love, manifested in the person of his well-beloved Son, the Lord might create unto himself a people who should for ever be one, akin unto himself, and like unto the Well-beloved.[72]

The lead in this exploration was taken by spiritual experience; it was frequently apparent even to Spurgeon himself that his theological cartography was severely stretched and at times quite unable to keep up.

Turning first to the divine dimension, Spurgeon believed that amid the growing anthropocentricity of contemporary theology it was above all necessary to return God to the centre of theology:

> To me, Calvinism means the placing of the eternal God at the head of all things. I look at everything through its relation to God's glory. I see God first, and man far down the list. We think too much of God to please this age; but we are not ashamed. Man has a will, and oh, how they cry it up! One said, the other day, - and there is some truth in it, too, - "I attribute a kind of omnipotence to the will of man." But, sirs, has not God a will, too? What do you attribute to that will? Have you nothing to say about its omnipotence? Is God to have no choice, no purpose, no sovereignty over his own gifts?[73]

Spurgeon maintained the absolute sovereignty of God over the moral universe, the physical universe, and human destiny. He held that God made the moral law, and that he could do as he willed, although his will was always in accord with that law.[74] His teaching on the physical universe was straightforwardly deterministic: 'The

---

[72] **No. 2418**, in *Christ's Relation to his People*, 39.

[73] Spurgeon, *An All-round Ministry*, 345.

[74] **No. 873**, in *The Passion and Death of Christ*, 57; *Pulpit*, 38 (1892), 15, quoted in Colquitt, 'Soteriology of Spurgeon', 37.

omniscient Lord of all appoints the date of every event; all times are in his hand, none are left to chance. ... The great clock of the universe keeps perfect time, and the whole machinery of providence moves with unerring punctuality.'[75]

God's sovereignty over human destiny was evidently a subject he found difficult. Approaching it from the theoretical angle of absolute sovereignty, he surmised that God could easily have converted the world on the day of Pentecost, and found it a mystery why he chose not so to do.[76] The view from the empirical angle was different: events bore some relation to the circumstances that preceded them, showing that sovereignty was not exercised arbitrarily,[77] and also that the freedom of the human will was compatible with predestination:

> When we look at matters of fact ... we see God predestinating and man premeditating; God knowing fully, yet man acting freely; God ordaining every circumstance, yet man manoeuvring to encompass his own projects; in short, we see man accurately, but unconsciously, fulfilling all that was written in the wisdom of God; and without any impetus of the Almighty upon his mind inciting him to do so.[78]

This coexistence of predestination and free will was not without tension,[79] but the question of election, together with its corollary regeneration, in which Spurgeon believed free will had no place, was for that reason even more problematic.[80] In defence of election Spurgeon argued that it was not unjust, for none deserved it; that all who wished for it obtained it, and those who did not desire it should not begrudge it to those who did;[81] that God was not responsible for the sin and the lostness of those who did not believe; and that God's

---

[75] *'Good Tidings of Great Joy'. Christ's Incarnation the Foundation of Christianity* (London: Passmore & Alabaster, 1901), 24.

[76] **No. 986**, in *The Messiah*, 474; *ST*, 9 (1873), 113.

[77] Spurgeon, *Lectures*, second series, 190.

[78] *Storm Signals* (London: Passmore & Alabaster, 1885), 19.

[79] E.g. in **no. 696**, in Nicoll (ed.), *Sermons*, 182-3.

[80] Spurgeon, *Storm Signals*, 18.

[81] Spurgeon believed that the Holy Spirit awakened the desire for salvation in the first place, as sinners are incapable of even wanting to be saved, and that this was an integral part of God's work of conversion (*Faith*, 19-20; *Pulpit*, 4 (1858), 138, quoted in Colquitt, 'Soteriology of Spurgeon', 44).

universal call to repent and believe was sincere though ineffectual.[82] However satisfied he may have been with this defence of the theory of election Spurgeon was troubled by its record in history. He believed that the saved should outnumber the lost, and yet felt obliged to conclude that Satan had triumphed so far. He consoled himself by looking to those who died as infants, who he believed made up the great majority of the elect, and to a time in the future when there would be a great gathering of the elect, while taking his habitual refuge in human ignorance and God's hidden wisdom.[83]

Spurgeon's attempts to relate divine sovereignty to human affairs were beset with problems, and fully bear out his admissions that here were things he could neither understand nor reconcile. The confidence and power he exhibited when he turned to the opposite pole, human sin and its punishment, stood out in contrast. As with other important doctrines, the experience and thought of his conversion moulded all his subsequent ideas. During the unhappy years preceding that event his sense of guilt had been accompanied by a conviction that God's justice required that his sin be punished. He longed for the power to live a righteous life and for the assurance that God accepted him, but his conscience insisted that the demands of justice could not be bypassed: God could not clear the sinner by a sovereign act of mercy, for that would impugn his justice and virtually annul his law.[84] 'Sin must be punished, or God must cease to be.'[85]

Astonishingly for one who already possessed such an acute sense of sin, Spurgeon's attitude to it hardened radically in his conversion: 'When I believed that Jesus was the Christ, and rested my soul in him, I felt in my heart from that moment an intense hatred to sin of every kind. ... When I at any time transgressed I felt an inward grief and horror at myself for doing the things that aforetime I had allowed and even enjoyed.'[86] This led him to the view that one of the effects of sin was to hide from people the extent of their sinfulness, an ignorance that could only be partially dispelled even in the believer: 'Oh, my dear brethren and sisters, if you have never seen God, if you have never had a faith's view of him, you have not seen

---

82 **No.303**, in *Holiness*, 12-16; *Election* (**nos. 41-42**), 11; *Pulpit*, 5 (1859), 130, quoted in Colquitt, 'Soteriology of Spurgeon', 149.

83 Spurgeon, *Infant Salvation: a Sympathetic Word to Bereaved Parents* (London: Passmore & Alabaster, n.d.), 13-17; *ST*, 5 (1869), 243-4.

84 Spurgeon, *All of Grace* (London: Passmore & Alabaster, 1886), 26-7; **no. 942**, in *The Messiah*, 412; **no. 1447** in *Pulpit*, 24 (1878), 678.

85 *Pulpit*, 8 (1862), 638, quoted in Colquitt, 'Soteriology of Spurgeon', 52.

86 **No. 1239**, in *Twelve Sermons on Sanctification* (n.d.), 341.

yourselves: you will never know how black you are till you have seen how bright he is; and inasmuch as you will never know all his brightness, so you will never know all your own blackness.'[87]

The theological counterpart of these convictions of conscience and experience was a doctrine of the intrinsic incompatibility of human sinfulness and divine holiness: 'Brethren, a holy God cannot endure sin: he cannot have fellowship with it, or with those who are rendered unclean by it, for it would be inconsistent with his nature so to do. On the other hand, sinful men cannot have fellowship with God: their evil nature could not endure the fire of his holiness.'[88] It followed from this assemblage of ideas that many of the most fertile fields of nineteenth century theological endeavour were dismissed by Spurgeon as altogether out of bounds. He rejected anything involving an implication that God might tolerate sin, all attempts to make out that the punishment of sin might be less than an eternal hell, any theory involving the cancelling of sin by subsequent righteousness, indeed the very idea that goodness latent within human nature might have a constructive theological role.[89] Spurgeon's views on holiness and sin sufficed unaided to set up a barrier between himself and the entire spectrum of contemporary liberal theological revision.

Spurgeon's tendency to set different lines of theological argument alongside each other with little of the synthesis that might reduce their tension was nowhere more evident than in his christology. In this case the weaknesses associated with the practice were more prominent than the strengths. As usual with the more theoretical, as opposed to experiential, areas of theology, the young Spurgeon absorbed and taught historical orthodoxy on the subject. In this case it was the patristic emphasis on the distinctness of Christ's divine and human natures: 'When Christ in past years did gird himself with mortal clay, the essence of his divinity was not changed; flesh did not become God, nor did God become flesh by a real actual change of nature; the two were united in hypostatical union, but the Godhead was still the same.' [90] And, again as usual, it was not long before he showed solidarity with his age by substituting spirituality for metaphysics:

---

[87] *ST*, 16 (1880), 495.

[88] **No. 1923**, in *Pulpit* 32 (1886), 541.

[89] *Pulpit*, 20 (1874), 676, quoted in Colquitt, 'Soteriology of Spurgeon', 178; **no. 661**, in *The Messiah*, 216; **no. 942**, in *ibid.*, 411-12; **no. 1540**, in *ibid.*, 192.

[90] *Pulpit*, 1 (1855), 2, quoted in Colquitt, 'Soteriology of Spurgeon', 67.

> Beloved, this is a mystery surpassing all comprehension. If any man should attempt to explain, or even to define the union of the divine and human in the Lord Jesus, he would soon prove his folly. The schoolmen of the dark ages were very fond of asking puzzling questions about what they called the hypostatical unity of the deity and humanity of Christ. They could not cast so much as a ray of light upon the subject; they amused themselves in enigmas and lost themselves in labyrinths. It is enough for us to know that the incarnation is a glorious fact, and it suffices us to hold it in its simplicity.[91]

Yet in reality Spurgeon was no more able to stop at the simple 'fact' of incarnation than any other theologian, and his frequent comments on christological themes reveal that despite the change in language the same patristic ideas maintained their place in his thought. He often emphasized the distinction between Christ's deity and humanity, going so far as to imply that Christ had separate divine and human consciousnesses.[92] He ascribed episodes in Jesus' life to his manhood or his Godhood as entities operating independently, the former usually being on view, but with the latter responsible for working miracles.[93] It is significant that in a sentence echoing the prologue of John's Gospel Spurgeon spoke of the Word being *united* to flesh rather than *becoming* flesh.[94]

One by-product of his difficulties in holding his christology together in the centre was a freedom to develop both Christ's deity and humanity. Spurgeon believed that all the attributes of God could be seen in Jesus, though veiled in flesh.[95] He also participated fully in the contemporary stress on Jesus' humanity. He was often at pains to point out that Jesus' humanity was absolutely ordinary with the single exception of its sinlessness; he included worship and faith among the shared experiences.[96] In one late sermon Spurgeon even

---

[91] *Pulpit*, 13 (1867), 699, quoted in Colquitt, 'Soteriology of Spurgeon', 68.

[92] **Nos. 1153-4**, in *Christ's Relation to his People*, 76; **no. 1968**, in *ibid.*, 684; *ST*, 14 (1878), 45.

[93] **No. 957**, in *Christ's Relation to his People*, 304. 'It is my solemn conviction that the deity co-worked with his humanity in the wondrous passion by which he has sanctified his elect.' *Pulpit*, 26 (1880), 161-2, quoted in Colquitt, 'Soteriology of Spurgeon', 68.

[94] **No. 724**, in *The Messiah*, 140.

[95] Spurgeon, 'Good Tidings', 126. For omniscience see *ST*, 3 (1867), 541; for omnipotence see **no. 1121**, in *Christ's Relations to his People*, 283.

[96] **No. 1099**, in *The Messiah*, 328-9; **no. 2418**, in *Christ's Relation to his*

began sketching an intriguing revision of the doctrine of Jesus' sinlessness:

> But when he took manhood into union with himself, he took therewith all that belonged to manhood. Now, sin having attached itself to manhood, the Christ, in becoming man, took our sin upon himself, as it is written, 'The Lord hath laid on him the iniquity of us all.' He could not be actually guilty – God forbid the thought! – but he became legally amenable to the penalty due for our transgression.[97]

This idea feeds directly into Spurgeon's doctrine of atonement. It was potentially useful to his three central themes on the subject – union, representation and substitution – but its most direct relevance was to his belief that reconciliation with God was through Christ's life of obedience to the law, which established a righteousness he could give to his people, as well as through his death.[98] He had always held this up as the historic doctrine in opposition to a modern restriction of Christ's atoning activity to his death.[99] The new thinking on sinlessness reinforced his position by fastening the atoning life firmly to the incarnation, thereby cementing that unity of incarnation and atonement as one great fact which he had earlier proclaimed.[100]

Atonement, the third frontier of theology that Spurgeon explored, was perhaps the one on which he concentrated most of all, for in it the other two met: sin was destroyed and the elect entered into God's holiness. His understanding of atonement was characteristic in being permanently anchored to strong convictions closely associated with his conversion. This was particularly true of his most prominent idea, substitution, which, though long familiar to him, he said came as a revelation to him upon his conversion.[101] He considered it the only possible explanation of his experience of loving acceptance by God, and believed it to be affirmed by the Bible, and witnessed to inwardly by the Holy Spirit; 'there is a chasm that no man yet has been able to bridge without it; it lightens our conscience, gladdens our hearts, inspires our devotion, and

---

People, 42-3.

97 **No. 2117**, in *Pulpit*, 35 (1889), 650.

98 **No. 395**, in *The Messiah*, 223-6.

99 **No. 1486**, in *ibid.*, 344; **no. 1527**, in *Sanctification*, 159-60.

100 Spurgeon, 'Good Tidings', 188-9.

101 Spurgeon, *All of Grace*, 28.

elevates our aspirations; we are wedded to it, and daily glory in it.'[102] Its importance to him was all the greater because of the way he insisted that a doctrine he considered essential to the Christian faith must be believed in order for a true faith to exist: 'The whole pith and marrow of the religion of Christianity lies in the doctrine of "substitution," and I hesitate not to affirm with conviction that a very large proportion of Christians are not Christians at all, for they do not understand the fundamental doctrine of the Christian creed.'[103] In consequence substitutionary atonement took its place alongside biblical inspiration as one of the two principle doctrines Spurgeon defended most stoutly against theological revision.[104]

Yet substitution was by no means the sum total of Spurgeon's doctrine of atonement; it was its usual public face, but he found it needed to be interpreted and enriched by other ideas. One of these, representation, had been associated with substitution from the first. Spurgeon adopted a classic Calvinist federal and covenant theology by which he sought to demonstrate the justice of a substitutionary punishment.[105] The federal theology was itself integrated into his third major idea, union with Christ, with which he tried to penetrate beyond the legal realm into an actual, vital process: 'There is yet another word higher than "substitution," higher than "representation," and that is "union". We are one with Christ, joined to him by a union that can never be broken. Not only does he do what he does, representing us, but we are joined unto him in one Spirit, members of his body, and partakers of his glory.'[106] During most of his life Spurgeon's discussions of union with Christ were directly associated only with regeneration, leaving the participation of the elect in atonement on the legal level of representation; but there are indications that some of his late thought transcended this limitation: 'Brethren, as many of us as are joined unto the Lord by a living faith are one with Jesus, by eternal union one. When he died, we died; when he rose, we rose; we were condemned and justified in him; and now that the Father loves him, we also are beloved in him.'[107] Having delved as far as he could, Spurgeon recognized that there was more to the atonement than he could understand: 'I feel that the

---

[102] **No. 1447**, in *Pulpit*, 24 (1878), 677.

[103] **No. 873**, in *The Passion and Death of Christ*, 62.

[104] **No. 2296**, in *Christ's Relation to his People*, 414.

[105] *All of Grace*, 28; *ST*, 1 (1865), 374-5.

[106] **No. 1862**, in *Christ's Relation to his People*, 558. Compare Spurgeon, *Christ's Glorious Achievements* (1877), 111-16.

[107] **No. 2117**, in *Pulpit*, 35 (1889), 655. He was nearly as explicit a decade earlier in **no. 1411**, in *Christ's Relation to his People*, 488-9.

idea of substitution does not cover the whole of the matter, and that no human conception can completely grasp the whole of the dread mystery. It was wrought in darkness because the full, far-reaching meaning and result cannot be beheld of finite mind.'[108]

Spurgeon's treatment of atonement was different to that of most of his contemporaries, and yet there was a certain amount of convergence, for example with Dale's theology of solidarity.[109] The divergence arose because Spurgeon's fundamental convictions, that retributory punishment was essential to the maintenance of justice and that penal substitution was biblical and axiomatic, were alien to the liberal ethic that in one way or another moulded the majority of the creative theology of the period. The element of convergence can largely be accounted for by Spurgeon's agreement with two of the main concerns behind liberal theological revision, the demand for reality rather than fiction, and righteousness uncompromised by legal sleight of hand or anything else. He rebutted the charge that imputation involved pretence by insisting that there was a genuine transfer of sin, not just punishment, from the elect to Christ, and of righteousness, not merely life, from Christ to the elect – 'only as righteous ones can we be saved'.[110] He even turned criticisms back onto their authors, saying that Dale's idea that righteousness could be attained by submission to its ideal manifestation in Christ was fictitious.[111] But he realized that his efforts to demonstrate the righteousness of his own theory could not completely satisfy all questioners, and so he fell back on his twin convictions that imputed righteousness was biblical and therefore revealed by God, and that God's righteousness was unimpugnable even where incomprehensible.[112]

Spurgeon's doctrine of union with Christ lay at the heart of a radical doctrine of regeneration: 'Now the life which grace confers upon the saints at the moment of their quickening is none other than the life of Christ.'[113] The old life, crucified with Christ, was dying a lingering death. The new life was an entirely new creation: spiritual,

---

108 Fullerton, *Spurgeon*, 181-2.

109 See p. 72, above.

110 Spurgeon, *Christ's Glorious Achievements*, 19, 'Good Tidings', 147-8, and *Faith*, 52-3. Spurgeon was at times uneasy about the word 'imputation', conscious that there was something intrinsically fictitious about it in contemporary definitions, but he found no real solution to the problems this occasioned (**no. 991**, in *The Messiah*, 586).

111 *ST*, 19 (1883), 643-4.

112 **No. 1771**, in *Pulpit*, 30 (1884), 162; **no. 1889**, in *Pulpit*, 32 (1886), 142.

113 *ST*, 1 (1865), 378.

partaking in the divine nature, and separated from the old life by a gulf as great as that between the latter and animal existence, it was higher than man's state prior to the fall. In its deeper sense Spurgeon restricted the fatherhood of God to the regenerate.[114]

Sanctification was by no means for Spurgeon the optional extra some evangelical theologies could allow it to become: he was quite as anxious as Baldwin Brown or Dale to ground it in atonement and declare it essential for salvation. He argued that Jesus conquered the world for his people and that they conquered the world for him; so if the members of Christ's body did not in fact overcome the world then the victory of their head would itself be compromised.[115] Elsewhere he declared:

> We preach salvation *from sin*; we say that Christ is able to save a man; and we mean by that that he is able to save him from sin and to make him holy; to make him a new man. No person has any right to say, 'I am saved,' while he continue in sin as he did before. How can you be saved from sin while you are living in it?[116]

Jesus came to remove the power and presence of sin, as well as its penalty; 'justification without sanctification would not be salvation at all'.[117]

Outside its central themes of a holy God, sinful humanity, and their reconciliation, Spurgeon's theology was weaker. Nowhere was this more evident than in his ecclesiology, where, in spite of the high practical importance he attached to the Church's fellowship and work, he was capable of thoroughly dismissive language:

> We are always talking about the church doing this and that today – what is the church? I believe there is a great deal too much said, both of bad and good, about that abstraction; the fact is, we are individuals. The church is only the aggregation of individuals, and if any good is to be done it must be performed by individuals.[118]

There were unresolved tensions in Spurgeon's mind concerning the relations that should pertain between the Church and the world.

---

[114] Spurgeon, *Christ's Glorious Achievements*, 119-22, **no. 1029**, in *Holiness*, 58, 'Good Tidings', 46, and **no. 942**, in *The Messiah*, 415.
[115] Spurgeon, *Christ's Glorious Achievements*, 100-02.
[116] **No. 618**, in *The Messiah*, 488.
[117] Spurgeon, *All of Grace*, 34.
[118] **No. 1099**, in *The Messiah*, 337-8.

He affirmed that all of nature was worthy of attention because it had been created by God and sanctified by Christ's presence,[119] yet wrote that 'the best we can do with this world is to get through it as quickly as we can, for we dwell in an enemy's country'.[120] His exhortations reflected this dichotomy: on one occasion he taught 'The salt of the earth should be well rubbed into the meat, and so the Christian should mingle with his fellow men, seeking their good for edification. We are men, and whatever men may lawfully do, we do; wherever they may go, we go';[121] on another he quoted 'Come ye out from among them: be ye separate' as the only way of dealing with evil.[122] There is evidence that involvement in the world was the dominant theme in the late 1860s, whereas the relative position was clearly reversed in Spurgeon's last years; this correlates with his overall frame of mind during the respective periods.[123]

A similar process was at work in Spurgeon's eschatology. At the outset of his ministry he looked for an imminent outpouring of the Spirit on the Church that would usher in Christ's kingdom;[124] but by 1861 he had adopted a pre-millennial eschatology which allowed him in one of his last sermons to envisage the Church's degeneration to the point of merging into the world prior to the day of judgement, a day which he had begun to hope was near.[125] However neither the bright early vision nor the dark late one encroached far into his ministry, during most of which he pictured the end of the age as distant and remote.[126] Death seemed much nearer, and, inseparably joined to judgement, was always prominent in Spurgeon's preaching. He never wavered in his allegiance to two ideas he considered demonstrably scriptural: that nothing – whether repentance, reparation or mercy – could intervene between death and judgement, and that the verdict of that judgement upon all who heard but did not receive the Gospel would be eternal punishment.[127] Yet he was not immune to the influences that led contemporaries away from these beliefs; the freedom and even relish of some of his early references to

---

119 *ST*, 1 (1865), 265; Spurgeon, *An all-round Ministry*, 44.

120 Spurgeon, *All of Grace*, 113.

121 **No 781**, in *Christ's Relation to his People*, 120.

122 **No. 2106**, in *ibid.*, 203.

123 **No. 655**, in *The Messiah*, 366-7; *ST*, 6 (1870), 529.

124 **No. 30**, in *The Holy Spirit*, 25-6.

125 Spurgeon, *Pulpit*, 7 (1861), 346, quoted in Colquitt, 'Soteriology of Spurgeon', 260, **no. 2200**, in *The Holy Spirit*, 130, and *An All-round Ministry*, 397-8.

126 E.g. **no. 986**, in *The Messiah*, 475-6.

127 **No. 2013**, in *Pulpit*, 34 (1888), 154-5.

judgement did not outlast the 1850s, and were a subject of regret in later years.[128] He declined to predict a verdict of guilty on those who had not heard the Gospel, and left to God the vindication of a doctrine to which he virtually confessed a dislike by concurring with a statement of Henry Ward Beecher's:

> 'I do not accept the doctrine of eternal punishment because I delight in it. … I would destroy all faith in it; but that would do no good; I could not destroy the thing itself. ...'
>
> Thus does Henry Ward Beecher exactly and forcibly express our own thoughts upon the matter. Not without the bitterest anguish of spirit do we contemplate the future state of the finally impenitent.[129]

This instance of a gap between Spurgeon's understanding and his belief, though among the more acute, was by no means unusual. Far from being bothered by this, as many would have been, in a curious way he revelled in it: the greatness of God, the awfulness of opposition to him, and the wonder of the grace that overcame it were all enhanced through leaving human reason floundering out of its depth. Regions beyond the frontiers of the intellect were opened up by his decision to believe all he found in the Bible; and he exulted in the freedom this accorded to spiritual experience. It is possible that this delight even took the edge off his theological appetite. Spurgeon's greatest achievements were as a preacher and mystic, rather than as a theologian, but Kruppa is wrong to accept his own modest disclaimer of any accomplishments in the latter field: 'I am content to live and die as a mere repeater of scriptural teachings; as a person who has thought out nothing and invented nothing.'[130] Robertson Nicoll's assessment is better: 'A great and trained theologian, master in every part of his own system, he preached nothing that he had not proved.'[131]

---

[128] 'In my own hearing, while a student, Mr. S. in the most moving words I ever heard him speak referred with regret and recoil to his early utterances on this question.' G. Tooley to Messrs Gracey and Ferguson, 25 February 1888, MS letter in Spurgeon's College.

[129] Preface, in William Baker, *The Duration of Future Punishments* (London: Passmore & Alabaster, 1865), v. Also **no. 2400**, in *Decision*, 151; *Pulpit*, 49 (1903), 609, quoted in Colquitt, 'Soteriology of Spurgeon', 275.

[130] Spurgeon, *Messages to the Multitude*, p. 269, quoted in Kruppa, 477.

[131] Introduction, in Nicoll (ed.), *Sermons*, 8.

Influence

The one thing responsible for Spurgeon's dramatic rise to fame upon his arrival in London was his preaching. Crowds flocked to hear it, and this drew publicity; the publicity in turn multiplied the crowds, and the increase of his congregation became self-perpetuating. At first press reports were mainly hostile, culminating in some offensive reporting of the Surrey Gardens disaster of October 1856, but in 1857 the tide turned, helped by the smoothing down of some of the rough edges of his preaching, but mainly because Spurgeon's integrity and refusal to descend to the level of his opponents set their distortions and animosity in sharp relief. The most obvious sign of the transition from notoriety to general acceptance was the presence of increasing numbers of people of high social standing in his congregations.[132]

Preaching never strayed from its central place in Spurgeon's life and work: it must be the starting point for an examination of the various means by which his influence made itself felt. Both the extraordinary initial impact and the unparalleled sustained success that followed can be attributed to a combination of four elements. The first was a voice remarkable in both power and quality. The second was his style, in which he aimed to replace conventionality, affectation and oratory, words which possessed a negative connotation for him, with reality, manliness and naturalness. John Clifford made the exaggerated claim that Spurgeon thus initiated a revolution in the spirit and aims of Christian preaching that he set alongside the Oxford Movement as one of the two most influential religious developments of his time in relation to worship.[133] Reality and manliness were general preoccupations of Spurgeon's generation, although naturalness was a rarer quality, one conspicuously absent from the influential writings of Thomas Carlyle. Yet there were others, notably Charles Kingsley, who communicated effectively in a style that combined the three qualities before Spurgeon did.[134] Spurgeon should be placed in the front rank

---

[132] *Spurgeon Autobiography*, I, 464, 469.

[133] John Clifford, *Typical Christian Leaders* (London: H. Marshall & Son, 1898), 92; cf. pp. 89-90. Idem., *God's Greater Britain* (London: James Clarke & Co., 1899), 158-9.

[134] Spurgeon did not physically embody the Victorian manliness epitomized by Kingsley, but in many respects his outlook was similar to that of the man of whom he wrote: 'he had very little of the heretic about him but the growl.' *ST*, 16 (1880), 619. See Norman Vance, *The Sinews of the Spirit: The Ideal of Christian Manliness in Victorian Literature*

of influential early exponents of a new style of preaching without being assigned the entire credit for developing it. The third feature of Spurgeon's preaching was its content. He attached great importance to depth and variety of thought: it was his belief that the decline of the evangelical party in the Church of England was the result of failure in this respect.[135] There can be few greater tests of a man's ability to continue thinking than publishing a sermon a week for decades. The substance of the gospel Spurgeon preached scarcely altered, but the impact of the series was not progressively blunted by staleness or repetition. The last element that made Spurgeon's preaching so successful was its spirituality. The act of preaching was itself a spiritual stimulus to him, and his fluency and lack of reserve helped him communicate his experience of God with remarkable clarity. Alexander McLaren's comment after reading some of his sermons was that 'there is a passion of love to Jesus, and a grand fullness of trust in Him which have stirred and rebuked me'.[136]

There was much variety in Spurgeon's preaching, but two features were rarely absent: he maintained close contact with his text, attaching importance to the way he broke it up for exposition, and he threw himself single-mindedly into pointed application. An 1881 sermon on Acts 2.2-4 entitled 'The Pentecostal Wind and Fire'[137] is as typical as any, offering in addition some interesting comments on preaching. Like most of his sermons, it had a carefully prepared introduction, in which he declared his aim to be to talk of the coming of the Holy Spirit as a fact bearing on the present rather than as history. There were four sections, each subdivided: the symbols of the Holy Spirit – wind and fire; the effects of his descent – filling and utterance; the themes of this utterance – redemption, regeneration and remission of sin; and its results, under which heading he summed up the end of the chapter in ten paragraphs. The first of these contrasted the deep feeling at Pentecost with the tendency in his own day to treat preaching like music or drama as a performance whose merits could be discussed, and concluded with the

---

and Religious Thought (Cambridge: Cambridge University Press, 1985).

[135] *ST*, 17 (1881), 109-10.

[136] E.T. McLaren, *Dr McLaren of Manchester: A Sketch*, (London: Hodder & Stoughton, 1912[3]), 244-5. 'For my own part when the Lord helps me to preach, after I have delivered all my matter, and have fired off my shot so fast that my gun has grown hot, I have often rammed my very soul into the gun, and fired my heart at the congregation, and this discharge has, under God, won the victory.' *ST*, 3 (1867), 106. Cf. *Spurgeon Autobiography*, II, 355.

[137] **No. 1619**, in *The Holy Spirit*, 91-103.

understanding of preaching of which he never for a moment lost sight: 'The object of all true preaching is the heart: we aim at divorcing the heart from sin, and wedding it to Christ. Our ministry has failed, and has not the divine seal upon it, unless it makes men tremble, makes them sad, and then anon brings them to Christ, and causes them to rejoice.'[138] He had already concentrated on the need to communicate rather than perform in discussing preaching method:

> I should think from what I know of some preachers that when they had their Pentecost the influence sat upon them in the form of tongues of flowers; but the apostolic Pentecost knew not flowers, but flames. What fine preaching we have nowadays! What new thoughts, and poetical turns! ...
>
> The Holy Ghost calls us not to this mode of speech. Fire, intensity, zeal, passion as much as you will, but as for aiming at effect by polished phrases and brilliant periods – these are fitter of those who would deceive men than for those who would tell them the message of the Most High. The style of the Holy Ghost is one which conveys the truth to the mind in the most forcible manner, - it is plain but flaming, simple but consuming.[139]

Printing extended the influence of Spurgeon's preaching beyond his live congregations, limited as these were by the size and immobility of the Metropolitan Tabernacle. The weekly printed sermons rose from an initial circulation of under 2000 to an average to 25,000 by 1871; this level was still being maintained in 1904 using a stock of Sunday evening and weekday sermons.[140] The sales of volumes of the American edition of his sermons reached half a million by 1879, but their appropriation by dozens of religious papers contributed more to making Spurgeon, according to Dr Stanford Holme, the preacher with the most extensive hearing in the United States. Large number of sermons were translated into only a

---

[138] *Ibid.*, 100.

[139] *Ibid.*, 95.

[140] F.B. Meyer, *Charles Haddon Spurgeon* (London, 1892), 12-13; *ST*, 7 (1871), 1-3; W.C. Wilkinson, *Modern Masters of Pulpit Discourse* (New York: Funk & Wagnalls, 1905), 207. The regular readership was augmented occasionally by exceptional sales of individual sermons, the record being the 350,000 notched up by the 'Baptismal Regeneration' sermons of 1864 – *ST*, 1 (1865), 347.

few languages, notably Dutch and Welsh, but Spurgeon's influence must have been felt in many other countries, including Russia, where a million copies of a few sermons were circulated with the blessing of the censor and the official approval of the Orthodox Church.[141] Almost every day Spurgeon received letters from appreciative readers of his sermons, many of them telling of conversions. At times such letters arrived at the rate of twenty a week, and known conversions through a few sermons numbered in the hundreds: what proportion remained unreported it is impossible to say. Some of the choicer stories were related in *The Sword and the Trowel,* including that of a major-general in India who was converted mainly through the sermons and subsequently sent off for large supplies to distribute in the army, as well as organising contributions to Spurgeon's college and orphanage.[142]

Spurgeon's influence was at its most concentrated in his own church, where his authority was absolute: near the end of his ministry he said that he had never known any appeal from his decisions.[143] The congregation that regularly stretched the 6500 capacity of the Metropolitan Tabernacle was predominately lower middle class, with men outnumbering women by about two to one. Membership rose inexorably for a quarter of a century before stabilising above five thousand in the 1880s. A total of 14,691 – an average of more than one per day – joined the church during Spurgeon's ministry.[144] It was a working church with an immense list of activities: in 1884 a leading deacon said that at least a thousand Tabernacle people were out conducting meetings on Sunday evenings.[145]

The Pastors' College was much the most important of the church's agencies, and was also uniquely Spurgeon's own, not being adopted

---

141 *Spurgeon Autobiography,* II, 353-4. Dr Geoffrey Rowell informs me that the monks of St. Macarios Monastery in Egypt told him that they appreciated Spurgeon's sermons.

142 *ST,* 11 (1875), 6; 8 (1872), 1, 140. Spurgeon's other publications do not compare with the sermons, yet they were numerous and influential, ranging from *The Treasury of David,* a multi-volume work on the Psalms, to a collection of rustic moral wisdom, *John Plougham's Talk;* the former sold 125,000 volumes by 1892, and the latter 400,000 copies – *From the Pulpit to the Palm-branch,* p. 198; Williams, *Personal Reminiscences,* 286-7.

143 Kruppa, *Preacher's Progress,* 156.

144 *The New York Examiner,* quoted without criticism in *ST,* 5 (1869), 38 also *ST,* 13 (1877), 40; Spurgeon, *Storm Signals,* 99; George Rogers in *ST,* 1 (1865), 30-31; *Spurgeon Autobiography,* II, 292, 355, 505.

145 Dallimore, *Robertson Nicoll,* 159.

by the Tabernacle until some years after he started it. It emerged from his desire to help some of his young converts, who were determined to preach but were hampered by a lack of education. He decided against using existing colleges because of their cost and doubts about their theology and fervour. From 1856 he placed students in the care of George Rogers, a Congregational minister whose outlook closely matched his own; within a decade the number had grown to nearly a hundred, taught by several lecturers.[146] Spurgeon thus pioneered the provision of cheaper, briefer, and less academic courses of study for the ministry aimed at making preachers rather than scholars out of candidates of moderate talent and humble social background. There were no educational and financial qualifications but as a rule students were required to be Baptists and Calvinists, and to show that they had already preached effectively for some time.[147]

Although the time Spurgeon spent with his students was normally limited to a lecture and counselling on Friday afternoons, his influence was still paramount, persisting after his students settled in the churches to which he personally assigned them. His policy was to give priority to the foundation of new churches, but he also received numerous applications from existing churches, typically from declining ones that hoped that a minister from Spurgeon's school would bring them renewed growth. In this way there developed an informal connexion within the Baptist denomination, maintained on an entirely voluntary basis.[148] Membership statistics conveyed the satisfying message of a rate of growth in these churches in excess of that of the denomination as a whole, so that by 1881 they made up one sixth of the denomination.[149]

Continuing loyalty was fostered by the annual conferences of the Pastors' College Association, founded by Spurgeon in 1865. This brought former and current students together with the aim of maintaining their distinctive theology, strengthening relationships, and encouraging evangelism. For many 'conference week', and

---

[146] *ST*, 1 (1865), 462; 6 (1870), 145-6.

[147] *ST*, 7 (1871), 221-7.

[148] *ST*, 7 (1871), 221-8; 1 (1865), 430; 14 (1878), 239.

[149] *ST*, 9 (1873), 148; John Clifford (ed.), *The English Baptists, Who They Are and What They Have Done*, (London: E. Marlborough, 1881), 28. The proportion was much higher in the home counties, where the bulk of Spurgeon's church-planting had been done: over two hundred churches in the region during his lifetime, much of it by students during their studies – E.W. Hayden, *A History of Spurgeon's Tabernacle* (Pasadena: Pilgrim Publications, 1971), 68.

especially Spurgeon's presidential address, was the highlight of the year[150]. Nonconformist colleges all had their spheres of influence, usually local, and prominent ministers exercised an episcopal role through personal ties with some ministers and churches, but no one brought these two informal mechanisms together as Spurgeon did or operated them on anything like the same scale. His own assessment was that 'we sometimes think the work of training ministers to be superior to all other services done to the Lord and his church', and he once called his college 'our greatest life work'.[151]

In 1866 a commentator suggested that as Spurgeon displayed the organising capacity required to follow Wesley's example, after twenty years' further development his network might, should circumstances warrant, become a sect called Spurgeonism.[152] Spurgeon repudiated vehemently both the name and the intention,[153] but the Downgrade Controversy of 1887-88 brought about such circumstances at the forecast time. In that crisis five-sixths of the members of the Pastors' College Association who responded swiftly indicated their personal and theological loyalty to Spurgeon by voting in favour of its reconstitution as the Pastors' College Evangelical Association,[154] but Spurgeon refrained from subjecting their loyalty to the still greater test of demanding that they follow him out of the Baptist Union; the vast majority stayed in, and the PCEA could not therefore become the nucleus of a new denomination.[155] The climate was not favourable to such an enterprise; on the crucial subject of the basis of communion Spurgeon's students did not follow their leader's way of thinking.

The monthly Spurgeon edited, *The Sword and the Trowel,* was launched in the same productive year as the Pastors' College Association, 1865, and with the complementary aim of reporting the work and advocating the principles of the churches connected to his

---

150 *ST*, 25 (1889), 284.

151 *ST*, 18 (1882), 260; 4 (1886), 473.

152 M. Coit Tyler in the *New York Independent*, quoted in *ST*, 2 (1866), 138.

153 *Ibid*.

154 434 out of 520 replies; only 24 of the remainder were outright 'no' votes – pencilled notes of the tellers, Spurgeon's College archives. Others joined the PCEA subsequently – *ST*, 24 (1888), 314.

155 A letter dating from soon after the end of the controversy shows that Spurgeon thought that the new Surrey and Middlesex Association might take on this role – Spurgeon to Isaac Near, 16 June 1888, quoted in E.A. Payne, 'The Down Grade Controversy: A Postscript', *BQ*, 28 (1979), 154 – but he proceeded cautiously, and no real progress toward a new denomination was evident before his final illness began in 1891.

own, in order to arouse readers to action, particularly of an evangelistic character. But another role soon assumed an equal priority, for the magazine also served a wider group of sympathizers in other denominations, many of them already readers of his sermons, and proved a useful means of channelling funds into Spurgeon's enterprises. Circulation rose from an initial ten thousand to level out around fifteen thousand about five years later.[156] The magazine was at the heart of the whole Spurgeonic network, and its circulation probably represented quite accurately the size of the wealthier section of the disparate community in whose lives Spurgeon's influence was considerable.

1865 was an important year for Spurgeon's relationship with the wider Baptist denomination as well as for the organization of his own network. That year he attended the autumn meetings of the Baptist Union in Bradford, thereby ending a decade during which he had taken no part in its affairs. He came away full of enthusiasm:

> Our own heart was brimming with love to all the brethren, we took the most public opportunity of expressing it, and we feel constrained again to say that if we have in any measure been an impediment to the forming of our Churches into a compact phalanx, it has not been our intention, and it shall not be the case in the future[157].

Enthusiastic reviews of Union meetings continued to appear at intervals in *The Sword and the Trowel,* but he never served on the committee, avoided denominational political matters such as the choice of a new secretary, and often stayed away from its assemblies.[158] One factor was slight awkwardness arising from his

---

[156] *ST,* 1 (1865), 1-2; 2 (1866), iii-iv; 6 (1870), iv; 1 (1865), iii; 5 (1869), 382; 7 (1871), 3.

[157] *ST,* 1 (1865), 504. The importance of this turning point in Spurgeon's career has been insufficiently appreciated: the Calvinist/Arminian debate of his youth was relegated to a subordinate place as he made Catholicism and Ritualism his main target. Thus William Landels, with whom he had crossed swords over election in 1859, became his friend in 1863, an ally in the Baptismal Regeneration controversy of 1864, and a colleague in the foundation of the London Baptist Association in 1865. See Michael Nicholls, 'The Downgrade Controversy: A Neglected Protagonist', *BQ,* 33 (1988), 268.

[158] *ST,* 2 (1866), 521; 13 (1877), 284; 11 (1875), 545; 16 (1880), 191; Fullerton, *Spurgeon,* 309.

extraordinary standing within the denomination – though there was very little resentment; but the main reason why he limited his involvement was that he was already overstretched by more immediate commitments.[159] Signs that this period of greatest contact with the denomination at large, and hence of greatest opportunity to influence it, would not last appeared in the 1870s when critical remarks began to accompany commendatory ones about Baptist Union meetings in *The Sword and the Trowel*. He decided to cease to attend them in 1883 when it became clear to him that liberal theology was beginning to find support among Baptists.[160] At the end of his ministry he was further from the Baptist Union than at its beginning; while even when he was closest to it his theological influence only operated in a limited way.

* * *

In 1880 Spurgeon paid a business visit to a chapel vestry while the Wesleyan Conference was in session. He was pounced upon, led in front of the assembly, and moved to tears by their welcome. He gave an impromptu talk, listened to some warm replies, and left with a deep sense of gratitude.[161] This incident conveys an impression of the sort of regard in which Spurgeon was very widely held. The depth of national feeling became apparent during his serious illness in 1891, when prayers for him were offered by people from all denominations, including opponents in the Downgrade Controversy, Gladstone, the two English archbishops, the Chief Rabbi, and even the Prince of Wales. It was still more evident after his death: on 9 February 1892 up to sixty thousand people filed past his coffin, and on the following day four thousand clergy and ministers attended a memorial service; Randall Davidson, then Bishop of Rochester, pronounced the benediction at the graveside.[162] Robertson Nicoll summarized this feeling boldly: 'It may well be doubted whether any other man of our time has so conquered prejudice, has so won for himself a deep and silent and universal

---

[159] *ST*, 2 (1866), 281-82.

[160] This is discussed in chapter 7. *ST*, 8 (1872), 530; 14 (1878), 469-71.

[161] *ST*, 16 (1880), 487. Compare the *Methodist Recorder*, 2 Feb. 1888: 'There is no man outside our communion to whom Methodism owes more than to CHARLES HADDON SPURGEON.' – in Spurgeon's College, Spurgeon Scrapbooks.

[162] *ST*, 27 (1891), 465; Spurgeon, *From the Pulpit to the Palm-branch*, 95, 125, 211.

regard, a regard in multitudes of cases that passed into reverence.'[163]

There was a catholic streak in Spurgeon that helped nurture this respect; this developed most in his last years when he more or less broke off hostilities on the Catholic front to concentrate his firepower on what he considered the more serious and dangerous errors of liberalism. He had long recognized spirituality in the High Church when he had come into contact with it,[164] but his last years of controversy and illness brought glimpses of something more:

> During the past year I have been made to see that there is more love and unity among God's people than is generally believed. ... I feel myself a debtor to all God's people on this earth. ... We mistake our divergencies of judgment for differences of heart; but they are far from being the same thing. In these days of infidel criticism, believers of all sorts will be driven into sincere unity. ... Their different modes of external worship are as the furrows of a field; the field is none the less one because of the marks of the plough. Between rationalism and faith there is an abyss immeasurable; but where there is faith in the Everlasting Father, faith in the Great Sacrifice, and faith in the Indwelling Spirit, there is a living loving, lasting union.[165]

But Spurgeon's general influence was very diffuse in comparison to that he exerted in the much narrower sphere of his own network. Two factors combined to incline him to concentrate heavily on the latter, the first being his preference for working on his own. '"Lead me not into temptation" means, to me, Bring me not into a comm.-ittee', was a saying of his.[166] He strongly believed that anything worthwhile was done by one man, and sought to apply this principle by rarely consulting others and making up his mind in advance even when he did.[167] He did some theological theorising to vindicate this practice:

> A minister fully equipped for the work, will usually be a spirit by himself, above, beyond, and apart from others. ... The man whom the Lord raises as leader becomes, in the same degree in which he is a superior man, a solitary man. ... No one knows, but he who has

---

163 *BW*, 1 March 1900, 457.

164 Shown in a number of book reviews in *ST*, e.g. 16 (1880), 532.

165 31 December 1891 address in *From the Pulpit to the Palm-branch*, 25-6.

166 Williams, *Personal Reminiscences*, 172.

167 *Spurgeon Autobiography*, II, 392; Douglas, *Prince of Preachers*, 186-7.

> endured it, the solitude of a soul which has outstripped its fellows in zeal for the Lord of hosts.[168]

The second factor that tended to narrow his influence was the rare seriousness with which he addressed the New Testament theme of rejection by the world. He saw that what he termed the 'theory of universal charity' was the modern way to reputation, and that persecution, false accusations and loss of reputation would result from the controversies into which his conscience drove him, but accepted these as normal features of authentic Christianity.[169]

That a man with such an approach to his fellows and society could enjoy such wide esteem is remarkable: there can be no better tribute than this to the strength of his more attractive qualities. But few outside his own circle were prepared to take Spurgeon undiluted, most feeling constrained to pick and choose between what they saw as the commendable and unacceptable in Spurgeon. On extreme versions such as that of Joseph Parker in 1890 this became to all intents and purposes a schizophrenic assessment. In Spurgeon's later years his theology was generally one of the first things to be discarded: Parker's dismissal of his Calvinism was unusual only for its coarseness.[170] The situation had seemed rosier to Spurgeon in 1874, before his retreat from involvement with main-stream Nonconformity began. In that year he took exception to Dale's analysis that it was only his own influence among Baptists that prevented Calvinism's obsolescence proceeding as smoothly in that denomination as among Congregationalists. Spurgeon maintained that in his experience his own moderate Calvinism – that which was prepared to welcome Arminian emphases alongside the five points of Calvinism – was a growing force, and that Calvinism was currently in a healthier state than at any time during the century. The arguments with which he supported this analysis reveal its limitations. His belief that the mood on both sides of the theological division was becoming more irenic than ever was not mistaken, but in his position it was easy to attach exaggerated significance to a theologically superficial acknowledgement of the

---

168 *Lectures* [first series], 170. He took this aloofness even further after the Downgrade Controversy, in which his sense of desertion by man was accompanied by an ecstatic experience of God alone – **no. 2053**, in Nicoll (ed.), *Sermons*, 459-60.

169 **No. 577**, in *Pulpit*, 10 (1864), 365-6, 372-3; **no. 1486**, in *The Messiah*, 349.

170 'When people ask me what I think of Spurgeon, I always ask which Spurgeon – the head or the heart – the Spurgeon of the Tabernacle or the Spurgeon of the Orphanage?' *BW*, 25 April 1890, 413.

force of the more attractive arguments of Calvinism. What he interpreted as a cause for optimism was only a limited and deceptive lull that merely eased a decline in the fortunes of Calvinism that Dale had accurately observed.[171] Spurgeon gave Calvinism a rallying point, but his achievement lay simply in keeping the retreat from degenerating into a rout: mounting a counter-attack was beyond his powers. Robertson Nicoll related that Spurgeon's sermons exerted an important conservative influence on Dr James Denney's theology, after his wife had persuaded him to read them,[172] but this was unusual: Spurgeon's theology was rarely taken seriously other than by people who were predisposed to be sympathetic to it.

Selectivity in appreciation was the norm even within Spurgeon's circle, resulting from failure to understand him in his many-sidedness rather than hostile reaction to any particular aspect. Many admirers concentrated on one of Spurgeon's major themes, and having isolated it went on to distort it further by treating it in a popular or conventional manner. Those who were inspired chiefly by Spurgeon's passion for evangelism found the 'simple gospel' evangelism of such as D.L. Moody especially attractive. To others 'the main characteristic of Mr. Spurgeon's influence lay in his spirituality',[173] and some of these were drawn by the 'higher experience' typified by the Keswick convention. Spurgeon's spirituality and evangelistic exploits amply qualified him for hero-status in both schools – Moody himself had idolized him, and Andrew Murray was among the prominent Keswick figures who greatly admired his preaching. While he welcomed some aspects of these movements and criticized others he did nothing to disavow the honorary status he was commonly accorded in each.[174]

---

[171] Spurgeon, 'The Present Position of Calvinism in England', *ST*, 10 (1874), 49-53; R.W. Dale, 'The Nonconformists', in *Christianity in Britain: an Outline of its Rise, Progress, and Present Condition* (London: Hodder & Stoughton, 1874), 136-7. By 1881 Spurgeon had given up contesting the point with Dale (*ST*, 17 (1881), 85).

[172] Cited in Fullerton, *Spurgeon*, 216.

[173] Douglas, *Prince of Preachers*, 145.

[174] *Spurgeon Autobiography*, II, 396-7; Andrew Murray, preface to *Christ's Relation to his People*. Spurgeon's comments on full-blown perfectionism were invariably caustic: 'Though they persuade themselves that their sins are dead, it is certain that their carnal security is vigorous enough, and highly probable that the rest of their sins are only keeping out of the way to let their pride have room to develop to ruinous proportions.' **No. 1114**, in *Sanctification*, 286 (page numbering not consecutive). However he gave a guarded welcome to the 1875 Brighton convention for the

Spurgeon's circle thus reflected the experiential and activist emphasis of the age; theology was at a discount. Although Spurgeon could write in 1881 that nearly all his former students were faithful to the Puritanic theology they had learnt at college,[175] few accorded it the importance their leader attached to it, and hardly any approached his mastery of it. Spurgeon's theological influence even on his own students was all the more superficial because he had little to contribute to two of the most prominent theological preoccupations of evangelicals at the close of the century: countering biblical criticism, the most urgent priority of conservative scholars, and dispensationalist eschatology, the favourite field of popular research. It did not help that Spurgeon made a thorough appreciation of his theology difficult: he left his best work in odd corners of his voluminous writings, its presentation spiritual rather than logical, the exposition biblical rather than systematic.

No one was able to assimilate all of Spurgeon. The difference between the two men who absorbed contrasting aspects of him affords some glimpse of what would have been required to do that. Archibald Brown, the son of a Metropolitan Tabernacle deacon and a product of the Pastors' College, was a close and loyal associate, one of the few to follow Spurgeon's resignations in the Downgrade Controversy, and the pronouncer of his graveside orations; his preaching and caring gifts, spiced with an unconventional personality, helped make his East London Tabernacle a church whose statistics in the denomination were second only to those of the Metropolitan Tabernacle.[176] William Robertson Nicoll, never involved in Spurgeon's network, was familiar with him first and chiefly through his sermons, of which his knowledge and admiration were equally exceptional: his keen mind and Scottish ministerial education made him rarely qualified to appreciate their theology.[177] What both these men – and indeed all who were seriously influenced by Spurgeon – had in common was a spiritual appreciation of his rich experience of God. 'This spirituality is so

promotion of Scripture holiness – *ST*, 11 (1875), 445. For the Moody style of evangelism see Iain Murray's discussion in *The Forgotten Spurgeon* (London: Banner of Truth, 1973[2]), 223-33.

175 *ST*, 17 (1881) 302.

176 G.H. Pike, *The Life and Work of Archibald Brown, Preacher and Philanthropist* (London: Passmore & Alabaster, 1892), passim. Spurgeon wrote of him, 'I am not able to take much credit for bringing you up, but I am about as proud as I dare to be.' *Spurgeon Autobiography*, II, 112; also pp. 506-7.

177 Darlow, *Robertson Nicoll*, 103-4, 402-3.

rare in a man of great powers that it is invariably the way to influence. It inspires a kind of awe.'[178]

It is not therefore surprising that Spurgeon never had a true successor. Archibald Brown might have come closest, but the succession became a Spurgeon family squabble and Brown's brief pastorate at the Metropolitan Tabernacle only came after much damage had been done and when he was in his sixties and in poor health. Spurgeon himself did not make things any easier: he believed that 'God can raise up a successor to each man, but the man himself is not to worry about that matter, or he may do harm.'[179] He made no provision for any aspect of his ministry beyond his death, with the slight exception of an expression of contentment that his publishers had sufficient supplies of (unrevised) sermon manuscripts to last for years after his death.[180] A temporary arrangement was made immediately after Spurgeon's death, under which his brother and assistant, J.A. Spurgeon, was pastor-in-charge, with A.T. Pierson, an American Presbyterian who had supplied the pulpit during Spurgeon's final months of absence in Mentone, as officiating minister. A division quickly arose between a faction supporting this arrangement and another advocating the appointment of Spurgeon's son Thomas. The latter won, but bad feeling became a lasting feature of a church that had known exceptional unity during a long pastorate. However neither side kept very close to Spurgeon's spirit, aims and theology; the true loyalists were a small rump led by his widow Susannah and secretary Joseph Harrald. The main fruit of their collaboration was the *Autobiography*. Harrald also continued revising Spurgeon's sermons for publication until his death in 1912.[181] Yet they were not able to provide any fresh forward impetus for Spurgeon's kind of Christianity: their work amounted to little more than a literary embalming of his memory.

The level of sales of Spurgeon's writings was maintained for a number of years after his death. Indeed, in 1900 it was believed that their circulation was actually greater than during his lifetime.[182] But after the First World War the picture was very different: comparatively few survived who had known Spurgeon, liberal theology was in the ascendant, and a biographer declared that 'his sermons are not

---

[178] Nicoll in Nicoll (ed.), *Sermons*, 9-10.

[179] *Spurgeon Autobiography*, II, 392.

[180] **No. 2230**, in *Christ' s Relation to his People*, 524.

[181] *From the Pulpit to the Palm-branch*, 60; A Harwood Field, *The Revd. Joseph William Harrald* (1918), 108-14; Murray, *Forgotten Spurgeon*, ch. 10.

[182] *Spurgeon Autobiography*, II, 432.

read today, 1933 is not 1855.'[183] Yet this was not to be the last word, for another generation later Helmut Thielicke wrote:

> It is evidence of the substance and also the excellence of form in Spurgeon's sermons that – removed from the situation in which they were originally preached, and also from the magnetism of Spurgeon's personality! – they lose very little in print. Not for a moment do they give the impression that we are reading merely historical testimonies to which we no longer have any immediate access and which come alive only in the act of reinterpretation. ... And I venture to ask: Of what other preacher of the nineteenth century could this be said? I would not know of a single one, even among the greatest.[184]

Since then the complete *New Park Street* and *Metropolitan Tabernacle Pulpits* have been republished in the United States, and a number of volumes in Britain. This reflects the resurgence of Calvinism in the second half of the twentieth century, but is also a tribute to Spurgeon's genius and spirituality. Furthermore, it was something he had anticipated: 'For my part, I am quite willing to be eaten of dogs for the next fifty years, but the more distant future shall vindicate me.'[185]

Clyde Binfield has suggested that Spurgeonism – Spurgeon's followers rather than the man himself – was the cause of the widening of the gap between the Baptist and Paedobaptist wings of Congregationalism during the twentieth century.[186] There is something in that, though analysis of 'Spurgeonism' shows that it cannot be divorced from Spurgeon himself. For one thing, the gap was already clearly visible in Spurgeon's lifetime, and Spurgeon reflected this when in the Downgrade Controversy he condemned trends in Congregational theology more comprehensively than Baptist ones. Spurgeon's most powerful legacy to his denomination was not his Calvinist theology but an attachment to evangelical values that operated directly as well as being mediated by his disciples. Though this could be called vague, it produced a measure of emotional,

---

183 F.C. Spurr, 'Charles Haddon Spurgeon 1834-92', in R.S. Forman (ed.), *Great Christians* (London: Ivor Nicholson & Watson, 1933), 523.

184 Helmut Thielicke, *Encounter with Spurgeon*, John W. Doberstein (tr.) (London: James Clarke & Co., 1964), 3.

185 1889 address in Spurgeon, *An All-round Ministry*, 368.

186 J.C.G. Binfield, 'Congregationalism's Two Sides of the Baptistry – A Paedobaptist View', *BQ* 26 (1975), 130.

though not intellectual, immunity to the attraction of liberalism. It was inspired by the example of his ministry more than by his theology, and perhaps most of all – more intensively though less broadly – by his personality and spirituality. Charles Williams, a leading Baptist minister of Spurgeon's generation, alluded to this warmly even while opposing him in the Downgrade Controversy: 'No other man that I know more completely wins the confidence and love of those who meet him face to face in familiar and frank converse. There is a charm about his manner, an absence of self-assertion in private talk, a noble simplicity and unreserve'.[187] The impact was greatest on his disciples, for whom the memory of Spurgeon was a dominant influence long after his death; it shines through the conclusion of W.Y. Fullerton's biography: 'To me he is master and friend. I have neither known nor heard of any other, in my time, so many-sided, so commanding, so simple, so humble, so selfless, so entirely Christ's man. Proudly I stand at the salute!'[188]

---

[187] *The National Baptist*, 9 February 1888, in Spurgeon's College, Spurgeon Scrapbooks.
[188] Fullerton, *Spurgeon*, 346.

CHAPTER 6

John Clifford (1836-1923)

Introduction

John Clifford was born on 16 October 1836 in Sawley, Derbyshire. Both his parents were manual workers in the lace industry, his father in factories and his mother mainly at home. After some meagre education in the different localities in the Trent valley to which they moved during his childhood, John began factory work alongside his father at about the age of ten. It was demanding work in difficult conditions: at the best of times he was fourteen hours away from home, and on occasions had to work through the night and on into the next day. It was in this setting that he espoused his father's Chartist politics, thus acquiring a radical outlook that he retained throughout a long life in a different milieu. Yet in other respects his mother's sympathetic personality marked him more than did his father's harsh one. Her working class credentials were unconventional, for she had three brothers in the General Baptist ministry; she it was who led the religious life of the home, bringing her son up in her own denomination rather than his father's Wesleyanism.[1]

It was in the Baptist church at Beeston in November 1850 that five or six months of misery and struggle to be freed from guilt were brought to an end by a sudden experience of spiritual emancipation: 'it seemed as though a light shot from the very face of Jesus Christ

[1] C.T. Bateman, *John Clifford, MA, BSc, LLB, DD, OM, Free Church Leader and Preacher* (London: National Council of the Evangelical Free Churches, 1904), 1-14; this is the only one among the three major biographies compiled with Clifford's personal help. Sir James Marchant had the advantage of access to Clifford's personal documents for his *Dr John Clifford* (London: Cassell & Co., 1924). M.R. Watts' 'John Clifford and Radical Nonconformity, 1836-1923' (unpublished DPhil dissertation, University of Oxford, 1966) is based on the most exhaustive study of the sources. Other biographical works add little to these.

into my heart.'[2] This typical evangelical conversion was soon followed by a desire to enter the ministry; and the local preaching he began when only fifteen years old, together with strenuous efforts to improve his education (aided by his Sunday School teacher and an ability to read while operating his machine), convinced his church that they should support his application to the General Baptist College at Leicester. He began three years of concentrated study there in September 1855, the last of which was in Nottingham following the college's move.

It had been Clifford's intention to continue his education at Glasgow University, but in September 1858 he accepted a unanimous invitation from a church at Praed Street, Paddington, whose pulpit he had supplied during that summer vacation. The church that was to be the setting for his life's ministry had an inglorious history spanning a single generation, into which it had contrived to cram both rise and decline: Clifford inherited a depleted congregation and a dilapidated building. He was determined not to let this decision curtail his education. His acceptance was conditional on being allowed time to study at London University. There he proceeded to string together an extraordinary series of degrees for a working minister: within eight years of arriving in London he could append to his name BA, BSc, MA, and LLB, gained with numerous honours and prizes. He refrained from taking outside engagements during this period, and his church showed no signs of neglect, growing strongly from the outset. Within three years the 500 capacity of Praed Street was proving awkward; the expansion plan eventually decided upon was acquisition of a new site in Westbourne Park in 1870, followed by the enlargement of the Praed Street chapel in 1872, and the opening of a chapel with a capacity of 1400 on the new site in 1877. Until the closure of Praed Street in 1908 the two churches were run jointly, often with an assistant mainly responsible for the older building. Clifford succeeded in communicating his own enthusiasm for work to his church. Amongst the most notable of the immense variety of activities were a mission in a neighbouring slum and the Westbourne Park Institute, which in its heyday held over 60 weekly classes.[3]

---

[2] Marchant, *Dr John Clifford,* 14. See also pp. 12-15; Bateman, *Clifford Leader,* 15-40.

[3] H.E. Bonsall, *The Dream of an Ideal City: Westbourne Park 1877-1977* (London: Westbourne Park Baptist Church, 1978), 239; Bateman (1904), 41-58, 73-7, 116-21; Bateman, *John Clifford, MA, BSc, LLB, DD* (London, 1902), 45; Clifford, 'The dedication', in *The Church of Christ; its Work, Character, and Message* (London: Yates & Alexander, 1877); Marchant, *Dr*

Robertson Nicoll remarked on Clifford's 'stupendous energy': Gladstone was the only contemporary he thought comparable in this respect.[4] This was the product not of an extraordinary constitution but of immense will-power and self-mastery. This is illustrated by a story Clifford himself told about a time early in his ministry when he was worried and depressed as he struggled to combine his pastorate and examination preparation; his wife told him that worry was wasteful, and he had never worried since.[5] His strength and self-discipline showed in the way he spent his working days: not only did he work long hours, but he concentrated on the matter in hand and made sure that odd minutes were well spent, whether in some useful activity or in the naps he was able to take at will.[6] Yet, impressive though his energy was, those who knew Clifford agreed that his most characteristic and powerful qualities were his remarkable humility and selflessness, highlighted by an engagingly childlike simplicity.[7] These combined with his gentleness, sincerity, and sensitivity[8] to make up the private face of Clifford's personality. An aspect of his character far more prominent in public was his combativity, which shines through his statement, 'Nothing thrills like a battle. Each man is a born fighter.'[9]

Clifford was aged seventy-nine when he retired from his ministry at Westbourne Park in 1915; enough of the old energy remained to keep him active during the eight remaining years of his life. His death took place quietly during a debate in the Baptist Union Council on 20 November 1923.[10]

John Clifford, 34, 63; Watts, 'Radical Nonconformity', 12. Further information on Clifford's career is contained in the section on his influence.

4 'Introduction', in Bateman, *Clifford Leader,* xi.

5 Isaac Foot, *John Clifford – The Bible and the Common People* (London: Brotherhood Movement, 1938), p. 7. Clifford married Rebecca Carter, a Berkshire doctor's daughter, in 1862; she died in 1919. Two daughters and three sons survived into adult life; the latter went into medicine, dentistry and electrical engineering; one of the former became a nurse, and the other acted as her father's secretary. Marchant, *Dr John Clifford,* 316-20. Bateman *Clifford Leader,* 315-16;

6 *Ibid.,* 318-20.

7 *Ibid.,* 'Introduction', p. xv; J.C. Carlile, 'John Clifford', in R.S. Forman (ed.), *Great Christians* (London: Ivor Nicholson & Watson, 1933), 140; Watts, 'Radical Nonconformity', 500.

8 Foot, *Bible and the Common People,* 8; Carlile, 'John Clifford', 134.

9 Clifford, *Daily Strength for Daily Living* (London: E. Marlborough & Co., 1885), 57.

10 Marchant, *Dr John Clifford,* 199, 284.

Theology

In 1891 Clifford told F.B. Meyer that for thirty years he had been preaching that life and service should be put before creed and system.[11] As he practised what he preached throughout his ministry it is necessary to explore the basic convictions that made up Clifford's worldview before examining the dogmatic structure in which he articulated these.

There is no more appropriate place to start the exploration than that at which he himself chose to begin the autobiographical fragments he wrote in the last year of his life:

> I began life in a factory and I have never forgotten the cruel impressions I received there of men and work. Ebenezer Elliott's prayer was on our lips daily – 'When wilt thou save the people?' Chartists were alive and eloquent. ... So I came to have sympathy with the working classes, of which I was one, ... and I have it still and I have never lost it after eighty years, and I feel it stronger today than ever.[12]

1848 came:

> I was only a lad of twelve, but I could not and did not escape the infection. It was revolutionary. The factory was full of it. Lads talked about the fall of kings as though they were ninepins, and expressed strange and wild hopes about the future. The Midland towns and the villages close to them were in a state of ferment, scarlet rhetoric abounded. ... What a world to live in![13]

Further encouraged by his father, a member of the Leicester Chartist Association, the young Clifford built his life's vision around radical socio-political aspirations.

Clifford's version of the Chartist programme always incorporated a passionate concern for the individual: 'The Chartist activities were all directed toward securing opportunity for the development of the individual and specially of the weakest and most wronged individual. They aimed at securing a fine and free life for each one. And that I wanted.'[14] A joint emphasis on the collective and the individual remained fundamental to Clifford throughout his life.

---

[11] Watts, 'Radical Nonconformity', 198.
[12] Marchant, *Dr John Clifford*, 1.
[13] *Ibid.*, 4.
[14] *Ibid.*, 6.

Nothing did more to develop the individualist side of his thought than Ralph Waldo Emerson's *Essays*, given him by his Sunday School teacher in 1854, and read repeatedly until the last week of his life. Clifford called its author 'the freshest and most suggestive thinker this century has seen'[15] and 'one of the most potent forces on shaping my life'.[16] Emerson's 'Trust thyself; every heart vibrates to that iron string'[17] was one of Clifford's favourite quotations; he once called it an echo of the great words of Christianity.[18] The *Essays* were the main vehicle for the influence of the Romantic Movement on him, inspiring Clifford with the same life-shaping vision of what he himself might be and do as Carlyle's *Sartor Resartor* gave to Baldwin Brown and Dale.[19] But it is significant that where there was a clash it was Emerson and not Clifford's social dream that yielded: whereas Emerson scornfully compared society to a joint-stock company in which the members agreed to surrender their liberty and culture in order the better to secure their bread, Clifford appropriated this illustration in a positive sense to present the Church as a joint-stock company in which the members provided for one another's needs.[20]

Optimism and a belief in progress were essential to Clifford's vision for personal and social development, imparting to it a triumphalist crusading drive. He claimed to have learnt this optimism from a saying of Emerson's he often quoted, 'Don't be a cynic and disconsolate preacher. Don't bewail and bemoan. Omit the negative propositions. Nerve us with incessant affirmatives.'[21] But Clifford's optimism was far broader and stronger than Emerson's, and ran completely counter to the latter's denial of real advance in society and morals.[22] Clifford defended Christianity as 'vindicated and illuminated optimism'[23] and questioned 'the right of the pessimist to be regarded as a Christian in the true and full sense of

---

15 Clifford, *Daily Strength*, 381.

16 Marchant, *Dr John Clifford*, 12. See also G.W. Byrt, *John Clifford: A Fighting Free Churchman* (London: Kingsgate Press, 1947), 22.

17 R.W. Emerson, *Essays* (London: James Fraser, 1841), 47.

18 Clifford, *The Ultimate Problems of Christianity* (London: Kingsgate Press, 1906), 292.

19 Clifford read this while at college, whereupon Carlyle's influence joined and reinforced that of Emerson (Watts, 8).

20 Emerson, *Essays*, 50; Clifford, *The Christian Conception of Society* (London: Alexander & Shepheard, 1891), 8.

21 Bonsall, *Dream of an Ideal City*, 105; compare Clifford, *Is Life Worth Living?* (London: E. Marlborough & Co., 1880), iv.

22 Emerson, *Essays*, 85.

23 Clifford, *The Pulpit and Human Life* (London: J. Clarke & Co., 1890), 16.

the word.'[24] His belief that 'the growth of goodness from age to age is undeniable'[25] could not even be threatened by the First World War, which he enclosed within vast brackets, as 'only a stupendous interlude ... a tragic episode, separable from the main currents of human experience'.[26]

Clifford's belief in individual and social development was not just concerned with the present life rather than eternity. Even within that there was a singular immediacy of focus: not for him distant utopias. 'The question of futurity rarely enters into my calculations. I am so engrossed in the "Everlasting now," and for everything that makes the present rich in moral energy, in broadening sympathy, and in increasing availableness to our fellows of any powers we may have.'[27]

In his dissertation on Clifford, M.R. Watts rightly stresses the importance of what he terms Clifford's 'this-worldliness', but in attributing it to the influence of Alexandre Vinet he fails to reach the heart of the matter. In his *Vital Christianity*, the work that impressed the young Clifford, Vinet did not marginalize judgement, heaven and hell as Clifford did;[28] he did not even spell out an eschatology in which God's triumph was to occur in the course of history rather than by bringing it to an end – an essential feature of Clifford's theology. Watts failed to recognize that although Christianity was integrated into Clifford's worldview from the earliest stages of its development, its basic structure – complete before he started his ministerial training – was assembled in a non-theological way.

This was only possible because Clifford had an unusually independent approach to Christianity; however superficially similar the result, tearing evangelical doctrine out of its native worldview and grafting it into a very different one necessitated major adjustments. It is characteristic of Clifford that the things that influenced him most profoundly occurred early in his life and were prominent in the reminiscing of his old age. A saying of his mother's that stands out among these shows how she encouraged that independence:

---

[24] Clifford, *God's Greater Britain* (London: James Clarke & Co., 1899), 170.

[25] Clifford, *Daily Strength*, 108.

[26] Quoted in Alan Wilkinson, *Dissent or Conform? War, Peace and the English Churches 1900-1945* (London: SCM, 1986), 67.

[27] Bateman *Clifford Leader*, 332.

[28] Translated by Robert Turnbull (1846). Vinet's declaration that family, country, arts, knowledge, industry, society are necessary conditions of man's existence, but that the end of man's being is in heaven (p. 180) was foreign to Clifford's way of thinking.

> When I was a lad of 13, she said to me, 'John, as you go out into the world, take care to carry the Gospels with you. Read them, and try to understand what Jesus means by what He says, and then, when you know what he wants you to do, go on to do it whatever it costs. Don't be afraid of what others say to you or about you, but be brave in following Him.' This message of my mother has been ever since a stimulus and an inspiration to me.[29]

His mother's seminal saying also indicated the method his independent approach would follow: by pointing him directly to the Jesus of the Gospels she helped him obtain swift access to his own version of New Testament Christianity without having to directly engage with the one that surrounded him during his formative years.[30]

Prior to the Downgrade Controversy the radicality involved in this approach was often cloaked by Clifford's reluctance to draw attention to his divergence from conventional evangelicalism, but it is clear enough in a sermon occasioned by Carlyle's death. This portrayed Carlyle as a New Testament Christian, suggesting that the content of Christianity was righteousness and power obtained by faith, self-renunciation and work, along with faith in and worship of Christ.[31]

> The chief thinker of this century ... has set out the facts and principles of the Eternal Religion of the Son of God – yea, moreover he has, with a voice of 'authority,' called men away from the Paganized, unreal, and corrupt accretions about Christianity to the simple essence, strong energy and practical aims of the

---

[29] Henry Cowell, *John Clifford as I knew Him* (London: Baptist Union Publications Department, 1936), 8-10. Another time he recounted this story he dated it to when he went to college (Marchant, *Dr John Clifford,* 93). In a letter he wrote that this instruction 'had more influence on me than all the theologians and bishops and ecclesiastics I have known' (Byrt, *Fighting Free Churchman,* 13)

[30] He did not avoid his evangelical forebears entirely, but derived from them primarily inspiration rather than theology, valuing their biography (to which he said he owed his greatest debt as a Christian) more than their writings. 'Denis Crane', *John Clifford: God's Soldier and the People's Tribune* (London: Edwin Dalton, 1908), 297-8; Clifford, 'Baptist Theology', *Contemporary Review,* 53 (1888), 510.

[31] Attributing the latter to Carlyle was a characteristically generous error. Clifford, *Typical Christian Leaders* (London: H. Marshall & Son, 1898), 183-9.

> Christianity of the New Testament and of Jesus Christ.[32]

A later comment on Greek and Scandinavian mythology revealed more starkly the gulf that separated his theology from that amid which he had grown up: 'Those old myths and tales throb with the deep religion of humanity, a religion more akin to the heart of Christianity than that which was dominating the Churches of England in the middle of our nineteenth century.'[33]

This analysis of Clifford's worldview is corroborated by his first annual church report, which shows that in 1859 individual and social development were already side by side the goal of his ministry, with the gospel seen as a means rather than as itself containing the end: 'We have a private object – the consolation and help of each other in the endeavour after spiritual manhood. We have a public object, the decrease of the evils of society, and the increase of individual and social good by the dissemination of the Gospel of Christ.'[34] It also accords with Michael Walker's view: 'The central motif in Clifford's theology was his prophetic vision of a brotherhood bound together in sacrificial service under the Christ of Calvary. It is perhaps inaccurate to describe it as theology. It was more the personal credo of a practical man caught up in the religious movements of his time.'[35] Walker has discerned well that Clifford's life project was not primarily theological in inspiration.

* * *

While at college Clifford went through a six month period of severe doubt provoked by the atmosphere prevalent among the students (a high proportion of his contemporaries became Unitarians or abandoned their studies for theological reasons) and his own reading of Theodore Parker and Orville Dewey. 'The only thing I could say for myself was that I believed in right; whether there was a God of Right or not I could scarcely say, so thoroughly was my confidence shaken.'[36] This experience did not substantially change the simple experiential faith that co-existed somewhat uneasily with

---

[32] *Ibid.*, 190.

[33] *Ibid.*, 263.

[34] Marchant, *Dr John Clifford*, 40.

[35] Michael J Walker, *Baptists at the Table: The Theology of the Lord's Supper amongst English Baptists in the Nineteenth Century* (Didcot: Baptist Historical Society, 1992), 193.

[36] Marchant, *Dr John Clifford*, 24. Other references are to Bateman *Clifford Leader*, 29-32; Clifford, *Pulpit and Human Life*, 19.

his Chartist- and Emerson-inspired worldview, but it obliged him to address the question of authority and work out a basis on which it could rest. He later described the formula he had found helpful, having in the meantime applied it successfully to other doubters. Its first component was 'external',[37] an ethical examination of history that concluded that the perfect founder of a religion that demonstrated moral progress must be supernatural; its second element was internal, faith leading to spiritual experience.[38]

In reality Clifford's treatment of the question of authority was more complex and confused; this is best illustrated by an 1886 publication on the subject, *How to Be Sure of the Voice of God*.[39] He began this with a rejection of all external authorities, including the Bible, as inadequate. Whenever he perceived rivalry between the internal and external Clifford never hesitated in siding with the former. His alternative to these he termed a scientific method of verification; this worked by observation and experiment, supplemented where necessary by reasoning and the consciousness of humanity.[40] This effectively gave back to external authority the place he had just denied it. He then maintained that the result of his method was acceptance of Christ, which led to 'an inward Sovereign and authoritative witness, in immediate contact with the soul, as the metals and gases of the laboratory are with the tests of the chemist'.[41] Conscious of the weakness of the results of an analysis of this witness (they really did not add up to more than conscience), he then swung back to the external realm by advocating scientific study of the Bible, especially of the New Testament, whose picture of Christ 'carries us to the fullness of the Godhead, the final, absolute test of the movements of the Divine Spirit in our age'.[42] He finally brought his wanderings to a close by returning to the place where he felt most secure, 'self-evident, necessary, and universal truths',[43] his description of presuppositions he believed verified 'by the

---

[37] I will follow Clifford's use of 'external' and 'internal' or 'inward', the keywords he used in his analysis of the nature of authority.

[38] Clifford, *Is Life Worth Living?*, 130-31.

[39] Unless otherwise specified, all references in this paragraph are to this pamphlet.

[40] Clifford believed that it was science that had made the demand of religious certainty one of the outstanding features of the period (*The Christian Certainties*, [London: Isbister & Co., 1893], 9). He had approved Huxley's demand for verification as early as 1873 (*The Living Christ*, [Nottingham: J. & J. Vice, 1873], 8).

[41] Clifford, *How to be Sure*, 13.

[42] *Ibid.*, 21.

[43] *Ibid.*, 23; compare p. 11.

individual and collective consciousness of humanity'.[44] This category included human freedom, the existence of God, and the independent existence of the moral law.[45] The impression conveyed by the pamphlet, and reinforced by other references to the subject of authority, is that nothing seemed able to support the entire structure, so as many factors as were to hand were made to support each other in the hope that between them the faith would somehow be propped up.

In all this Clifford was feeling his way toward a christological theory of authority, the key to which lay in proceeding from Jesus as found in the Bible to Jesus known in Christian experience: 'Our reliance is not on the book but on Him through it, having its beginning, indeed, in the outward facts of His wondrous life, but extending, deepening, and fortifying itself from day to day by communion with the living Saviour.'[46] This approach depended on the maintenance of an adequate biblical 'launching-pad'. Clifford thought it possible to know Christ personally through accepting the scriptural picture and interpretation of his life without necessarily believing in biblical inspiration,[47] but he also mapped out areas of the Bible unsullied by criticism, in which he could find the same sort of comforting confidence that Spurgeon had in the entire book. In 1888 he declared the Bible's 'total freedom from moral and religious error';[48] in 1892 he said criticism, concerning itself with form rather than substance, did not touch the saving ideas and central facts of the Bible: thus Christ and his work were unaffected, as were its 'spiritual communications' generally.[49] This position was easy to maintain during the lull that occurred in new challenges from New Testament criticism in the 1880s and 1890s, but was vulnerable to the new wave that broke at the beginning of the twentieth century. The Jesus of history/Christ of faith debate made Clifford retreat from the confidence of his presidential address to the Baptist Union in 1888 – 'our nineteenth century has nothing in all its wide sweep, more

---

[44] *Ibid.*, 11.

[45] Clifford, *Daily Strength*, 438-9.

[46] Clifford, *Christian Certainties*, 233.

[47] Clifford, 'Inspiration', in Frederick Atkin (ed.), *Biblical Difficulties and How to Meet Them* (London: S.W. Partridge & Co., 1891), 10-11.

[48] Clifford, *The Battle of the Sacred Books* (London: E. Marlborough & Co., 1888), 13.

[49] Clifford, *The Inspiration and Authority of the Bible* (London: J. Clarke & Co., 1892), 34, 40-41.

indestructible or more indubitable than the history of Jesus'[50] – to the view that Jesus' character and spirituality, though not his function, were immune to the current revision.[51] One new issue, the rediscovery of the eschatological emphasis of Jesus' teaching, threatened the very heart of Clifford's worldview and prompted sharp resistance instead of his usual orderly retreat.[52] His authority structure was beginning to look somewhat the worse for wear.

* * *

Clifford published little before the 1870s, so there is little evidence on which to judge his early theology. However there are some indications that in the 1860s he had only partially adapted a rather conventional theology to make it dovetail more neatly into his unconventional worldview. An 1868 pamphlet displays features that contrast markedly with his later writings, including the rhetorical question, 'Is not the worship of Almighty God the supreme purpose, the final cause of every provision the gospel contains?'[53] His later emphasis was consistently anthropocentric, culminating in an explicit subordination of acts of worship to reverence for man as man.[54] Whereas in 1868 he told his fellow General Baptists that 'our theological faith is, of course, within an ace of perfection itself'[55] five years later he was saying that theology must be progressive, as Christ was providing new material and there was a need for new expositions of the fundamental facts.[56]

Clifford continued to believe this to the end of his life, and it was therefore quite consistent of him to consider his theology provisional in nature. Even as an octogenarian he struck a new note, declaring in 1919 that the current 'movement for unity will slough the obsolete accretions of the past and unite the religions of the world'.[57] In the 1880s he shared the widespread feeling that a second Reformation was needed, led by a great theologian who could fashion a new

---

[50] Clifford, *Christian Certainties*, 126-7. That address assumed that the Christianity of Christ and that of the first forty years of the Church's history were one and the same (pp. 113-14).

[51] Clifford, *The Ultimate Problems of Christianity* (London: Kingsgate Press, 1906), 55-60.

[52] *Ibid.*, 214-6.

[53] Clifford, *The Non-attendance of Professed Christians at Public Worship* (Leicester: Winks & Son, 1868), 65.

[54] Clifford, *Ultimate Problems*, 327.

[55] Clifford, *Non-attendance*, 70.

[56] Clifford, *The Living Christ*, 22-3.

[57] Marchant, *Dr John Clifford*, 207.

systematic theology in response to the current dissatisfaction with the Protestant theology of the previous two centuries; and, being the optimist he was, he proclaimed in 1891 that this already existed subconsciously and was on the point of breaking through into consciousness.[58] The method to be followed was his own, an 'advance to the theology of the New Testament', outflanking all intervening theologies: 'We do not refute Augustine and Pelagius, Calvin and Arminius; we study them, thank them, and leave them.'[59] The result could be systematic because Clifford believed that theology was a science, interpreting facts and forces into a coherent system. 'Christianity is real, and the real is the reasonable and may be reasoned. A doctrine is self-condemned if it eludes the intelligence.'[60]

Clifford was not himself able to create the 'severely-reasoned, compact, and luminous system'[61] which he believed desirable and imminent. What theological activity he did engage in was largely derivative in nature and even then concentrated in a few areas, following the emphases of his worldview. Thus Clifford's concentration on the short-term future in this world meant that, in spite of searching thoroughly, Watts came up with few clues as to his views on future punishment, even though this was one of the most discussed doctrines of the period.[62]

His treatment of atonement may be taken as representative of his work on doctrines that did not fire his imagination. Misgivings about substitutional atonement are apparent in a confused discussion of 1880, the upshot of which was that Christ removed guilt but could not remove blame – and yet the guilty were still in reality guilty, though treated as though they were not.[63] By 1885 substitution was abandoned, leaving him in a limbo, unsatisfied with the subjective theory but unable to discover an objective theory that did not include some kind of illicit legal sleight of hand. He resorted to

---

[58] Clifford, *The Dawn of Manhood* (London: Christian Commonwealth, 1886), 81, 'The Great Forty Years', in *Baptist Handbook* (1889), 56, and *The Coming Theology* (London: James Clarke & Co., 1891), 16.
[59] *Ibid.*, 11, 15.
[60] Clifford, *Christian Certainties*, 29: there are echoes of Hegel here. 'The Great Forty Years', 55.
[61] Clifford, *Our Churches and Colleges and the Ministry of the Future* (Derby, 1892), 17.
[62] Watts, 'Radical Nonconformity', 438-9.
[63] Clifford, *Is Life Worth Living?*, 111.

making vague statements of the fact of atonement and minimising the importance of theories.[64]

Significant development in his theology was largely in areas that integrated best with his vision for social progress. In 1872 Clifford was already suggesting that '*Jesus Christ and Modern Social Life is the supreme question of the present hour*',[65] in an address that stated that God's plan was to build a regenerate society by first renewing individuals in Christ and then renewing structures through them.[66] This movement from the individual to the social level remained the basic framework of his social thought through all its later elaboration: he maintained to the end of his life the balance between the two he first established as a teenager.[67]

Although that remained unchanged, the growing popularity of social matters in the 1880s did affect Clifford in three ways: it encouraged him to address the subject with renewed vigour and frequency; it gave him a new theological language, that of the kingdom; and it led him away from laissez-faire and towards socialism. Westcott's social gospel was one influence: its language coloured Clifford's second presidential address to the Baptist Union in 1888, and Clifford acknowledged the debt three years later.[68] But Westcott was by no means the only person heralding a 'social gospel', and Clifford had espoused a theology of the kingdom at least a year before Westcott coined his expression.[69]

Clifford's version of this theology still had room for the old dissenting idea of the gathered church, alongside an increasingly

---

[64] Clifford, *Daily Strength*, 33, 'Baptist Theology', 523-4, and *The Religious Life of England during the Reign of Queen Victoria*, reprinted from *The Christian World*, n.d. but ?1887, 7-8, cited in John Briggs, *The English Baptists of the Nineteenth Century* (Didcot: Baptist Historical Society, 1994), 24. One such recurrent statement can be found in Clifford, *The Coming Theology*, 35, *Pulpit and Human Life*, 9, and *Ultimate Problems*, 245. Clifford published a sermon entitled *Theories of the Atonement* in 1894, immediately after reading a theory Gladstone had published, but there are no signs that his enthusiasm for it had any lasting impact.

[65] Clifford, *Jesus Christ and Modern Social Life* (London: E. Marlborough & Co., 1872), 3.

[66] *Ibid.*, 5, 31.

[67] It is typical that the two great causes of his last years were personal evangelism and the brotherhood movement (Marchant, *Dr John Clifford*, 206-16).

[68] Clifford, *The New City of God* (London: Alexander & Shepheard, 1888), 37; David Thompson, 'John Clifford's Social Gospel', *BQ*, 31 (1986), 207.

[69] Clifford, *Daily Strength*, 80. Westcott invented the phrase 'social gospel' in an 1886 sermon published in *Social Aspects of Christianity* (Thompson, 207).

rare emphasis on conversion. He held that the Christian idea of society was the only true one, and that 'the ideal Church is the Ideal of Society. ... Sociology is a branch of New Testament ecclesiology.'[70] This meant that though science, the state, art and literature had a part to play, the Church was the prime agent in ushering in the kingdom.[71] But the Church could only approach its own ideal and fulfil this role if all its members had 'a conscious relationship to Christ Himself';[72] and so far as he was concerned this began in the traditional and by now unfashionable way: 'The reality of religious conversion is as indisputable now as ever, and as evident as the ebb and flow of the tides. Men are radically and really changed, swept out of all their past passions and pursuits, and set with the entire force of a living consecration to a new and purer destiny.'[73] It is illuminating to pinpoint the reason why Clifford stood by conversion while the very word fell into disuse among most fellow liberals. He had adopted the same theology of universal fatherhood as they, according to which 'Sin may destroy the sense of our relation to God; but it cannot destroy the Father's relations to us.'[74] But whereas contemporaries tended to accentuate the universality of the latter part of the statement, dwelling on the relief it gave from the horrifying prospect of eternal punishment, Clifford concentrated on the first clause, because his programme was to build a new society rather than to open heaven to all comers.[75] Sin was therefore still, though in a different way than in traditional evangelical theology, a barrier whose removal by conversion was an urgent necessity.

But the Church's importance was only as a means: it was not an end. The two poles of Clifford's thought were the individual and society, with the Church a mere lever wielded by collected individuals in their efforts to yank society into the desired state. So he

---

[70] Clifford, *The Coming Theology*, 36. Clifford, *The Sevenfold Law of Ministerial Training* (London: E. Marlborough & Co., 1887), 23 shows how theocratic Clifford's vision could be.

[71] Clifford, *New City of God*, 36, and *Christian Conception of Society*, 8.

[72] Clifford, *The Renewal of Protestantism* (London: J. Clarke & Co., 1895), 13.

[73] Clifford, *Christian Certainties*, 211. In 1909 Clifford gave doubts over conversion as a major cause of Baptist decline (Watts, 446-7). Watts is unjustified in perceiving tension between this and Clifford's judging the Church by its contribution to a new society.

[74] Clifford, *Ultimate Problems*, 255.

[75] Universal brotherhood was more prominent than universal sonship in Clifford's exposition of the doctrine in *The Christ of the Coming Century* (Veal, Chifferiel & Co., 1899), 13-15.

maintained that Christ's goal was the kingdom, but that Christians had turned Church history into a struggle between that and their own primary focus on churches.[76] Near the end of his life Clifford reverted to other language in making a similar point: 'The Free Church conception is that Religion is first and always first, and the Church is nothing more than the means by which Christianity is expounded and enforced, and applied in the life of the individual and of the nation.'[77] That 'religion' could substitute for 'kingdom', giving his reductionist ecclesiology a still more alarming aspect, is a sign that Clifford never really had a theology of the kingdom – it was just a label for a social vision bathed in religiosity.

Even Clifford's optimism yielded its distinctive theological fruit in the prominence he accorded to the biblical word 'joy'. The motto he took for his first complete year of ministry was 'The joy of the Lord is your strength' (Nehemiah 8:10), and when he recalled that fact half a century later he added that this had been the keynote of his ministry.[78] He held that Christ's future predominance was guaranteed by the joy he gave his people; that Christ's two great commands were to repent and rejoice; and that the latter was unique to Christianity.[79]

The emphasis on progress in his worldview meant that Clifford was predisposed to welcome anything that could be construed as offering support to this, yet it was nearly thirty years after the publication of *The Origin of Species* before he began to exploit the possibilities presented by evolution. Far from ushering in evolutionary optimism, the lessons he drew from Darwin's work in a sermon marking the scientist's death, notably on the Pauline doctrine of the travail of creation and man's solidarity in sin through heredity, pointed backward toward orthodoxy.[80] But within five years Clifford's attitude to evolution had undergone a major transformation: in 1887 he declared that 'the certainty of progress

---

[76] Briggs, *English Baptists of the Nineteenth Century*, 23, citing Clifford, 'The Place of Baptists in the Evolution of the Churches', *Religious Systems of the World*, 1892 edition, 559.

[77] Clifford, *Anglicanism, Romanism and National Character* (1920), 15, quoted in Walker, *Baptists at the Table*, 185. He was contrasting the Free Churches favourably with Tractarianism on this point.

[78] Watts, 'Radical Nonconformity', 454.

[79] Clifford, *The Future of Christianity* (London: Yates & Alexander, 1876), 21-2.

[80] Clifford, *Evolution and Christianity* (London: Griffiths & Co., 1882), 5, 9-10.

towards a nobler stage and the prophecy of a divine and glorious consummation'[81] were among the most fruitful ideas of science.

He began to apply evolution everywhere, and ended up adopting the popular Darwinistic ideas of Henry Drummond, whose *The Ascent of Man* argued that the moral side of humanity and social and religious history were included in human evolution, and that 'the struggle for life' was really an altruistic 'struggle for the lives of others'; in Clifford's own words, 'Man ... is altruistic in the soul of him, in a world that is founded on altruism.'[82] The man who had once argued that Darwin's work only necessitated minor adjustments to the first two chapters of Genesis ended up rewriting the third chapter, replacing a sudden fall from perfection by a series of checks on an upward spiritual evolution in a world in which 'the entire scheme of things is one connected evolution, in which God manifests Himself in, and to, His creatures; that in the fullness of time He may reconcile all things to Himself.'[83]

This far-ranging vision did not disturb Clifford's lifelong focus on the here and now: to the end of his life he continued to see eschatological significance in current events. Thus the Anglo-American alliance was 'a sign of the advancement of the Kingdom of God upon the earth'.[84] His most extravagant hopes were in 1919, when he expressed the opinion that humanity had entered the final stage in its life, the international, and that the kingdom would really come.[85]

Three themes together made Clifford's theology *look* increasingly different from the old evangelicalism in the late 1880s, thereby making the image it conveyed more faithful to the underlying reality than had previously been the case. Evolutionism has already been discussed; the others, immanence and incarnation, were also much in vogue and fitted well with Clifford's emphasis on the present life. In 1890 Clifford linked the two, arguing that God's immanence in human life conferred on it a divinity that was revealed in the

---

[81] Clifford, *Sevenfold Law*, 24.

[82] Clifford, *Ultimate Problems*, 270, and *Typical Christian Leaders*, 248-52. I follow James Moore's useful distinction between Darwinism, Darwin's own thought and its implications, and Darwinisticism, which describes anything beyond this and notably evolutionary metaphysics (*The Post-Darwinian Controversies* (Cambridge: Cambridge University Press, 1979), 116). For the popularity of Drummond's views in the 1890s see Ian Sellers, *Nineteenth-Century Nonconformity* (London: Edward Arnold, 1977), 62.

[83] Clifford, *Ultimate Problems*, 216, also 268-9, and *Evolution and Christianity*, 14.

[84] Clifford, *God's Greater Britain*, 181.

[85] Watts, 'Radical Nonconformity', 475-6.

incarnation.[86] Much of his immanental language simply conveyed a sense of God's active involvement in the world – indeed, he spoke in this way of the immanence of Christ – even when it was mediated by man.[87] There was a similar concern behind his use of incarnation: it demonstrated that God was thoroughly and permanently involved in the great human struggle for deliverance from sin and death and for renewal in righteousness and holiness.[88] In contrast with his extreme evolutionism, Clifford had reasons to avoid the more radical forms of both immanence and incarnation. In the case of the former the impediment was his firm emphasis on the personal, which persisted in his late accounts of the doctrine of God. Although he showed solidarity with R.J. Campbell during the New Theology controversy, he did not hide his disagreement with his friend's pantheistic streak: 'Our peril is our loss of the great truth that whilst God is in all and through all, He is also over all, and above all.'[89] The chief restraint on incarnationalism was his pre-occupation with experience. Though he had acquired an incarnational theology of the relationship of all people to God in Christ, his deepest concern was that this should become conscious through the redemptive process. Thus his last major theological work maintained that 'the whole scheme of things is redemptive.'[90]

Clifford's radical worldview gave him an opportunity to break new ground in his theology, but instead of attempting original work in the main he contented himself with rather crude adaptation of old ideas until he came across new ones that better suited his outlook. To disappointment at the absence of an innovative spirit must be added dissatisfaction with detailed elements of his theological work. The idea of development was so ingrained in him that he could declare human beings to be 'of *infinite* and *ever increasing* worth and preciousness'[91] with no sense of incongruity. That illustrates the sloppiness of which he was capable, which was marked for a man of considerable ability and exemplary application – he read the Old

---

86 Clifford, *Pulpit and Human Life*, 8-9; compare p. 12.

87 Clifford, *God's Greater Britain*, 135-6, *Christian Conception of Society*, 3, and *Typical Christian Leaders*, viii.

88 Clifford, *The Coming Theology*, 34-5. Here Clifford followed Westcott in arguing that the incarnation was integral to God's plan, and not contingent on sin.

89 *Baptist Times*, 8 February 1907, quoted in Alan Sell, *Theology in Turmoil* (Grand Rapids: Baker Book House, 1986), 36. Compare Watts, 'Radical Nonconformity', 444-5. Clifford, *Ultimate Problems*, chapter 6 is the best expression of Clifford's late doctrine of God.

90 *Ultimate Problems*, 300.

91 *Ibid.*, 342; italics mine.

Testament in Hebrew regularly and followed German theological literature closely in the midst of a very full ministerial and political programme.[92] A less than admirable characteristic was his frequent use of that dubious theological shorthand which curtails theological argument by throwing in positively or negatively loaded words, as when he talked of giving up 'the *metaphysic* of universal sovereignty' in favour of 'the *fact* of universal fatherhood'.[93] He had just summarily dismissed sovereignty as a concept borrowed from Roman law and empire – having earlier in the same book discussed Jesus' prominent use of the phrase 'the kingdom of heaven'.[94]

But compensation for the lack of innovation and significance in Clifford's theology is provided by the presence of these qualities in his worldview. In many respects he was typical of his generation. His was a spirituality in the evangelical tradition, grounded in a conversion experience that gave liberation from guilt, and nourished in an intensely personal relationship with God; he shared its inspiring sense of mission in which a range of influences mediated by the Romantic Movement coalesced; he participated in the widespread ethical dissatisfaction with important aspects of received evangelical doctrine; and he was in the vanguard in terms of readiness to welcome and integrate into his thinking advances in history, science, and other academic disciplines. But in one important respect he stands out from his peers. This was not his interest in politics, or even the possession of a theology that did not obstruct such an interest – it is a myth that the evangelical theology of Wilberforce and Spencer Percival contained anything inherently antagonistic to full involvement in politics;[95] rather it was such an accentuation of working for this world as to marginalize completely working for eternity. This was not only something the old theology could not countenance, but went way beyond the general position of the political Nonconformity of such as Dale and Guinness Rogers. It as so radical that it did not really have an appropriate theological vehicle in England before the social gospel of the 1890s, although a preconditional anthropocentricity had been developing in various ways for some time. Clifford had this worldview before it became articulate, which helps account for the unusual phenomenon of his

---

[92] Bateman, *Clifford Leader*, 107-8.

[93] Clifford, *Ultimate Problems*, 246-7; italics mine.

[94] *Ibid.*, 195ff; compare p. 230.

[95] This needs to be exploded, as it still has plenty of life in it – it is a crucial assumption in the main thesis of Mark Johnson's *The Dissolution of Dissent, 1850-1918*, (New York: Garland, 1987).

flourishing more in the environment of the early twentieth century than in that of his prime.

Influence

On one occasion Clifford said that 'my highest ambition is to secure the application of the principles and forces of Christianity to the whole life of man',[96] adding that preaching seemed the best method of accomplishing this aim, but that personal intercourse was an important complement to it. He considered his own church the proper sphere for both these principal means of influence: he avoided outside engagements while pursuing his studies at London University, and when he accepted them later it was with a degree of reluctance and not without questioning the wisdom of so doing.[97] He was a modest man, and genuinely preferred investing himself in a worthwhile manner in his own church to spreading himself thinly around the country. The impact of his preaching and personal work at Praed Street and Westbourne Park is therefore a good place to start to assess Clifford's influence.

Clifford approached his ministry with a powerful sense of vocation, embodying his own teaching on the subject: 'Of all ideas that of God is first and chief; and next unto it, is that of a PERSONAL VOCATION. Feel that strongly, and heroism is born. Give it free scope, and obstacles are overcome. Make it the ruler of your thinking, and you become real, true, daring, invincible.'[98] This combined with his energy and joy to produce a characteristic style of preaching, whose main feature has been variously described as 'vehemence' by Watts and 'abandon' by Bateman.[99] 'His pulpit utterances are delivered with an overflowing eloquence which carries him with irresistible force from point to point until he reaches the climax of the peroration.'[100] Critics complained of excessive 'glow', and that the presentation made the difficult material even harder to cope with, but the enthusiasm and positiveness of his tone were appealing nonetheless.[101] His congregation appreciated listening to a preacher who could be inspirational while showing that he was alive to all the problems of the real world in which they lived.

[96] Bateman, *Clifford Leader*, 114.
[97] *Ibid.*, also 58.
[98] Clifford, *Daily Strength*, 234.
[99] Watts, 'Radical Nonconformity', 258; Bateman, *John Clifford*, 153.
[100] Bateman, *Clifford Leader*, 99.
[101] *Ibid.*; also 135.

But Watts has rightly pointed out that Clifford's printed sermons do not in general read well, his success as a preacher owing more to the impact of his personality than to his material.[102] As with most contemporaries in the nonconformist ministry, the bulk of his publications were sermons; and they were not particularly successful. Even his bestselling work *The Inspiration and Authority of the Bible* only sold five times as many copies as the size of his congregation when it went on the market in 1892, with sales in the following decade equivalent to three more congregations.[103] His journalistic output must not be omitted when evaluating the impact of his writings; it included some leading articles for *The Christian World* and *The Freeman* amongst contributions to other titles, but only his editing of *The General Baptist Magazine* from 1870 to 1884 constituted a major supplement to the influence he exerted though his regular preaching ministry.[104]

In Clifford's own estimation the best work he had done was personal work; and J.C. Carlile thought he had a genius for helping others, and that his greatest achievements were in character building. Among the foundations of this personal work were his unselfishness – Spurgeon said he never knew a more unselfish man – and the methodical approach to pastoral visitation he maintained throughout his ministry.[105] In spite of his working class background and his ability to capitalize on this in political contexts, the backbone of the church in which he exercised his ministry was made up of the well-to-do middle class, and the constituency he attracted was weighted towards the young and educated: students, 'intelligent' young businessmen, 'superior' artisans.[106] His most important personal work was concentrated among people in these categories.

The outstanding quality that Clifford brought to his work with young people, and especially young men, was a perennial youthfulness of his own. He had a freshness, simplicity, frankness and enthusiasm that put him on the same wavelength as them.[107] He catered for the demand for counselling by regularly setting aside his Friday evenings: in this way he helped twenty or thirty young people each week in the 1870s and 1880s, the biggest single problem

---

[102] Watts, 'Radical Nonconformity', 260.

[103] Bateman, *Clifford Leader,* 163, 174; 'Crane', *God's Soldier,* 174. My calculations are based on a conservative congregation figure of 1200.

[104] Bateman, *Clifford Leader,* 174; Byrt, *Fighting Free Churchman,* 101.

[105] Byrt, *Fighting Free Churchman,* 80; Carlile, 'John Clifford (1836-1923)', 140; Watts, 'Radical Nonconformity', 73.

[106] Bateman, *Clifford Leader,* 109.

[107] Byrt, *Fighting Free Churchman,* 82-3; Cowell, *Clifford as I Knew Him,* 7.

for whom was the doubt-laden atmosphere of the time.[108] 'Denis Crane' recalled that Clifford's reputation was widely discussed by the young well beyond the circles directly acquainted with him; it was through this oral network that he himself decided at one difficult moment that Clifford was the only preacher in London who could help him.[109] Isaac Foot's is an unexceptional case: drawn into Clifford's orbit as a sixteen-year-old fresh from west country Methodism, he at first found services at Westbourne Park rather dubious, but there was something appealing about the preacher that persuaded him to keep on coming:

> I was a young man with no claims upon him, living in a distant part of the country, not a member of his own denomination, and yet he went out of his way to give me encouragement at a time when his help meant a great deal to me. And what he did for me he did for so many others. Is it any wonder that to so many of us he became our hero, and that we rejoiced in his leadership?[110]

Some who came under Clifford's influence in this way became Baptist ministers or missionaries; they were known as 'Clifford's boys' and maintained links with him and one another. The most distinguished of the twenty-six members of this group active in 1902, J.H. Rushbrooke and Newton Marshall,[111] had similar effusive testimonies to what Clifford had done for them. Rushbrooke wrote that Clifford had led him through dangerous years of questioning, helping him by always being positive; that Clifford's idealism, devotion to Christ and crusading energy were qualities that aroused hero-worship; that Clifford had always responded to later requests; and that any usefulness in his ministry was due to Clifford's life-shaping influence.[112] Marshall testified that instead of being frightened of his crude heresies as others had been, Clifford had cheered him on and set him to work till a more vigorous moral life made a clearer religious insight possible; that he had continued to exercise

---

[108] Cowell, *Clifford as I Knew Him*, 22.
[109] 'Crane', *God's Soldier*, 83.
[110] Foot, *Bible and the Common People*, 8; also 5-6.
[111] Bateman, *John Clifford*, 63ff. Rushbrooke was president of the Baptist Union in 1926 and very influential in the Baptist World Alliance in the inter-war period; when Marshall died in 1914 aged only 41 Clifford wrote that 'more hopes gathered about him for the future of the Baptist and Free Churches than about any other minister of our time' (Watts, Radical Nonconformity, 458).
[112] Byrt, *Fighting Free Churchman*, 91-2; Bateman, *Clifford Leader*, 136.

pastoral guidance at a distance through genuine letter-writing; and that it was to Clifford he owed a purpose and mission in life.[113] There are no better indicators than these of the quality of Clifford's personal influence.

Clifford provided organisations for the young as a supplement to his more informal support. He gave basic training to prospective ministers in the Preachers' Institute that he started in 1879. On a larger scale was the Westbourne Park Institute, started in 1885 to cater for the broader educational and recreational interests of the young people Clifford drew into the church. Its rapid growth indicates just how strong that draw was: by 1892 its membership had reached 1500.[114] But that was its peak, and thereafter it followed the downward trend of church membership, where the maximum figure of 1406 had been attained in 1889. There was a steady decline in membership throughout the rest of Clifford's ministry, a trend that was not disturbed when he took a back seat as honorary pastor in 1915: it dropped below a thousand in 1903, to 753 in 1910, and to 596 in 1920 – which brought the church back to the level obtaining at Praed Street prior to the opening of Westbourne Park in 1877. Watts suggests that the church failed to attract the new working class population entering the area by the turn of the century as the middle class left.[115] This is a valid point, but other churches – including those of Dale and Spurgeon – had run into similar inner city problems earlier and yet maintained membership levels, in part through commuting: there must have been additional factors. It is significant that his church's growth was heavily dependent on his ministry's appeal to the mobile, educated and doubt-beset young church-going population of the capital, something difficult to maintain with advancing age in fast-changing times.[116] Although he had a record in this field that few could rival, it is likely that by his late fifties even Clifford was finding the going harder amid growing competition from new young nonconformist stars such as Silvester Horne and R.F. Horton.

---

[113] Bateman, *Clifford Leader,* 125-7; Byrt, *Fighting Free Churchman,* 89.

[114] Bateman, *Clifford Leader,* 129; Marchant, *Dr John Clifford,* 62; Watts, 'Radical Nonconformity', 252.

[115] Watts, 'Radical Nonconformity', 12, 264, 429-30, 478; Bonsall, *Dream of an Ideal City,* 241; Bateman, *Clifford Leader,* 71.

[116] The experience of Clifford's contemporary A.M. Fairbairn at Mansfield College is instructive: after being the great guru of its early students he was dismissed almost contemptuously by their successors less than twenty years later (W.T. Pennar-Davies, *Mansfield College, Its History, Aims and Achievements* (Oxford: [Mansfield College], 1947), 30-31).

* * *

However much Clifford preferred to concentrate on the ministry he exercised in his own church, he nonetheless had a parallel career at a much more public level, which must have been a vehicle of influence. It began quietly: in the 1860s and 1870s he was little known beyond General Baptist circles and the London Baptist Association. When that began in 1865 he did not even rate one of the fifteen places on the committee, though he did stand out enough for Spurgeon to ask him to write an article for *The Sword and the Trowel*.[117] At that time the idea of drawing comparisons between the two men, as was commonly done a quarter of a century later, would have seemed most incongruous in spite of the mere two years that separated them in age. The shape of Clifford's public career was nearly as unorthodox as that of Spurgeon. Whereas Baldwin Brown and Dale peaked conventionally in their forties and fifties, Spurgeon's remarkable fame was gained when he was still in his twenties, and Clifford's greatest public success did not come until his late sixties.

In 1882 *The Christian Globe* did a feature article on Clifford, regarding him as the leading Baptist theological liberal:[118] this was a significant pointer to the way in which Clifford was beginning to emerge on the national nonconformist scene in the 1880s. Few things could be more helpful in establishing liberal credentials than a dose of conservative opposition, and this was something that both Clifford's major publications of the decade managed to attract.[119] Helped by this exposure, Clifford managed to gain a place alongside Spurgeon and McLaren as one of the top three Baptist preachers, according to a March 1887 survey of readers of the inter-denominational *British Weekly*.[120] At the same time as this proof of national prominence among Nonconformists, he was awarded the highest honour his own denomination could bestow, the vice-presidency of the Baptist Union, with only eight militant

117 Clifford, 'The Utilization of Church-power', *ST*, 1 (1865), 307.

118 Watts, 'Radical Nonconformity', 72.

119 Several Christian newspapers criticized Clifford's sermon 'Abraham's mistake in the offering of Isaac' from *Daily Strength for Daily Living* (1885); Clifford responded in an appendix (see p. 425). Robertson Nicoll attacked *The Dawn of Manhood* (1886) in the first issue of *The British Weekly* (see Nicoll to Spurgeon, 29 August 1887, MS letter in Spurgeon's College).

120 Watts, 'Radical Nonconformity', 119.

conservatives voting against.[121] Other rewards began to flow in. An important measure of his new standing was the number of invitations he received to speak at the annual meetings of Nonconformist colleges: the Independent College at Bangor and Rawdon Baptist College opened his account in June 1887, and others followed over the next few years.[122]

The Downgrade Controversy suddenly broke in August 1887 and caught Clifford up along with the rest of the denomination. He did rather well out of it: their long-standing relationship helped ensure that he was exempted from Spurgeon's attacks, which gave him some opportunity to play a statesmanlike role. This culminated in his very successful presidential address at the climax of the controversy, which helped him emerge from the episode with a higher profile than any of the other defenders of the unity of the Baptist Union; this soon led to misleading but flattering 'Spurgeon versus Clifford' interpretations of the controversy. In 1889 it was reported that Clifford was accorded the sort of welcome by a Baptist Union assembly that had previously been reserved for Spurgeon.[123] In the ensuing years Clifford's public theological activity was at its height, its centrepiece being *The Inspiration and Authority of the Bible* (1892); so too was the conservative rearguard action against him in a succession of minor controversies, all of which helped raise his profile still further.[124] But it was a question of the moment making the man rather than vice versa. Clifford undoubtedly did some leading of opinion, but the late 1880s and early 1890s were the years in which matters at issue between conservatives and liberals came to a head, especially as they touched on biblical criticism and authority, and Clifford happened to be the Baptist best placed to incorporate and express a shift that was taking place very widely for deep-seated reasons.[125]

It looked as though the high-point of Clifford's public career had coincided with that of his church. He continued to be active through the 1890s, publishing and collecting further honours – President of the National Free Church Council in 1898, President of the Baptist

---

[121] On a previous occasion he had declined this honour (which automatically led to the presidency a year later). Bateman, *Clifford Leader,* 144; Watts, 'Radical Nonconformity', 120-21.

[122] Clifford, *Can We Be Sure of God*? (London: E. Marlborough & Co., 1887), 1, and *Sevenfold Law,* title page.

[123] 'An Old Baptist', *Freeman,* 18 October 1889.

[124] These are discussed in Watts, 'Radical Nonconformity', chapter 8.

[125] See Willis Glover, *Evangelical Nonconformists and Higher Criticism in the Nineteenth Century* (London: Independent Press, 1954), chapter 7.

Union for a second time in 1899.[126] But then came events that persuaded Charles Bateman to publish two biographies of Clifford in quick succession; that of 1902 called Clifford the Baptist equivalent of Dale, but by 1904 he had become the chief of Nonconformists.[127] Others showed even less restraint in the adulation they heaped upon him: comparisons were freely drawn between Clifford and Gladstone, and he was called 'the greatest Protestant since Cromwell'.[128] The reason for all this was that Clifford had thrown himself heart and soul into leading both the opposition to the 1902 Education Bill and the passive resistance movement that followed its enactment. This put him at the head of a movement that gave Nonconformists as high a political profile in the nation as any their ancestors had enjoyed since the time of Cromwell – hence the comparisons. The power and the mood were dissipated so dramatically that historians have been tempted to question their reality, but nothing can alter the fact that in the years leading up to the great election victory of 1906 Clifford was a national Liberal celebrity.

Watts is right to call this the peak of Clifford's career, but this was so politically more than religiously, and certainly not theologically. His most systematic theological work, *The Ultimate Problems of Christianity*, appeared in 1906, but this was an isolated event, and he admitted in the preface that these Angus lectures delivered at Regent's Park College would have been revised at leisure, never to see the light of day, had not publication soon after delivery been a condition of the lectureship.[129] Few would judge that the theological world would have been any poorer without them.

David Thompson has declared that Clifford 'had a theological as well as a social influence on a whole generation of Baptist ministers';[130] this is a somewhat bold conclusion, taking him beyond the scope of his discussion of Clifford's social gospel. J.C. Carlile's theological assessment seems safer: 'I do not think the Doctor added much to constructive theology. He was a profound reader and a keen student; his published works, though numerous, could hardly

---

[126] The circumstances of this unusual honour were special: the Vice-President (J.A. Spurgeon) died just before he was due to become President, and Clifford was brought in at short notice after Charles Williams had turned down an approach (Watts, 292-3).

[127] Bateman, *John Clifford*, 127, and *Clifford Leader*, xvii.

[128] Quoted in Foot, *Bible and the Common People*, 13; see also Watts, 'Radical Nonconformity', 334.

[129] Clifford, *Ultimate Problems*, xi.

[130] Thompson, 'Clifford's Social Gospel', 210.

be described as productions of first-class importance.'[131] If theology is to be defined narrowly Carlile is right, but that was not Clifford's way of looking at it. His theology was governed by social concerns; he would have seen the encomium that he had 'done more than any single man to fulfil Palmerston's famous prophecy that "in the long run English politics will follow the consciences of the Dissenters"'[132] as quite as complimentary to the theology that animated him as to the political activity that flowed from it. Clifford was a pioneer of this kind of theology among Baptists. He was also widely revered by a large proportion of more than one generation of Baptist ministers. Furthermore, the theology of many of these had more than a passing resemblance to Clifford's. But more than that is hard to prove: there was no self-consciously 'Cliffordian' theological movement. He even had a hard time finding his successor at Westbourne Park. He had been on the look-out for several years before he settled on S.W. Hughes, a Birmingham Baptist minister with good oratorical and political credentials, and someone who shared his own characteristic qualities, joyfulness and energy.[133]

One change in Baptist church practice possessing theological overtones can be ascribed with confidence to Clifford's influence. This was the introduction of the practice of dedicating infants, at first in the home, but in the church services from 1887.[134] Little more than a century later few Baptists would imagine that things had ever been done any other way. But assessing Clifford's overall influence is less easy. *The Daily Chronicle*'s obituary writer pointed to it as well as anyone: 'There was no man of his time who did so much to infuse zeal into the cause of Nonconformity, and none, perhaps, outside Parliament who did so much for the cause of Liberalism.'[135] Here is a generous tribute to his political influence, associated with a comment that points to the heart of his religious influence, in which his personality played a larger part than his ideas.

---

[131] Carlile, 'John Clifford (1836-1923)', 138.

[132] *British Congregationalist,* quoted in Bonsall, *Dream of an Ideal City,* 18.

[133] Byrt, *Fighting Free Churchman,* 169; Watts, 'Radical Nonconformity', 468.

[134] Horton Davies, *Worship and Theology in England. Vol. 4: From Newman to Martineau, 1850-1900* (Princeton: Princeton University Press, 1962), 238; 'Crane', *God's Soldier,* 77.

[135] Quoted in Bonsall, *Dream of an Ideal City,* 112.

CHAPTER 7

The Downgrade Controversy (1887-88)

Introduction

The Downgrade Controversy of 1887-88, the biggest conservative rearguard action against the growth of liberal theology in Victorian England, took its name from the titles of two articles that appeared in *The Sword and the Trowel* in March and April 1887. Their principal theme was the 'down grade' of eighteenth century dissenting theology, but when Spurgeon borrowed the title for the article in the August edition that launched the controversy his intention was to protest directly and forcibly against contemporary theological trends.

The author of the original unsigned articles was Robert Shindler, yet in his doctoral dissertation on Spurgeon H.F. Colquitt not only assumes that Spurgeon wrote them, but that these were the articles that launched the controversy; and having started his chapter in this fashion he never looked back.[1] Not all historical treatments of the Downgrade Controversy have been quite as feeble, but the overall quality is disappointing, with the entire controversy too often misconceived as an attempt by Spurgeon to preserve the Baptist Union from the widespread contemporary movement towards a more liberal theology. That the Downgrade Controversy arose from Spurgeon's concern about this trend is not in dispute, but it will be argued here that his intention was protest and not reform, a distinction that places the whole controversy in a new light.

Several factors account for the picture of disarray presented by the historiography of the controversy. The basic problem has been its complexity and confusion: participants were quite as lost at the time as historians have been since. This has been compounded by the

---

[1] H.F. Colquitt, 'The Soteriology of Charles Haddon Spurgeon Revealed in his Sermons and Controversial Writings' (unpublished DPhil. dissertation, University of Edinburgh, 1951), 114-28.

reticence of the people who knew most. Spurgeon's widow Susannah was 'led to allow the shadow of the past to rest upon it in a measure, and to conceal, under a generous silence, most of the documentary and other evidence that could be produced'.[2] It was natural that those close to Spurgeon should be reticent about this unhappy period in his career, but Baptist leaders were equally sensitive, for the slightest indiscretion might jeopardize the slow healing of the wounds the Baptist Union had itself suffered.[3] One consequence is that knowledge of some episodes died with their participants, leaving gaps in the documentation of the controversy. This irremediable difficulty has been compounded by inadequate use, neglect or ignorance of the most important archival sources, held by Spurgeon's College and the Baptist Union. Some of the most important evidence held by the Baptist Union did not come to light until the early 1990s.[4] Working on a complex subject with inadequate materials, the majority of committed commentators have exacerbated their difficulties by allowing their bias to become a handicap. Finally, there have been subjects, especially the correspondence between Spurgeon and Samuel Harris Booth, the secretary of the Baptist Union, on which misunderstandings and mistakes have developed by transfer from one writer to another, culminating in completely mythological interpretations.

Because of its complexity and the confusion of its historiography the Downgrade Controversy requires a more extensive treatment than it is possible to offer here, even when interesting sub-plots are set on one side in order to concentrate on the main events. In consequence I neglect somewhat Spurgeon's opponents, having subjected them to more detailed examination elsewhere,[5] and

[2] Susannah Spurgeon and Joseph Harrald *(eds.)*, *C.H. Spurgeon Autobiography*, revised edition, 2 vols. (London: Banner of Truth, 1962, 1973), II, 469.

[3] E.A. Payne, *The Baptist Union, A Short History* (London: Carey Kingsgate, 1959), 127. In 'The Down Grade Controversy: A Postscript', *BQ*, 28 (1979), 146, Payne states that strong feelings on the Downgrade Controversy still persisted in 1951, and as late as the 1980s his main study, 'The Down Grade Controversy' (1955), remained a typescript in Baptist Church House to which access was restricted. It is now in the Angus Library at Regent's Park College (Lewis Drummond, *Spurgeon Prince of Preachers* [Grand Rapids: Kregel Publications, 1992], 673).

[4] I presented the most significant new information and its implications for the understanding of the controversy in 'The Down Grade Controversy: New Evidence', *BQ* 35 (1994), 262-78.

[5] *Ibid.*, and also Mark Hopkins, 'Spurgeon's Opponents in the Down-

reserve most of my attention for Spurgeon and his supporters. The first major theme of this historical section is a reassessment of Spurgeon's aims, showing that his intention was to protest against burgeoning liberal theology and not to reform the Baptist Union; the second is the highlighting of another key factor that has been inadequately appreciated, the gap that existed between Spurgeon and his supporters, one that involved differences of goal as well as failures in communication.

* * *

The years preceding the controversy are as important as the period of the controversy itself for understanding Spurgeon's mind. For many years Spurgeon had not been too troubled by the existence in his own denomination of people holding views he considered unacceptable because he had been able to dismiss them as a tiny fringe. When his attention was drawn to a Baptist minister of suspect theology in 1877 Spurgeon replied that 'there are not above a dozen loose men among us to my knowledge, but an attack upon one might make a martyr of a party, and cause a world of trouble to the many faithful ones among us'.[6] His character was not of the compulsively combative type, and he realized how counter–productive heresy hunting had become in an age in which such ideas as freedom and tolerance had attained unprecedented ideological supremacy.

The great shift in his attitude came not in 1887 but in 1883. Intriguingly, it was prompted by incidents at the Baptist Union's autumn meetings at Leicester, where the Congregationalists had run into difficulties six years earlier.[7] Afterwards Spurgeon, who had not been present, tried to reassure Archibald Brown, using the same argument he had employed in 1877, only to be told, 'I wish I could believe that the spirit of the age has only tainted about a dozen men amongst us. If so they are able to make a wonderful noise in the way of applause at every "broad" statement.'[8] This was not just a *coup de grâce* for Spurgeon's argument: the crisis thus precipitated nearly

grade Controversy', *BQ*, 32 (1988), 274-94.

[6] Quoted in Iain Murray, *The Forgotten Spurgeon* (London: Banner of Truth, 1973[2]), 185.

[7] The most complete published account of this crisis is in Patricia Stallings Kruppa, *Charles Haddon Spurgeon: A Preacher's Progress* (New York: Garland, 1982), 421-3.

[8] Brown to Spurgeon, 16 October 1883, MS letter at Spurgeon's College.

resulted in Spurgeon resigning from the Baptist Union. The advice of friends and the persuasive powers of the president and secretary of the Union kept him from taking that step, but he never attended Union meetings again and its leaders stepped very carefully for four years, trying to avoid anything that might lead Spurgeon to change his mind and resign after all.[9]

The only public intimation of these dramatic events was a note in *The Sword and the Trowel.* This 'public protest' revealed his attitude in the years immediately preceding the Downgrade Controversy:

> In all Christian associations there should be sufficient opportunities for differences of opinion upon matters not essential; and I trust that I should be the last to complain of the unrestrained use of this liberty, but when truths which are viewed as vital by a large portion of any society are trifled with by others, there is so far an end of fellowship, or else of conscientiousness. I, for one, have no Christian fellowship with those who reject the Gospel of our Lord Jesus Christ, neither will I pretend to have any.[10]

He was concerned only with denial of what he considered to be fundamental truths, and he planned to demonstrate his concern in two ways: by protesting against the beliefs in question, and by withdrawing from fellowship with those who held them.

However these two were not equal partners. Spurgeon stood firmly by his decision to decline fellowship where unacceptable views were openly tolerated – he never returned to Baptist Union meetings after 1883. But he was more reluctant and hesitant when it came to the other aspect of what he conceived to be his duty, namely protesting, as a letter he wrote to his brother-in-law in November 1883 indicates:

> I have fired the first shot, and the battle is beginning – see 'Xtn World' of this day. We shall see who loves the truth and who is a traitor ... I think I must personally withdraw from the Baptist Union. I do not care to fight, but can be rid of the responsibility by retiring.[11]

---

[9] Hopkins, 'Spurgeon's Opponents', 275; part of the 1883 correspondence survives at Spurgeon's College.
[10] *ST*, 19 (1883), 607.
[11] Spurgeon to W. Jackson, 8 November 1883, quoted in Payne, 'Down

Paradoxically Spurgeon was proposing to fight and run at the same time, a policy he acted upon faithfully in the Downgrade Controversy itself. Protest was a duty, a necessary preliminary that would allow him to justify withdrawal, the more congenial part of the package. Then his responsibility would be ended and with it the pressure from his conscience and other people to maintain the protest. The longing to escape burdensome responsibility was a theme that recurred in Spurgeon's writings during these years:

> For what may be said or done at the debating meetings we have no sort of responsibility, for we have ceased to attend them.[12]

> Our day-dreams are over: we shall neither convert the world to righteousness, nor the church to orthodoxy. We refuse to bear responsibilities which do not belong to us, for our real responsibilities are more than enough. Certain wise brethren are hot to reform their denomination. They ride out gallantly. Success be to the champions! They are generally wiser when they ride home again. I confess great admiration for my Quixotic brethren, but I wish they had more to show for their valour. I fear that both church and world are beyond us; we must be content with smaller spheres. Even our own denomination must go its own way. We are only responsible so far as our power goes, and it will be wise to use that power for some object well within reach. For the rest, let us not worry and weary about things beyond our line.[13]

This last quotation is from an address given at a time when Spurgeon was in great pain. It was at such times that his pessimism and inclination to retreat stood out most starkly, although his analysis of the theological scene was never bright after 1883. In contrast his protests, including the article that launched the Downgrade Controversy, were issued during intervals of good health, though indications of optimism as to their effectiveness were even then few and slight. Therefore suggestions that his strong language was the product of a mind unbalanced by pain were misguided.

Beyond these protests Spurgeon did not have any plan of action to suggest to his supporters. Naturally an optimist, at times he

---

Grade Controversy: Postscript', 148-9.

[12] *ST*, 21 (1885), 595. The meetings in question were those of the Baptist Union.

[13] *ST*, 22 (1886), 255.

hoped that the situation would improve, but never, before, during, or after the controversy, did he believe it possible to win a fight against the liberal trend: on that score he displayed a consistent pessimism that events proved to be justified. He had no enthusiasm for reform or schism as ways of establishing a satisfactory basis of fellowship. He was sceptical about the effectiveness of creeds, the obvious tool of would-be reformers, knowing that people found ways to get round them;[14] and as for schism,

> Divisions we have had enough of already, and more would be calamitous in the highest degree, and would, in the long run, bring no relief; but plain, honest, outspoken witness-bearing is a more Scriptural line of action, and if it be coupled with a decided withdrawal from fellowship with error, it may in due time work for good.[15]

There are no grounds for believing that any of these attitudes of the mid-1880s had changed when Spurgeon's first Downgrade article appeared in the August 1887 number of *The Sword and the Trowel*. This was simply another in the series of protests he had issued since 1883, very similar in tone and content to previous ones, the difference being that this time attempts to prevent the development of a major controversy failed. By way of explanation for the series of articles, Spurgeon complained to his friend James Douglas about Christians in other denominations whose letters to him showed they regarded him as the custodian of truth among Baptists. '"I am not that," he said; "it is too bad to hold me responsible for all that may occur."'[16] 'Responsibility' is still the key word. He did not like it, but correspondents jogged his conscience, which also told him it was his responsibility to protest against current theological trends in Nonconformity. Such was the background to the Downgrade Controversy. In the light of it the general assumption that Spurgeon was fighting for control over the basis of faith of the Baptist Union immediately becomes suspect: that would have required a thorough change not only in his programme but in the outlook that inspired it.

---

[14] *ST*, 19 (1883), 607.
[15] *ST*, 22 (1886), 108.
[16] Douglas, *The Prince of Preachers: a Sketch; a Portraiture; and a Tribute* (London: Morgan & Scott, [1893]), 163.

History

The August article was followed by three more in successive months; these were later reprinted and circulated to all Baptist ministers.[17] Their main preoccupation was with doctrinal decay, the usual theme of his occasional protests. Three particularly important points of doctrinal difference were mentioned in all the articles: 'We cannot hold the inspiration of the Word, and yet reject it; we cannot believe in the atonement and deny it; ... we cannot recognize the punishment of the impenitent and yet indulge the "larger hope."'[18] There was also a subsidiary theme, that departure from gospel truth was leading to a decline in spirituality, shown in the decline of prayer meetings and an increase in theatre-going.[19]

Convinced that nonconformist theology and life were entering on a very dangerous phase, and seeing little being done about this, Spurgeon's purpose in writing was to warn people by focusing attention on the problem:

> A little plain-speaking would do a world of good just now. These gentlemen desire to be let alone. They want no noise raised. Of course thieves hate watch-dogs, and love darkness. It is time that somebody should spring his rattle, and call attention to the way in which God is being robbed of his glory, and man of his hope.[20]

This message was directed at evangelical Nonconformity in general, but especially at Congregationalists. He indicated that 'the Baptists are by no means so far gone as the Independents'[21] and later went so far as to say he 'did not at first aim at the Baptist body, for we

---

[17] Spurgeon, in *Baptist*, 23 December 1887 (in Spurgeon's College, Spurgeon Scrapbooks (hereafter cited as SS). After I worked with them, the bound scrapbooks were taken apart and their contents transferred to ring binders, in the process invalidating my volume and page references. The order of newspaper cuttings seems to have been preserved, and these can be located by date without great difficulty; but unfortunately other material, including valuable manuscript letters and notes, most of which was loose but inserted at appropriate pages, has been completely disassociated from the cuttings and may not be easy to locate.

[18] *ST*, 23 (September 1887), 465; see also (August), 397, (October), 513, and (November), 558-9.

[19] *ST*, 23 (August 1887), 397-8, (September), 461, and (October), 511, 514.

[20] *ST*, 23 (August 1887), 400; see also (September), 465.

[21] *ST*, 23 (September 1887), 464.

thought most hopefully of it'.[22]

The very first paragraph gives a fair sample of the tone he maintained throughout:

> Read those newspapers that represent the Broad School of Dissent, and ask yourself, How much farther could they go? What doctrine remains to be abandoned? What other truth to be the object of contempt? A new religion has been initiated, which is no more Christianity than chalk is cheese; and this religion, being destitute of moral honesty, palms itself off as the old faith with slight improvements, and on this plea usurps pulpits which were erected for gospel preaching.[23]

The language in which Spurgeon sought to convey his warning was unrestrained and devoid of theological precision and argument; it reflected his sense of outrage and determination to overcome the silence that had engulfed his earlier protests.

Baptist leaders in particular were not easily drawn into crossing swords with Spurgeon. It takes two sides to make a controversy, and since they had nothing to gain and potentially much to lose from engaging in one – Spurgeon's resignation from the Union was an immediate threat, and its possible repercussions did not bear thinking about – they remained silent, hoping that peace and quiet would eventually return as on previous occasions. Their hopes were dashed because of a single paragraph in the middle of Spurgeon's article in which the current state of Dissent was compared unfavourably with that of the Church of England.[24] Virtually all the limited press debate of the first Downgrade article was accounted for by various Anglican newspapers seizing on such useful ammunition for their ongoing rivalry with Nonconformity. Leading Nonconformists were stung into replying, uniformly accusing Spurgeon of being too gloomy – not difficult in view of Spurgeon's imprecise and immoderate language. Spurgeon found himself prime witness to one side and principal traitor to the other in a dispute that did not interest him. Instead of hearing echoes of his own concern and discussion of what could be done, he found himself drawn into an

---

[22] *ST*, 24 (May 1888), 249. Most historians of the controversy have realised this inadequately, if at all.

[23] *ST*, 23 (August 1887), 397. *The Christian World* was the main newspaper he had in mind

[24] *ST*, 23 (August 1887), 398-9. The points in this paragraph are developed and documented in Hopkins, 'Spurgeon's Opponents', 275-81.

unfruitful debate over how many Nonconformists had fallen away from evangelical faith, the new subject chosen by the champions of Nonconformity. In September and October more and more Nonconformists closed ranks against Spurgeon as exploitation of his articles, especially by Anglicans, made itself increasingly felt in the country. Meanwhile Spurgeon found some strange allies in his unenviable position, when liberal Nonconformists started to add their voices to the debate: at complete cross-purposes with their denominational leadership, they concurred with Spurgeon that the theological differences between them were as radical as he made out.

The later Downgrade articles were shaped by the developing debate – Spurgeon made much of the liberal manifesto that appeared in *The Christian World* – but overall they followed the pattern of earlier protests,[25] notably in their dearth of constructive proposals. In the first of the series he suggested an informal alliance of people who could protest, if little else,[26] but in the following ones he had less rather than more to propose:

> Let us, as many as are of one mind, wait upon the Lord to know what Israel ought to do... What each man's place and course should be the Lord will make clear unto him.[27]

> What action is to be taken we leave to those who can see more plainly than we do what Israel ought to do.[28]

> During the past month many have put to us the anxious question, *'What shall we do?'* To these we have had no answer to give except that each one must act for himself after seeking direction of the Lord.[29]

It is difficult to see how it could have been otherwise. He rejected one course of action proposed to him, naming individuals and producing evidence against them,[30] and he still lacked enthusiasm

[25] *CW*, 1 September 1887, (in SS); *ST*, 23 (September 1887), 513.
[26] *ST*, 23 (August 1887), 400.
[27] *ST*, 23 (September 1887), 465.
[28] *ST*, 23 (October 1887), 515.
[29] *ST*, 23 (November 1887), 560.
[30] This was not just because of his abhorrence for personal quarrels (*ST*, 23 (October 1887), 513), but because he was quite as aware as many of those who pressed him to name names of the disastrous consequences that would accrue to him through creating martyrs.

for credal reform and schism, the two strategies that might have led to a satisfactory basis of communion:

> The Union, as at present constituted, has no disciplinary power, for it has no doctrinal basis whatever, and we see no reason why every form of belief and misbelief should not be comprehended in it so long as immersion only is acknowledged as baptism. There is no use in blaming the Union for harbouring errors of the extremest kind, for, so far as we can see, it is powerless to help itself, if it even wished to do so. Those who originally founded it made it 'without form and void,' and so it must remain. At least, we do not see any likelihood of a change...
>
> *Why not start a new Denomination?* This is not a question for which we have any liking. There are denominations enough. If there were a new denomination formed the thieves and robbers who have entered other 'gardens walled round' would climb into this also, and so nothing would be gained.[31]

Having blocked off these avenues, Spurgeon was left with withdrawal of fellowship, the usual concomitant of his protests. Intimations that he refused to have fellowship with those who had adopted the views he was denouncing were the main feature of the conclusions of each of the four articles in *The Sword and the Trowel*, with an increasing emphasis that culminated in the announcement of his resignation from the Baptist Union in the November edition.[32]

Spurgeon had never been far from taking this step since 1883, and was finally led to take it by the reaction to his Downgrade protest. What took him aback most was the widespread refusal of the defenders of Nonconformity to acknowledge that there was a significant theological problem:

> Our warning was intended to call attention to an evil which we thought was apparent to all: we never dreamed that 'the previous question' would be raised, and that a company of esteemed friends would rush in between the combatants, and declare that there was

---

[31] *ST*, 23 (November 1887), 560; emphasis Spurgeon's.

[32] *ST*, 23 (August 1887), 400, (September), 465, (October), 515, and (November), 560. The announcement in *The Sword and the Trowel* was quoted in the newspapers on 27 October, prior to Spurgeon's official letter of resignation of 29 October.

> no cause for war, but that our motto might continue to be 'Peace, peace!'[33]

The last straw for Spurgeon was what happened at the Baptist Union's autumn assembly at Sheffield early in October 1887. In a published letter Spurgeon referred to three matters in and around these meetings that influenced his decision to resign: a report in *The Freeman* that apparently treated the Downgrade Controversy as a joke; uncomplimentary allusions to his protest by E.G. Gange, one of his leading former students; and above all the general silence of the assembly on the subject of his protest. The policy of silence that had been responsible for the slow start to the debate in August became obvious for the first time at Sheffield, prompting the following comment from one journalist:

> Now, it was curious to observe that, while the recent utterances of the greatest of living Baptist leaders were evidently present to all minds, these being the conversational staple at every interval, there was a tacit understanding that Mr. Spurgeon should be ignored throughout the occasion. We confess that though this excessive caution may easily be understandable on certain grounds, it is difficult either to admire it on the one hand, or to believe in its wisdom on the other... Now, in various quarters Mr. Spurgeon's attitude is regarded as a most serious sign of the times. But we think that we mark a still more serious sign of the times when we see the leaders of a great evangelical denomination vainly emulating the poor ostrich. A great difficulty is upon them, and they evade it by burying their intellects in any little bush that happens to be at hand.[34]

Spurgeon's own conclusion was that 'the whole together made it clear to me that no one thought my appeals worthy of notice'.[35]

---

[33] *ST*, 23 (October 1887), 509.

[34] *Christian Commonwealth*, 13 October 1887 (in SS). Samuel Harris Booth, the Secretary of the Baptist Union, told T.R. Stevenson, a Council member, that he had kept Downgrade off the agenda in Sheffield in the hope that Spurgeon would calm down – and was annoyed with him for publishing this comment in the *Derby Daily Telegraph*. Stevenson to Booth, 18 November 1887, MS letter in BU Downgrade archive, held in the Angus Library at Regent's Park College, Oxford.

[35] In *The Baptist*, 23 December 1887 (in SS); the reference to the Downgrade Controversy as a joke was in *The Freeman*, 7 October 1887 (in SS).

Spurgeon's resignation from the Baptist Union was a turning point in the controversy. He had put all his energy into an impassioned and sustained protest; its failure had allowed him to take this step to complete his withdrawal from fellowship with what he considered vital error, thereby gaining for himself some relief from his burdensome sense of responsibility. He concluded the article in which he announced his resignation by describing the independency into which he was retreating, its loneliness relieved by a catholic vision:

> In the isolation of independency, tempered by the love of the Spirit which binds us to all the faithful in Christ Jesus, we think the lovers of the gospel will for the present find their immediate safety. Oh, that the day would come when, in a larger communion than any sect can offer, all those who are one in Christ may be able to blend in manifest unity! This can only come by the way of growing spiritual life, clearer light upon the one eternal truth, and a closer cleaving in all things to him who is the Head, even Christ Jesus.'[36]

The article he wrote for the December issue of *The Sword and the Trowel* was of a different character to the four Downgrade articles: instead of protest and debate he addressed the need for revival in response to scepticism.[37] On 7 November Spurgeon left for his customary two months' winter break at Mentone on the Franco-Italian border in the comforting conviction that the Downgrade Controversy was by then over.

* * *

But, far from ending, the controversy was thrust into a new and still more acrimonious phase by Spurgeon's resignation: to his great dismay Spurgeon was not permitted to retreat unmolested. The initiative was now mainly in the hands of his opponents, though it lay to some extent also with his friends.

In order to understand the six-month heart of the Downgrade Controversy, the period that lay between Spurgeon's resignation from the Baptist Union and the Union's April meetings, it is necessary to analyse the various positions adopted and their

---

[36] *ST*, 23 (November 1887), 560.
[37] *ST*, 23 (December 1887), 605ff.

different agenda in a more sophisticated way than has been attempted before. This analysis presents four main positions, three among those whose primary allegiance was to the Union, and the other among those whose primary allegiance was to Spurgeon, and also notes the presence of small, uninfluential groups at the two extremes. The first group considered Spurgeon's protest and resignation completely out of order, and wanted the Union to close ranks against him. Their leaders were the President and Vice-President of the Union that year, James Culross (Principal of Bristol Baptist College) and John Clifford, backed up by Culross's fellow Bristol man Richard Glover. Their initial inclination was to continue the policy of silence, but when others ruled that out they adopted a strategy of insisting that Spurgeon attempt to substantiate or withdraw his charges, and of censuring him when he failed to do either. They believed he deserved reprimand for slandering the denomination with unsubstantiated, offensively worded, and probably groundless accusations, rendered doubly wounding by his resignation. A second group accepted that Spurgeon had gone over the top, but felt that there were some genuine grounds for concern, and that the denomination should address these, in the process hopefully establishing a basis for eventual reconciliation. This party was led by Charles Williams, the immediate past President of the Union, and included (Glover apart) most of the active former Presidents, notably Joseph Angus and Alexander McLaren. Their policy was to get the Union to adopt declarations vindicating its evangelical faith. Union Secretary S.H. Booth is not assigned to either group because he was drawn in both directions at different points (and had an uncomfortable time as a result). [38] In between these two groups lay a more amorphous mass without clear leadership, of well-meaning but ill-informed people who initially thought that the whole controversy was a tissue of misunderstandings and precipitate actions susceptible of resolution by personal contact and calm discussion. With Samuel Vincent as spokesperson, they emerged from between the other groups to carry the day at the Baptist Union Council in December with their resolution to send a delegation to confer with Spurgeon. After the failure of that initiative they became little more than floating voters for the two groups that knew their mind to vie for. The vast majority of

---

[38] The composition and agenda of these two groups have become considerably clearer with the emergence of the new Baptist Union material lodged in the Angus Library at Regent's Park College, notably S.H. Booth's correspondence.

Spurgeon's supporters made up the fourth and last major block in the denomination. There was a wide measure of agreement between them and Williams' group: they too hoped that the Baptist Union would declare its evangelical basis, and thereby reopen the door to Spurgeon – not appreciating that Spurgeon himself had no desire to walk back in. But there were still significant differences, notably in primary loyalty – for the one group to the Union, for the other to Spurgeon – and especially as to whether the declarations would vindicate the evangelical nature of the Union or restore it, whether it would continue with its existing membership or show liberals out through one door while welcoming Spurgeon back through the other. This meant subtle differences in the content each group had in mind for the declarations. These four major groups apart, there was a small group of liberals who were not ashamed of parading their radical disagreement with Spurgeon's theology in the columns of *The Christian World*, while at the same time largely accepting his analysis; and a similarly small group of Spurgeon loyalists who followed him into an early exile from the Union. Neither of these groups had much influence on the course of the controversy. When the story has been told, it will be seen that the crucial factor in the main outcome, the prevention of large-scale disruption in the Union, was the ultimate preponderance of Williams' moderate group over the radical approach of Culross and Clifford.

If Spurgeon's articles had sent shock waves through Nonconformity, his resignation had the effect of concentrating these on his own denomination and multiplying their strength. There have been attempts to represent the resignation as a tactical ploy, intended to generate a greater response to his charges. Spurgeon himself interpreted it in this way some weeks after the event in a letter to his wife: 'I ... only left the Union when nothing could be done. Now, something will be done. Not until I took the decided step could I effect anything.'[39] But this came at a time when his resignation was being heavily criticized, largely on the ground that he had not made adequate efforts to do something about the situation he was unhappy with before giving up, and Spurgeon was doing his best to justify himself. Three considerations support the contention that this quotation was an exercise in self-justification. Firstly, Spurgeon had not done everything possible: most obviously he had neither gone to Sheffield nor even attempted to get his Downgrade protest a place on the agenda of the meetings there. Secondly, he was not in the

[39] In *Spurgeon Autobiography*, II, 471.

forefront of the initiatives that followed his resignation, as he surely would have been had his main aim been to ensure that 'something will be done'. Thirdly, if Spurgeon had been intent on reforming the Baptist Union his decision to abandon his army on the field once hostilities were fairly under way would have been peculiar, to say the least. But he had no such intention. In reality his main interest in resigning was escape – from fellowship with people who in his view denied the gospel, from the responsibilities involved in membership of the Baptist Union, and even from the effort and pain involved in theological conflict.

Spurgeon's resignation deepened the gap that separated him from his own supporters. This was not just a communication gap, but a difference of outlook and aim. It had already existed at the Sheffield Assembly, where Spurgeon's friends made no attempt to put his protest on the agenda, believing that it was up to him to take the lead.[40] James Douglas, the most outspoken of conservative Baptists in the Baptist Union, and a neighbour and close associate of Spurgeon, was not consulted about the resignation and did not approve of it either:

> We received the news of the decision to which he had come with deep regret. ... Mr. Spurgeon left the Baptist Union before we did or were prepared to follow him. So far from having sought to influence him in that direction, we should have advised – had our advice been asked - his staying on and waiting the course of events in hope of better days. As a matter of fact, the step was taken and the die was cast before we even knew that the purpose had formed in his mind.[41]

This surprise and regret were shared by the vast majority of Spurgeon's supporters. Even the handful who resigned – who included his son Charles and Archibald Brown – probably acted more out of loyalty than conviction.

The shock administered to them by Spurgeon's resignation prompted his supporters to begin to organize themselves. Their first concerted action in the controversy was a meeting of the London members of the Pastor's College Association held on 18 November 1887, at which about a hundred former students of Spurgeon were present. They passed three resolutions nearly unanimously. One

---

[40] William Cuff, in *BW*, 21 October 1887 (in SS).

[41] Douglas, *Prince of Preachers*, 166.

expressed sympathy and support for Spurgeon, another stated that resignation from the Union should be a matter of individual conscience and the most significant one was a request to Council to try to see how to get Spurgeon to reconsider his resignation.[42] This was in contradiction with Spurgeon's request in his letter of resignation that no one should ask him to reconsider.[43]

The means by which the Council might persuade Spurgeon to reconsider his resignation was receiving attention at the same time. It was also on 18 November that David Davies, minister of Regent's Park Chapel and a member of the Council, had a letter published in *The British Weekly* in which he proposed that notice should be given at the Spring Assembly of the Union for constitutional revision in the autumn; this would involve a basis of faith on cardinal truths with legislative authority over the churches.[44]

Davies obtained from Spurgeon permission to quote an endorsement of his plan in a published letter: '"It would give me unfeigned pleasure if there could be a Baptist Union founded upon evangelical principles – say the basis of the Evangelical Alliance. I wish you every success in your desire to bring the present Union to that state."'[45] 'If' is the operative word: he would not have resigned when he did had he seen any likelihood of the Baptist Union adopting a doctrinal basis, a point he explained to Dr Culross:

> The 'Metropolitan men' in London request the Union to devise some way by which I, with others, can return to it. This is very right from their point of view, but I wish you to understand, as President of the Union, that *the request is not mine.* I do not ask you to do what I am sure you cannot do. If I had thought that you could have done anything which would enable me to return if I retired, I should have asked you to do it before retiring
>
> So long as an Association without a creed has no aliens in it, nobody can wish for a creed *formally*, for the spirit is there; but at a time when 'strange children' have entered, what is to be done? Whatever may theoretically be in your power, you *practically* have

---

[42] *BW*, 25 November 1887 (in SS).

[43] The letter is quoted in *Daily News*, 3 November 1887 (in SS).

[44] *BW*, 18 November 1887 (in SS).

[45] *Baptist*, 9 December 1887 (in SS). The doctrinal basis of the Evangelical Alliance, a prominent feature of conservative thinking during the controversy, is included as Appendix 2.

> no power whatever.[46]

Spurgeon explained how he could justify his supporters' making an effort he believed doomed to failure in a letter to the secretary of the Pastors' College Association:

> It was incumbent on *me* to leave the Union, as my private remonstrances to officials, and my repeated printed appeals to the whole body had been of no avail ... but *you* have made no such appeals, and might not be bound to do as I have done till you have had my experience of failure.[47]

Spurgeon believed it would only be wrong to pursue such objectives if the Union positively decided that people who held doctrines he considered unacceptable should be allowed to stay.[48]

Spurgeon's supporters were not the only ones to be stirred into action by his resignation. A slight majority of the Baptist Union Council did not believe that the situation warranted a special meeting,[49] but a small group of ex-presidents of the Union led by Joseph Angus, the Principal of Regent's Park College, ensured that one took place nevertheless. Angus succeeded in persuading the committee of officials and former presidents to approve his plan, which was to pass a declaration reaffirming the evangelical character of the Union and send a deputation with this to Spurgeon in the hope that he would withdraw his resignation. When they met on 13 December 1887, it became clear that many Council members were unhappy with the resemblance of the declaration (of which they had had no notice) to a creed, and that they thought a discussion with Spurgeon might prove all that was needed to restore him to their fellowship. Consideration of the declaration was deferred, and it was resolved to send a delegation made up of Culross (President), Clifford (Vice-President), Samuel Harris Booth (Secretary) and Alexander McLaren to confer with Spurgeon at Mentone on 'how the unity of our Denomination in truth, and love, and good works

---

[46] Spurgeon to Culross, 26 November 1887, quoted in *Spurgeon Autobiography*, II, 478 (emphasis original).

[47] Spurgeon to Mackey, 23 November 1887, quoted in *CW*, 1 December 1887 (in SS; emphasis original).

[48] *ST*, 24 (January 1888), 44.

[49] For the figures see Mark Hopkins, 'The Down Grade Controversy: New Evidence', *BQ*, 35 (1994), 263.

may best be maintained'.[50]

Informed by telegram of this resolution, Spurgeon was perplexed:

> I don't quite see what it all means. ... If they really mean brotherly conference, I will see them when I return, right gladly; that is to say, if I find any use in it. Now I shall need wisdom. I do not fear four doctors, but I think it a very wise move on their part. If it means that they will surrender, it is well; but if it is meant to fix on me the odium of being implacable, it is another matter.[51]

In that last sentence Spurgeon alluded to his fear that the delegation would try to score off him by reopening the question of his resignation, something that he was determined to forestall. This thought vied for prominence in his correspondence with Booth with his desire not to be seen to be uncooperative by refusing to contribute positive thoughts on how the Baptist Union might put its house in order. This hitherto undescribed correspondence – no account of the controversy has hinted that it survived, and few have even alluded to it – is worth quoting at length because it largely accounts for Spurgeon's bitterness in the latter stages of the controversy. Spurgeon's reply to the telegram informing him of the Council's resolution included the following:

> If the resolution sent me meant only what it says, I rejoice in it: the object proposed for deliberation is as dear to me as to any of you. To talk it over with any one or all of you would be most pleasant. ...
>
> If you are going to discuss the question of my action towards the Union, I decline an interview ... If the object is anything beyond a friendly deliberation as to future action, I decline to meet the deputation either here or anywhere else for an unreported conversation. ...
>
> If the Deputation only intends to seek my aid in proposing a way

[50] 'Special Meeting of the Council, Tuesday 13 December 1887', 5, in Baptist Union, Minute Book 1887-89 (hereafter cited as MB), 166. See also the rest of this document. A fuller account of this Council meeting and its background is contained in Hopkins, 'New Evidence', 262-5, which updates idem., 'Spurgeon's Opponents', 282-4.

[51] Spurgeon to Mrs Spurgeon, 14 December 1887, quoted in *Spurgeon Autobiography*, II, 472.

> for future united action, I could have but one feeling, and that would be to meet you most heartily.[52]

In his reply Booth acceded to Spurgeon's request that the delegation should not travel to Mentone, and said that he would need a few days to consult its other members about Spurgeon's letter before making any reply, should one be necessary at all before Spurgeon's return early in January.[53] In the event the response of both Culross and Clifford to the awkward conditions was to counsel waiting; restraining his impatience, Booth did not reply until Spurgeon was back in London. All four members of the delegation were then involved in the protracted drafting process. It was McLaren who suggested the softer line that helped keep negotiations open, though the others then sailed even closer to the wind by dropping all direct reference to Spurgeon's December conditions.[54] So instead of clarifying the deputation's understanding of the terms of reference for the proposed meeting, Booth ended up merely commenting, 'I trust that whatever hesitation you have felt is removed, and you are able to name a time when the conference may be held which the Deputation was instructed to seek',[55] and repeated the words of the resolution.

Spurgeon consulted his brother before replying as follows:

> In my letter I laid down very explicit conditions upon which I can consent to see the Deputation, and I will not see the deputation unless those conditions are understood and accepted.

> I wish your letter had not avoided my demand, for it is not lightly made. The wording of the resolution is kind enough, but if it does

---

52 Spurgeon to Booth, 14 December 1887, MS letter in BU Downgrade archive. 'Council of Baptist Union Re Withdrawal of Rev. C.H. Spurgeon', 1-2, in MB, 176, a printed transcript (hereafter referred to as 'transcript') of the entire correspondence between Spurgeon and Booth leading up to the meeting with the 'four doctors', is marked 'Strictly Private and Confidential, for the use of Special Committee only – S. H. B[ooth].' This was the committee of officers and ex-presidents, which met on 16 January 1888.

53 Booth to Spurgeon, 16 December 1887, MS letter in BU Downgrade archive.

54 Hopkins, 'New Evidence', 266-7.

55 Booth to Spurgeon, 6 January 1888, in 'transcript', p. 3.

> not mean what it says I have no care for verbiage. If it means what I judge it to mean then it includes my conditions.[56]

On this occasion there was a clear three-way division in the delegation. McLaren favoured going ahead with the meeting accepting Spurgeon's conditions, and Booth was inclined to postpone the meeting till they had reported back to the special committee of officers and ex-presidents, but Culross and Clifford were determined to make another attempt to get Spurgeon to express himself in such a way as to allow them to raise issues such as the resignation at the meeting. Booth was talked round, while McLaren, sick and working by correspondence, was circumvented.[57] Booth's next letter asked Spurgeon whether two statements in his letter of 14 December meant that he 'intended to preclude all reference to the past'.[58] Spurgeon's reply was the final letter in the correspondence, written only the day before the provisional date set for the meeting:

> I very much regret that if my letter needed explanation you did not seek it at once. Your avoiding allusions to my conditions in yours of January 6 forced me to request an explicit answer. These delays and hesitancies make me feel that you put a different meaning on the Resolution of the Council to what I do. I had some reason to think so at the first, and it has been confirmed.
>
> I will try to be as plain as I can in this instance. Of course I would not 'preclude all reference to the past.' It would be unreasonable and impossible.
>
> But I wished you to be quite clear that I have quitted the Baptist Union for good reasons, and have given those reasons to the world, and as I have not changed in reference to them, I decline to go over them in private before four persons. ...

---

[56] Spurgeon to Booth, 9 January 1888, MS letter in BU Downgrade archive. See also Spurgeon to Booth, 7 January 1888, in 'transcript', 3.
[57] Hopkins, 'New Evidence', 267-8. Had McLaren been healthy and fully involved, it is likely that this pivotal episode would have taken an entirely different course.
[58] Booth to Spurgeon, 11 January 1888, in 'transcript', 4. The two statements are the second and third paragraphs in my quotation of the letter, above.

> ... If you mean more than the plain words [of the resolution] bear, I do not see the use of our meeting.
>
> This is not to withdraw anything in former letters, but to explain.[59]

Booth's reply simply named a time and place for the meeting.[60]

Whereas Spurgeon arrived at the meeting on 13 January 1888 armed merely with a statement suggesting that the Baptist Union would do well to adopt a doctrinal basis along the lines of that of the Evangelical Alliance, the three members of the Union delegation[61] turned up with a far from unexceptionable document. Drawn up by John Clifford, it began by tearing right through the barrier Spurgeon thought he had erected against discussion of his resignation:

> 1. We are to deliberate with you on the *maintenance* of the union in truth and love and good works of the Baptist Union.
>
> 2. The circumstance that threatens that unity with a breach is the resignation of C.H.S.[62]

The document went on to explore the possibility of Spurgeon reconsidering his resignation, and then asked him either to substantiate or to withdraw his charges against the Baptist Union. Spurgeon replied to the first point in the negative; on the second he offered some explanation of his language but declined to name individuals.[63]

Spurgeon had no time to recover from this shock before another one rocked him: at its meeting on 19 January 1888 the Council

---

[59] Spurgeon to Booth, 12 January 1888, MS letter in BU Downgrade archive.

[60] Booth to Spurgeon, 12 January 1888, MS letter in BU Downgrade archive.

[61] Ian Sellers' suggestion that McLaren's absence from the delegation was because he thought it would only widen the breach is incorrect: he excused himself on the ground of ill-health. Sellers, 'Other Times, Other Ministries: John Fawcett and Alexander McLaren', *BQ*, 32 (1987), 194; Hopkins, 'New Evidence', 269.

[62] Cited in Bateman, *John Clifford, MA, BSc, LLB, DD, Free Church Leader and Preacher* (London: National Council of the Evangelical Free Churches, 1904), 145-6; emphasis original. Spurgeon's prepared statement is included in 'Council Re Withdrawal of Spurgeon', 6.

[63] 'Council Re Withdrawal of Spurgeon', 6.

followed up its delegation's meeting with Spurgeon by passing a resolution which rapidly became known as the 'vote of censure':

> That the Council recognizes the gravity of the charges which Mr. Spurgeon has brought against the Union previous to and since his withdrawal. It considers that the public and general manner in which they have been made reflects on the whole body, and exposes to suspicion brethren who love the truth as dearly as he does. And, as Mr. Spurgeon declines to give the names of those to whom he intended them to apply, and the evidence supporting them, those charges, in the judgement of the Council, ought not to have been made.[64]

Spurgeon's sense of betrayal fuelled some bitter comments on the Council in *The Sword and the Trowel*.[65] Previous attempts to assess Spurgeon's reaction to the censure have been unbalanced owing to not having taken into account the negotiations of the terms of reference for his meeting with the Union deputation.[66] It was not just the heaviness of the blow that rocked him, but the fact that he believed it to have been beneath the belt – and the correspondence does show that the deputation resorted to dubious negotiating ploys. They avoided divulging their interpretation of the resolution appointing them, aware of the fact that had Spurgeon known it he would have considered that his conditions were not fulfilled and would therefore have declined to meet them, and they employed casuistic methods to get round the plain sense of Spurgeon's conditions: their performance was neither straightforward nor commendable.

The considerations that influenced events during the middle

---

[64] Published in Sir James Marchant, *Dr John Clifford* (London: Cassell & Co., 1924), 160. See Hopkins, 'New Evidence', 270 for the toning down of William Landels' original draft of this resolution at a meeting of ex-presidents and officials on 17 January.

[65] 24 (February 1888), 81-3, 91.

[66] Even Payne's 'The Down Grade Controversy', the only account of the controversy to have subjected the minutes to 'careful examination' ('The Down Grade Controversy: A Postscript', 147), strangely neglects to discuss this important correspondence. The source for Charles Bateman's suggestive statement that 'after much further correspondence *and the removal of considerable misunderstandings* they met' (italics mine) is clearly Clifford himself (*John Clifford, MA, BSc, LLB, DD* [London, 1902], 74).

phase of the controversy between Spurgeon's resignation at the end of October 1887 and the adoption of a declaration by the Council in February 1888 were complex, resulting in confusion among participants and historians alike. A leading cause of this has been a failure to differentiate two distinct debates, the main one concerning the accuracy of Spurgeon's charges, and a subsidiary one over the justification of his resignation. Denial of the charges and challenges to Spurgeon to substantiate them by naming individuals to whom he considered them applicable were the principal theme of the main debate, but consideration of them will be easier once the features of the debate over the resignation have been delineated.

Spurgeon justified his resignation in two ways: he argued that the Baptist Union was powerless to preserve itself from error,[67] and he stressed that he only resigned after numerous public protests and private remonstrances with Union officials had failed. The main challenge to this defence occurred at the Council meeting of 13 December 1887. A former friend and theological ally of Spurgeon's named William Lockhart, displaying a convert's zeal in his new role as opponent, posed searching questions to present and former officials of the Union concerning Spurgeon's private remonstrances. All denied that they had withheld anything that ought to have been brought to the notice of Council. Booth mentioned his communication with Spurgeon over the Leicester Assembly of 1883 but said that Spurgeon had accepted the explanation offered. He then read extracts from letters dated 30 March and 25 April 1887 which showed that Spurgeon still supported the work of the Baptist Union although he was no longer attending its meetings. Lockhart concluded that Spurgeon had not done what he thought he had done, and Spurgeon's brother James stormed out of the meeting.[68] Spurgeon reacted angrily to the reports that reached him in France: 'For Dr. Booth to say I never complained, is amazing. God knows all about it, and he will see me righted'.[69]

This episode is of considerable historiographical importance as it furnished the main historical basis for a mythical interpretation of the controversy that is still very much alive. Its main author was J.C. Carlile, who was just enough in the know to gather that Spurgeon's correspondence with Booth was a significant factor, but had only vague information as to its timing and content – he even thought

67 See Hopkins, 'Spurgeon's Opponents', 286 for more on this constitutional debate.
68 *CW*, 15 December 1887 (in SS).
69 *Spurgeon Autobiography*, II, 472.

that Booth continued to share with Spurgeon information and disquiet about theological change during and after the controversy.[70] It is possible that there is a factual basis for his contention that Booth denied Spurgeon permission to publish their correspondence, for it is feasible that Spurgeon might have thereby wished either to vindicate his claim to have remonstrated with Union officials before resigning, or to expose the tactics of the Union delegation. But Carlile failed to distinguish concern about the conduct of the controversy (the matter at issue between Spurgeon and Booth) from the debate on the veracity of Spurgeon's charges, which enabled later historians, mainly ones sympathetic to Spurgeon, to develop his myth with the argument that refusal of permission to use the Booth correspondence meant that Spurgeon was unable to verify his charges.[71] They had found an explanation for the failure of Spurgeon's attempt to reform the Baptist Union that exonerated its author, when they ought to have questioned their assumption that Spurgeon was seriously pursuing reform.

Spurgeon's resignation altered the main thrust of the response to his charges from the numerical issue – how many Nonconformists were no longer evangelical – to general denials. This was desirable because a greater threat required a more robust defence, and feasible because Baptists were more conservative theologically than Congregationalists. A common practice was to select for comment the vaguest and most offensive passages in Spurgeon's articles.[72] The main difficulty, the acknowledgement by some liberals earlier in the controversy that Spurgeon's facts were accurate, was tackled from both ends: the more orthodox distanced themselves and the Baptist Union from such views, and liberals changed their language to help build a united front against Spurgeon.

This defence was turned into counter-attack by calling upon Spurgeon to prove his allegations by naming the people at whom they were levelled. The call was not prompted by a quest for knowledge, for the names of the Baptist liberals Spurgeon could

---

[70] A recent biography has this version of the myth (Arnold Dallimore, *Spurgeon* [Edinburgh: Banner of Truth, 1985], 209-10) as does the more scholarly biography of Kruppa, *Preacher's Progress*, (pp. 427-8).

[71] Carlile, *C.H. Spurgeon, An Interpretative Biography* (London: Religious Tract Society, 1933), 244-50. Lewis Drummond, *Spurgeon Prince of Preachers* (Grand Rapids: Kregel Publications, 1992), 684, 697, 714 provides a recent example of this myth.

[72] This and other points in this and the following paragraph are developed and documented in Hopkins, 'Spurgeon's Opponents', 284-6.

have divulged were well known to all – and the very insistence of the call indicated confidence that there would be no embarrassing surprises. It was, rather, a tactic designed to place Spurgeon in an impossible situation: if he named anyone he would be overwhelmed by the sympathetic support a martyr could expect, while if he refused he was wide open to accusations of cowardice, having no evidence, and slandering a denomination.

Hard pressed by the Council and its delegation, and suffering even more acute agonies in trying to exclude his opponents from the Pastors' College Association, Spurgeon still tried hard to resist the demand for names. He reiterated his objection to introducing personalities and argued for a basis of faith as an alternative strategy, while incidentally showing that he was aware of the consequences of giving way to the call for names:

> The last thing we should care to see would be trials for heresy. These do more harm than good. But there is no need for them. If there be certain definite doctrines laid down, men who honestly differ will go; and if they do not, their remaining will not be the fault of their brethren. The Baptist Union could readily clear itself without going into personal details. Let it tell the world what it believes.[73]

But behind these defiant words Spurgeon's resolve to abstain from naming individuals was in fact seriously shaken. James Spurgeon revealed at the January meeting of Council that he and his brother had considered mentioning names, and that he would be the one to do so should it prove necessary,[74] while shortly afterward a letter shows that Charles was wavering 'They keep on clamouring for names. You can give me names. I don't want anyone to be drawn into personalities; but if they cry "names," we shall have enough to give them!'[75]

There exists a scrap of paper in the handwriting of Joseph Harrald, Spurgeon's private secretary, which may date from the time of the Downgrade Controversy, and could therefore have been

---

[73] *ST*, 24 (February 1888), 91. Compare 23 (October 1887), 513; *Baptist*, 9 November 1888 (in SS).
[74] *Baptist*, 20 January 1888 (in SS).
[75] Spurgeon to Joseph, 8 February 1888, quoted in Kruppa, *Preacher's Progress*, 441. The recipient was probably Charles Joseph, a Pastor's College trained Birmingham Baptist minister.

Spurgeon's list of names.[76] The first five names on it – J.G. Greenhough, Roger Littlehales, Henry Leonard, James Thew, and B.F. Jones – were all known liberal Baptist ministers. At the end came 'Remembering Uzza', the title of the article with which *The Freeman,* the most influential Baptist weekly, entered the controversy; this had been of importance in the original arousal of opposition to Spurgeon. In between came two more names, those of William Lockhart and James Guinness Rogers, who were both friends of Spurgeon who had written him supportive letters in the early stages of the controversy, but who had later became among his most persistent opponents. There is an interesting note, again in Harrald's writing, pencilled at the top of the letter from Lockhart: 'Please return this to C.H.S. He says, "Do not show it unless you are pressed."'[77] The letter in question did not contain any significant information, and could only have been of use to expose Lockhart's volte-face in some kind of personal counter to the Liverpool minister's harrying of Spurgeon in Council. As no alternative theory carries any conviction it is tempting to consider this as an instruction to James Spurgeon, possibly for use at a Council meeting. If so, it stayed in his pocket, for, after toying with the idea of yielding to the call for names, the Spurgeons stuck to their first convictions and gave none.

The retreat upon which Spurgeon had embarked by resigning had failed to give the peace and quiet for which he longed. Only the postman had interrupted the calm of Mentone, and at the meeting celebrating his return Spurgeon was still able to enjoy passivity: 'I do not see my way at all – do not know what is going to be done. I don't want to see ... I desire to follow in the way He leads, and I doubt not He will work in his infinite wisdom in a way which we little dream of.'[78] But the mauling he soon faced, culminating in the 'vote of censure', spurred him to fight back. He began to show far more enthusiasm than previously for the campaign to give the Baptist Union an evangelical basis of communion, expressing a hope that

---

[76] The argument hinges on the existence of a separate scrap with another list on the back of a printed circular dated 23 January 1888, and the addition *at the bottom* of Harrald's list of names of an entry in a different hand on the same subject as the list on the dated scrap.

[77] Lockhart to Spurgeon, 26 August 1887, MS letter in Spurgeon's College, which also holds the MS of Rogers to Spurgeon, 4 September 1887. Rogers' appreciation was much more qualified.

[78] *Baptist,* 13 January 1888 (in SS).

churches would keep on trying, even if it took twenty years.[79] After being a spectator for a while he showed willingness to act as a consultant, if not quite a coach: his resignation disallowed him from being a player. At the same time he tried to bring attention back to the theological issues with which he had begun his protest. The difference was that he now focused on the most palpable area of theological change specifically as it affected the basis of communion of the Baptist Union:

> Now that the offensive personage has been finished off, it will be well to forget *him*, and go to the main question. *Does the Baptist Union hold the doctrine of future probation?* Many of its members avow it. Members of its high-handed Council glory in it. It could somewhat clear its blurred reputation if it passed a resolution setting forth that it rejected the dream of future probation and restoration as unscriptural, unprotestant, and a stranger among Baptists.[80]

His opponents had little constructive to say in reply, for they had a vested interest in reducing theological debate to a minimum. There were no conceivable advantages to be gained through it, and every reason to fear the divisions that might result from the spotlighting of theological differences. Some deduced from Spurgeon's concentration on one doctrine that he had virtually abandoned all his other charges,[81] but Spurgeon denied the soundness of their conclusion: 'We have directed particular attention to the post-mortem salvation and purgatory heresies, because the existence of these needs no proof, for they are openly avowed; but other errors are also rife enough.'[82] There is no evidence that Spurgeon acknowledged that any of his charges had been unjustified; on the contrary, in the later stages of the controversy he was convinced that he had earlier on underestimated the spread of unacceptable theology among Baptists.[83]

---

[79] Spurgeon to Diss Baptist Church, 27 January 1888, quoted in *Baptist*, 10 February 1888 (in SS).
[80] *ST*, 24 (February 1888), 91; emphasis Spurgeon's.
[81] T.R. Stevenson in *CW*, 23 February 1888 (in SS); William Landels in *Freeman*, 10 February 1888 (in SS). This argument has been endorsed by M.R. Watts in 'John Clifford and Radical Nonconformity (1836-1923)' (unpublished DPhil dissertation, University of Oxford, 1966), 157.
[82] *ST*, 24 (March 1888), 147.
[83] *ST*, 24 (June 1888), 249.

Spurgeon was thus already moving towards the debate over doctrinal declarations at the Union Assembly in April, which was to be the climax of the Downgrade Controversy, but the end of the middle phase of the controversy is best situated at the Council meeting on 21 February 1888. There William Lockhart proposed a second and more severe censure of Spurgeon for remarks he had made following the first; its defeat by twenty-three votes to sixteen marked the end of the cycle of recrimination on the Union side.[84] Spurgeon broke the cycle on his own side: his brother had taken the lead in a campaign to reverse the 'vote of censure' at the Union Assembly, but Spurgeon never endorsed it, and the idea disappeared from view as soon as he expressed the hope that it be dropped.[85]

* * *

The field was at last clear for the discussion of the doctrinal declaration that had been postponed in both December and January. It was a welcome change for Spurgeon, after four months on the defensive against concerted assaults on his words and deeds, as well as against challenges to carry on the combat on ground chosen by his enemies and favourable to them, amid which the theological issues he had wanted to highlight had been neglected.

Even before Council met Spurgeon wrote that 'there are signs of a better spirit with some on the Council, and I am hopeful'.[86] The reason for this encouragement was that Joseph Angus had communicated with him and consulted with his brother James in preparing the new version of his declaration that he moved in the Council on 21 February 1888, where James Spurgeon supported it.[87] The different terms used for the two Spurgeons are significant: the meeting with the Baptist Union delegation and the 'vote of censure'

---

[84] 'Minutes of Adjourned Meeting of Council ... 21st February 1888', 5, in MB, 194.

[85] MB, 188-9; *ST*, 24 (April 1888), 197-8.

[86] Spurgeon to Stockwell (editor of *The Baptist*), 14 February 1888, quoted in Kruppa, *Preacher's Progress*, 441.

[87] *Baptist*, 24 February 1888 (in SS); 'Minutes of Council, 21 February 1888', 4, in MB, 194. The declaration as proposed in February is on pp. 3-4 of this document; the December version is in 'Special Meeting of Council, Tuesday 13th December 1887', 3-4, in MB, 166; the January version is in 'Agenda for Adjourned Meeting of Council, Wednesday, 18 January 1888', in Spurgeon's College.

had reinforced Charles' inclination to avoid direct involvement in Union affairs. This continued standing off from the action is more eloquent than the odd expression of confidence that the Baptist churches would shake off error and unite in the truth.[88] These were defiant statements into which Spurgeon channelled feelings which might have found more destructive outlets in the immediate aftermath of the 'vote of censure'. More true to his real pessimism was his confident prediction in *The Sword and the Trowel* prior to the February Council meeting that there was no likelihood of the Baptist Union obtaining a scriptural basis.[89] Spurgeon knew that the Union would not agree to the sort of pruning of its membership that would accompany any basis of communion satisfactory to him.

The debate on the doctrinal declarations in Council exposed two major areas of controversy.[90] The first concerned their status: not everyone was satisfied by Angus's denial that the declaration amounted to a creed, or by James Spurgeon's assurance that his brother did not intend to use them against the unsound. The other subjects of concern were two doctrinal clauses, on the fall and future punishment. John Clifford suggested that a few changes could make the declaration satisfactory to all, an idea that was supported by William Cuff, a former student of Spurgeon's Pastors' College whose Shoreditch church was on of the largest in the denomination. A man of an irenical cast of mind, Cuff was representative of a major element among Spurgeon's supporters who did not attach much importance to defining theologically the limits beyond which they would not have fellowship. His loyalty to Spurgeon was strong, and buttressed by theological agreement, but these were tempered by some disagreement with Spurgeon's manner of proceeding in the controversy and a desire to avoid excluding anyone from the Baptist Union. Clifford produced his suggested changes on the spot: a new introduction which spelt out the non-credal status of the declarations in forthright terms, and new versions of the two controversial doctrinal clauses. Angus approved the former but contested the latter. The declaration was eventually passed after compromises were reached, that on future punishment restoring Angus's reference to eternal punishment in exchange for promoting

---

[88] Spurgeon to Paignton Baptist Church, 3 February 1888, quoted in *Baptist*, 10 February 1888 (in SS).

[89] *ST*, 24 (March 1888), 147 (this edition was in the press before the Council meeting).

[90] The main sources used for this meeting of Council are *CW*, 23 February 1888, and *Baptist*, 24 February 1888 (in SS).

his sentence on permissible alternative views from a footnote to the main body of the text.[91] The verdict of the conservative weekly *Word and Work* summed up the meeting well: 'The ruling desire was *compromise*. The aim of the majority was, not to find exact words to express a definite orthodox faith, but rather to discover language plastic enough to cover antagonistic beliefs.'[92]

Council's declaration did not satisfy James Spurgeon, who was among the five who voted against it; his brother was also critical of the alterations, assuring Booth 'that its form is totally different from that which was agreed upon by Dr. Angus and my brother. The preamble gives it another meaning altogether. It is an historical document, but it is not a basis of union such as I recommended.'[93] In response the two brothers decided to put before the Union Assembly an amended version that was unambiguously confrontational in character, published in *The Freeman* on 30 March. It combined all the most conservative elements of Angus's different versions, including a clause that stated that those who renounced the doctrines contained had no legitimate place in the Union. It also went a little further than Angus had ever gone, notably in omitting the reference to acceptable alternative views on future punishment.

C.H. Spurgeon was by now very eager to see doctrinal declarations discussed and voted on in the Union Assembly, not because he had revised his opinion that it was hopeless to press for reform, but in order to expedite the division he believed necessary: 'We have come to a parting of the ways, and the old school and the new cannot go much further in company; nor ought they to do so. Let them part with as little friction as possible.'[94] Though the fact was not obvious in all his language, his lack of illusions concerning the greater voting strength of his opponents was nonetheless evident:

> The question now before the Union ... will, as I believe, decide its history for many a year to come, and either leave it the warren of latitudinarians, or make it the stronghold of the Gospel. Some resolve to stay in the Union and contest the question for years, and this will probably be the case; but I much fear it will be a hopeless

---

[91] Clifford's suggested changes are in *Baptist*, 24 February 1888 (in SS); the final form of the Council declaration is in 'Minutes of Council, 21 February 1888', in MB, 194.

[92] 2 March 1888 (in SS); emphasis original.

[93] *Baptist*, 2 March 1888 (in SS).

[94] *ST*, 24 (April 1888), 198.

struggle.[95]

Allowing for those who would stay and fight even after losing the vote, Spurgeon thought he could still look forward to the consolation of many joining him in withdrawal from the Union. Even when he gave the greatest support to the reform movement he consistently stood by his conviction that the likelihood of satisfactory reform was negligible.

At the Council meeting on Friday 20 April 1888 it became clear that Spurgeon's friends there did not want a confrontation if it could be avoided. They still held out hopes of finding formulae that would secure Spurgeon's return while satisfying the Council. The difference in aim that had separated Spurgeon from the vast bulk of his supporters throughout the controversy was about to reap its harvest. The wording of the footnote on future punishment was changed so as to exclude 'the dogmas of Purgatory and Universalism' from the permitted alternative interpretations of Matthew 25:46. These were words used loosely in Spurgeon's circle to describe all views that envisage finite punishment after death and even vague universalist hopes, whereas opponents understood them to signify the Catholic doctrine of purgatory and dogmatic universalism, positions virtually if not entirely unknown among Baptist Union members. Spurgeon and his supporters did not begin to wake up to this difference until the debate in the Assembly on Monday 23 April.

The Spurgeon brothers conferred, and the outcome was that this change was insufficient for James Spurgeon to offer to withdraw his amendment. When Council learnt this on Saturday, Landels and Culross riposted by proposing that further mention be made of the insufficiency of Spurgeon's evidence – in effect another censure. Once more it was Williams who managed to head this off, thereby (as he justifiably pointed out afterwards) keeping the way open for compromise.[96]

It has become possible to reconstruct most of the story of the final compromise since the following letter from J.A. Spurgeon to Booth came to light in the discovery of fresh archival material on the Downgrade Controversy in the Baptist Union:

In haste but heartily I reply (tho' in the face of two or three

[95] Spurgeon, *Baptist*, 30 March 1888 (in SS).
[96] Williams to Booth, 28 April 1888, MS letter in BU Downgrade archive.

telegrams and your letter I am still a little in the dark without the whole documents as amended before me) yet if it is as I expect that in another form I get practically what I am aiming at; then of course I gladly comply. What am I to do? I presume, withdraw my amendment with my accustomed grace!!! and say all that I can that is healing and brotherly and in order as I do so.

I will run round by my brother's house and reach you as soon as I can, with the last and best news I can in God's name extract from him. God be praised if we have really escaped.

But only fancy what speech you have missed in losing mine!!! My wigwam will have many fewer scalps now I leave all yours on your heads in peace.[97]

This shows that the compromise formula – the removal of the part of Clifford's introduction that most detracted from the declaration's doctrinal authority – came from the Union side (though whether it was by or through Booth isn't clear). Though written on the day before the Union debate rather than at the last minute, the letter betrays the fact that J.A. Spurgeon was proceeding with speed and without the sort of careful consideration a matter of such consequence needed. It also sheds interesting light on the relationship between the Spurgeon brothers: James was pretty confident he could talk Charles round, a confidence that proved not to be misplaced.

Council agreed to this compromise in a specially assembled meeting literally five minutes before the debate was due to begin.[98] The final text of the declaration reads as follows:

Whilst expressly disavowing and disallowing any power to control belief or to restrict inquiry, yet, in view of the uneasiness produced in the Churches by recent discussions, and to show our agreement with one another, and with our fellow Christians on the great truths of the Gospel, the Council deem it right to say that –

(A) Baptized into the name of the Father, and of the Son, and of the

---

[97] J. A. Spurgeon to Booth, 22 April 1888, MS letter in BU Downgrade archive.

[98] 'Minutes of Meetings of the Council on 20, 21, and 23 April 1888', 13-15, in MB, 202.

> Holy Ghost, we have avowed repentance towards God and faith in the Lord Jesus Christ – the very elements of a new life; as in the Supper we avow our union with one another, while partaking of the symbol of the body of our Lord, broken for us, and of the blood shed for the remission of sins. The Union, therefore, is an association of Churches and Ministers professing not only to believe the facts and doctrines of the Gospel, but to have undergone the spiritual change expressed or implied in them. This change is the fundamental principle of our Church life.
>
> (B) The following facts and doctrines are commonly believed by the Churches of the Union: -
>
> (1) The Divine Inspiration and Authority of the Holy Scriptures as the supreme and sufficient rule of our faith and practice: and the right and duty of individual judgement in the interpretation of it.
>
> (2) The fallen and sinful state of man.
>
> (3) The Deity, the Incarnation, the Resurrection of the Lord Jesus Christ, and His Sacrificial and Mediatorial Work.
>
> (4) Justification by faith – a faith that works by love and produces holiness.
>
> (5) The work of the Holy Spirit in the conversion of sinners, and in the sanctification of all who believe.
>
> (6) The Resurrection; the Judgement at the last day, according to the words of our Lord in Matthew xxv. 46. *
>
> * It should be stated, as a historical fact, that there have been brethren in the Union, working cordially with it, who, while reverently bowing to the authority of Holy Scripture, and rejecting the dogmas of Purgatory and Universalism, have not held the common interpretation of these words of our Lord.[99]

The Spurgeons had made a bad bargain, for although the strongly anti-credal language was gone there was no credal language in its place, and the doctrinal clauses remained a simple statement of what was generally believed by members of the Baptist Union. In

[99] The sources are 'Council Report for 1887, Proof Copy for Council Members', and *CW*, 24 April 1888.

addition, the language of the motion he had agreed to second would hardly have enchanted J.A. Spurgeon had he succeeded in perusing it before being called upon to speak:

> That the Report of the Council, with the exception of Clauses I. and II. and the word 'But' in Clause III. of the Declaration of the Council, be adopted, and that in reference to so much of it as relates to recent discussions respecting the evangelical character of the Union, the Assembly places on record its judgement that there has been sufficient vindication by the Declaration of the Council and otherwise of the evangelical character of the churches of the Union and of their pastors, and that additional tests of membership are unnecessary, inasmuch as the Council and the Assembly have ample power under the Constitution to determine all questions of membership, and therefore can deal with the case of any church or person that may not hold evangelical sentiments.[100]

James Spurgeon's speech showed that doubts about the agreement he had accepted were already crowding into his mind. In proposing the motion, Charles Williams, had defended the legitimacy of the 'larger hope' in a speech that showed evident signs of having been prepared with a very different scenario in mind, and Spurgeon began by saying that he seconded the motion, but not the speech. He then observed that whereas Williams had had an hour to change his speech 'I think I have only had about a quarter of an hour since I really knew where we were'.[101] And he brought his speech lamely to an end by saying, 'I will not go further into any detail, because I always notice that when once you have come to an agreement if you begin to talk about it you will soon disagree, and, therefore, taking Mr. Williams's motion as it stands, I am very glad to be able now to second it.'[102] But he did *not* do what his elder brother told Williams *he* would have done if he had been in that situation, namely turn around and oppose the resolution after all.[103] So while his own verdict was that they had been 'entrapped by diplomatists',[104] in the final analysis it was his decision to withdraw

[100] 'Minutes of Council, 20, 21 and 23 April 1888', 15, in MB, 202.
[101] *CW*, 24 April 1888 (in SS).
[102] *Ibid*.
[103] Charles Williams in *The National Baptist*, Philadelphia, 31 May 1888.
[104] Spurgeon to Wright, 27 April 1888, quoted in Kruppa, *Preacher's Progress*, 442-3.

from the Union at a relatively early stage that proved decisive in his discomfiture.

* * *

One thing of which the compromise deprived the historian is a precise numerical measure of the strength of the sides in the Baptist Union. The next best thing is the results of the election for Council that took place while the debacle was underway – ballot papers were distributed before the compromise but collected after it. Supporters of the Union leadership could easily indicate this by voting back all those elected in 1887, thanks to Samuel Harris Booth's ploy of publishing their names separately from the list of new candidates. Spurgeon supporters knew their own 'slate' among the new candidates, and the level of liberal sympathies can be gauged by the size of the vote for their most high profile would-be newcomer, James Thew of Leicester. The second lowest scorer among existing Council members attracted about 51% of votes cast (the lowest scorer hadn't attended a single meeting during the year, a fact recorded on the ballot papers). New candidates who supported Spurgeon received on average about 27% of votes cast. Considering the 22% of voters remaining as liberal accords well with the approximately 25% vote for Thew.[105] These figures should be viewed with some caution, but they do sit well with the results of two further sets of independent calculations which set a realistic maximum of 44% and absolute minimum of 17% for the level of support for Spurgeon. These are provided respectively by subsequent Downgrade related votes in the London Baptist Association (where Spurgeon supporters were more numerous than in the denomination as a whole) and the level of support for Spurgeon among his own former students over introducing a new basis of faith for the re-formed Pastors' College Association.[106]

Social and geographical analysis of the two sides must be even

---

[105] Baptist Union Council voting returns, 1888, in the Angus Library, Regent's Park College. The figures are worked out in more detail in Hopkins, 'New Evidence', 272.

[106] For more detail on these calculations see Mark Hopkins, 'Baptists, Congregationalists, and Theological Change: Some Late Nineteenth Century Leaders and Controversies', (DPhil thesis, University of Oxford, 1988), 245. Though lacking access at that time to the Council returns, I there estimated Spurgeon's support as a quarter of the Union membership.

less precise. The investigations made on separate trains on the way to the Union's autumn meetings in Sheffield in October 1887 by the reporters of *The Baptist* and *The Freeman* make an interesting starting-point. The former found universal support for Spurgeon, while the latter heard derogatory comments about the controversy. After they compared notes *The Baptist's* correspondent accounted for the difference by the fact that his colleague was in a first class carriage.[107] Other evidence fits in with this suggestion that ministers of larger and richer churches were less likely to be sympathetic to Spurgeon than those at the other end of the scale. At less than 10%, support for Spurgeon in the Council, pre-eminently the preserve of the successful, was much lower than in the denomination as a whole. It is particularly noteworthy that in marked contrast to the national picture only two out of the ten Council members trained at the Pastors' College supported him.[108]

Glimpses of life in local churches confirm the contrasting attitudes of the wealthier and more cultured on the one hand, and the poorer and less educated on the other. A letter from a Weymouth minister educated at the Pastors' College is a good example:

> Personally I have suffered much from false doctrine in this church. The doctrine of everlasting punishment, which I unhesitatingly announce, is like gravel between the teeth of not a few among us, while some of our influential people have gone so far along the "down-grade", as to question and deny the deity of our Lord. I have had a hard time here, and even yet do not see how my position is to be long tenable. Often have I felt that I would sooner labour among the poorest and most ignorant, than among those in whom spiritual-carnal pride has wrought such havoc, and through whom a pestilential blight appears to rest upon Christian work.
>
> The only thing that has comforted me here has been the manifold blessing that has all along rested, and is still resting, upon my work at our Village Chapel at Putton. There, among a simple, true-hearted people, the gospel is precious, prayer abundant, and conversions numerous. There, it is a joy and a recreation to preach,

[107] *Baptist*, 7 October 1887; *Freeman*, 7 October 1887 (both in SS).

[108] Payne, 'The Down Grade Controversy', 35. The eight supporters of Spurgeon in the Council known to me by name are William Cuff, C.B. Sawday (the two Pastors' College men), J.A. Spurgeon, David Davies, James Dann, J. Baillie, William Stott and R. Cory. The last-named resigned.

> for the believers are hungry for the bread of life, and one is conscious of breathing a spiritual atmosphere. But here, at Bank Bldgs, there is a frost in the air that nips every bud of holy feeling, and makes it hard to work.[109]

The secretary of the Surrey and Middlesex Association, whose constituency was in the rural parts of the two counties, was well placed to observe and comment on the urban/rural divide. He believed that a large proportion of those who transferred to village churches from London or the larger towns were unhelpful, 'being either saturated with unsound doctrine or a worldly spirit, or both'; many found that the parish churches was more congenial. 'For these two reasons, country churches feel there is something wrong with the principles and spirit of many in the denomination, distrust the pastors of city churches, and are just in the state of mind to support anyone who would vigorously express dissatisfaction with the tendencies of the times'[110]

The limited regional evidence points in the same direction as the local evidence. So many individual churches were divided internally over the Downgrade Controversy that it is scarcely surprising that virtually all towns and regions were also. It is significant that the few near-exceptions were usually either very urban or very rural. Birmingham and Liverpool were major centres whose Baptist churches were virtually united in opposing Spurgeon.[111] On the other side, the rural Northern District of the Devon Association was unique in passing unanimously a resolution expressing 'hearty sympathy with the Rev. C.H. Spurgeon in his whole noble defence of Evangelical truth in the "Down Grade" articles in the Sword and Trowel'.[112] However the different ethos of urban and rural churches was not the only cause of regional variation in support for Spurgeon and the Council. Other reasons can be adduced for attitudes in the General Baptist heartland of the East Midlands, where it was claimed that no Derby minister approved of Spurgeon's resignation; F.M.W. Harrison's study of the Downgrade Controversy in

---

[109] George J. Knight to Profs Gracey and Fergusson, 11 February 1888, MS letter in Spurgeon's College.

[110] E.W. Tarbox, in *Freeman*, 6 April 1888 (in SS).

[111] George Samuel to Spurgeon, 20 March 1888, MS letter in Spurgeon's Pamphlets, VIII, no. 10; *Birmingham Owl*, no date (in SS); *Baptist*, 3 February 1888 (in SS).

[112] *Freeman*, 9 December 1887 (in SS).

Nottinghamshire also turns up little support for Spurgeon.[113]

The gap between town and country was social and economic, but also included a theological aspect linked to these factors. The evidence provided by the Downgrade Controversy supports the contention that the liberalizing process in theology was linked to ethical and intellectual changes in the more educated and cultured classes, thence filtering gradually down the social scale and out from the towns into the villages.

* * *

Though himself involved in engineering the rushed compromise that gave the course of the Downgrade Controversy its last and most dramatic twist, as soon as he saw how Charles Williams handled it in his speech C.H. Spurgeon was thoroughly put out. At several points in the controversy his low expectations had cushioned him from the shocks he received, but he had no such protection from the effects of this miscalculation. He reserved his most frank reactions for private correspondence: 'I feel so ill and utterly crushed by last Monday that I feel that I am only acting like a sensible man if I keep out of all Unions and associations henceforth. ... We are sold, not betrayed but entrapped by diplomatists.'[114] Knowing that victory was out of the question, Spurgeon had been looking forward to defeat in the Union, because it would have led to many joining him in resigning from the Union, vindicating his claim that proponents of the old and the new theologies could no longer remain in fellowship. At the last moment he had allowed himself to be persuaded down the different path of securing an adequate doctrinal basis for the Union, only to discover that it stopped short of the hoped for destination. Worse still, the compromise meant that the great majority of his loyal supporters did not feel themselves driven to choose between Spurgeon and the Baptist Union.

According to James Douglas, 'the crucial mistake lay in attempting to do by proxy a work, the responsibility of which required his own presence and lead on the field of action'.[115] In that assessment Spurgeon's precipitate resignation from the Baptist Union was a key

---

[113] W.R. Stevenson, in *Derby Daily Telegraph*, no date (in SS); F.M.W. Harrison, 'The Nottinghamshire Baptists. Church Relations: Social Composition: Finance: Theology', *BQ*, 26 (1975), 186-90.

[114] Spurgeon to Wright, 27 April 1888, quoted in Kruppa, *Preacher's Progress*, 442-3.

[115] Douglas, *Prince of Preachers*, 167.

error. However, while it is undeniable that Spurgeon made a series of tactical errors in his handling of the controversy, it is inadequate to consider his style of leadership as simply the greatest of these. He had shown a capacity for decisive leadership in reforming the Pastors' College Association. The contrast with his approach to the conflict in the Baptist Union can only partly be accounted for by his position of authority within his own organisation. It has been shown that by expressing distaste for schism and scepticism as to the efficacy of creeds before the Downgrade Controversy began, Spurgeon had declined to take either of the two obvious routes out of his predicament, instead settling on withdrawal from communion. Only when his resignation from the Baptist Union induced his friends to campaign for his return rather than follow his example, and furthermore worsened rather than ended the criticism to which he was subjected by fellow Baptists, did he take up the idea of seeking a satisfactory doctrinal basis for the Union. Even then his motives were to relieve the pressure of the criticism and provoke a disruption of the Union, not new hope that the method might yield a Baptist Union he would be happy to rejoin; and his caginess about direct involvement in implementing the plan reflected his dominant desire for escape.

What was changed by the bitter experience of the controversy was Spurgeon's attitude to schism: he did not come to like the idea, or become starry-eyed about its efficacy, but it did become more attractive than other conceivable futures. The difficulty was that its contemporary unpopularity was a powerful disincentive to coming out publicly in its favour, and the compromise in the Baptist Union, followed by another in the London Baptist Association, made it difficult for Spurgeon to make progress toward building a new network of fellowship. In June 1888 he was already privately entertaining the thought that the Surrey and Middlesex Association might form the nucleus of a new Baptist Union, and he joined it when it severed its links with the Baptist Union in October. But his church did not follow him until the spring of 1890, and the only significant further step taken by this association at Spurgeon's suggestion was to broaden its constituency by changing its name to the Home Counties Association in October 1890.[116]

Spurgeon did not make a better job of the bid to reform the

[116] Two June 1888 letters to Isaac Near, quoted by Payne in 'The Down Grade Controversy: A Postscript', 154; *Surrey Comet*, 3 November 1888 (in SS); *ST*, 26 (1890), 300, 680; Godfrey Holden Pike, *The Life and Work of Charles Spurgeon*, 3 vols. (London: Cassell & Co., [1892-93]), III, 314.

Baptist Union because that hadn't ever really been his aim. His conduct of the early stages of the controversy can only be understood in the light of his lack of a positive programme: all he intended was protest and withdrawal. The Downgrade Controversy was a calamity to him because of the failure of the plan he developed in its middle phase, which was to divide the Baptist Union and work toward an alternative organization of fellowship. Crucial to this failure was the fact that very few of Spurgeon's supporters had reached his firm conclusions on the total incompatibility of 'old' and 'new' theologies. Spurgeon tended to presume that their personal loyalty and substantial theological agreement with him meant that they shared his thinking on the limits of communion, whereas they were not as ready as he was to insist that the time had come for a barrier to be erected between the evangelical and liberal ideas of Christianity. This points to a second major weakness in Spurgeon's conduct of the controversy: he failed to develop a theological debate of any quality or amplitude on the matters at issue, namely the nature of evangelicalism and the basis of communion in a congregational polity.

Issues

Like the Leicester Conference Controversy, the Downgrade Controversy was all about religious communion. The same two aspects were present in the later controversy as in the earlier one: firstly, the theological definition of the limits of communion; and secondly, how these should be implemented within a congregational polity.

Theological

The greater conservatism of the Baptist denomination was reflected in the different focus of debate. Whereas Congregationalists had debated whether religious communion should be on a theological basis at all, Baptists were agreed not only that there should be a theological basis but also what kind of theology it should be: the word 'evangelical' was wielded like a banner on all sides. Spurgeon wrote, 'let the one question be discussed in all good temper, and let the truth be contended for in the name of our Lord Jesus Christ, *shall the Baptist Union be a resort for men of every school of thought, or shall it be declared to be an evangelical institution?*';[117] while from the other side, an editorial in *The Freeman* proclaimed that 'all that remains for any of us is to make the Baptist Union so Evangelical that non-Evangelicals will not care to be members of it'.[118]

The difficulty, and the matter at issue, was the meaning of 'evangelical'. Recent years had seen the development of a far greater diversity of theologies appropriating the evangelical label than had ever existed before, a fact illustrated by one prominent Congregationalist:

> I cannot but feel that a very great change indeed has come over the theological position of the Congregational ministry... It is the abandonment of what was once regarded as central and essential to the strength and vigour of the Christian religion; it is nothing less than the expulsion of the old bones of a formerly prevalent theology, the extraction of the very skeleton about which that theology was built up. Nevertheless, I am equally confident in the assurance that the change which has taken place has not involved any departure from the evangelical faith.[119]

Spurgeon expressed his agreement with the conclusion of a writer in *The Christian World* that in current usage 'Evangelicalism, on its intellectual side, lies neither here nor there, but is consistent with the most widespread differences of belief'.[120] This was one of a number of interesting points in the controversy at which the two extremes were at one with each other and at odds with the peacemakers in the middle, who in this instance tended to affirm that 'we do in heart understand what is meant by the word "evangelical"'.[121] The article in *The Christian World* went on to suggest that they were rapidly approaching Dean Farrar's position, 'when he maintains that Evangelicalism on its mental side merely implies honest search for truth, while in its deepest meaning it signifies integrity of purpose

---

117 Preface to [Robert Shindler], *Creed or No Creed? A Question for the Baptist Union* (London, 1888), 2.

118 27 April 1888 (in SS).

119 W.F. Adeney, tutor at New College, London, in *Congregational Review*, 1 (November 1887), 1058-9. There is a perceptive contemporary analysis of the role of uncertainty over the definition of evangelicalism in the controversy in *The Free Church of Scotland Monthly*, 1 December 1888 (in SS).

120 *CW*, 22 November 1888 (in SS); *ST*, 25 (January 1889), 40.

121 F.B. Meyer, in *Freeman*, 28 September 1888 (in SS).

and kindness of heart'[122] – a definition that might include atheists and Hindus equally well. The word 'evangelical', far from being an answer to the problems associated with rapid theological change, was itself a major casualty of that process. The days were over when it could preside unchallenged over harmonious fellowship in the Baptist Union.

This did not mean that the word had ceased to be useful. Baptists could still agree that acceptance of the authority of the Bible was fundamental to evangelicalism, and that 'the inspired Scripture of the Old and New Testament is the only complete, authoritative, and infallible exposition of evangelical doctrine'.[123] But that only brought them face to face with a further difficulty: major disagreements over biblical interpretation put paid to any hopes that the simple proclamation of biblical authority might suffice as a basis of communion. There was no substitute for a discussion of what the various parties believed to be fundamental doctrines.

Agreement on another distinguishing factor of evangelicalism was of no more practical use. Baptists were unanimous that evangelical faith was a living faith and not a merely intellectual one, its source being in personal communion with Jesus Christ: disloyalty to Christ put one beyond the pale.[124] But as with the Bible, so with Christ: different views of the Gospel meant that there was disagreement as to what was disloyalty. Here too the breakdown of the old evangelical consensus meant that an informal basis of faith was no longer workable, and neither the Baptist Union nor the London Baptist Association was able to resolve the controversy without drawing up simple doctrinal statements. Three doctrines dominated the debate: Scripture, the atonement, and future punishment.

On Scripture, the boundary outside which Spurgeon was unwilling to have fellowship was the doctrine of plenary inspiration.[125] An objective certainty on which to ground all else was a psychological necessity for him, and any doctrine that fell short of biblical infallibility appeared to involve the assertion of a superior – and in Spurgeon's eyes infallible – human authority. This was to remove the foundations of the faith:

---

[122] *CW*, 22 November 1888 (in SS).
[123] A declaration accepted by the London Baptist Association on 8 January 1889, quoted in *Freeman*, 28 December 1888.
[124] Aldis, Angus and Maclaren, in *BW*, 18 November 1887; *Freeman*, 12 October 1888 (both in SS).
[125] *ST*, 23 (November 1887), 558-9.

> When a man falls into an error, but reverently conceives that he finds it in his Bible, he is on a very different footing from the man who says that he judges by his moral consciousness, or some other unreliable standard, and declares that if the Bible contradicts him he will sooner renounce Scripture than change his opinions. We can have a measure of fellowship with a mistaken friend who is willing to bow before the teaching of Scripture if he can be made to understand it; but we must part company altogether with the errorist, who overrides prophets and apostles, and practically regards his own inspiration as superior to theirs. We fear that such a man will before long prove himself to be an enemy of the cross of Christ, all the more dangerous because he will profess loyalty to the Lord whom he dishonours.[126]

While Spurgeon believed that the question of authority came down to a simple choice between the infallibility of Scripture and its subjection to human authority, his opponents believed that recognition of biblical authority was compatible with denial of infallibility. The conventional way to attempt to substantiate this claim was to argue for different degrees of inspiration in different parts of the Bible, the aim often being to disallow error in matters of doctrine but admit its possibility in history or science. Spurgeon did not think this removed the difficulty:

> If the Bible is not infallible, we do not care a rush whether it is inspired or not. If writers are to take away this book and that from the canon, they may as well take the whole, for they are evidently greater authorities than the Scripture upon which they sit in judgement.[127]

Like many others in the controversy, this discussion did not proceed very far, mainly because Spurgeon's opponents feared that theological debate would exacerbate division.

Spurgeon's understanding of the atonement was founded on his belief that there was no possibility of sin being unpunished by a righteous and holy God, or that such a God would receive into his glory any but the completely righteous. Unless Christ had taken upon himself the sin of humanity and its punishment, and bestowed in exchange his own righteousness, Spurgeon could see no prospect

---

[126] *ST*, 24 (May 1888) 207.
[127] *ST*, 24 (July 1888), 378; compare *ST*, 24 (May 1888), 206.

for the human race save eternal condemnation: substitutionary atonement was an essential:

> The largest charity towards those who are loyal to the Lord Jesus, and yet do not see with us on secondary matters, is the duty of all true Christians. But how are we to act towards those who deny his vicarious sacrifice, and ridicule the great truth of justification by his righteousness? These are not mistaken friends, but enemies of the cross of Christ. There is no use in employing circumlocutions and polite terms of expression:- where Christ is not received as to the cleansing power of his blood and the justifying merit of his righteousness, he is not received at all.[128]

This he believed to be the centre of evangelical doctrine, and the main point at which it was under attack.[129]

Alexander Mackennal's remarks on atonement from the chair of the Congregational Union were typical of the current attitudes to which Spurgeon objected. In an address rewritten in order to discuss the theological issues raised by the Downgrade articles, Mackennal criticized the forensic theory, saying that the atonement was the weakest aspect of the preaching of the previous generation. He surveyed some efforts to construct an alternative, finding something to praise in Dale, McLeod Campbell, Horace Bushnell, and Baldwin Brown, but confessed that they did not yet have a solution.[130] Attempts were frequently made to alleviate the difficulty of this situation by drawing a distinction between the *fact* of atonement (which was believed) and *theories* of it (multiple and optional). It was held that Spurgeon erred through not recognizing that distinction.[131] But the difficulty inherent in this distinction was to know where fact ended and theory started. Even the most exiguous notion of the 'fact' of atonement contained ideas in addition to historical data concerning Jesus' death. A supporter of Spurgeon explored the problem:

> Mr. Spurgeon, with many others, believes with strong and deep conviction, that substitution and expiation are the main and central

---

128 *ST*, 23 (November 1887), 559.

129 *ST*, 24 (July 1888), 344; no. 2368, April 1888 sermon in Spurgeon, *Christ's Relation to his People* (London: Passmore & Alabaster, [1904]), 365.

130 Mackennal, 'The Life of the Spirit', in *CY* (1888), 56-8.

131 Roger Littlehales, in *CW*, 15 September 1887 (in SS).

ideas of the atonement; that these are as much facts revealed by the scripture as the death of Christ itself; that they are not merely theories of the atonement, but are factors so essential that without them there could be no atonement at all.[132]

In reality 'fact' was shorthand for the core belief required for fellowship, and 'theory' referred to the finer definition on which there could be freedom; as there was disagreement on the content of the two categories this language could not help furnish a basis of communion.

Yet, as Baptists could still unite in acknowledging the authority of Scripture, so did they preserve a consensus in favour of objective atonement. It is significant that the unacceptable positions on the atonement that conservatives highlighted during the controversy were held by Congregationalists, such as the man who did not accept all Paul said on the atonement, and the one who said that every act of self-sacrifice was an atonement. When students of Airedale and Rawdon Colleges debated the question, 'Does the doctrine of the Divine Fatherhood render the objective aspect of the Atonement necessary?', it was a Baptist who argued for and a Congregationalist against objectivity.[133] And, as with plenary inspiration, Spurgeon did not bid for an unambiguous statement of substitutionary sacrifice in the Baptist Union declaration. Among Baptists the structure of evangelical faith remained more or less intact – righteousness for the believer through Christ's death, the supreme authority of the biblical revelation – although the old theological foundations of imputation of sin and righteousness, and biblical infallibility were rapidly being undermined. Spurgeon found this cause for serious concern, but he chose to home in on a third doctrine, eschatology, the only area in which Baptists were openly dismantling the visible structure of traditional evangelical doctrine. Thus future punishment became the main theological battlefield of the controversy.

By the end of his series of Downgrade articles in *The Sword and the Trowel* Spurgeon had condemned most varieties of contemporary eschatology, but conditional immortality was conspicuously absent from the list even though he had often opposed it previously.[134] The

---

132 [George Lock], in *Spen Valley Times*, 13 January 1888 (in SS).

133 *Word and Work*, 11 May 1888 (in SS); *Cleakheaton Guardian*? May 1888 (in SS); *Freeman*, 11 December 1885, 833.

134 *ST*, 23 (September 1887), 465; (October), 513; (November), 558.

explanation was that it was the beneficiary of a unique extension of Spurgeon's basis of communion. This indicates where Spurgeon's priorities were on future punishment: he was not overly concerned about the natural immortality of man denied by conditional immortality, but he was adamant in outlawing any hope for sinners who died unrepentant. He called universalism 'the most deadly of all the errors which have plagued the church of God'[135] because he believed it had disastrous effects on the preaching of the Gospel. He appealed to Scripture in defence of his stand:

> It is of no avail to sit down and draw inferences from the nature of God, and to argue, "God is love, and therefore he will not execute the sentence upon the impenitent." He knows what he will do better than you can infer; he has not left us to inferences, for he has spoken pointedly and plainly. He says, "He that believeth not shall be damned," and it will be so, "For the mouth of the Lord hath spoken it." Infer what you like from his nature; but if you draw an inference contrary to what he has spoken, you have inferred a lie, and you will find it so.[136]

Spurgeon needed all the scriptural support he could muster because in some respects he was at his most vulnerable on future punishment. Endless punishment differed from most aspects of Spurgeon's basis of communion in that its status in evangelical Baptist tradition had not been unquestioned: as Clifford pointed out, neither Robert Hall nor John Foster had been of the opinion that eternal punishment should be a term of communion.[137] Spurgeon's second and more pressing problem was the way it was giving ground to other views. The process of change is not easy to chart – in 1888 of two Baptist ministers, both holding a form of the larger hope, one believed that the vast majority of Baptists still stood by eternal punishment, while the other thought that there no longer existed even a bare majority for the old view.[138] But though Baptists lagged behind Congregationalists it is clear that the larger hope was rapidly gaining ground, particularly among the young.[139] In 1885 it had

---

[135] *ST*, 24 (February 1888), 85.
[136] *Pulpit*, 34 (1888), 154; emphasis Spurgeon's.
[137] *Baptist*, 30 March 1888 (in SS).
[138] R. Scott Moncrieff, in *Freeman*, 2 March 1888; James Thew, in *Baptist*, 24 February 1888 (both in SS).
[139] One student at Bristol Baptist College in the mid-1880s believed his contemporaries without exception favoured some kind of larger hope –

taken both courage and tact in considerable quantities for James Thew to get away with airing the larger hope for the first time in a representative national Baptist meeting; but when Charles Williams proclaimed the legitimacy at least of its less adventurous versions three years later scarcely a voice was raised against him. The speed of change took many aback:

> It is agreed that the fact of the holding of either the larger hope or the ultimate annihilation of the wicked is not counted a disqualification for membership in the Baptist Union. Again I refrain from passing an opinion, but I confess to a bewildered feeling of amazement at these positions being so undoubtedly advanced and accepted. It surely indicates a very wonderful change of front, which has been quietly taking place in these last few years.[140]

Two contemporary assessments of Congregational beliefs agreed that the dogmatic viewpoints – eternal punishment, conditional immortality, universalism – were espoused by comparatively few; the great majority held to a vague 'larger hope' or were completely agnostic on the subject.[141] Baptists were abandoning eternal punishment more slowly, but the same trend was apparent. That trend was the result of a widespread dilemma: how could the Bible's authority cohere with the dictates of the contemporary liberal conscience? At one end of the scale, few cared to argue that dogmatic universalism was the consistent teaching of an authoritative Bible; at the other end, the preservation of the traditional interpretation of the Bible involved the rejection of basic convictions of the modern conscience. Comparatively few were prepared to resolve the tension by rejecting one or other of these authorities. It was hoped that the two could be found to agree.

People professing the most diverse views have succeeded in interpreting the Bible in such a way as to make it agree with them; it is therefore remarkable that so many Nonconformists of this period found themselves to a greater or lesser extent restrained by it from enlarging their hopes for the human race as much as they would

---

'Nemo' to Spurgeon, MS letter, in Spurgeon's College, Spurgeon Pamphlets, VIII, no. 12a.

140 *Christian*, 27 April 1888 (in SS).

141 C. Chapman, in *Congregational Review*, 1 (November 1887), 1054; Alexander Hannay, in F.A. Freer, *Edward White, His Life and Work* (London: Elliot Stock, 1902), 241-2.

have liked. Some managed to enjoy quite a buoyant hope by affirming texts that appeared favourable and developing ways of coping with difficult ones; others who would have liked to have made similar progress lacked the intellectual dexterity required and contented themselves with suspending judgement and trusting hopefully in God's love. Notable leaders found themselves stranded between their attraction to the larger hope and their understanding of the Bible.[142] Those who succeeded in resolving this dilemma did so by taking the ethical leap first and only then returning to the Bible with sufficient confidence in their new-found affirmations to apply one of the available methods of reinterpreting its awkward passages. The following account, by a theological student who went up to Regent's Park College from the sheltered valleys of Wales in 1888, vividly illustrates the priority of ethical considerations:

> Not long after I entered college one of the senior students did me the honour of asking me to go for a walk. In the course of the walk, this renowned and learned senior ventured to express some doubts about the eternity of hell. I can vividly recall the terrible shock I suffered. If he had confessed to a murder the shock would not have been so great. Yet I knew him to be helpful and Christian in his whole walk and conversation, and the perplexity of my soul was increased correspondingly. All this, however, gave me food for thought. Some few months later an old minister visiting the college was asked by the Principal to conduct morning prayers. He must have felt that the college, notwithstanding the unbending orthodoxy of the Principal, the venerable Dr. Angus, was under suspicion of heresy, and so thought it his duty to talk to the Almighty to say something that would help to keep us students in the straight path on this great issue. I can recall his words as if they were uttered yesterday, "And, Oh God," he tenderly pleaded, "when we hear the shrieks of the damned ascending from the everlasting flames of the bottomless pit, give us grace to shout, Hallelujah, Hallelujah." This was too much for me, and I came to the conclusion that I would rather risk sharing the agonies of the damned, than join in the Hallelujah of the saints.[143]

---

[142] E.g. Charles Williams, in *CW*, 24 April 1888 (in SS); James Guinness Rogers, *Present-day Religion and Theology Including a Review of the Down Grade Controversy* (London: T. Fisher Unwin, 1888), 159-61.

[143] George Howells, 'Christian Problems: Settled; and Awaiting Further

No reinterpretation of biblical eschatology was sufficiently convincing and attractive to rise above the confusion and take the dominant position that had once belonged to everlasting punishment. It was a situation parallel to that pertaining on Scripture and the atonement, and it gave further encouragement to the powerful reaction against dogmatic theology. D.W. Simon's long experience in Congregational theological education adds weight to his analysis of the situation in 1891:

> The theological tone of our colleges is, I believe, higher than it ever was; but the anti-theological and falsely practical current outside is so strong that even the best students have difficulty in stemming it – the majority prefer to float with it. ... Great interest, it is true, has been aroused in the three subjects of Inspiration, the Atonement, and Future Punishment – interest theological, no doubt, but very apt to rest in "the state of unreasoned sentimental conviction which is styled 'finding' or 'being found by' a truth."[144]

Spurgeon was loyal to a tradition in which doctrine had been defined but found himself living in an age that was dissatisfied with the old definitions but neither able nor often even willing to establish new ones. In the Downgrade Controversy Baptists were willing to affirm that their basis of communion was an evangelical one, but when it came to defining it doctrine by doctrine few were willing to be drawn into constructive theological debate. Instead, their main concern in formulating a doctrinal declaration was to find turns of phrase that would satisfy conservatives without embarrassing liberals: vagueness had become a virtue.

Ecclesiastical

The second part of the theological debate was a necessary complement to the first: once a basis of communion had been worked out it was necessary to decide how to publicize and implement it. As with the Congregationalists in the Leicester Conference Controversy, the debate turned largely on the tension between creed and freedom. Baptists agreed that a basis of communion involved doctrine, and that doctrine must be expressed

---

Exploration', *BQ*, 7 (1934), 107-8; quoted with the editor's permission.

144 F.J. Powicke, *David Worthington Simon* (London: Hodder & Stoughton, 1912), 166. It is interesting that he mentions the same three doctrines as pervaded the Downgrade Controversy.

in some way. 'Creed' is the obvious word which suggests itself in connection with doctrinal statement, and it wended its way through the thick of the fray much the same way as did 'evangelical', but with the difference that creeds were no more popular among Baptists than among Congregationalists.[145] Back in 1880 even Spurgeon shared the prevalent penchant for exalting freedom at the expense of creed:

> We have no defences for our churches, either in Acts of Parliament or enforced creeds; but the regenerated hearts and consecrated spirits of men, who resolve to live and die in the service of King Jesus, have hitherto sufficed, in the hands of the Spirit, to preserve us from grievous heresy.[146]

Some sought to rule out creeds by finding definitions such as 'a declaration of the faith made by the Church's authority'[147] that clearly did not fit in the congregational polity. More often the effort was made to work out the concept within the context of their own polity and theology. There was agreement across the battle lines of the controversy that an individual's creed was an organized expression of the sum of his beliefs.[148] Moving from the individual to the collective level introduced a new element, the distinction between prescriptive and descriptive statements of faith. The majority of Baptists joined with *The Christian World* on the one hand, and Spurgeon on the other, in differentiating between prescriptive creeds and descriptive declarations, and in considering that the Baptist Union Council's resolution of February 1888 fell into the latter category.[149] However, attitudes to it showed that even a descriptive declaration was not an innocuous document. A substantial minority on Council did their best to oppose the very idea of a declaration, and there was firm and successful resistance to conservative efforts to include in one any belief that was not universally held among members of the Baptist Union. Light is shed on these facts by Charles Williams:

---

145 See Joseph Angus, in *Freeman*, 13 April 1888 (in SS) for a critique of contemporary opposition to creeds.
146 Spurgeon, *An All-round Ministry: Addresses to Ministers and Students* (London: Passmore & Alabaster, 1900), 159.
147 H.C. Leonard, in *Baptist*, 10 November 1888 (in SS).
148 [Shindler], *Creed or No Creed*, p. 8; *CW*, 29 March 1888 (in SS).
149 *CW*, 1 March 1888; Spurgeon to Booth, in *Baptist*, 2 March 1888 (both in SS).

> Even though the constitution were not altered, a Declaration, if of any value, would decide who should be and who should not be members of the Union. Men with tender consciences would take the hint and leave the Union, and men with seared consciences would not, and, while we lost the former to our great regret, we should retain the latter to our reproach. A Declaration that would be inoperative, that would leave things as they are, that would affect no one, is not worth making... No one should vote for a Declaration who is not prepared to adopt a creed as a test of membership.[150]

In practice, therefore, the position of some conservatives, that 'creed' and 'declaration' were different names for the same thing, and that the real difference was between a declaration that was applied and one that was left on the shelf, had some force.[151]

This also strengthened the position of those who rejected both creeds and declarations. James Culross, the Baptist Union president in 1887, employed one of their favourite arguments when he informed Spurgeon that he would no more let a document come between himself and Scripture than hc would a priest.[152] Horace Noel, whose contributions to the conservative side of the debate were perhaps both the best and the least heeded, replied that an authoritative creed did not come between a believer and his Bible, but between the Baptist Union and those seeking admission.[153] Much less was made of arguments based on the premise that the Union was only a voluntary society than in the Leicester Conference Controversy, but one associate of Spurgeon did find an apposite quotation along these lines in the works of Andrew Fuller:

> If articles of faith be opposed to the authority of Scripture, or

---

[150] In *Baptist,* 20 April 1888 (in SS). His language is coloured by his desperate last-minute efforts to have the declaration dropped from the agenda, in order to prevent the disruption of the Union that was in prospect, but the point made stands nonetheless. Later *The Christian World* made the same point in connection with the London Baptist Association declaration, 25 October 1888 (in SS).

[151] [Shindler], *Creed or No Creed,* 7; Thomas Greenwood, in *Baptist,* 30 March 1888; Horace Noel, in *Baptist,* 2 November 1888; G.D. Hooper, in *Baptist,* 26 October 1888 (all in SS).

[152] Culross to Spurgeon, 22 November 1887, MS letter in Spurgeon's College. See also Angus, in *Freeman,* 13 April 1888 (in SS).

[153] Horace Noel, in *Baptist,* 20 January 1888 (in SS).

substituted in the place of such authority, they become objectionable and injurious; but if they simply express the united judgement of those who voluntarily subscribe to them, they are incapable of any such kind of imputation.[154]

Fuller accepted that no creed could partake in or mediate the Bible's authority in the Church, but maintained that associations of churches could use a credal interpretation of the Bible to regulate their own membership. However, this view was presented very inadequately in the controversy; even the man who quoted Fuller largely negated the force of his argument by concluding his pamphlet with a repetition of the dominant formula, that there must always be appeal from a declaration or creed to the Bible.[155]

As a rule, history was conspicuously absent from the debate, another area in which the Baptist controversy was poorer than its Congregational counterpart. Sheer ignorance prevailed to a surprising extent: *The Baptist* was convinced that no Baptist confession of faith existed outside the Bible, and when Spurgeon published the 1689 confession, a Baptist version of the Congregational Savoy declaration, it could not hide its surprise and discomfiture.[156] This exchange took place in 1889-90; during the main part of the controversy Spurgeon scarcely alluded to confessions of faith.[157]

Ignorance cannot however be proffered as an excuse for some of the inconsistency shown toward creeds in contemporary Baptist practice. One of the few things repeated clearly, frequently and unanswerably by supporters of Spurgeon was that the Baptist Union already had a creed, so that the question before them was not whether to have a creed, but what creed to have. A congregational polity and believers' baptism were written into the constitution, while an unwritten creed excluding non-trinitarian views was evidently in operation.[158] This was a necessary component of the argument that the Union already had sufficient powers to safeguard its evangelical nature, one that was of great importance to Spurgeon's opponents in the months following his resignation. But by the time of the Union debate in April 1888 anti-credalism was asserting itself strongly. The two currents were juxtaposed, with

154 Quoted in [Shindler], *Creed or No Creed,* 10.
155 [Shindler], *Creed or No Creed,* 11.
156 *Baptist,* 28 March 1890 (in SS). See also *ST,* 25 (1889), 618.
157 *ST,* 24 (February 1888), 82.
158 *Ibid.*; Robert Kerr, in Baptist, 20 January 1888 (in SS).

total disregard for the contradiction, in Charles Williams' speech proposing the compromise motion. Having been applauded for stating that a creed was unnecessary, he said that they should get their creeds from Christ alone; 'and because I go to Him alone I will never be a party to the formulating of any creed as a test of membership in any shape whatsoever'.[159] But, in an abrupt change, he concluded on the opposite tack:

> We are a Union of evangelical Christians, and we wish it to be known to all whom it may concern that the Council and the Assembly intend to maintain the evangelical character of the Baptist Union... We have the power under the Constitution to revise our list of members from time to time, and should we know of a man who is not evangelical in character we will say to him, "You have no place in an Evangelical Society".[160]

The problem that Spurgeon's opponents failed to resolve was the tension between their two yearnings: to be evangelical, and to be free. Even those who set the greatest store by freedom acknowledged a doctrinal standard of fellowship. In his comment on the controversy, John Hunter, the liberal Congregationalist, said that Congregational freedom meant far more to him than the Congregational polity, but added:

> While claiming this freedom and comprehensiveness for the Congregational body, I must at the same time testify that I have always and everywhere found it recognised by its most liberal and progressive ministers and members, that when a man lost his faith in the essential Deity of Jesus Christ, he had, and ought to have, no place among us as a recognised teacher and preacher.[161]

In a similar anti-credal vein, *The Baptist* proclaimed that it would be better to sacrifice the Union itself than freedom of conscience; yet it added immediately afterwards that there was a line beyond which liberty became license, and proceeded to sketch it in doctrinally.[162] Sweeping creeds aside in one paragraph, they brought them back in all but name in the next. Horace Noel's argument, that whenever

---

159 *CW*, 24 April 1888 (in SS).
160 *Ibid.*
161 In *BW*, 23 September 1887 (in SS).
162 11 November 1887 (in SS).

one distinguishes between beliefs compatible and incompatible with fellowship one brings in a test creed, is incontrovertible.[163] When the anti-credal rhetoric is taken away what remains is not a confrontation between free and doctrinally limited communion, but simply differences over where and how to trace the bounds within which freedom could be enjoyed.

Four ways of drawing the line can be distinguished. One was a peculiarly Baptist idea, with no parallels in the Leicester Conference Controversy. The idea of what might be described as a sacramental creed was that participation in believers' baptism and the Lord's Supper implied acceptance of the fundamentals of Christian faith that these embodied. The first of the two main sections of the Baptist Union declaration was an expression of this theory. But this was not really the more palatable alternative to a creed its supporters believed it to be. One problem was that the sacraments could mean different things to different people: the Unitarian General Baptists of the Old Connexion practised them. Another difficulty was to explain the difference between a statement of the doctrines taught or implied by these sacraments and any other doctrinal statement.

The second possibility was the method in operation up to the time of the controversy, the right of Council to delete names from the membership list subject to appeal to Assembly. This right, much publicized in order to refute Spurgeon's allegation that the Union had no doctrinal control over its membership, was only used on rare occasions when there was an overwhelming consensus as to the unacceptability of a particular view. Indeed, it relied on the existence of such a consensus for its effectiveness. So long as the theological basis of communion was informally decided by what J.A. Picton called the selective action of spiritual affinities the powers of Council could act as a final sanction to prevent any forcing of this otherwise unpoliced system. This was fine while the consensus lasted, but the Downgrade Controversy resulted from the decay of that consensus. In that new situation an informal, unwritten and flexible creed could hardly be counted adequate. The leaders thought they could broaden the basis of communion according to their own developing spiritual affinities while preserving the old informality, but they had no adequate sense of the consequences this had for a minority who were not prepared to go along with them. Though it opposed Spurgeon in the controversy, *The British Weekly* understood the hidden force that elicited his openly forceful response:

---

163 In *Baptist*, 20 April 1888 (in SS).

> When it is urged that this "wretched controversy" should cease, that churches may go on with their work, it is forgotten that new doctrines have been forced in upon the churches in the most vehement and brow-beating fashion, with small regard for unity and peace. Yet whenever remonstrance or resistance are made there is a cry for peace![164]

This leaves the third and fourth ways to draw the line, declaration and creed. Both were doctrinal summaries, the difference being in their constitutional status and authority. The declaration was an attempt to steer a middle course between an informal basis and a creed, aiming to reinforce a basis of communion acceptable to the current majority while exerting only a limited influence on the future. In practical terms there was probably little difference between the two, for like Congregationalists a decade earlier few Baptists were prepared to stomach that adjunct to creeds, excommunication.[165] In any case, the difference is only of academic interest, as conservatives failed to obtain declarations that excluded any of the views they would have liked to exclude. Their greatest success was in the secondary controversy in the London Baptist Association, whose declaration had a greater resemblance to a creed than the Union's; yet even there they could only draw the doctrinal net tight enough to allow next to no room for spiritual affinities to continue their process of expansion without considerable discomfort.

* * *

Few comments on the Downgrade Controversy are as telling as this one of Guinness Rogers: 'There are no controversies which are worse in themselves or more difficult to bring to any satisfactory conclusion than those in which the issues are not clearly stated and defined, and this is pre-eminently the case in the present instance.'[166] It was by and large an unsuccessful – and therefore not untypical – controversy. It was complex and emotive, for much was at stake; but it was bedevilled by a general inability to express positions clearly,

---

164 17 February 1888 (in SS).

165 See **no.1575**, in Spurgeon, *The Messiah* (London: Passmore & Alabaster, 1898), for Spurgeon's own coolness toward excommunication.

166 Rogers, *Present-Day Religion,* 139.

let alone attain a sympathetic understanding of the positions of opponents. Most participants were trained for the ministry, but when they became controversialists, whether eagerly or reluctantly, their lack of training in that field was alarmingly apparent. According to Spurgeon's student and biographer J.C. Carlile, 'The controversy known as the "Down Grade" was not a squabble between Spurgeon and the Baptist Union. It was one of those thought conflicts which reappear in history when opposing ideas can no longer refuse battle.'[167] It was indeed a thought conflict, but unfortunately one that was all but buried beneath a squabble.

[167] Carlile, *C. H. Spurgeon, An Interpretative Biography*, 243.

CHAPTER 8

Conclusion

The theological development of Baldwin Brown and Dale points unambiguously toward a single dominant factor motivating their theological journeys – journeys representative of those of others of their generation. Congregationalists growing up in the mid-nineteenth century were not reluctantly driven to the conclusion that some revision of Calvinist theology was made necessary by increasing pressure from critical, exegetical or scientific conclusions. They rejected a solidly constructed system with a well established appeal to Scripture, one with a long heritage going right back to Calvin, and addressed themselves to the task of constructing another that might bear comparison with it – a task that demanded all the piety, assiduity and ingenuity that were liberally bestowed upon it – because they were driven to do so by moral outrage. Beside that, all other motivations pale into insignificance. The God of Calvinism appeared monstrous, an absolute ruler who arbitrarily condemned people to an everlasting punishment totally out of proportion to their sin, while equally arbitrarily bestowing everlasting blessedness on others who were quite as sinful, justifying this by some legal sleight of hand in which the guilty got off scot-free after an innocent had been condemned. It was axiomatic that God must be better than humankind, and yet this God seemed clearly worse, and certainly not the God of love, mercy and forgiveness declared by the Bible.

This ethical revolution was no sudden new arrival on the scene: it had been gathering momentum over a very long period, with the cultured classes always in the vanguard. Evangelical Dissent had long kept it at bay by immersing itself in evangelism and sanctification, accompanied by withdrawal from the world; at a theological level the tension it created was maintained at a bearable level by such ideas as the governmental theory of the atonement. But the generation under consideration in this study came upon the scene at a critical stage. On the one hand the fires of revival were cooling, on the other hand the barriers that provided some protection against broader social influences were coming down as Nonconformity returned to greater participation in national life in a new political environment. The crucial element, however, coinciding with these developments, was the arrival in the mainstream of British culture of a new movement, Romanticism. The high Victorian generation that took over leadership of Nonconformity in the 1860s and maintained its hold through the 1880s was pre-eminently Nonconformity's Romantic generation. The tendency of Romanticism to internalize and subjectivize authority injected unprecedented pace into the ethical revolution, all the more powerfully among evangelicals since they had a traditional seriousness of their own which reinforced the new high seriousness of Romanticism. It was the ethical impact of Romanticism that created the urge to work out a new theology, the one that came to be labelled 'liberal' – it is anachronistic to bestow that label on any pre-Romantic theology. So it was this ethical imperative that gave liberal theology its essence, making it recognizable through all its many developments: if evangelical theology began with an authoritative biblical gospel, liberal theology started with authoritative moral axioms.

Within the broad movement that is Romanticism, the principal influence that led Baldwin Brown, Dale, Clifford and others like them to reject aspects of their theological heritage that had lasted since the Reformation can be identified more precisely. It would be hard to exaggerate the impact of Thomas Carlyle's vision of reality, righteousness and earnestness on their generation, although the complementary influence of others – for Clifford Ralph Waldo Emerson was paramount – should not be forgotten.

But theological guidance was one thing Carlyle could not offer to Nonconformists who felt that their faith must lie at the heart of the reality he advocated. A number turned to the only readily available guides who had prospected a route out of Calvinism that was as spiritual as it was ethical (for evangelical spirituality was not among the features of the movement the first generation of liberals were inclined to reject): Thomas Erskine, Alexander Scott and McLeod Campbell. F.D. Maurice's antecedents were more complex, but his larger corpus of writings and prominence in the Church of England gave him a wider influence than the Scottish friends whose concerns were so similar to his own.

Other features of liberalism – many would say, causes of liberalism – have had no place in this summary of its genesis in Nonconformity for the simple reason that they played little if any part in it. Though their seeds were present at an early stage, it was decades before the fruit appeared, sometimes only in a later generation. Early liberals conceived of life as an education and rejected the conventional distinction between justification and sanctification, but it was only in the 1870s that thoroughly developmental theologies began to appear when Herbert Spencer's philosophy had achieved its impact and it was realised that Darwinian evolution could give them a scientific cachet. Early liberals did relativize the Bible's authority – interestingly, by exploiting possibilities inherent in the old inductive approach of the Enlightenment, while it was conservatives who gradually took up the deductive thinking of plenary verbal inspiration and inerrancy as they too came under the influence of Romantic currents.[1] It is noteworthy that the concern that underlay this was largely with biblical ethics, and that early British liberals' interest in biblical criticism was minimal. This was the case with Erskine, Scott, McLeod Campbell, Maurice, Baldwin Brown, Dale and Clifford, and most of their prominent associates. None of them countered the mid-century vilification of German theology that helped insulate Britain from critical ideas emanating from that quarter for another quarter of a century. Those who lived to see the arrival of biblical criticism at the top of the agenda in the 1880s did not indeed fight it as an enemy, but nor did they greet it as a friend: rather, they treated it like a dubious stranger that needed to be disarmed before being allowed the run of the house. Lastly, even those who like Clifford affirmed the importance of the social dimension of the gospel in a way that evangelical Nonconformity had never done, did not do so at the expense of the individual dimension. That was only possible in a later generation that had not known the evangelical spirituality in which liberal pioneers had grown up.

This chronology, and hence hierarchy, of the causes and components of liberalism still needs to establish its place in the history of theology: a more diffuse movement, it has not been subjected to the intense analytical attention lavished on the Reformation, the Evangelical Revival, or the Oxford Movement. Evangelical folk history has tended to assume that the issues that assumed most prominence later, especially during the fundamentalist controversy – notably evolution and biblical criticism – had always been central to liberalism: in this it has been quite mistaken and still stands in need of correction.

Unlike liberals, conservatives had a clear doctrinal position to

---

[1] Robert Haldane, a notable pioneer of inerrantist thinking, published his views in 1816, the year in which his acquaintance with continental revival began – a movement influenced by Romanticism. The classic pre-Princeton statement of the position was by Louis Gaussen, a product of the Swiss revival. See D.W. Bebbington, *Evangelicalism in Modern Britain: A History from the 1730s to the 1980s* (London: Unwin Hyman, 1989), 86-91.

rally round, the common evangelical heritage embodied in the theological basis of the Evangelical Alliance; and in Nonconformity they also had a leader, Charles Haddon Spurgeon. Spurgeon's life and thought illustrate the fact that conservatives were not completely cut off from the currents of thought that gave birth to liberalism. Although his early years were spent in a more sheltered environment than those of the other leaders in this study, he displayed several of the qualities the three of them had in common. He shared their concern for reality, rooted in spirituality, and came out with similar criticisms of the shallowness of much contemporary evangelical religion; like them his enthusiasm for living, practical Christianity was accompanied by little involvement in the more technical domains associated with the faith, such as biblical criticism; he also went through his period of youthful doubt. Our study has shown that he was not even immune to the appeal of the moral considerations that shaped their theological revisions.[2] These similarities (and others might be added) show that Spurgeon was not immune to the Romantic tide that swept his generation.

But the key difference was in the way Spurgeon responded to that appeal: instead of rejecting aspects of his received theology, he studied the Bible and concluded that his theology was biblical, and that the Bible was God's word; and, sensing spiritual confirmation of both these conclusions, he decided that the reasonable thing to do would be to submit his reason and conscience to its authority. There was nothing innovative about the doctrinal defences with which he surrounded the Bible: plenary verbal inspiration, infallibility, no compromise, and very little debate. Believing that everyone who questioned the Bible had *ipso facto* committed the cardinal error of asserting his own authority over that of the Bible, he did not see any need for further argument. The haven that Newman found in the Catholic Church Spurgeon discovered in the Bible, confident that the Calvinist tradition had brought out most of its main themes, and that the key to the rest was to accept what the Bible said without excessive concern for system or consistency.

Spurgeon's position was similar to the general conservative pattern: experience was a rich source of assurance, and a world remained to be evangelized before the dramatic finale foretold by biblical prophecy. Above all, the Bible was declared sacrosanct: the only concession made was to ascribe infallibility to the original text in order to draw the sting of textual criticism. The thesis of Robert Shindler's original Downgrade articles, that any shift of position on the Bible might start one moving down a slippery slope to complete

---

[2] See p. 151 above

loss of faith, was widely shared.[3] True to its evangelical heritage, continuing conservatism was an even less intellectual movement than early liberalism; theology was considered a finished work, and biblical criticism an illicit one. Few tried to fight on at a scholarly level, and those who did achieved very little.[4] Spurgeon's unusual early exposure to the Puritans and subsequent love and study of them stimulated his theology and exegesis in a manner altogether untypical of the movement he headed.

As well as insights into the nature of mid-nineteenth century liberal and conservative theology, this study sheds some light on the similarities and differences at this period of the two denominations it covers. The different paths taken by the Baptist and Congregational Unions in the twentieth century, all the more intriguing in view of the similarities of their early history and the close historical link between the denominations, have drawn the attention of historians from both traditions. When, half way through the century, Ernest Payne listed reasons for the divergence, he put first the theological gap that had grown up, remarking that there were still many Baptists sympathetic to Spurgeon.[5] Twenty years later Clyde Binfield's explanation was similar, although he distinguished 'Spurgeonism' from Spurgeon, holding the former responsible.[6] Responding after another decade, John Briggs suggested that as Spurgeon's variety of late nineteenth century Nonconformity was closer to that of the earlier part of the century, it would be more accurate to say that it was the Congregationalists who parted company with the Baptists: he therefore invoked 'Baldwin Brownism' as the cause of the gap between the denominations.[7] Something can be said for both sides of that debate: a minority holding their station by swimming against the tide while the majority are drifting with it is certainly the more active group. There is no doubt that the tide was running toward liberalism, making

---

[3] *ST*, 23 (1887), 170.

[4] David Bebbington's attempt to say that evangelicals made a bigger intellectual contribution in this period than they are generally credited for, especially in theology, is one of the least successful arguments in his impressive study of British evangelical history. Bebbington, *Evangelicalism in Modern Britain*, 137-41.

[5] E.A. Payne, 'Baptist-Congregationalist Relationships', *CQ* 33 (1955), 222.

[6] J.C.C. Binfield, 'Congregationalism's Two Sides of the Baptistery – a Paedobaptist View', *BQ*, 26 (1975), 130.

[7] J.H.Y. Briggs, 'Charles Haddon Spurgeon and the Baptist Denomination in Nineteenth Century Britain', *BQ*, 31 (1986), 218-9, 228.

Baldwin Brown's task as a leader of thought easier than Spurgeon's, and therefore making Spurgeon's influence all the more worthy of the prominence it is accorded by all three commentators.

It would, however, be unwise to assign to Spurgeon the entire responsibility for the theological differences between the denominations without enquiring whether there was something about Baptists that made them more amenable to his conservatism. Briggs has suggested that believers' baptism was such a factor: it underlined the principle of the congregational polity, that church membership should be restricted to believers; it pointed to the priority of evangelism; and it was a natural companion to evangelical belief.[8] This must be acknowledged; and it might be added that believers' baptism also represented an additional element of divergence from the dominant Christian tradition, another handicap to be overcome in any bid to attain the respectability enshrined in the established church.

That last observation ties in with the fact that the overall social standing of the Congregationalists was higher than that of the Baptists. This assessment was commonplace among contemporaries as well as historians, and is not affected by Binfield's point that little distinguished the life of similarly placed churches of the two denominations.[9] The relative social and theological standing of the denominations fits with evidence from the Downgrade Controversy that liberalism was strongest in the urban middle class.

Yet Baldwin Brown was the only one among the four leaders studied to have come from the urban social elite of Nonconformity, the milieu most propitious to liberalism according to the theory entertained above. Dale and Clifford illustrate in different ways how that liberal ethos was accessible to intelligent youngsters from less privileged backgrounds – especially ones whose mothers encouraged them to aim for the ministry. Dale was brought up in a large London church where he could get alongside people whose status and values his mother was ambitious for him to share. Though rural, Clifford's background was industrial, animated by Chartism as well as chapel; a key factor in his case was the influence of the liberal-minded Sunday school teacher who supervised his self-education. Indeed, education was a key to upward social movement for both men. Something that should not be forgotten when the middle-classness of churches is discussed is the unrivalled opportunities they afforded for upward social mobility as a result of allowing unusually free inter-class contact.

---

[8] *Ibid.*, 236.
[9] Binfield, 'Congregationalism's Two Sides', 121.

A lesson from the two controversies was that in the 1870s and 1880s respectively the militant wings of both liberalism and conservatism lacked both the strength and the quality of leadership to prevail against the two denominational establishments in their rapidly expanding Unions. The two might proclaim their mutual incompatibility, but it arose too late for schism to be viable. The mid-century Methodist blood-letting marked the end of an era, with the latter part of the century seeing the dawn of the ecumenical age. In their first thirty years the Baptist and Congregational Unions were quite fragile, and might have snapped under pressures considerably less than those the Baptist Union survived in the Downgrade Controversy; but the ties with which they had since bound churches to themselves and each other, ties of loyalty and fellowship as well as financial ones, proved too strong. Ernest Payne, himself a secretary of the Baptist Union, drew attention to the importance of this fact, that denominations founded in rejection of institutionalized religion had suddenly, in the course of two or three generations, developed powerful institutions of their own.[10]

This process meant that Baptists and Congregationalists had to start to learn to live with the difficulties inherent in a broad and loosely defined basis of communion, with the like of which the Church of England had been coping for centuries. Both the Leicester Conference and the Downgrade Controversies illustrate that the pressure is felt most at the conservative end of the theological spectrum, where people like Spurgeon could believe that fundamental aspects of their faith were being denied at the opposite end of the spectrum. The two controversies also show that liberals were insensitive to the problems they were involuntarily causing. A conclusion that can be drawn from the debates is that it was impossible to retain all who felt they belonged in the denominational fellowship. One alternative was a tightly defined basis of communion that would exclude some on the liberal wing; the other possibility was an informal basis which would include some holding views that would lead conservatives with a rigorous approach to matters of fellowship to resign. In both denominations the latter solution was applied, with the result that in the decades that followed many conservatives either retreated to the fringes or withdrew altogether. Perhaps the idea of telling some they are not welcome has been considered more repulsive than that of placing others in a situation that induces them to retire of their own accord. This is a scenario that recurs perennially in different guises. It has not always been sufficiently appreciated that the result of the two

---

[10] Payne, 'Baptist-Congregationalist Relationships', 222-3.

alternative courses of action is the same.

While this book has clarified the theologies of some of the leaders of high Victorian Nonconformity, and removed the distortions that have plagued the historiography of the Downgrade Controversy, its most distinctive contribution may be in its understanding of liberalism in relation to Romanticism. I dissent from Bebbington's broad conclusion that evangelicalism continued to a large extent in an Enlightenment culture in Victorian Nonconformity, rather little influenced by Romanticism. Its weakness can be seen in his handling of Spurgeon: he cites Spurgeon's opposition to Gothic architecture, organs and gowns – all features of Romanticism – and takes them as typical of Nonconformity when in fact Spurgeon was in a shrinking minority on all three points. Furthermore, he neglects the more substantial areas in which Spurgeon joined fellow Nonconformists in following Romantic trends: preaching style, the cult of manliness, dress, sentimentalism, and also, on the conservative theological side, inerrancy and premillennialism.[11]

But my difference with Bebbington may not be so very great. I would argue that Romanticism was a major phase in Western culture, between Enlightenment and modernism/post-modernism, but one that did not end up achieving so great an impact as those two in the sense of changing the overall complexion and direction of culture. Only in its initial surges (in Britain to be dated to the early nineteenth century in high culture, around the 1820s for the culture of the elite, and in popular culture to mid-century) does one find a relatively pure Romanticism, sharply marked out from the preceding Enlightenment. Afterward there were cross-currents in which Enlightenment emphases returned, though not unaffected by the intervening Romantic tide. (This is in fact a recurring pattern in cultural change, and the label 'Romanticism' should still be used for the entire period before (post-)modernism, so long as the broader and narrow senses are distinguished.) Only considerable strength or marked isolation might have prevented Nonconformity from following the overall pattern – and neither of these did apply.

What of the value of the theological work of this Romantic generation? One reason why there have been so many varieties of liberal theology is that no dominant system arose in the movement's early years to give it a recognizable outline. In this respect Calvinism was a hard act to follow, and Dale was by no means the only one to rue the slow pace and provisional nature of theological

[11] David Bebbington, 'Gospel and Culture in Victorian Nonconformity', in Jane Shaw and Alan Kreider, eds, *Culture and the Nonconformist Tradition* (Cardiff: University of Wales Press, 1999), 57, 59.

reconstruction and the lack of interest in that process caused by the widespread contemporary denigration of theology. Towards the end of the century widespread calls for the rise of a great theologian were a symptom of dissatisfaction with the progress made. None emerged, nor was there any sense that a new system of any great robustness had been attained. Similar calls were not heard on the conservative side, but perhaps they should have been, as the pressure on traditional theology should not have been written off as merely due to aberrant cultural trends. My own engagement with this period began, as I suspect some others' has too, with a hope that the early history of theological problems whose impact I myself felt might hold clues to finding their answers. In a way I was disappointed: the answers are not embedded in the sediment of the nineteenth century waiting for the skilled or lucky theological archaeologist to uncover them, but thinking the thoughts of that Romantic generation after them with a mind that could draw on resources not available to them did prove helpful. But that will be another story.

Appendix 1

Declaration of the Faith, Church Order, and Discipline of the Congregational, or Independent Dissenters Adopted at the Annual Meeting of the Congregational Union, May, 1833.

THE CONGREGATIONAL Churches in England and Wales, frequently called INDEPENDENT, hold the following doctrines, as of Divine authority, and as the foundation of Christian faith and practice. They are also formed and governed according to the principles herein stated.

PRELIMINARY NOTES

1. It is not designed, in the following summary, to do more than to state the leading doctrines of faith and order maintained by Congregational Churches in general.
2. It is not proposed to offer any proofs, reasons, or arguments, in support of the doctrines herein stated, but simply to declare what the Denomination believes to be taught by the pen of inspiration.
3. It is not intended to present a scholastic or critical confession of faith, but merely such a statement as any intelligent member of the body might offer, as containing its leading principles.
4. It is not intended that the following statement should be put forth with any authority, or as a standard to which assent should be required.
5. Disallowing the utility of creeds and articles of religion as a bond of union, and protesting against subscription to any human formularies as a term of communion, Congregationalists are yet willing to declare, for general information, what is commonly believed among them, reserving to every one the most perfect liberty of conscience.

6. Upon some minor points of doctrine and practice, they, differing among themselves, allow to each other the right to form an unbiased judgment of the Word of God.
7. They wish it to be observed, that, notwithstanding their jealousy of subscription to creeds and articles, and their disapproval of the imposition of any human standard, whether of faith or discipline, they are far more agreed in their doctrines and practices than any Church which enjoins subscription and enforces a human standard of orthodoxy; and they believe that there is no minister and no church among them that would deny the substance of any one of the following doctrines of religion, though each might prefer to state his sentiments in his own way.

PRINCIPLES OF RELIGION

I. The Scriptures of the Old Testament, as received by the Jews, and the books of the New Testament, as received by the Primitive Christians from the Evangelists and Apostles, Congregational Churches believe to be Divinely inspired, and of supreme authority. These writings, in the languages in which they were originally composed, are to be consulted, with the aids of sound criticism, as a final appeal to all controversies, but the common version they consider to be adequate to the ordinary purposes of Christian instruction and edification.

II. They believe in one God, essentially wise, holy, just, and good; eternal, infinite, and immutable in all natural and moral perfections; the Creator, Supporter, and Governor of all beings, and of all things.

III. They believe that God is revealed in the Scriptures, as the Father, the Son, and the Holy Spirit, and that to each are attributable the same Divine properties and perfections. The doctrine of the Divine existence, as above stated, they cordially believe, without attempting fully to explain.

IV. They believe that man was created after the Divine image, sinless, and in his kind, perfect.

V. They believe that the first man disobeyed the Divine command, fell from his state of innocence and purity, and involved all his posterity in the consequences of that fall.

VI. They believe that, therefore, all mankind are born in sin, and that a fatal inclination to moral evil, utterly incurable by human means, is inherent in every descendant of Adam.

VII. They believe that God having, before the foundation of the world, designed to redeem fallen man, made disclosures of His mercy, which were the grounds of faith and hope from the earliest ages.

VIII. They believe that God revealed more fully to Abraham the covenant of His grace, and, having promised that from his descendants should arise the Deliverer and Redeemer of mankind, set that patriarch and his posterity apart, as a race specially favoured and separated to His service; a peculiar church, formed and carefully preserved, under the Divine sanction and government until the birth of the promised Messiah.

IX. They believe that, in the fulness of the time, the Son of God was manifested, being born of the Virgin Mary, but conceived by the power of the Holy Spirit; and that our Lord Jesus Christ was both the Son of man and the Son of God; partaking fully and truly of human nature though without sin – equal with the Father and "the express image of His person".

X. They believe that Jesus Christ, the Son of God, revealed, either personally in His own ministry, or by the Holy Spirit in the ministry of His apostles, the whole mind of God, for our salvation; and that, by His obedience to the Divine law while He lived, and by His sufferings unto death, He meritoriously "obtained eternal redemption for us"; having thereby vindicated and illustrated Divine justice, "magnified the law", and "brought in everlasting righteousness".

XI. They believe that, after His death and resurrection, He ascended up to heaven, where, as the Mediator, He "ever liveth" to rule over all, and to "make intercession for them that come unto God by Him".

XII. They believe that the Holy Spirit is given, in consequence of Christ's mediation, to quicken and renew the hearts of men; and that His influence is indispensably necessary to bring a sinner to true repentance, to produce saving faith, to regenerate the heart, and to perfect our sanctification.

XIII. They believe that we are justified through faith in Christ, as "the Lord our righteousness", and not "by the works of the law".

XIV. They believe that all who will be saved were the objects of God's eternal and electing love, and were given by an act of Divine sovereignty to the Son of God; which in no way interferes with the system of means, nor with the grounds of human responsibility; being wholly unrevealed as to its objects, and not a rule of human duty.

XV. They believe that the Scriptures teach the final perseverance of all true believers to a state of eternal blessedness, which they are appointed to obtain through constant faith in Christ, and uniform obedience to His commands.

XVI. They believe that a holy life will be the necessary effect of a true faith and that good works are the certain fruits of a vital union to Christ.

XVII. They believe that the sanctification of true Christians, or their growth in the graces of the Spirit, and meetness for heaven, is gradually carried on through the whole period during which it pleases God to continue them in the present life, and that, at death, their souls, perfectly freed from all remains of evil, are immediately received into the presence of Christ.

XVIII. They believe in the perpetual obligation of Baptism and the Lord's Supper; the former to be administered to all converts to Christianity and their children, by the application of water to the subject, "in the name of the Father, and of the Son, and of the Holy Ghost", and the latter to be celebrated by Christian churches as a token of faith in the Saviour, and of brotherly love.

XIX. They believe that Christ will finally come to judge the whole human race according to their works; that the bodies of the dead will be raised again; and that, as the Supreme Judge, He will divide the righteous from the wicked, will receive the righteous into "life everlasting", but send away the wicked into "everlasting punishment".

XX. They believe that Jesus Christ directed His followers to live together in Christian fellowship, and to maintain the communion of saints; and that, for this purpose, they are jointly to observe all Divine ordinances, and maintain that church order and discipline which is either expressly enjoined by inspired institution, or sanctioned by the undoubted example of the apostles and of apostolic churches.

PRINCIPLES OF CHURCH ORDER AND DISCIPLINE

I. The Congregational Churches hold it to be the will of Christ that true believers should voluntarily assemble together to observe religious ordinances to promote mutual edification and holiness, to perpetuate and propagate the Gospel in the world, and to advance the glory and worship of God, through Jesus Christ; and that each society of believers, having these objects in view in its formation, is properly a Christian Church.

II. They believe that the New Testament contains, either in the form of express statute, or in the example and practice of apostles and apostolic churches, all the articles of faith necessary to be believed, and all the principles of order and discipline requisite for constituting and governing Christian societies; and that human traditions, fathers and councils, canons and creeds, possess no authority over the faith and practice of Christians.

III. They acknowledge Christ as the only Head of the Church, and the officers of each church under Him, as ordained to administer His laws impartially to all; and their only appeal, in all questions touching their religious faith and practice, is to the sacred Scriptures.

IV. They believe that the New Testament authorises every Christian church to elect its own officers, to manage all its own affairs, and to stand independent of, and irresponsible to, all authority, saving that only of the Supreme and Divine Head of the Church, the Lord Jesus Christ.

V. They believe that the only officers placed by the apostles over individual churches are the bishops or pastors and the deacons; the number of these being dependent upon the number of the church; and that to these, as the officers of the church, is committed respectively the administration of its spiritual and temporal concerns – subject, however, to the approbation of the church.

VI. They believe that no persons should be received as members of Christian churches, but such as make a credible profession of Christianity, are living according to its precepts, and attest a willingness to be subject to its discipline, and that none should be excluded from the fellowship of the church, but such as deny the faith of Christ, violate His laws, or refuse to submit themselves to the discipline which the Word of God enforces.

VII. The power of admission into any Christian church, and rejection from it, they believe to be vested in the church itself, and to be exercised only through the medium of its own officers.

VIII. They believe that Christian churches should statedly meet for the celebration of public worship, for the observance of the Lord's Supper, and for the sanctification of the first day of the week.

IX. They believe that the power of a Christian church is purely spiritual and should in no way be corrupted by union with temporal or civil power.

X. They believe that it is the duty of Christian churches to hold communion with each other, to entertain an enlarged affection for each other, as members of the same body, and to co-operate for the promotion of the Christian cause; but that no church, or union of churches, has any right or power to interfere with the faith or discipline of any other church further than to separate from such as, in faith or practice, depart from the Gospel of Christ.

XI. They believe that it is the privilege and duty of every church to call forth such of its members as may appear to be qualified by the Holy Spirit to sustain the office of the ministry; and that Christian churches unitedly ought to consider the maintenance of the Christian ministry in an adequate degree of learning as one of their especial cares, that the cause of the Gospel may be both honourably sustained and constantly promoted.

XII. They believe that church officers, whether bishops or deacons, should be chosen by the free voice of the church; but that their dedication to the duties of their office should take place with special prayer, and by solemn designation, to which most of the churches add the imposition of hands by those already in office.

XIII. They believe that the fellowship of every Christian church should be so liberal as to admit to communion in the Lord's Supper all whose faith and godliness are, on the whole, undoubted, though conscientiously differing in points of minor importance; and that this outward sign of fraternity in Christ should be co-extensive with the fraternity itself, though without involving any compliances which conscience would deem to be sinful.

(Source: Albert Peel, *These Hundred Years: A History of the Congregational Union of England and Wales, 1831-1931* (London: Congregational Union of England and Wales, 1931), 69-74).

Appendix 2

The Basis of Faith of the Evangelical Alliance (1846)

'That the parties composing the Alliance shall be such persons only as hold and maintain what are usually understood to be Evangelical views, in regard to the matters of Doctrine understated, namely: -

'1. The Divine Inspiration, Authority, and Sufficiency of the Holy Scriptures.

'2. The Right and Duty of Private Judgement in the Interpretation of the Holy Scriptures.

'3. The Unity of the Godhead, and the Trinity of the Persons therein.

'4. The utter Depravity of Human Nature, in consequence of the Fall.

'5. The Incarnation of the Son of God, His work of Atonement for sinners of mankind, and His Mediatorial Intercession and Reign.

'6. The Justification of the sinner by Faith alone.

'7. The work of the Holy Spirit in the Conversion and Sanctification of the sinner.

'8. The Immortality of the Soul, the Resurrection of the Body, the Judgment of the World by our Lord Jesus Christ, with the Eternal Blessedness of the Righteous, and the Eternal Punishment of the Wicked.

'9. The Divine institution of the Christian Ministry, and the obligation and perpetuity of the ordinances of Baptism and the Lord's Supper.

'It is, however, distinctly declared: - First, that this brief Summary is not to be regarded, in any formal or Ecclesiastical sense, as a Creed or Confession, nor the adoption of it as involving an assumption of the right authoritatively to define the limits of Christian Brotherhood; but simply as an indication of the class of persons whom it is desirable to embrace within the Alliance: - Second, that the selection of certain tenets, with the omission of others, is not to be held as implying that the former constitute the whole body of important Truth, or that the latter are unimportant.'

(Source: David King, *Historical Sketch of the Evangelical Alliance, Consisting of Two Papers Read in Freemasons' Hall, London, August 19, 1846, and August 20, 1851* (Glasgow: S. & T. Dunn, 1851), 34-5).

Bibliography

With very few exceptions, this bibliography is limited to works cited. Books by Charles Haddon Spurgeon marked with an asterisk denote collected editions of sermons originally published in the *New Park Street Pulpit* and *Metropolitan Tabernacle Pulpit* series.

Manuscripts and Typescripts

Baptist Union Archive, Angus Library, Regent's Park College, Oxford. Material related to the Downgrade Controversy, principally the correspondence of Samuel Harris Booth, the Secretary, and the Council Minute Book, 1887-89.

Dale, Robert William, letters to, in the University of Birmingham Library. The most useful correspondence was that from Henry Wace.

Payne, Ernest A., 'The Down Grade Controversy' (1955), typescript in the Angus Library, Regent's Park College, Oxford.

Spurgeon's College Archive. In an uncatalogued and disorganized state; a wide variety of material was used, including a considerable body of Spurgeon's correspondence. The following is the most important single element:

Spurgeon Scrapbooks, Downgrade vols 1-6, and various other volumes covering 1883-93, in Spurgeon's College. Compiled by Spurgeon's secretary, Joseph Harrald, these have unfortunately been dismembered since I worked on them. The press cuttings that were the main element have been transferred to ring binders, but the manuscript letters and other insertions are no longer associated with them.

Theses

Colquitt, Henry Franklin, 'The Soteriology of Charles Haddon Spurgeon Revealed in his Sermons and Controversial Writings' (PhD, University of Edinburgh, 1951).

Gould, William Blair, 'The Theological Contribution of Robert William Dale' (PhD, University of Edinburgh, 1955).

Johnson, Mark David, 'The Dissolution of Dissent: A Social and Institutional History of Congregational Theological Accommodation, 1850-1918' (PhD, University of Toronto, 1982).

Newell, J. Philip, 'A.J. Scott and his Circle' (PhD, University of Edinburgh, 1981).

Sellers, Ian, 'Liverpool Nonconformity (1786-1914)' (PhD, University of Keele, [1969]).

Watts, Michael R., 'John Clifford and Radical Nonconformity (1836-

1923)' (DPhil, University of Oxford, 1966).

Newspapers and Periodicals

Baptist Handbook, 1884, 1888-1914.
British Quarterly Review, The, 1877-78.
British Weekly, The, 1887-91, 1907.
Christian World, The, 1877-79, 1883-84, 1887-90.
Congregational Review, 1887-88.
Congregational Yearbook, The, 1851-1914.
English Independent, The, 1877-79.
Evangelical Magazine, The, 1877-78.
Freeman, The, 1883, 1885-89.
Leicester Chronicle and Leicestershire Mercury, 1877-78.
Nonconformist, The, 1877-79.
Nonconformist and Independent, The, 1884, 1887-88
Sword and the Trowel, The, 1865-91. (Includes numerous signed articles by C.H. Spurgeon not entered individually).

Books, Pamphlets and Articles

Bateman, Charles T., *John Clifford, M.A., B.Sc., LL.B., D.D.* (London, 1902).

—*John Clifford, M.A., B.S., LL.B., D.D., Free Church Leader and Preacher* (London: National Council of the Evangelical Free Churches, 1904).

Bebbington, David W., *Evangelicalism in Modern Britain: A History from the 1730s to the 1980s* (London: Unwin Hyman, 1989).

—'Gospel and Culture in Victorian Nonconformity', in Jane Shaw and Alan Kreider (eds), *Culture and the Nonconformist Tradition* (Cardiff: University of Wales Press, 1999), 43-59.

— *The Nonconformist Conscience: Chapel and Politics, 1870-1914* (London: Allen & Unwin, 1982).

— 'Spurgeon and British Evangelical Theological Education', in D.G. Hart and R. Albert Mohler, Jr. (eds), *Theological Education in the Evangelical Tradition* (Grand Rapids: Baker, 1996), 217-34.

Binfield, J. Clyde G., 'Congregationalism's Two Sides of the Baptistry – A Paedobaptist View', *Baptist Quarterly*, 26 (1975), 119-33.

— (ed.), 'The Cross and the City: Essays in Commemoration of Robert William Dale 1829-1895', Supplement to the *Journal of the United Reformed Church History Society* 6 Supplement no. 2 (1999).

Bonsall, H. Edgar, *The Dream of an Ideal City: Westbourne Park 1877-1977* (London: Westbourne Park Baptist Church, 1978).

Bradley, W.L., *P.T. Forsyth: The Man and his Work* (London: Independent Press, 1952).

Bradstock, Andrew, '"A Man of God is a Manly Man": Spurgeon, Luther and "Holy Boldness"', in *idem. et al* (eds), *Masculinity and Spirituality in Victorian Culture* (Basingstoke: Macmillan, 2000), 209-25.

Briggs, John H.Y., 'Charles Haddon Spurgeon and the Baptist Denomination in Nineteenth Century Britain', *Baptist Quarterly*, 31 (1986), 218-36.

Briggs, John H.Y., *The English Baptists of the Nineteenth Century* (Didcot: Baptist Historical Society, 1994).

Brown, Elizabeth Baldwin (ed.), *In Memoriam: James Baldwin Brown B.A., Minister of Brixton Independent Church; Born August 19, 1820, Died June 23 1884* (London: J. Clarke & Co., 1884).

Brown, James Baldwin, *The Battle and Burden of Life* (London: Hodder & Stoughton, 1875).

—*The Divine Life in Man* (London: Ward, 1859).

—*The Divine Life in Man* (London: Ward, 1860[2]).

— *The Divine Mystery of Peace* (London: Jackson, Walford & Hodder, 1863).

— *The Divine Treatment of Sin* (London: Jackson, Walford & Hodder, 1864).

— *The Doctrine of Annihilation in the Light of the Gospel of Love* (London: Henry S. King, 1875).

— *The Doctrine of the Divine Fatherhood in Relation to the Atonement* (London: Ward & Co., 1860).

— *First Principles of Ecclesiastical Truth: Essays on the Church and Society* (London: Hodder & Stoughton, 1871).

— *The Fullness of Time; or, the Advent of the Lord the Divine Key to History* (London, 1856).

— *The Gospel of the Son of Man. A Sermon Preached on Behalf of the London Missionary Society at Surrey Chapel* (London: J Clarke, 1875).

— *The Higher Life: Its Reality, Experience, and Destiny* (London: H.S. King, 1874).

—*John Leifield, D.D.: A Sketch of his Character and Ministry. With Brief Notes of His Last Days* (London: Ward & Co., 1862).

— *Light on the Way: Brief Discourses*, Elizabeth Baldwin Brown (ed.) (London: J. Clarke & Co., 1886).

— *Misread Passages of Scripture* (London: Hodder & Stoughton, 1869).

— *Misread Passages of Scripture, Second Series* (London: Hodder & Stoughton, 1871).

—'Our Theology in Relation to the Intellectual Movement of Our Times', *Congregational Yearbook* (1879), 51-77.

— 'The Perfect Law of Liberty', *Congregational Yearbook* (1879), 79-98.

—'The "Religious Life" and Christian Society', in H.R. Reynolds (ed.), *Ecclesia* (London: Hodder & Stoughton, 1870), 131-84.

— *The Risen Christ the King of Men*, Elizabeth Baldwin Brown (ed.) (London: R. Fischer Unwin, 1887).

— 'The Soul and Future Life', *Nineteenth Century*, 2 (1877) 511-17.

— *Studies of First Principles* (London: the Author, 1848-49). (Six tracts republished as a book).

— *Thomas Raffles, D.D., LL.D.; a Sketch* (London: Jackson, Walford & Hodder, 1864).

Brown, James Baldwin, *The Way of Peace for the Congregational Union;*

with Remarks on the Morale of its Religious Literature, the So-called Young School, and Negative Theology: a Letter to the Members (London: Ward, 1857).

— *The World-Religion* (London: Ward & Co., 1851).

— *The Young Ministry: its Relation to the Age. A Lecture for the Times* (London: John Snow, 1847).

Byrt, G.W., *John Clifford: A Fighting Free Churchman* (London: Kingsgate Press, 1947).

Campbell, Donald, (ed.), *Memorials of John McLeod Campbell, D.D., Being Selections from his Correspondence* (London: Macmillan, 1877).

Campbell, John McLeod, *The Nature of the Atonement and Its Relation to Remission of Sin and Eternal Life* (London: Macmillan, 1867[2]).

Carlile, J.C., *C. H. Spurgeon, An Interpretative Biography* (London: Religious Tract Society, 1933).

— 'John Clifford (1836-1923)', in R.S. Forman (ed.), *Great Christians* (London: Ivor Nicholson & Watson, 1933), 131-41.

Clifford, John, 'Baptist Theology', *Contemporary Review*, 53 (1888), 503-25.

— *The Battle of the Sacred Books* (London: E. Marlborough & Co., 1888).

— *Can We Be Sure of the Voice of God?* (London: E. Marlborough & Co., 1887).

— *The Christ of the Coming Century; or, the Primitive Christian Faith in its Application to the Institutional Life of Man* (London: Veal, Chifferiel & Co., 1899).

— *The Christian Certainties. Discourses and Addresses in Exposition and Defence of the Christian Faith* (London: Isbister & Co., 1893).

— *The Christian Conception of Society* (London: Alexander & Shepheard, 1891).

— *The Church of Christ; Its Work, Character and Message. An Address Delivered at the Dedication of Westbourne Park Chapel, September 30, 1877* (London: Yates & Alexander, 1877).

— *The Coming Theology or, the Primitive Christian Faith; the Source and Basis of a Living and Progressive Christian Theology. The Address from the Chair of the General Baptist Association, held at Burnley, June 23-25, 1891* (London: James Clarke & Co., 1891).

— *Daily Strength for Daily Living. Twenty Sermons on Old Testament Themes* (London: E. Marlborough & Co., 1885).

— *The Dawn of Manhood. Twelve Sermons* (London: Christian Commonwealth, 1886).

— (ed.), *The English Baptists, Who They Are and What They Have Done* (London: E. Marlborough, 1881).

— *Evolution and Christianity* (London: Griffiths & Co., 1882).

— *The Future of Christianity; or, Jesus Christ, the Eternal King of Men. Preached before the Baptist Missionary Society, 26th April 1876* (London: Yates & Alexander, 1876).

— *God's Greater Britain. Letters and Addresses* (London: James Clarke & Co., 1899).

— 'The Great Forty Years; or, the Primitive Christian Faith in its

Application to the Institutional Life of Men', in *Baptist Handbook* (1889), 25-58.
— *How to Be Sure of the Voice of God* (London: E. Marlborough & Co., 1886).
— 'Inspiration', in Frederick Atkin (ed.), *Biblical Difficulties and How to Meet Them* (London: S.W. Partridge & Co., 1891).
— *The Inspiration and Authority of the Bible* (London: J. Clarke & Co., 1892).
— *Is Life Worth Living? An Eightfold Answer* (London: E. Marlborough & Co., 1880).
— *Jesus Christ and Modern Social Life* (London: E. Marlborough & Co., 1872)
— *The Living Christ: or Christ's Present Work an Answer to Modern Doubt* (Nottingham: J. & J. Vice, 1873).
— *The New City of God; or, the Primitive Christian Faith as a Social Gospel* (London: Alexander & Shepheard, 1888).
— *The Non-attendance of Professed Christians at Public Worship* (Leicester: Winks & Son, 1868).
— *Our Churches and Colleges and the Ministry of the Future* (Derby, 1892).
— *The Pulpit and Human Life; or, the Minister as the Interpreter of Human Life. An Address Delivered to the Students of the Lancashire Independent College, Manchester, at the Forty-seventh Seasonal Anniversary, June 19th, 1890* (London: J. Clarke & Co., 1890).
— *The Renewal of Protestantism* (London: J. Clarke & Co., 1895).
— *The Sevenfold Law of Ministerial Training. An Address Delivered to the Students of Rawdon College, Leeds, at the Annual Meeting Held June 29th, 1887* (London: E. Marlborough & Co., 1887).
— *Theories of the Atonement. A Sermon Preached at Westbourne Park Chapel, Sunday Evening, September 9, 1894* (London: J. Clarke & Co., 1894).
— *Typical Christian Leaders* (London: H. Marshall & Son, 1898).
— *The Ultimate Problems of Christianity. Eight Lectures Delivered in 1906, at Regent's Park College, London* (London: Kingsgate Press, 1906).
— 'The Utilization of Church-Power', in *The Sword and the Trowel*, 1 (1865), 307-11.
Collings, J., *Conservatism in Religious Worship and Belief* (June 25 1883 Midland Baptist Association Meetings, reprinted from Leamington Chronicle).
Cowell, Henry J., *John Clifford as I Knew Him: A Commemorative Tribute* (London: Baptist Union Publications Department, 1936).
'Crane, Denis', *John Clifford: God's Soldier and the Peoples' Tribune* (London: Edwin Dalton, 1908).
Currie, Robert, Alan Gilbert and Lee Horsley, *Churches and Churchgoers: Patterns of Church Growth in the British Isles since 1800* (Oxford: Clarendon, 1977).
Dale, A.W.W., *The Life of R.W. Dale of Birmingham* (London: Hodder & Stoughton, 1898.
Dale, Robert William, 'The Alleged Reaction in the Theology of Congregationalists', *Congregationalist*, 2 (1873), 55-59.

— *The Atonement. The Congregational Union Lecture for 1875* (London: Hodder & Stoughton, 1878[7]).
—'The Bible – a Library Not a Book', *Congregationalist*, 2 (1873), 51-55.
— *Christ and the Controversies of Christendom* (London: Hodder & Stoughton, 1869).
—*Christ and the Future Life* (London: Hodder & Stoughton, 1897[3]).
— *Christian Doctrine. A Series of Discourses* (London: Hodder & Stoughton, 1896).
— 'The Church the Fullness of Him that Filleth All in All', *Congregationalist*, 1 (1872), 454-60.
— 'Congregationalism', *British Quarterly Review*, 73 (1881), 1-12, 265-87.
— *Discourses Delivered on Special Occasions* (London: Jackson, Walford & Hodder, 1866).
— *The Epistle of James and Other Discourses* (London: Hodder & Stoughton, 1895.)
— *The Epistle to the Ephesians: Its Doctrine and Ethics* (London: Hodder & Stoughton, 1882).
— *The Evangelical Revival and Other Sermons: with an Address on the Work of the Christian Ministry in a Period of Theological Decay and Transition* (London: Hodder & Stoughton, 1880).
— 'The Expiatory Theory of the Atonement', *British Quarterly Review*, 46 (1867), 463-504.
— 'The Faith Once Delivered to the Saints', in *Mansfield College, Oxford: its Origin and Opening* (1890).
— *Fellowship with Christ and Other Discourses Delivered on Special Occasions* (London: Hodder & Stoughton, 1891).
— 'George Dawson: Politician, Lecturer, and Preacher', *Nineteenth Century*, 2 (1877), 44-61.
—'Have We Forgotten Christ?' *Congregationalist*, 1 (1872), 705-10.
— *History of English Congregationalism*, ed. and completed by A.W.W. Dale (London: Hodder & Stoughton, 1907).
— 'The History of Spring Hill College', in *Mansfield College: its Origin and Opening* (1890).
—'The Idea of the Church in Relation to Modern Congregationalism', in H.R. Reynolds (ed.), *Ecclesia: a Second Series of Essays on Theological and Ecclesiastical Questions* (London: Hodder & Stoughton, 1871), 355-412.
— *The Jewish Temple and the Christian Church. A Series of Discourses on the Epistle of Hebrews* (London: Hodder & Stoughton, 1896[10]).
— *Laws of Christ for Common Life* (London: Hodder & Stoughton, 1884).
— (ed.), *The Life and Letters of John Angell James: Including an Unfinished Autobiography* (1861[2]).
— *The Living Christ and the Four Gospels* (London: Hodder & Stoughton, 1890).
— *A Manual of Congregational Principles* (London: Hodder & Stoughton, 1884).
— 'Maurice on the Gospel of St. John', *Eclectic Review*, new series 2 (1857), 45-53.
— 'Memoir', in Henry Rogers, *The Superhuman Origin of the Bible Inferred*

from Itself (London: Hodder & Stoughton, 1893[8]), vii-lxvii.
—'Mr Matthew Arnold and the Nonconformists', *Contemporary Review*, 14 (1870), 540-69.
—'The Moral View of the Atonement', *British Quarterly Review*, 44 (1866), 410-52.
—'The New Birth', *Congregationalist*, 1 (1872), 325-32.
—*Nine Lectures on Preaching. Delivered at Yale, New Haven, Connecticut* (London: Hodder & Stoughton, 1877).
—'The Nonconformists', in *Christianity in Great Britain: an Outline of its Rise, Progress, and Present Condition. A Series of Articles Contributed to "The Daily Telegraph"* (London: Hodder & Stoughton, 1874), 113-62.
—*The Old Evangelicalism and the New* (London: Hodder & Stoughton, 1889).
—'On Some Present Aspects of Theological Thought among Congregationalists', *Congregationalist*, 6 (1877), 1-15.
—'The Positive Side of Modern Deism', *Eclectic Review*, new series 3 (1858), 253-65.
—'Prayer in Relation to Revival', *Congregationalist*, 3 (1874), 1-6.
—*Protestantism: Its Ultimate Principle* (London: Hodder & Stoughton, 1874).
—'The Seat of Authority in Religion', *Contemporary Review*, 58 (1890), 389-411.
—*The Talents: or, Man's Nature, Power, and Responsibility* (London: Aylott & Jones, 1846).
—*The Ten Commandments* (London: Hodder & Stoughton, 1871).
—'Thomas Carlyle', *Congregationalist*, 10 (1881), 205-17, 285-92.
—'Unitarian Criticism of the Congregational Union Lecture for 1875', *Congregationalist*, 5 (1876), 153-67, 203-12, 278-87.
Dallimore, Arnold, *Spurgeon* (Edinburgh: Banner of Truth, 1985).
Darlow, T.H., *William Robertson Nicoll: Life and Letters* (London: Hodder & Stoughton, 1925).
Davies, Horton, *Worship and Theology in England. Vol. 4: From Newman to Martineau, 1850-1900* (Princeton: Princeton University Press, 1962).
Douglas, James, *The Prince of Preachers: a Sketch; a Portraiture; and a Tribute* (London: Morgan & Scott, [1893]).
Drummond, Lewis, *Spurgeon Prince of Preachers* (Grand Rapids: Kregel Publications, 1992).
Emerson, Ralph Waldo, *Essays* (London: James Fraser, 1841).
Fairbairn, Andrew Martin, sermon in *Memorial Services Preached in Carr's Lane Chapel, on the Occasion of the Death of Dr. R. W. Dale...* (Birmingham: Hudson & Son, 1895), 12-21.
Field, A. Harwood, *The Rev. Joseph William Harrald* (London: A.H. Stockwell, 1918).
Foot, Isaac, *John Clifford – The Bible and the Common People* (London: Brotherhood Movement, 1938).
Forsyth, Peter Taylor, *Baldwin Brown: a Tribute, a Reminiscence, and a Study* (London: James Clarke & Co., 1884).
Freer, Frederick Ash, *Edward White, His Life and Work* (London: Elliot

Stock, 1902).
Fullerton, William Young, *C. H. Spurgeon: A Biography* (London: Williams & Norgate, 1920).
—*F. B. Meyer: A Biography* (London: Marshall & Co., 1929).
[—]*From the Pulpit to the Palm Branch: a Memorial of C. H. Spurgeon* (London: Passmore & Alabaster, 1892).
Glover, Willis, B., *Evangelical Nonconformists and Higher Criticism in the Nineteenth Century* (London: Independent Press, 1954).
Gordon, James M., *Evangelical Spirituality: From the Wesleys to John Stott* (London: SPCK, 1991).
Grant, John, W., *Free Churchmanship in England 1870-1940 with Special Reference to Congregationalism* (London: Independent Press, 1955).
Hanna, William, (ed.), *Letters of Thomas Erskine of Linlathen from 1800 till 1840* (Edinburgh: David Douglas, 1877).
Harrison, F.M.W., 'The Nottinghamshire Baptists: Church Relations: Social Composition: Finance: Theology', *Baptist Quarterly*, 26 (1975), 169-90.
Hart, Trevor, (ed.), *Justice the True and Only Mercy: Essays on the Life and Theology of Peter Taylor Forsyth* (Edinburgh: T & T Clark, 1995).
Hayden, Eric W., *A History of Spurgeon's Tabernacle* (Pasadena: Pilgrim Publications, 1971[2]).
Hinton, John Howard, *Strictures on Some Passages in the Rev. J. B. Brown's "Divine Life in Man"* (London: Houlston & Wright, 1860).
Hopkins, Mark, 'Dale, Robert William', in Timothy T. Larsen (ed.), *Biographical Dictionary of Evangelicals* (Leicester: IVP, 2003), 175-8.
—'The Downgrade Controversy: New Evidence', *Baptist Quarterly*, 35 (1994), 262-78.
—'Spurgeon's Opponents in the Downgrade Controversy', *Baptist Quarterly*, 32 (1988), 274-94.
Hough, Lynn Harold, *Dr. Dale after Twenty-five Years. An Address Given at Carr's Lane Chapel, Birmingham. July 5th, 1922* (Birmingham: Cornish Bros., 1922).
Hough, Lynn Harold, 'R. W. Dale', *Congregational Quarterly*, 7 (1929), 417-24.
Howells, George, 'Christian Problems. Settled; and Awaiting Further Exploration', *Baptist Quarterly*, 7 (1934), 106-22.
Hunter, Leslie Stannard, *John Hunter, D.D.: A Life* (London: Hodder & Stoughton, 1921).
Johnson, Dale A., *The Changing Shape of English Nonconformity, 1825-1925* (New York/Oxford: Oxford University Press, 1999).
Johnson, Mark David, *The Dissolution of Dissent, 1850-1918* (New York: Garland, 1987).
—'Thomas Gasquoine and the Origins of the Leicester Conference', *Journal of the United Reformed Church Historical Society*, 2 (1982), 345-52.
Johnson, W. Charles, *Encounter in London. The Story of the London Baptist Association 1865-1965* (London: Carey Kingsgate Press, 1965).
Jones, R. Tudor, *Congregationalism in England 1662-1962* (London: Independent Press, 1962).

Kennedy, John, *The People Called Independents: with Relation to their Doctrinal History and Beliefs* (London: John Snow & Co., 1878).

King, David, *Historical Sketch of the Evangelical Alliance, Consisting of Two Papers Read in Freemasons' Hall, London August 19, 1846, and August 20, 1851* (Glasgow: S. & T. Dunn, 1851).

Kirkby, Charles, *The Late Baldwin Brown's Pulpit: a Protest and a Defence Addressed to the Congregational Ministers of England and Wales* (London: Christian Union Office, 1886).

Kruppa, Patricia Stallings, *Charles Haddon Spurgeon: A Preacher's Progress* (New York: Garland, 1982).

Mackennal, Alexander, 'The Life of the Spirit', in *Congregational Yearbook* (1888), 50-61.

Mansfield College Oxford: Its Origin and Opening, October 14-16, 1889 (London: James Clarke, 1890).

Marchant, James, *Dr John Clifford* (London: Cassell & Co., 1924).

McLaren, E.T., *Dr. McLaren of Manchester: A Sketch* (London: Hodder & Stoughton, 1912[3]).

Meyer, Frederick Brotherton, *Charles Haddon Spurgeon* (London, 1892).

Moberly, R.C., *Atonement and Personality*, (London: John Murray, 1913).

Moore, James R., *The Post-Darwinian Controversies: A Study of the Protestant Struggle to Come to Terms with Darwin in Great Britain and America, 1870-1900* (Cambridge: Cambridge University Press, 1979).

Mozley, John Kenneth, 'R. W. Dale 1829-95', in R.S. Forman (ed.), *Great Christians*, (London: Ivor Nicholson & Watson, 1933), 161-74.

Murray, Iain H., *The Forgotten Spurgeon* (London: Banner of Truth, 1973[2]).

Nicholls, Mike, *C.H. Spurgeon the Pastor Evangelist* (Didcot: Baptist Historical Society, 1992).

—'The Downgrade Controversy: A Neglected Protagonist', *Baptist Quarterly*, 33 (1988), 260-74.

Nicoll, William Robertson, *Princes of the Church* (London: Hodder & Stoughton, 1921).

'Onlooker', *The Theological Chaos and the "Congregational" Crisis* (London: n.p., 1878).

The Ordination Services of the Rev. R. W. Dale, M.A., to the Co-Pastorate of the Congregational Church Assembling at Carr's Lane Chapel, Birmingham. November 22, 1854 (includes answers to questions by Dale).

Paton, John Brown, *The Reasonableness of the Evangelic Faith* (Nottingham: Arthur Johnson, 1895).

Payne, Ernest A., 'Baptist-Congregationalist Relationships', *Congregational Quarterly*, 33 (1955), 216-26.

— *The Baptist Union: A Short History* (London: Carey Kingsgate, 1959).

— 'The Development of Nonconformist Theological Education in the Nineteenth Century, with Special Reference to Regent's Park College', in *idem.* (ed.), *Studies in History and Religion* (London: Lutterworth Press, 1942).

— 'The Down Grade Controversy: A Postscript', *Baptist Quarterly*, 28 (1979), 146-58.

Peel, Albert, *These Hundred Years: A History of the Congregational Union of England and Wales, 1831-1931* (London: Congregational Union of England and Wales, 1931).

—and J.A.R. Marriott, *Robert Forman Horton* (London: G. Allen & Unwin, 1937).

Pennar-Davies, W.T., *Mansfield College, Its History, Aims and Achievements* (Oxford: [Mansfield College], 1947).

Pike, Godfrey Holden, *James Archer Spurgeon, D.D., LL.D., Preacher, Philanthropist and Co-Pastor with C. H. Spurgeon at the Metropolitan Tabernacle* (London: 1892).

— *The Life and Work of Archibald G. Brown, Preacher and Philanthropist* (London: Passmore & Alabaster, 1892).

— *The Life and Work of Charles Haddon Spurgeon*, 3 vols (London: Cassell & Co., [1892-93]).

Porritt, Arthur, *More and More of Memories* (London: G. Allen & Unwin, 1947).

Powicke, Frederick J., *David Worthington Simon* (London: Hodder & Stoughton, 1912).

— 'Frederick Denison Maurice (1805-1872): A Personal Reminiscence', *Congregational Quarterly*, 8 (1930) 169-84.

Public Conference on the Terms of Religious Communion (1878).

Rogers, James Guinness, 'The Congregationalism of the Future', in H.R. Reynolds (ed.), *Ecclesia* (London: Hodder & Stoughton, 1870), 463-531.

—two sermons in *Memorial Services Preached in Carr's Lane Chapel, On the Occasion of the Death of Dr. R. W. Dale...* (Birmingham: Hudson & Son, 1895).

— *Present-Day Religion and Theology Including a Review of the Down Grade Controversy* (London: T. Fisher Unwin, 1888).

Rogerson, John, *Old Testament Criticism in the Nineteenth Century: England and Germany* (London: SPCK, 1984).

Rowell, D. Geoffrey, *Hell and the Victorians. A Study of the Nineteenth Century Theological Controversies Concerning Eternal Punishment and the Future Life* (Oxford: Clarendon, 1974).

Scott, Alexander J., *Discourses* (London: Macmillan, 1866).

Sell, Alan P.F., *Theology in Turmoil: The Roots, Course and Significance of the Consevative-Liberal Debate in Modern Theology* (Grand Rapids: Baker Book House, 1986).

Sellers, Ian, *Nineteenth Century Nonconformity* (London: Edward Arnold, 1977).

— 'Other Times, Other Ministries: John Fawcett and Alexander McLaren', *Baptist Quarterly*, 32 (1987), 181-98.

[Shindler, Robert], *Creed or No Creed? A Question for the Baptist Union* (London, 1888).

Skeats, Herbert S., and Charles S. Miall, *History of the Free Churches of England 1688-1891* (London: Alexander & Shepheard, 1891).

Spurgeon, Charles Haddon, *All of Grace. An Earnest Word with Those who Are Seeking Salvation by the Lord Jesus Christ* (London: Passmore &

Alabaster, 1886.
—*An All-round Ministry: Addresses to Ministers and Students* (London: Passmore & Alabaster, 1900).
—*Christ's Glorious Achievements. Set Forth in Seven Sermons* (London: [1877]).
—**Christ's Relation to His People* (London: Passmore & Alabaster, [1904]).
—*The Clue of the Maze* (Pasadena, n.d.).
—*Commenting and Commentaries. Two Lectures Addressed to the Students of the Pastors' College, Metropolitan Tabernacle, together with a Catalogue of Biblical Commentaries, and Expositions* (London: Passmore & Alabaster, 1876).
—**Election* (Welwyn: Evangelical Press, 1978).
—*Faith; What It Is, and What It Leads to* (London: Passmore & Alabaster, 1903).
—*"Good Tidings of Great Joy". Christ's Incarnation the Foundation of Christianity* (London: Passmore & Alabaster, 1901).
—*The Greatest Fight in the World* (London: Passmore & Alabaster, 1892).
—*Infant Salvation. A Sympathetic Word for Bereaved Parents* (London: Passmore & Alabaster, n.d.).
—*Lectures to my Students: a Selection From Addresses Delivered to the Students of the Pastors' College, Metropolitan Tabernacle* (London: Passmore & Alabaster, 1875).
—*Second Series of Lectures to My Students: Being Addresses Delivered to the Students of the Pastors' College, Metropolitan Tabernacle* (London: Passmore & Alabaster, 1877).
—**The Messiah. Sermons on Our Lord's Names, Titles and Attributes* (London: Passmore & Alabaster, 1898).
—*The Metropolitan Tabernacle Pulpit*, 11, 24, 30, 32, 34, 35 (London: Passmore & Alabaster, 1865, 1878, 1884, 1888, 1889).
—'Preface', in William Barker, *The Duration of Future Punishments. Two Lectures to the Students at the Metropolitan Tabernacle...* (London: Passmore & Alabaster, 1865), pp. v-vii.
—*The Saint and His Saviour: the Progress of the Soul in the Knowledge of Jesus* (London: Hodder & Stoughton, 1889).
—**Sermons,* William Robertson Nicoll (ed.) (London: Thomas Nelson, 1910).
—*Storm Signals: Being a Collection of Sermons Preached on Sunday and Thursday Evenings at the Metropolitan Tabernacle* (London: Passmore & Alabaster, 1885).
—**Twelve Sermons on Decision* (Grand Rapids, 1971).
—**Twelve Sermons on Holiness* (1937).
—**Twelve Sermons on the Holy Spirit* (1937).
—**Twelve Sermons on the Passion and Death of Christ* (Grand Rapids, 1971).
—**Twelve Sermons on the Resurrection* (Grand Rapids, 1968).
—**Twelve Sermons on Sanctification* (n.d.).
Spurgeon, Susannah and Joseph Harrald, *C. H. Spurgeon Autobiography*, revised ed., 2 vols (London: Banner of Truth, 1962, 1973).

Spurr, Frederic C., 'Charles Haddon Spurgeon 1834-92', in R.S. Forman (ed.), *Great Christians* (London: Ivor Nicholson & Watson, 1933), 515-23.

Thielicke, Helmut, *Encounter with Spurgeon*, John W. Doberstein (tr.) (London: James Clarke & Co., 1964).

Thompson, David M., 'John Clifford's Social Gospel', *Baptist Quarterly*, 31 (1986), 199-210.

Underwood, A.C., *A History of the English Baptists* (London: Carey Kingsgate, 1947).

Vance, Norman, *The Sinews of the Spirit: The Ideal of Christian Manliness in Victorian Literature and Religious Thought* (Cambridge: Cambridge University Press, 1985).

Vinet, Alexandre, *Vital Christianity: Essays and Discourses on the Religions of Man and the Religion of God*, Robert Turnbull (tr.) (Edinburgh, 1846).

Walker, Michael J., *Baptists at the Table: The Theology of the Lord's Supper amongst English Baptists in the Nineteenth Century* (Didcot: Baptist Historical Society, 1992).

Watts, Michael R., *The Dissenters. Vol. I: From the Reformation to the French Revolution* (Oxford: Clarendon, 1978).

Westcott, Brooke Foss, *The Epistles of St. John: the Greek Text with Notes and Essays* (London: Macmillan & Co., 1883).

Wilkinson, Alan, *Dissent or Conform? War, Peace and the English Churches, 1900-1945* (London: SCM, 1986).

Wilkinson, William Cleaver, *Modern Masters of Pulpit Discourse* (New York: Funk & Wagnalls, 1905).

Williams, William, *Personal Reminiscences of Charles Haddon Spurgeon* (London: Religious Tract Society, 1895[2]).

Index

Studies in Evangelical History and Thought

(All titles uniform with this volume)
Dates in bold are of projected publication

Andrew Atherstone
Oxford's Protestant Spy
The Controversial Career of Charles Golightly

Charles Golightly (1807–85) was a notorious Protestant polemicist. His life was dedicated to resisting the spread of ritualism and liberalism within the Church of England and the University of Oxford. For half a century he led many memorable campaigns, such as building a martyr's memorial and attempting to close a theological college. John Henry Newman, Samuel Wilberforce and Benjamin Jowett were among his adversaries. This is the first study of Golightly's controversial career.

2006 */ 1-84227-364-7 / approx. 324pp*

Clyde Binfield
Victorian Nonconformity in Eastern England

Studies of Victorian religion and society often concentrate on cities, suburbs, and industrialisation. This study provides a contrast. Victorian Eastern England—Essex, Suffolk, Norfolk, Cambridgeshire, and Huntingdonshire—was rural, traditional, relatively unchanging. That is nonetheless a caricature which discounts the industry in Norwich and Ipswich (as well as in Haverhill, Stowmarket and Leiston) and ignores the impact of London on Essex, of railways throughout the region, and of an ancient but changing university (Cambridge) on the county town which housed it. It also entirely ignores the political implications of such changes in a region noted for the variety of its religious Dissent since the seventeenth century. This book explores Victorian Eastern England and its Nonconformity. It brings to a wider readership a pioneering thesis which has made a major contribution to a fresh evolution of English religion and society.

2006 */ 1-84227-216-0 / approx. 274pp*

John Brencher
Martyn Lloyd-Jones (1899–1981) and Twentieth-Century Evangelicalism

This study critically demonstrates the significance of the life and ministry of Martyn Lloyd-Jones for post-war British evangelicalism and demonstrates that his preaching was his greatest influence on twentieth-century Christianity. The factors which shaped his view of the church are examined, as is the way his reformed evangelicalism led to a separatist ecclesiology which divided evangelicals.

2002 / 1-84227-051-6 / xvi + 268pp

July 2005

Jonathan D. Burnham

A Story of Conflict

The Controversial Relationship between Benjamin Wills Newton and John Nelson Darby

Burnham explores the controversial relationship between the two principal leaders of the early Brethren movement. In many ways Newton and Darby were products of their times, and this study of their relationship provides insight not only into the dynamics of early Brethrenism, but also into the progress of nineteenth-century English and Irish evangelicalism.

2004 / 1-84227-191-1 / xxiv + 268pp

Grayson Carter

Anglican Evangelicals

Protestant Secessions from the Via Media, c.*1800–1850*

This study examines, within a chronological framework, the major themes and personalities which influenced the outbreak of a number of Evangelical clerical and lay secessions from the Church of England and Ireland during the first half of the nineteenth century. Though the number of secessions was relatively small—between a hundred and two hundred of the 'Gospel' clergy abandoned the Church during this period—their influence was considerable, especially in highlighting in embarrassing fashion the tensions between the evangelical conversionist imperative and the principles of a national religious establishment. Moreover, through much of this period there remained, just beneath the surface, the potential threat of a large Evangelical disruption similar to that which occurred in Scotland in 1843. Consequently, these secessions provoked great consternation within the Church and within Evangelicalism itself, they contributed to the outbreak of millennial speculation following the 'constitutional revolution' of 1828–32, they led to the formation of several new denominations, and they sparked off a major Church–State crisis over the legal right of a clergyman to secede and begin a new ministry within Protestant Dissent.

2007 */ 1-84227-401-5 / xvi + 470pp*

J.N. Ian Dickson

Beyond Religious Discourse

Sermons, Preaching and Evangelical Protestants in Nineteenth-Century Irish Society

Drawing extensively on primary sources, this pioneer work in modern religious history explores the training of preachers, the construction of sermons and how Irish evangelicalism and the wider movement in Great Britain and the United States shaped the preaching event. Evangelical preaching and politics, sectarianism, denominations, education, class, social reform, gender, and revival are examined to advance the argument that evangelical sermons and preaching went significantly beyond religious discourse. The result is a book for those with interests in Irish history, culture and belief, popular religion and society, evangelicalism, preaching and communication.

***2005** / 1-84227-217-9 / approx. 324pp*

Neil T.R. Dickson

Brethren in Scotland 1838–2000

A Social Study of an Evangelical Movement

The Brethren were remarkably pervasive throughout Scottish society. This study of the Open Brethren in Scotland places them in their social context and examines their growth, development and relationship to society.

2003 / 1-84227-113-X / xxviii + 510pp

Crawford Gribben and Timothy C.F. Stunt (eds)

Prisoners of Hope?

Aspects of Evangelical Millennialism in Britain and Ireland, 1800–1880

This volume of essays offers a comprehensive account of the impact of evangelical millennialism in nineteenth-century Britain and Ireland.

2004 / 1-84227-224-1 / xiv + 208pp

Khim Harris

Evangelicals and Education

Evangelical Anglicans and Middle-Class Education in Nineteenth-Century England

This ground breaking study investigates the history of English public schools founded by nineteenth-century Evangelicals. It documents the rise of middle-class education and Evangelical societies such as the influential Church Association, and includes a useful biographical survey of prominent Evangelicals of the period.

2004 / 1-84227-250-0 / xviii + 422pp

Mark Hopkins
Nonconformity's Romantic Generation
Evangelical and Liberal Theologies in Victorian England

A study of the theological development of key leaders of the Baptist and Congregational denominations at their period of greatest influence, including C.H. Spurgeon and R.W. Dale, and of the controversies in which those among them who embraced and rejected the liberal transformation of their evangelical heritage opposed each other.

2004 / 1-84227-150-4 / xvi + 284pp

Don Horrocks
Laws of the Spiritual Order
Innovation and Reconstruction in the Soteriology of Thomas Erskine of Linlathen

Don Horrocks argues that Thomas Erskine's unique historical and theological significance as a soteriological innovator has been neglected. This timely reassessment reveals Erskine as a creative, radical theologian of central and enduring importance in Scottish nineteenth-century theology, perhaps equivalent in significance to that of S.T. Coleridge in England.

2004 / 1-84227-192-X / xx + 362pp

Kenneth S. Jeffrey
When the Lord Walked the Land
The 1858–62 Revival in the North East of Scotland

Previous studies of revivals have tended to approach religious movements from either a broad, national or a strictly local level. This study of the multifaceted nature of the 1859 revival as it appeared in three distinct social contexts within a single region reveals the heterogeneous nature of simultaneous religious movements in the same vicinity.

2002 / 1-84227-057-5 / xxiv + 304pp

John Kenneth Lander
Itinerant Temples
Tent Methodism, 1814–1832

Tent preaching began in 1814 and the Tent Methodist sect resulted from disputes with Bristol Wesleyan Methodists in 1820. The movement spread to parts of Gloucestershire, Wiltshire, London and Liverpool, among other places. Its demise started in 1826 after which one leader returned to the Wesleyans and others became ministers in the Congregational and Baptist denominations.

2003 / 1-84227-151-2 / xx + 268pp

Donald M. Lewis

Lighten Their Darkness

The Evangelical Mission to Working-Class London, 1828–1860

This is a comprehensive and compelling study of the Church and the complexities of nineteenth-century London. Challenging our understanding of the culture in working London at this time, Lewis presents a well-structured and illustrated work that contributes substantially to the study of evangelicalism and mission in nineteenth-century Britain.

2001 / 1-84227-074-5 / xviii + 372pp

Herbert McGonigle

'Sufficient Saving Grace'

John Wesley's Evangelical Arminianism

A thorough investigation of the theological roots of John Wesley's evangelical Arminianism and how these convictions were hammered out in controversies on predestination, limited atonement and the perseverance of the saints.

2001 / 1-84227-045-1 / xvi + 350pp

Lisa S. Nolland

A Victorian Feminist Christian

Josephine Butler, the Prostitutes and God

Josephine Butler was an unlikely candidate for taking up the cause of prostitutes, as she did, with a fierce and self-disregarding passion. This book explores the particular mix of perspectives and experiences that came together to envision and empower her remarkable achievements. It highlights the vital role of her spirituality and the tragic loss of her daughter.

2004 / 1-84227-225-X / xxiv + 328pp

Donald J. Payne

The Theology of the Christian Life in J.I. Packer's Thought

Theological Anthropology, Theological Method, and the Doctrine of Sanctification

J.I. Packer has wielded widespread influence on evangelicalism for more than three decades. This study pursues a nuanced understanding of Packer's theology of sanctification by tracing the development of his thought, showing how he reflects a particular version of Reformed theology, and examining the unique influence of theological anthropology and theological method on this area of his theology.

***2005** / 1-84227-397-3 / approx. 374pp*

Ian M. Randall

Evangelical Experiences

A Study in the Spirituality of English Evangelicalism 1918–1939

This book makes a detailed historical examination of evangelical spirituality between the First and Second World Wars. It shows how patterns of devotion led to tensions and divisions. In a wide-ranging study, Anglican, Wesleyan, Reformed and Pentecostal-charismatic spiritualities are analysed.

1999 / 0-85364-919-7 / xii + 310pp

Ian M. Randall

Spirituality and Social Change

The Contribution of F.B. Meyer (1847–1929)

This is a fresh appraisal of F.B. Meyer (1847–1929), a leading Free Church minister. Having been deeply affected by holiness spirituality, Meyer became the Keswick Convention's foremost international speaker. He combined spirituality with effective evangelism and socio-political activity. This study shows Meyer's significant contribution to spiritual renewal and social change.

2003 / 1-84227-195-4 / xx + 184pp

James Robinson

Pentecostal Origins

Early Pentecostalism in Ireland in the Context of the British Isles

Harvey Cox describes Pentecostalism as 'the fascinating spiritual child of our time' that has the potential, at the global scale, to contribute to the 'reshaping of religion in the twenty-first century'. This study grounds such sentiments by examining at the local scale the origin, development and nature of Pentecostalism in Ireland in its first twenty years. Illustrative, in a paradigmatic way, of how Pentecostalism became established within one region of the British Isles, it sets the story within the wider context of formative influences emanating from America, Europe and, in particular, other parts of the British Isles. As a synoptic regional study in Pentecostal history it is the first survey of its kind.

2005 / 1-84227-329-1 / xxviii + 378pp

Geoffrey Robson

Dark Satanic Mills?

Religion and Irreligion in Birmingham and the Black Country

This book analyses and interprets the nature and extent of popular Christian belief and practice in Birmingham and the Black Country during the first half of the nineteenth century, with particular reference to the impact of cholera epidemics and evangelism on church extension programmes.

2002 / 1-84227-102-4 / xiv + 294pp

Roger Shuff

Searching for the True Church

Brethren and Evangelicals in Mid-Twentieth-Century England

Roger Shuff holds that the influence of the Brethren movement on wider evangelical life in England in the twentieth century is often underrated. This book records and accounts for the fact that Brethren reached the peak of their strength at the time when evangelicalism was at it lowest ebb, immediately before World War II. However, the movement then moved into persistent decline as evangelicalism regained ground in the post war period. Accompanying this downward trend has been a sharp accentuation of the contrast between Brethren congregations who engage constructively with the non-Brethren scene and, at the other end of the spectrum, the isolationist group commonly referred to as 'Exclusive Brethren'.

2005 / 1-84227-254-3 / xviii+ 296pp

James H.S. Steven

Worship in the Spirit

Charismatic Worship in the Church of England

This book explores the nature and function of worship in six Church of England churches influenced by the Charismatic Movement, focusing on congregational singing and public prayer ministry. The theological adequacy of such ritual is discussed in relation to pneumatological and christological understandings in Christian worship.

2002 / 1-84227-103-2 / xvi + 238pp

Peter K. Stevenson

God in Our Nature

The Incarnational Theology of John McLeod Campbell

This radical reassessment of Campbell's thought arises from a comprehensive study of his preaching and theology. Previous accounts have overlooked both his sermons and his Christology. This study examines the distinctive Christology evident in his sermons and shows that it sheds new light on Campbell's much debated views about atonement.

2004 / 1-84227-218-7 / xxiv + 458pp

Kenneth J. Stewart

Restoring the Reformation

British Evangelicalism and the Réveil at Geneva 1816–1849

Restoring the Reformation traces British missionary initiative in post-Revolutionary Francophone Europe from the genesis of the London Missionary Society, the visits of Robert Haldane and Henry Drummond, and the founding of the Continental Society. While British Evangelicals aimed at the reviving of a foreign Protestant cause of momentous legend, they received unforeseen reciprocating emphases from the Continent which forced self-reflection on Evangelicalism's own relationship to the Reformation.

2006 */ 1-84227-392-2 / approx. 190pp*

Martin Wellings

Evangelicals Embattled

Responses of Evangelicals in the Church of England to Ritualism, Darwinism and Theological Liberalism 1890–1930

In the closing years of the nineteenth century and the first decades of the twentieth century Anglican Evangelicals faced a series of challenges. In responding to Anglo-Catholicism, liberal theology, Darwinism and biblical criticism, the unity and identity of the Evangelical school were severely tested.

2003 / 1-84227-049-4 / xviii + 352pp

James Whisenant

A Fragile Unity

Anti-Ritualism and the Division of Anglican Evangelicalism in the Nineteenth Century

This book deals with the ritualist controversy (approximately 1850–1900) from the perspective of its evangelical participants and considers the divisive effects it had on the party.

2003 / 1-84227-105-9 / xvi + 530pp

Haddon Willmer

Evangelicalism 1785–1835: An Essay (1962) and Reflections (2004)

Awarded the Hulsean Prize in the University of Cambridge in 1962, this interpretation of a classic period of English Evangelicalism, by a young church historian, is now supplemented by reflections on Evangelicalism from the vantage point of a retired Professor of Theology.

2006 */ 1-84227-219-5 / approx. 350pp*

July 2005

Linda Wilson

Constrained by Zeal

Female Spirituality amongst Nonconformists 1825–1875

Constrained by Zeal investigates the neglected area of Nonconformist female spirituality. Against the background of separate spheres, it analyses the experience of women from four denominations, and argues that the churches provided a 'third sphere' in which they could find opportunities for participation.

2000 / 0-85364-972-3 / xvi + 294pp

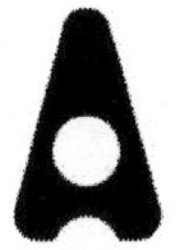

Paternoster
9 Holdom Avenue,
Bletchley,
Milton Keynes MK1 1QR,
United Kingdom
Web: www.authenticmedia.co.uk/paternoster

July 2005